PUBLIC SERVICE TRADE UNIONISM
AND RADICAL POLITICS

To Mavis, Megan and Laurie,
who tolerated this intrusion in their lives

Public Service Trade Unionism and Radical Politics

CHRIS MILLER
University of the West of England, Bristol, UK

Dartmouth

Aldershot • Brookfield USA • Singapore • Sydney

Published by
Dartmouth Publishing Company Limited
Gower House
Croft Road
Aldershot
Hants GU11 3HR
England

Dartmouth Publishing Company
Old Post Road
Brookfield
Vermont 05036
USA

British Library Cataloguing in Publication Data
Miller, Chris
  Public Service Trade Unionism and
  Radical Politics
  I. Title
  331.8811352041

Library of Congress Cataloging-in-Publication Data
Miller, Chris, 1949-
    Public service trade unionism and radical politics / Chris Miller.
      p.   cm.
    Includes bibliographical references and index.
    ISBN 1-85521-641-8
    1. Trade-unions–Government employees–England–London–Political
  activity–History–20th century.   2. Islington (London, England)
  3. National Association of Local Government Officers–History.
  I. Title.
  HD8005.2.G73L665   1996
  331.88'113520421–dc20
                                                                    95-39634
                                                                    CIP

ISBN 1 85521 641 8

Printed in Great Britain by Ipswich Book Co. Ltd., Ipswich, Suffolk.

Contents

Appendices

Acknowledgements

This book began life as a thesis and involved the support and participation of a large number of NALGO officers and activists, especially in the London Borough of Islington, as well as access to NALGO documentation. For that my thanks and I hope that I have accurately reflected their views, although responsibility for their interpretation rests entirely with me. I want too to acknowledge the invaluable support and supervision given by Paul Hoggett and the advice offered by Allan Cochrane. Again though the final product, and any weaknesses, is my responsibility. Last but not least I would like to thank Jan Green who took on the task of converting the draft into the final typescript.

Introduction

This book is concerned with the nature of public service white-collar trade unions and particularly those within local government. As with all trade unionists, public service workers have a need to organise collectively to promote and defend their interests at the workplace. However, it is argued that, unlike other workers, the human product of their labours gives the production process and its output a heightened significance that sits uneasily within capitalist labour relations. It is also a relationship that places pressure, and sometimes actual restrictions, on the kind of behaviours deemed as acceptable for those organisations representing public service workers.

The late 1960s and early 1970s was a period of significant growth in British public service trade union organisation. Moreover, the politics of public service trade unionism underwent a transformation that was not far short of revolutionary in which the concept of public service was increasingly replaced for a growing and influential section of the membership by a self-perception that was more aggressively militant and workerist. The key issue was seen to be the conflict between public service workers and their employers. The emphasis was on the improvement of service conditions, through strong trade union organisation and a repertoire of industrial conflict strategies, rather than the quality of service provision or the relationships with service users. Yet this continuing neglect of the quality of service provision has had damaging repercussions for collectively provided social welfare. The responsibility for any loss of faith in welfare services clearly does not rest entirely, or even primarily, with public service workers and their trade unions. Nevertheless, it is suggested that the kind of trade unionism that emerged during this period did close down what few opportunities there were for building a defensive alliance to protect public services, based not on past practices but on future possibilities.

Since the mid-1970s the UK post-war settlement in the organisation and delivery of British welfare services has faced mounting criticism from both the left and right of the political spectrum. Indeed many of those employed within the welfare services, and committed to their preservation, have been at the forefront of such criticisms. However, since the 1979 election of the Conservatives under Margaret Thatcher the primary attack has been driven by a right-wing agenda intent on the marketisation and restructuring of social welfare. Yet the early 1980s also saw the election in many of Britain's major urban conurbations of radical left-wing Labour councillors committed to protecting welfare services but in a re-organised decentralised form to make them more democratically accountable and more able to meet the needs of service users. Indeed for a brief period until the 1987 election of the Conservatives for their third term of office, local government experienced a radical political renaissance, was a site for experimentation in policy initiatives, and became the centre of opposition to central government policies.

For the socialist councillors elected during this period, such plans of resistance and the development of alternative welfare strategies were to be built around a loose alliance between themselves, service users, community organisations, the new social movements, and public service trade unions. A series of measures were to be introduced that made service providers more accountable to users but also recognised the important contribution of front line workers to policy formulation. A commitment to high quality public services and an extension of democracy within the local state was to hold the alliance together, along with a common antipathy towards the new-right central government and the prospect of a future radical Labour government.

For many such local authorities at the centre of these initiatives was the decentralisation of local government services coupled with increased user control over their delivery. Decentralisation was hailed as the basis of a new partnership between elected members, service users, and public service workers. Yet to succeed it required a transformation in the way white-collar public service workers saw themselves, both in relation to their professional practices and their position as workers. Above all it required them to step outside and beyond the normal industrial relations discourse and enter into a political dialogue aimed at building a new agenda for social welfare. Negotiating such a dialogue, on which so much appeared to depend, was never going to be easy for any of the stakeholders. Indeed it can be argued that such essentially local initiatives were doomed to failure unless they could be matched by similar transformations and leadership at a national level.

This book explores the role played by the National Association of Local Government Officers (NALGO), the principal white-collar public service union, in relation to these elected urban left radicals and their decentralisation strategy. This turbulent decade in local government, as well as demonstrating the key but often undervalued role of public service workers, proved to be a testing ground for their trade union politics. By focusing on a local authority proposing and implementing one of the most radical decentralisation initiatives both the limitations of such trade unionism and some possible future patterns are highlighted.

White-collar trade union reaction to these radical initiatives in local government proved to be essentially conservative and defensive. Nevertheless this can be argued as understandable given their actual experience of the new, mainly inexperienced, councillors and the practical consequences of the new policies that largely fell upon their shoulders. Indeed, the subsequent retreat from the urban left agenda and the failure of the proposed alliance would suggest to some that the union's politics were perfectly attuned to the circumstances. Nevertheless, whilst giving full acknowledgement to the pressures and risks facing the white-collar public service workers, the question is raised as to how far NALGO was able to break with a style of unionism increasingly modelled on their blue-collar colleagues in manufacturing, and what else they might have done to fully exploit the albeit limited opportunities to develop a socialist vision of public welfare.

Public service front-line workers have a wealth of information, knowledge, and experience to bring to the policy process and are essential to ensuring high quality service delivery. As public service trade unions increasingly engage in a proactive way with the policy debate a new form of trade unionism needs to be developed. As well as advancing the role of workers in the formulation and management of policies and ensuring that they can play a full part in the overall management of welfare provision, this also needs to give full recognition to the rights of service users and their role in managing services. The post-war welfare settlement built upon a partnership between the state and the assumed expertise of the professional, already fatally wounded by the new-right, still needs to be reconstructed by the left. A new democratic mandate for collective welfare is required that involves service users, welfare workers, and elected members as equal partners. Public service trade unions, as much as anyone, need to re-evaluate their priorities and strategies.

1 White-collar workers and white-collar unions

The new public service white and blue-collar union, UNISON, is the largest trade union in Britain with a membership of 1.4m. However, in exploring the politics of public service white-collar unions our focus is on the National Association of Local Government Officers (NALGO), one of the three founder members of UNISON, along with the National Union of Public Employees (NUPE) and the Confederation of Health Service Employees (COHSE). At the time of the merger, in 1993, NALGO was itself the third largest union in Britain, with 0.75 million members, and the largest white-collar trade union in Europe. It is in the context of this growing strength of public service unionism, their increasingly active role in social policy debates, and their willingness to adopt militant action, that the nature and character of their trade unionism needs to be understood.

In exploring these issues the decade of the 1980s provides opportunities to gauge trends and indicate future developments within the new union. This is an especially significant period for two reasons. Firstly, following the 1982 local government elections, a number of local authorities found themselves governed by what has been referred to as the new urban left. Those identifying with this label saw the need to develop an alliance of opposition to the then still young Thatcher government as the major task confronting them. The urban left elected into office were committed to pursuing new socialist policies, defending existing welfare services, challenging central government, and saw themselves as part of a broad alliance, in which they would have a leading role, of public service users, voluntary and community organisations, social movements, labour party activists, and the public service trade unions. Secondly, and as part of the urban left's strategy, a number of policy measures were initiated during this period that challenged existing relationships between public service workers, local government managers, and service users. For many authorities radical versions of the decentralisation of service provision, containing a commitment to extend local democracy, stood at the heart of their strategy. Such decentralisation policies are here used as a litmus test of white-collar public service trade unionism. It is suggested that an examination of union action via this particular configuration of local government politics and policies provides useful insights into the general nature of public service trade unionism. However, our starting point is to review work done to date in exploring the emergence of white-collar trade unionism and its relationship to the structural position of white-collar workers, as this provides a useful contextual framework in which to consider the specificity of events in what was a turbulent decade of local government politics.

This chapter traces briefly the overall growth of white-collar work, highlighting the heterogenous nature of the category, and the parallel growth in white-collar trade unionism and its militancy. It then attempts to summarise the ongoing and complex debates concerning the class position of white-collar workers and its relationship to trade unionism. It is suggested, however, that such theories have tended to neglect the particular nature of public service work and the consequences of state employment. Finally, it draws together some general comments on the potential nature of white-collar unionism. However, understanding the nature of white-collar unionism is acknowledged as a complex process. Thus whilst the relationship between objective class places, class consciousness, trade unionism and its character is worthy of detailed study, no automatic link between these can be assumed and any understanding of structural location whilst important is insufficient for an account of collective action. In addition to class place, any analysis must take account of factors concerned with class formation. Thus those who occupy such places, how they perceive themselves in relation to other social categories and the extent to which such categories as gender and race mediate their life chances are all considered important. Again the significance of class place must be measured against how "fixed" it is likely to be for particular occupants, or whether it simply represents a resting place on the way to somewhere else in the social structure. Further, the prior experiences people bring to their class place, along with contemporary experiences in other aspects of their lives and, for human service workers, their relations with the political process, also need to be taken into account. Equally, when considering the collective organisations of any group of workers, the history of that organisation and the role played by key actors are important in shaping its current character, as is the membership's assessment of the likely success of any proposed set of actions within a particular context.

No automatic link, therefore, is made between growing trade unionism and an emergent working class consciousness amongst white-collar workers. However, the sociological tradition that acknowledges a link between the changing structural position amongst occupational groups and their potential trade unionism is felt to be most useful in explaining these developments. Public service workers are here viewed as belonging to a category of white-collar work, ambiguously located performing functions that reproduce the capitalist social formation but often utilising criteria that are inimical to capitalism, and having to respond to pressure from social categories whose interests are objectively in conflict with those of capital.

Expansion of white-collar work

The overall expansion of white-collar work has resulted from a number of developments within the production process including: its increasing complexity; advances in technology; an increased division of labour; the expansion of specialised work sectors; the need for greater co-ordination and administration; the growth of managerial and supervisory functions; and the development of the service sector and decline in manufacturing. In particular, the post-war expansion of state activities especially in the areas of social welfare and the management of urban life has been crucial to this process. Bain et al. (1973) notes that between 1911 and 1966 white-collar workers increased by 176%, to represent 38.3% of the total labour force, as compared with an increase of only 5% amongst blue-collar workers. Such trends have continued across all sections of white-collar employment (Goldblatt 1983, Heath and McDonald 1987, Halsey 1987), affecting all social classes (Goldthorpe and Payne 1986), so that non-manual workers now make up the majority of the workforce. Such trends are powerfully evident within the public services, with employment within local government increasing by more than 100% between 1949 and 1974 (Fryer 1975, 1989, Buck 1985). By 1979, 29.8% of the workforce were to be found within the public sector, 12.3% working in local government. However, Price (1983), correctly warned against assuming such trends would continue uninterrupted as reductions in public services, the stabilisation of white-collar work in manufacturing, and the impact of new technology on routine non-manual jobs all led to a decline in this sector. Indeed Beaumont (1992) using Flemings's (1989) figures points out that public sector employment reached a peak in 1979, and between 1979-89 declined by 18% so that its overall figure dropped to 24.9% of the workforce. However, within local government numbers fluctuated during the 1980s with 1988 their highest point (3,081,000 employees), although across the whole decade there was a decline of 2.1%. Beaumont also points out that there was some considerable variation within these categories such that whilst overall employment in local authority education declined by 6.4% social service employment increased by 19.5%.

A fractionalised workforce

Yet such overall figures can create a false sense of homogeneity amongst this category of white-collar worker and their organisations (Hyman 1980), masking what Fryer describes as a "compounded fragmentation of labour" (Fryer et al. 1975). Such heterogeneity makes an understanding of those organisations such as NALGO, representing diverse segments of white-collar workers particularly difficult. Although there continues to be significant differences between white and blue-collar workers in respect of their market and work situations, typically for example, over average earnings, holiday entitlements, hours worked, sick pay, pensions, internal career prospects, autonomy over one's work and levels of authority over other workers (Stewart et al. 1980), there is considerable overlap between those at the bottom of the white-collar and the top of the blue-collar sectors, leaving Price (1983) to refer to "a more or less favoured non-manual group". Others, such as Braverman (1974) and Crompton and Jones (1984) consider these overlapping white and blue-collar workers as objectively occupying the same class positions. However, this may not be the final occupational destination, especially for men, for those within the bottom of the white-collar category, as many begin a lengthy but ultimately privileged career structure in relatively menial roles (Goldthorpe 1987), resulting overall in a less stable social identity. Furthermore, there are significant forms of differentiation within the white-collar category itself, not only in relation to market and work situation, but also on the basis of gender and race.
  The non-manual sector is thus acknowledged to be segregated by gender both horizontally and vertically. Women dominate both particular occupations, usually low paid and low status (McDowell 1989), a process that has taken place over a short period of time (Hakim 1979), and different types of work (Walton 1975, Howe 1986). They are also likely to experience vertical segregation within those occupations where both men and women are employed (Crompton and Jones 1984, Beechey 1982). Within the UK public sector women workers made up 54.3% in 1977 reflecting both an overall

expansion in employment during the 1970s, and especially a growth in part-time employment. Thus by 1981, some 49.7% of women employed in local government were in part-time jobs (Beaumont 1992). Similarly a report of the Equal Opportunities Commission (1993) noted that women remain under-represented in management and professional occupations. In 1992, although women represented 47% of all employees, they made up 32% of employees in managerial and administrative occupations and 40% of those in professional work (see Social Trends 1995). Similarly the report pointed out that those women within management continue to be found mainly at the lower levels of management, although some improvement in this since the 1970s is acknowledged. Nevertheless we can agree with Marshall et al. (1988) who conclude that "class systems are structured by sex in ways that clearly affect the distribution of life chances, class formation and class action among both women and men alike" (p 73).

A similar division exists in relation to the racial composition of white-collar work. Thus, despite the fact that as race has shifted from the periphery toward the centre of politics, and a "partial racialisation of policy" (Mitchell and Russell 1989) has been evident via "municipal anti-racism" (Gilroy 1987) resulting in increased public service employment opportunities and a channel for internal mobility for some black workers (Sivanandan 1983, Stubbs 1985), two basic points need to be made. Firstly, black people remain under-represented in white-collar jobs, and secondly, where black workers are so employed they are nearly all in lower paid positions (Doyal et al. 1981, CRE 1982, Brown 1984, Gordon and Newham 1986). Thus Ouseley et al. (1981) found that, despite its commitment to race equality, black workers in the Borough of Lambeth Social Work Directorate, were under-represented within senior management, specialist, professional and practitioner posts.   Overall, some 80% of the black staff were concentrated in the lowest three, non-social work grades. More recent research (Stubbs 1985 and Dominelli 1992) confirm this picture, arguing that not only are there relatively few black workers within social services but that where they are found they occupy lower status positions. However Brown (1992) notes that whilst in the mid-1970s, "the low penetration of white-collar occupations was the most striking characteristic of the black and Asian labour force ..." (p 52), some recent figures suggest otherwise but he challenges the impression given by current Labour Force survey statistics, that for example show a higher proportion of those of Indian origin than whites in professional jobs (Department of Employment 1991). These, he argues, are distorted due to the high proportion of those of Indian origin in self-employment, but included within the employee figures, and high numbers of black unemployed who, if in work, would be counted in manual occupations. Brown concludes that, "among black and Asian workers there is still a disproportionately large number of semi-skilled and unskilled manual workers ... At all levels of employment ... evidence of continuing widespread discrimination" (pp 60-61).

In addition to any differentiation based on gender and race, public service workers are here understood as a significant category in their own right (Carpenter et al. 1987), distinct from the general category of white-collar. Their human 'product' is often intangible, involving a change in attitude, behaviour, or circumstance in one or more people following their interaction with the worker. Unlike industrial production, the process of production and the quality of the product is a central concern within human service work. Here production and consumption occur simultaneously, "The client ... is both the consumer ... and the primary raw material being processed ..." (Prottas 1978 p 289). Further, such workers are distinguished by their relationship with state power itself. They sell their labour power for the production of social use values, in the reproduction of the social formation. Such use values are largely determined in the political process and consequently attention must be paid to the relationship between the service producers and elected representatives as each appeals to a different source for their legitimacy (a democratic mandate or political programme vs. possession of professional knowledge and credentials). Since the early 1980s the conventional pattern within local government of elected members leaving day-to-day welfare practice to the professionals, and looking for guidance on policy development to senior professional management, the central state, and to their political parties at national level, has been dramatically broken by both 'municipal socialists' and 'new right' councillors prepared to intervene both at the level of policy and practice (Livingstone 1982, Seabrook 1984, Boateng 1985). Nevertheless, the identification of use values, and clarity over how these should be met, is rarely straightforward so that such workers often experience high levels of autonomy, flexibility, and ambiguity within the labour process, which allows for a range of often opposing ideas and practices to be injected (Prottas 1978, Lipsky 1980, Pithouse 1990).

For Johnson and O'Donnell (1981), human service work potentially contains, "the germ of a new society, one which is organised to collectively produce, distribute and consume values in a human, rational and egalitarian form ..." (p 42). For others (O'Connor 1973, Offe 1975) state welfare provision not only reproduces capitalist social relations but also negates them by introducing new and additional social relations of production. Human service workers can then be placed along a continuum ranging from those primarily concerned with social control, or social reproduction, to the meeting of collective and individual need. However, such distinctions are not always clearly demarcated for contradictory functions are usually contained within the same job description. The significance of such functions, which confer relative degrees of power, has been a neglected area in the white-collar literature. Thus, although writers such as Bain and Price (1972) refer to the relative possession of, or proximity to, authority, as being a differential factor within white-collar work, they are primarily concerned with authority in relation to other workers rather than control exercised over other citizens in the policing and social reproduction of people and social relations. Moreover the contradictory nature of such work, and its transformative possibilities, has undoubtedly been an attraction for a significant number of those employed therein and this may also predispose them to trade union membership. Thus Carpenter et al. (1987) suggest it is the "growing contradictions between the 'caring' image and the reality ... which creates the spaces favourable to trade unionism, which may be expressed either as alienation and growing instrumentalism and/or a desire to recapture 'caring' values" (p 36). Yet Martin (1984), argues that as a consequence of their caring functions, such social service workers can be viewed by the public as forfeiting their right to pursue their own material interests. Further, workers may themselves accept this, thereby restricting the range of organisational tactics available to them. Yet their unions may, equally, use a 'nature of the work' argument as a justification to press for better conditions, hoping this will reassure workers who believe that consumers deserve a 'proper service', and are concerned with the ethical implications of prioritising their own material interests.

The Islington research tends to confirm such contradictions and tensions, in the relationship between the worker and their product. This is illustrated by comments from current or former NALGO shop stewards. Some expressed it, as Carpenter et al. argued, as a tension between their belief in the service and their growing inability to deliver it,

I have a strong sense of sympathy, and I care very much about the poverty and difficulties people have to face but I'm not quite sure how much longer I can go on working in the public services, on the front line, dealing with people's problems ...

I feel somewhat burnt out ...
(Welfare Rights Worker - female)

I am quite happy to work outside my contract. All I want is to get the job done.
I'm there to provide a service ... Most people want to get the job done effectively.
Council often wants to cut corners."
(Housing Improvement Worker- male)

Many highlighted the conflict between being a trade unionist and delivering public
services,

You try to provide a good service, but as a trade unionist you try to protect yourself,
but part of that is fighting for a better service. If you're fighting for better pay you
are also fighting to retain the best staff to deliver the service.
(Housing Estate Manager- male)

If I've had to go out on strike I just try to make sure things will be okay, and hope
and pray nothing happens (to clients) even if that means working harder between now
and when the strike takes place.
(Social Worker - female)

Others saw the union as a vehicle for arguing for better quality services,

... the reality of the product that was on offer (decentralisation) was not what it was
being presented as, so I felt I had a duty, as a trade unionist, to fight this through the
union ... the trade union becomes a very important political tool to fight back and
present your views on welfare ...
(Social Worker- male)

A minority said they would even be prepared to sacrifice some of their benefits as
workers for a better service to users,

I think the union should be involved in service delivery. It is quite a legitimate role,
for a group of organised workers with experience of the services, to feed into
discussions about policy changes because there is obviously a lot of expertise ...
Providing a better service may mean giving things up as workers ... I feel we should
emphasise a good positive environment for the public. We're providing a public
service.
(Housing Estates Manager- male)

Many simply emphasised the commitment to public service provision,

If you work in a job that provides a service to the public you obviously feel that what
you do is useful.
(Administrative Worker - female)

It's rather hard to be a trade union member with socialist ideals, wanting to see
things progress, to see services delivered to working class people ... Workers feel
they have a duty to serve the public ... a lot of people in the public services are
really committed to helping people, to deliver a service to people less fortunate than
themselves ...
(Housing Advisory Worker- male)

Such comments illustrate the difficulty for public service workers of detaching
themselves from their product, and separating or prioritising their material conditions of
work over the quality of service provision. The centrality of the service user, in the

labour process of public service work, means that the social relations involved are a distinctive feature, "... only for human service workers do there exist social relations with the human object of their labours" (Stevenson 1976, p 82). This is not to argue that such concerns could not be found in other work and indeed there have been examples where such feelings have been expressed (Collective Design Projects 1985). It is, however, suggested that, unlike normal capital-labour relations, such tensions are central to the principles of collectivised social goods based on need.

Yet such caring relationships should not be idealised, nor the assumption made that workers alone can define the nature of the product, committed though they might be, rather than their managers, elected members, users, consumer groups, social movements or the public. Indeed, one of the arguments advanced by the proponents of decentralisation was precisely that public service workers should be more accountable to the user and have closer contact in order to better identify and respond to social needs: a position that finds resonance in the demands of many user and community groups. Moreover, historically public service unions have paid relatively little attention to the transformation of worker-user relations or the development of alternative models of service deliver. Clearly a change in the power relations with users could have a profound impact on the labour process of public service workers and there are signs that users are increasingly unwilling to accept existing relations (Small 1987, Gyford 1991).[1] Yet ironically, as users begin to demand a relationship based more on principles of partnership, negotiation, democratic accountability and control, so workers demmonstrating an increasing defensiveness, begin to define their collective interests in part on the basis of the 'otherness' of the user, presenting them as threatening, troublesome, with complex problems that demand high levels of skill and an ever-increasing level of resources. Indeed, there is some evidence of a distinction between the trade unionism of public service workers and that of other workers, the latter, it is suggested, having a more developed sense of "societal unionateness" (Prandy et al. 1983) and which is said to explain an apparently lower commitment to the wider labour movement amongst public service unionists, despite higher levels of membership. Thus Rallings (1983) concludes that, "white-collar workers' involvement in trade unionism seems to be based on instrumental not ideological considerations. There is little basis ... for sentiments consistent with a proletarian or even collective type of class consciousness" (p 65).

Human service work is thus premised on a set of values that contain a point of opposition to existing market values. Yet is also dependent upon continuing capital accumulation by the market to secure its existence and its primary function remains that of social reproduction. Workers both meet need and manage it, strive to empower people but reproduce patterns of dependency and powerlessness. Such work may be attractive to those who espouse socially oriented values but they must do so within the requirements of capitalist legitimation and social reproduction. As workers, they also have their own group interests and organise collectively to defend and promote these, especially when the state proves less than willing to provide the status, personal rewards, and resources they believe justifiable to support their work and position. Such interests, however, may often conflict with those of their human products, to whom they are also committed. Thus human service workers are both a distinct sector of white-collar work and ambiguously located, faced with conflicting functions, sources of legitimacy and accountability, commitments and loyalties.

The state

Discussion of the state is well documented elsewhere (Dunleavy and O'Leary 1987).

Yet if the actions of public service workers are to be fully understood it is necessary to give some consideration to the nature and role of the state and the extent to which it determines their structural location and opportunities for social action (Fairbrother 1980). This is also particularly important in the context of the new urban left as it emerged in the early 1980s for, as Gyford (1985) comments, "One should not underestimate the importance which many of them attached to a correct theoretical underpinning to their work" (p 37). Although our main focus will be on the local state, this cannot proceed without some initial reference to the overall state.

The concept of 'the state' is here understood as a shorthand description for both a set of social relations (Poulantzas 1975, CSE State Group 1979, London to Edinburgh Weekend Return Group 1980) and a complex set of institutions (Miliband 1969), with different functional requirements, internal relations, and distinct patterns of social relations in their interventions in civil society. It is neither "autonomous of society ... (nor) ... is it wholly determined in form and function by society ..." (Hall 1984, p 23). Within the state there are a number of competing and consciously mobilised interest groups, but they nevertheless act within, and are dependent upon, certain economic imperatives, and are not free to act in any way they want (Offe 1982). There are also boundaries to the state although not narrowly confined to the governmental machinery, and within these it performs functions that do not always comfortably co-exist, but rather display contradictions and tensions between them, not only reflecting competing interests within the state system and external demands to pursue conflicting objectives (Poulantzas 1972, 1975, Offe and Ronge 1975, Hall 1984) but also, as O'Connor has argued, inherent contradictions between the functions of capital accumulation and legitimacy. To that extent it is possible to talk of 'the state' without having to accept that life within it reflects a single-mindedness of purpose, or that real and significant changes cannot be brought about either from within it, or through pressure from without. Nor does is assume, however, except in specifically transformative moments, that such changes, once achieved, will remain in place without being subjected to efforts to remove or reformulate them in ways that render them unrecognisable to their original form or intention.

The state then is not a free-floating subject, but an aspect of class society, emerging over time, and firmly located within a particular mode of production. It is a central mechanism for ensuring the conditions for capital accumulation, "the cohesive factor of the entire social formation" (Poulantzas 1975, p 156). Its contradictory character is to be found in that it both defends and is often peopled by those specific interests sustaining a mode of capitalist production but gives legitimacy to a social system that offers competing possibilities and conflicting demands (O'Connor 1973). It performs these functions in a number of ways including: maintaining law and order; fostering social harmony and consensus, ensuring the reproduction of the social formation; protecting and furthering the interests of the nation, as expressed by the dominant social class; and directly intervening in the economic process (Poulantzas 1975, Offe 1984). Within this a crucial role for the state is to act as though it represents the general interests, acting neutrally as if classes did not exist, whilst simultaneously preserving the overall interests of the dominant class (Offe and Ronge 1975, Hall 1984).

Purely functionalist models (Poulantzas 1975), provide only an inadequate understanding of the state, and have rightly been subjected to much criticism for the limited scope ascribed to working-class organisation (Gough 1979, Held 1987), obscuring the boundary between state and civil society (Miliband 1972), giving insufficient recognition to the diversity and competing perspectives within the state, not providing an historical account of how the state came into being in the particular form it did (Saville 1975, Hall 1984), and not explaining how it is that the state behaves in ways that guarantee the conditions for capital accumulation (Offe and Ronge 1975). It is not then its functions that ensure the state's relative autonomy. Equally, the state is not simply an instrument of a dominant class (Miliband 1969, 1972). Rather the state is concerned with the interests of all members of a class society and must be able to respond to competing demands and pressures from what is a complex contradictory social structure, whilst striving to maintain capitalist accumulation; a process which constantly requires the state to intervene in a partisan way, and in so doing undermines the commodity form (Offe and Ronge 1975). Moreover, opportunities exist for conflicting interests both within and external to the state, to sometimes form cross-class alliances powerful enough to secure reforms against the interests of other fractions including the dominant ones (Hall 1984). Yet what is not clear is the extent of such autonomy (Gough 1979), for this will be determined by a number of factors including, the ability of the state to effectively anticipate and respond to needs or conflicts, successful intervention in the market, the degree of convergence between competing interests, and ultimately by the balance of forces between those competing social formations in struggle with each other (Offe and Ronge 1975, Gough 1979, Offe 1982). Yet the state also has very powerful forces at its disposal which can be mobilised for explicitly repressive purposes when required. However, this is not the usual response within social democracies, as the state is concerned with projecting an image of free and equal citizens (CSE State Group 1979). In turn this, "opens up the possibility of ... oppositional space within the state" (CSE, p 19) and permits the development of alternative forms of organisation and transformative political practices that can challenge the fragmentation imposed by the state (London-Edinburgh Return Group 1980), and which can be achieved by working from within state, as well as from the outside. However, radicals attempting to act progressively within the state should not ignore the ways in which state workers themselves participate in coercive and controlling relationships (Fairbrother 1980).

The primary role of the local state is one concerned with the reproduction of capitalist relations, by ensuring that labour power has the capacity to produce, and giving legitimacy to the social formation. In this respect, the post-war welfare consensus gave the local state the central responsibility for delivering welfare services and whilst this has been challenged and undermined since the 1979 election of Margaret Thatcher it continues to play a major role in orchestrating, if not always directly providing, such services. However, it is not as Cockburn (1977) argued, simply an instrument of capitalism, an agency of the national state. As a number of writers have pointed out (Dearlove 1979, Lojkine 1981, Byrne 1982, Duncan and Goodwin 1982, Cochrane 1989, Goodwin 1989), such functionalism again ignores the space for independent working class action, the specifically local factors involved in the formation of local states which itself generates conflict between local and central state institutions, or the possibility that groups will be able to organise to secure their interests. These need not be directly linked to the reproduction of capital, and may result in concessions being won from the dominant class, which can be expressed as local interests in opposition to the centre. Thus, local politics should be understood as being exceedingly difficult to manage, for as Cooke (1989) notes, they are "the sum of social energy and agency resulting from the clustering of diverse individuals, groups, and social interests ... centres of collective consciousness" (p 296).

Equally, however, one should not overestimate the importance of local politics, or underestimate the significance of national influences (Dunleavy 1980, 1984, Rhodes 1985, Stoker 1988), despite the often fragmented and divided nature of many of these nationally structured networks, segments of which may be actively opposed to the dominant formation.   Nevertheless, there have been attempts to construct locally determined alternatives in economic development and political life (Goodwin 1989), and local traditions, cultures, and practices, within some geographic areas have contributed to sustaining collectivist values in the face of a new right government committed to a individualist competitive market ideology. However, this has often not only highlighted the vitality and diversity of localism but also the weakness of territorial interests and the power of the centre to impose policies and thus, the limits of localist politics. Nevertheless, as Johnston (1990) summarises,

> Spatial uniformity is not the dominant characteristic of civil society ... places differ. Capitalism is characterised by uneven spatial development producing a map of places that differ not only in their productive characteristics ... (but) in how production is organised ... how social life ... is structured ... Thus local circumstances vary and with them the needs for state activity (both qualitatively and quantitively). (p 63)

There are then opportunities at the level of the local state to articulate and mobilise around alternatives to capitalist relations, citizenship and different visions of the state itself. However, locality politics should not be seen as so powerful in themselves, or sufficiently autonomous, as to create 'islands of socialism' (CSE 1979, Cooke 1989). Yet what is often absent from those emphasising the potential of local politics, and indeed from the politics of the urban left, is a sufficient recognition of the need for a national body that can effectively mobilise, co-ordinate, articulate, generalise, and where necessary, transcend such locally specific initiatives, yet without losing sight of local differentiation and local need (Murray 1988). However, as Offe (1984) argues, whilst there needs to be a revolutionary agency for the winning of state power, this must also revolutionise itself, and there is much that can be learnt from the new social movements in this respect. Initiatives such as those of radical decentralisation are particularly challenging because they are focused on the relationships and practices of potential partners in an alliance for social transformation and require their transformation if they were to succeed. However, in the absence of a general and widespread social crisis, such alliances are likely to be constrained in their efforts of self transformation.

The growth of white-collar trade unionism

Alongside the overall expansion of white-collar work, there has been a parallel growth in the membership and density of white-collar trade unionism, although a number of unions have their origins in the last century. More recently an increasing number have developed organisational structures similar to those found in their blue-collar counterparts and have been prepared to engage in militant forms of unionism to secure their interests (Beaumont 1992). Such growth in white-collar trade unionism has been at a steady rate, but not uniformly present across all groups, although Clegg (1985) notes that in 1910 and 1933 local government was one of the ten most unionised industries in Britain. It is estimated that 75% of all white-collar employees are members of an organisation concerned with employment, with 55% in full trade unions, but only 31% and 24% respectively are from the private sector (Prandy et al. 1983). The public sector is now the most highly unionised in the economy, with all groups of workers associated with this growth. More significantly, white-collar trade unionism has been less badly affected by the overall decline since 1979 in trade union membership. Thus in 1979, public service unionism had four million TUC affiliated members, and accounted for

37.4% of all trade unionism, a sharp contrast with its 14.3% share in 1911. This represented a ten-fold increase in membership, as against an overall four-fold increase in all trade unions (Fryer 1989). Nevertheless, such growth represented only an increase in union density from 33% to 44% between 1948 and 1979, and remained weak relative to manual workers (Rawlings 1983, Crompton and Jones 1984).

Three stages in the growth of union density have been identified by Price and Bain (1983), who highlighted a period of rapid increase after the First World War, a period of stability between 1950-1966, and a further phase of rapid growth 1969-1980, during which time, whilst there was an overall expansion in trade union membership, white-collar union growth accounted for slightly more than two-thirds of the total. Since 1980, the trade union movement has experienced a fourth stage during which many of the gains made in the 1970s had been lost by the mid-1980s. In 1980-81 alone, trade unions lost 1.3m members, almost 40% of the membership gained in the previous decade, with falls in membership outstripping falls in employment (Allen 1989). In the period 1979-88 the trade union movement as a whole lost some 3m members, a decline of more than 25% (Beaumont 1992), so that between 1978-91 membership dropped from a position where 53.1% of the employed population were union members, to one where only 37.7% were at the end of the period (HMSO 1995). However, most of the membership losses occurred in manufacturing whilst a number of white-collar unions continued to grow, including NALGO (up 0.20%).

Within these general trends union growth has been quite spectacular in some areas, and most notably in the public services (Fryer et al. 1975). Thus, NALGO increased its membership from 146,324 in 1966 to 231,790 in 1975 (a 58% increase) and overall Fryer (1989) estimates that in a 35 year period, 1950-1985, NALGO experienced a growth of 282%. Despite cuts in public expenditure and the general decline in trade union membership, NALGO still managed a 1985 membership level of over 75,000, 71% higher than in 1970. At the point of merger in 1993 with COHSE and NUPE, into what is now the largest union in Britain 'UNISON', NALGO was itself the third largest union, and had retained its female majority (409,000 women members compared to 387,000 male members in 1982). Yet not only was the period 1969-1979 one of rapid white-collar union growth, it was also a decade characterised by an increase in militant action among those in local government employment (Joyce et al. 1988). Walsh (1982) dates this change in character from 1969, noting that this was not so much in relation to the number of strikes, but rather for strikes to last longer and involve more days lost. In addition, Walsh suggests that other tactics, including boycotting, go-slows, working to rule, and demonstrations became part of the weaponry of local government unions, all of which contrasted with the situation prior to 1961 when NALGO's rules forbade members to take strike action.

White-collar unions

How can this growth in membership, and increasing militancy, amongst white-collar public service trade unionists be explained and what might it represent? There are two broad schools of thought to this issue of the nature of trade unions in general and white-collar unions in particular: the industrial relations approach and the sociological tradition. Despite some overlaps between the two approaches (Carpenter et al. 1990), there are also some marked differences. The former, led by Bain and his associates (Bain 1970, 1972, 1973, Bain and Elias 1985) rejects any connection between increasing white-collar trade unionism and the class position of such workers. The sociological tradition, within which there are a number of competing analyses, stresses a strong relationship between social class, union membership and union character, so that, "an understanding of the white-collar class situation is essential to any interpretation of white-collar behaviour" (Crompton 1976, p 412).   Equally, however, it is long acknowledged that, "there is no inevitable connection between unionisation and class consciousness" (Lockwood 1958).   The sociological tradition attempts to explain the growth of white-collar trade unionism by reference to the system of social stratification and the class place of white-collar workers within it.   Central to this is the view that trade unions have historically had a dual role of both defending and promoting sectional interests, as much in relation to other workers as in respect of management, but are also linked to a labour movement and, therefore, have a more generalised collective consciousness. Thus their emergence may symbolise a consciousness of class, weak and inconsistent though that might be, and consequently any substantial increase in the number of white-collar trade unionists is to some extent a reflection of both their changing class position and the development of a class consciousness. Crompton (1976), for example, notes, "to the extent that the class situation of the white-collar worker ... approaches that of the manual worker, so will the likelihood of union membership increase" (p 412).   Thus, there is an attempt to demonstrate that collective action is a recognition that groups of workers have interests in common, although these may be restricted to occupational rather than universalistic interests, which are in conflict with those of the employer, and which cannot always effectively be resolved via individualistic strategies or through appeals to common interests. Such a consciousness may also recognise that other workers share similar interests, and that the trade union movement is the most effective vehicle, at least on an instrumental level, for the expression and promotion of those work-based interests.

The industrial relations school of white-collar trade unionism

For some writers explaining the growth of white-collar trade unionism has been relatively straightforward and Bain and his associates (1970, 1972, 1973) have presented what continues to be an influential 'industrial relations' model. Underlying their work is the view that there is no relation between social class and white-collar unionism. Instead, three 'strategic variables' are identified to explain aggregate white-collar unionism in Britain: employment concentration linked to bureaucratic organisational patterns; employer recognition; and favourable government action. Later, Bain modified this by introducing economic factors to explain the pace and direction of white-collar union growth both prior to recognition, by providing an immediate motivational drive, and post recognition, by influencing the continued need for growth and development. Thus Beaumont (1992) concludes that, "the major cause of the changed character of public sector, white-collar unions in Britain from the late 1960s has been the operation of income policies" (p 56). Price (1980) suggests that other variables, such as gender and race, could also be added as key mediating factors in workers' reactions without disturbing the Bain's model.

For Bain (1972), white-collar workers are motivated to join unions primarily, "to control more effectively their work situation" (p 188). This need arises as a consequence of the increasing bureaucratisation and concentration of their employment situation, thereby reducing their ability to influence the labour process through other means. However, a combination of such circumstances and motivational drive are seen as insufficient in themselves since, "their growth will not be very great unless their recognition by employers is extended ... the strength of these unions will generally not be sufficient in itself to persuade employers to concede recognition; this will require the help of government. In short, future white-collar unionism is largely dependent upon government action to encourage recognition" (p 188). Managerial policies are important because Bain assumes that white-collar workers are unlikely to risk the loss of their personal and collective rewards, actual or anticipated, through a collective struggle around union recognition. Similarly, he believes that it is indeed in the interests of management to grant such recognition and, operating within a social democratic framework, sees the state as a mediator in such conflicts, assisting management to see the benefits of co-operation in the interests of economic success.

There are, however, a number of difficulties with the Bain's overall approach (Adams 1977). For example, in relation to the role of the state Bain suggests that not only do white-collar workers need state support if their unionisation is to proceed but also that the state is motivated both by a desire to be a good employer and to see the development of trade unionism as linked to economic prosperity. Such views are difficult to sustain and Bain appears to make the mistake of universalising state motivation conceived within a pluralist and corporatist framework from one specific historical moment. Although the state may indeed play an influential role this can be both in encouraging or undermining unionisation, as the Thatcherite period visibly testifies. Similarly, state support for unionisation may occur for other reasons such as in response to increasing militancy amongst manual workers (Smith 1987), or as an attempt to institutionalise social conflict. In addition other concerns with Bain's model include: the lack of recognition given to the other sources of support for white-collar unionisation; the assumption of an almost permanent relationship of dependency by white-collar workers in relation to management and the ascription of a universally limited motivational drive amongst them and conversely its neglect of the potential for collective strength and identity to develop amongst white-collar workers as a consequence of their engagement with both management and the state, and especially the role of the white-collar activist in promoting and sustaining trade unionism. One can indeed point to circumstances where the state has encouraged union growth, granted union recognition in its capacity as employer, or legitimised unions by according them high status. However, encouragement by the state at a particular time towards a trade union may in fact be perceived in such a way as to both inhibit the growth of membership and negatively influence how others relate to it. Similarly, the model tells us little of what might happen if recognition or support is subsequently withdrawn. The implication must be that white-collar unions would enter a period of decline yet as we have seen this has not been their universal reaction despite sustained and extreme hostility from the state during the 1980s.

As Carpenter (1987) points out, the state and management are just as likely to be influenced by the unions as they are to adopt a Bain-like posture of making a rational assessment on the merits of collective organisation for workers and the management of conflict. The lines of influence are thus complex, interactive and changing rather than the one-directional route suggested by Bain. Carpenter (1989) illustrates this point in relation to the creation of the health service unions in 1919, suggesting that recognition can only be understood in the context of a combination of favourable economic and political conditions, a group of activists able to respond effectively to relevant issues, the failure of existing professional bodies, and a lengthy period of local and national conflict with a threatened national strike. In addition there was also the general growth in trade union membership nationally, which leapt from 2.5 million in 1910 to 8.3 million by 1920, and the growing political confidence of labour. However, important to both developments, was the ending of the war which provided unions with additional strength as the government was keen to avoid industrial unrest and was willing to make concessions.

Management, as Bain argues, clearly does enjoy considerable power, and its willingness or refusal to grant recognition is indeed likely to be important for the future development of a union. However, as with the state, management is not always united: divisions exist over appropriate strategies to both control labour and extract the highest return (Friedman 1989). Similarly, workers can themselves influence the way management perceives how its interests are best realised. Bain suggests that, as a consequence of worker concentration and bureaucratisation, it is in managements' interests to pursue a corporate strategy, thus recognising unions, in order to produce a rational, structured and institutionalised framework within which dialogue can take place, or in Lumley's words "for this conflict to be contained, controlled and eventually resolved" (1973, p 57). However, management may believe, as the new public sector managerialism has revealed, that its interests are better served through other strategies such as: resisting workers' pressure; forestalling future pressure by trading off concessions; exploiting divisions amongst workers; promoting other avenues of representation; or pursuing tactics of intimidation and refusing to compromise. Yet workers will not necessarily passively accept whatever strategy management adopts nor will the outcome be entirely dependent upon the narrow relationship between management and union as both are influenced by wider political and economic events.

Bain's starting point is the isolated individual worker making rational choices who is thus unwilling to forsake their career prospects by engaging in collective struggle. This, however, ignores the transformative possibilities in both the consciousness and confidence of the individual worker inherent in the coming together of groups of workers seeking union recognition. Further, it does not allow for the possibility that such collective strength might indeed be enhanced by a refusal of recognition rather than it always being dissipated. Bain takes insufficient account of the collective learning processes in a struggle for recognition, and the impact these can have both on the individual, and crucially, on the collective. It is this sense of collectivity that in practice will support and enable individuals to overcome those fears, anxieties and uncertainties that are experienced by both white and blue-collar workers. Bain is mistaken to assume that only white-collar workers feel they are entering a high-risk area when seeking recognition or taking union action: such feelings can be present throughout the production process.

The sociological tradition

In surveying the diversity of white-collar work it is generally acknowledged that there are essentially three distinctive groups of workers: the de-skilled proletarianised workers who in all respects, other than perhaps consciousness, are part of the working class; those in senior managerial and comparable white-collar work who appear to be closely associated with the bourgeoisie or dominant class; and finally an intermediate group over whom there is most dispute but who are generally thought of as being ambiguously located in class terms. Amongst those writing about class there appear to be four broad categories: firstly between those who adopt either a marxist and weberian definition of class which also includes a group who attempt to work between such divisions; secondly, amongst both marxists and weberians there are those who emphasise class structure, usually linked to occupational differences, stressing the workers' relation to production, functions performed and market or work situation, and those who are more concerned with class formation with again those who seek to explore the relationship between both. Finally, in terms of the overall approach to the debate there are those who attempt to develop a more theoretical approach and those who have given emphasis to exploring the development and practice of specific trade unions or the position of particular white-collar occupations within a work setting, drawing out general conclusions from their case studies (Crompton 1993). Whatever their disagreements, most writers acknowledge the pioneering work done by Lockwood. For Lockwood (1958), influenced by both Marx and Weber, the most significant factor in the growth of clerical trade unionism was the increasing bureaucratisation of the workplace, which brought workers into closer proximity and subjected them to union rules. The actual character from any resultant collective organisation would, however, be determined by changes in their work and market situation, and by the social consciousness of the members. This was predicted to alter as the growing numbers of clerical positions meant that the social background of the workforce altered to include members of the working class.

The first category of white-collar workers, those understood to represent, as a consequence of their class place, the functions performed, or because of their privileged market and work conditions, a new and distinctive class, 'in and for themselves', are not our main concern. However, it is worth noting that they might be variously described. Thus Poulantzas, using a very much criticised narrow structural definition, labels them as the new petty bourgeoisie (Poulantzas 1972, 1973, 1975) where class places "... designated certain objective places occupied by the social agents in the division of labour: places that are independent of the will of these agents ... distinct from the class origin, the social origin of the agents" (1975, pp 14-17). Whilst Poulantzas ascribed all white-collar workers as part of this category he too acknowledged the significance of intra-class divisions, or fractions, within it which might ally themselves to other classes and taking "an important role as social forces" (1973, p 108). The American marxists B. and E. Ehrenreich (1977) describe these intermediate white-collar occupations as a distinctive albeit derivative class, "a professional-managerial class" based on the functions they perform in the reproduction of capitalist culture and class relations and "objectively antagonistic to both the working class and capitalists alike". The weberian writers, with a much greater concern for class formation, Goldthorpe (1982), Abercrombie and Urry (1985) and Carter (1985), drawing upon the earlier work of Renner (1978), identify state officials, managers and administrators in private business as belonging to a 'service class' who perform the "functions of control, reproduction and conceptualisation - necessary functions for capital in relationship to labour," (Carter 1985, p 122). Goldthorpe ascribes this designation to a wide range of occupations but distinguishes between two service classes. A central requirement within the service class is that of trust within the employment contract arising from the need in a complex society to delegate authority and for some to have specialised knowledge and expertise for which autonomy and discretion in work is required and substantial rewards are offered along with well-organised careers and predictable trajectories underpinned by professionalism. Their trade unionism is understood as an occupational strategy for both defending and promoting their existing privileges, and its character has little to do with a working class consciousness.

Goldthorpe is nevertheless reluctant to predict the nature of any socio-political activity by this class but suggests that it will be essentially conservative, pursuing a strategy of exclusion by credentialism, as it attempts to further its material interests through organisation and various forms of trade union action. However, if the service class needs to organise in this way to defend and promote its interests it raises the question of what will be the consequences for that relationship of trust on which the class was initially founded, highlighting the dysfunctional aspects of delegated, or borrowed, authority. Goldthorpe goes on to suggest that any workplace action will be narrowly focused, for to identify with or generalise issues to include other workers could only be threatening for the service class implying, as such action ultimately might, a greater degree of control from below. Thus, he argues, white-collar radicalism will remain "minoritarian, intermittent and localised", being "channelled into single issue movements or into forms which avoid direct involvement in questions of class inequalities in distribution or production" (p 183).

Thus, whilst the boundaries around the service group are often unclear, and therefore there are difficulties in respect of its self-identity and collective purposes, it is nevertheless proposed that this class can increasingly identify its own interests, and for which they would organise collectively in order to protect and promote them. Thus, its actions will be protective and group oriented, and there would be little about their trade unionism that was associated with a wider labour movement, although this would not necessarily mean that they would be unwilling to pursue tactics similar to those of the trade union movement if these were deemed to be most appropriate. However, as has already been indicated, the injection of workers into these places who hold opposing political values along with the hostility shown toward state employees at all levels during the last 15 years may have a destabilising effect, especially when this class can no longer be guaranteed continuity of reward. Similarly the injection of general private sector managers into the state suggests, perhaps, that there has not been the degree of trust in the ability of this sector as accredited by service class theorists to deliver the new managerialism required in the restructuring of welfare.

Whilst writers such as Goldthorpe would include public service workers within the service class and other service class writers (Abercrombie and Urry 1983) acknowledge the vulnerability of some such workers to the dangers of proletarianisation, still others (Callinicos 1988) are much clearer that public service workers have indeed already been deskilled and are now located within the working class. Indeed, the most popular explanation offered for a growing trade union consciousness amongst public service workers is that of the proletarianisation thesis. Braverman (1974) argued that the developmental logic of the capitalist mode of production was to create a universal market, resulting in an increasing loss of control by the direct producers over the production process. A worker's broad knowledge of the production process is removed and embodied in a management controlled organisation, so that workers are faced with a progressive reduction in skills through both advances in technology and consciously designed managerial strategies, producing, "an immense mass of wage workers", and "the sub-divided detail worker" (p 315). The result is said to be an increase in capital's control over production, a cheapening of labour, and an increased rate of exploitation. More recently these arguments have been extended to suggest that a fiscal crisis of the state will not only advance this process but will lead to greater consciousness of class (O'Connor 1973, Crompton and Gubbay 1977, Frankel 1979, Robinson 1981, Fairbrother 1984). However Braverman did not suggest that all white-collar jobs had been so altered but that there remained a range of intermediate categories, "sharing the characteristics of worker on the one side and manager on the other to varying degrees ... the position of such functionaries may best be judged by their relations to the power and wealth that commands them from above, and to the mass of labour beneath them which in turn they help to control, command and organise" (pp 404-406). This as Hyman (1980) suggests, indicates that for Braverman the middle layers neither constitutes a distinct class nor have they been (or would be) fully proletarianised but are located ambiguously.

A number of writers have applied this analysis to public service workers in the UK. Thus Corrigan, quoted by Sharron (1980), argues that the Seebohm reforms of the personal social services, "helped to produce a radical divide between planners ... and doers, and a degrading of the skills formerly required ... This process ... deskilling, turned social workers into simple, commanded, servants of the state who could more easily see that they were only there to plug certain gaps in the system" (p 9). It has become relatively commonplace for commentators within social work to refer to the supposed proletarianising features of the 'Seebohm factories' with their increased individualisation, atomisation, greater employer control, worker conformity to rules and procedures, and which are, for one writer, "little dissimilar from the impact of the introduction of the assembly line by Henry Ford" (Simpkin 1983, p 19). Others have argued a similar case for other public service occupations (Hart-Landsberry 1981, Weinstein 1986). Public sector workers, according to these arguments, are firstly deskilled, proletarianised and unionised, but then secondly, in the context of a fiscal crisis, become increasingly militant. Now they not only defend their interests, but become aware of and defend the universalistic principles of their work against market criteria, and thereby adopt a more class conscious position.

There have been a number of general criticisms levelled against Braverman, such as that the theory is over-deterministic, assuming that unionisation can be deduced from social position, that it overestimates the power of management and conversely underestimates the capabilities, bargaining position, and ways of resisting management by the direct producers (Buraway 1979, Giddens 1980, Westwood 1984, Littler and Salamon 1984, Cooley 1985). Similarly, it is difficult to impute motives as to why workers who face deskilling join trade unions, which may be as a means of combatting deskilling rather than a sign of class consciousness. Again workers may use the strength of their union not to advance class interests but against the interests of other groups of workers, maintaining old skill divisions and fragmentation within the working class (Rubery 1978, Stark 1980, Beechy 1982). Similarly management are not so strategically organised as Braverman implies and have controlling options other than deskilling, not least of which are those of 'responsible autonomy' or a core/periphery model (Friedman 1976, 1986, Wood and Kelly 1982, Childs 1985) as well as having other concerns such as profit maximisation which may generate different strategies (Wood and Kelly 1988). Moreover the exercise of power within organisations is clearly more complex and relational than Braverman suggests (Lukes 1974, Walsh et al. 1981). Braverman also technicizes 'skill' and insufficiently acknowledges its social construction (Carpenter et al. 1990, Cockburn 1983). Beechey (1982) identifies this skill-defining process as crucial in relation to women's work noting how so much of it has escaped such classification. Furthermore, she argues that trade unions have actively participated in this process of denial. Cockburn (1983) notes that the designation of skill attached to a job is not so much a reflection of the intrinsic difficulty of performing it as of the degree of organisational bargaining power of its holder. Additionally, Braverman neglects the possibility of any reskilling or skill enhancement, which may indeed be initiated by management in order to combat or undermine growing worker solidarity, increase those areas over which they have control, or redirect energies into areas newly defined as skilled but also more individualistically oriented.

There are also some specific difficulties when the argument is applied to public service workers. For example, it is not always easy to see which skills have been lost, or how to measure these against any new skills, specialisms, autonomy, or the drive towards increased training and professionalism that emerged with Seebohmisation (Carpenter et al. 1990). Again, the interpretation of events is not always clear. Thus, worker anxiety over the Seebohm reforms could be said to be at least in part associated with coping with new skills and working in unfamiliar areas. Further, whilst professional managerial control was undoubtedly extended, it is possible to interpret such increased supervision, form filling, and bureaucratic procedures as producing greater accountability, to the benefit of the service user, and ultimately as a protection for the worker against unjustified criticism or complaint, rather than a deskilling process. Moreover, some writers have argued that a loss of autonomy has not been an issue for workers. Pithouse (1990) in his research on a decentralised social services office, found there to be "considerable areas of practitioner autonomy which are the outcome of both covert and explicit negotiations within the organisation", and that such self-regulation, "contains certain disadvantages in that scrutiny and assessment of practice suffers in the contest over the control of work" (p 42). Indeed, he argues similarly to Lipsky (1980), that social workers do not complain about an excessive hierarchy but rather, "visit consumers according to priorities they set themselves. They apply their own preferred modes of intervention ... They ration their time and pace their energies ... redefine claims made upon them as legitimate or not" (p 45). Pithouse found that senior management were seen as removed from practice and, therefore, having no legitimacy to impose criteria for processing work, a position supported by local management. Consequently, he argues, "The claim made by practitioners to self-regulation requires that questions of competence are rarely examined openly" (p 50).

There may also be real limitations on how far management may be able to deskill particular groups of workers, however determined they may be, because of the nature of the work in question. Carpenter et al. (1990), for example, make the point that the uncertain and contradictory tendencies in state welfare work, and specifically the need for such work to be organised in a way that is sensitive to the individual needs of the user place certain restrictions on controlling mechanisms. Others (Prottas 1978, Lipsky 1980, Ferner 1985) have also highlighted the continuing autonomy and influence of front-line workers, the practical difficulties involved in managing them and the limitations on deskilling imposed by the complex and individually responsive nature of the job. Prottas (1978) explores the policy-making role of front-line welfare workers, suggesting, "To a considerable degree, caseworkers make welfare policy. They do so not merely in the context of their formal responsibilities, but in the context of their interactions with clients and to further their work-generated ends. They are not in-dependent actors but they do have considerable independence of action" (p 287). Prottas argues that, "despite the massive mechanisms designed to control and direct their behaviour" (p 288) front-line workers retain autonomy because they define the relationship of the client to the welfare agency, mediating "the transmogrification of citizens into simple, more orderly creatures" (p 189). Furthermore, their ability to define the client not only gives them power over the client but also, as a consequence of the label they have applied, places demands and expectations on the agency itself. Prottas makes the additional point that the nature of the social programmes themselves are complex and controversial ensuring that agency goals are multiple, contradictory and vague, making it difficult to police, despite large numbers of regulations. In addition, management has to deal with the attempts by other external forces, such as professional bodies and trade unions, to define acceptable behaviour for front-line workers. Finally, the behaviour to be controlled often takes place in places that are inaccessible to supervisors and the agency must often rely upon the front-line workers to say what they are doing and to reassure the agency that they are doing the correct thing. Indeed, the state to some extent depends upon such workers (Hoggett 1990), and their continuing autonomy and skill may well serve the interests of management rather than threaten them (Marshall et al. 1987).

Despite such modifications and criticisms, it is nonetheless acknowledged that a number of white-collar occupations have experienced deskilling (Crompton and Jones 1984, Carter 1985, Cousins 1987). However, as Carchedi (1977) argues, it is still a mistake to confuse the economic process of proletarianisation with the ideological and political requirements of becoming proletariat. The significance of what happens to a particular type of work may be relatively unimportant if the current occupants both expect to be and are upwardly mobile, final destinations being more important than current realities (Goldthorpe 1980). Although Braverman argues that he was only concerned with class places (1974, pp 26-27), his work only confirms the inherent weakness of attempting to consider class structure independent of class formation.

The idea that some workers, such as those found within human service work, are best considered to be in ambiguous, or contradictory, class places has been advanced by Wright (1977, 1985, 1989) and Crompton and Jones (1984). Initially, Wright (1977) began by using a class structure approach and focused on the contradictory interests within class places for those workers who sell their labour power but also dominate other workers within production. He identified three clusters of contradictory locations: managers and supervisors; semi-autonomous employees, with employed professionals the most cited example of those who retain high levels of control over their immediate labour process; and small-scale employers. Wright concluded that it was the class struggle that would determine whether or not such workers joined with the working class. His earlier work was heavily criticised for both over-emphasising relations of domination rather than those of exploitation, assuming that occupations could be ranked unproblematically and ignoring the functional nature of specific occupations (Crompton and Gubbay 1977, Roemer 1982, Abercrombie and Urry 1983). In response, Wright (1985) revised his class map, arguing that it was exploitation through the possession of effective control over productive assets that was the principal basis of the capital-labour relation. However, Wright highlighted other exploitative processes, suggesting that both organisational assets (defined as "effective control over the co-ordination and integration of the division of labour" (p 151) and skill/credential assets (measured by a combination of occupational job traits and autonomy) were important. He argued that structural changes within capitalism have impacted unevenly on different groups of workers producing a non-coincidence between the three key assets underpinning capitalism and resulting in class locations with "multiple class character" (1985, p 43). Wright also specifically included the state sector, acknowledged the importance of individual class trajectories in determining class and suggested that class positions must be viewed ultimately in "probalistic terms" (p 185). The inclusion of the state sector as a distinct feature of advanced capitalism is a useful advance in that it requires an understanding of the relations between human service workers and the users of state services in an analysis of the former's class position.

Thus, as a consequence of an uneven distribution of these different assets, Wright concluded that some workers would be in "objectively contradictory locations within exploitation relations" (p 87) and that managers and state bureaucrats occupied the principal contradictory location because "they embody a principle of class organisation which is quite distinct from capitalism and which potentially poses an alternative to capitalist relations" (p 89). The political implications of this for Wright, along with Goldthorpe, is that,

The heart of the positive struggle for socialism is radical democracy ... radical democratic control over the physical and organisational resources used in production ... Arguments for socialism in terms of the quality of life, the expansion of real freedom, the reduction of violence and so on, provide a basis for building class coalitions for socialist objectives. (1985, pp 287-289)

Again Wright faced criticism (Marshall et al. 1988) partly over what was perceived as an unacknowledged weberian shift in his work but primarily over the central place given to conceptual autonomy in a job for determining skill assets, resulting in some rather unusual occupational codings, the functionalist and overly deterministic nature of his argument, the difficulty of resolving the relationship between a class structural map and class formation, and the failure to acknowledge mediating factors other than class structure. Wright's (1989) subsequent revisions have attempted to acknowledge the, "temporal indeterminancy in the class location of people" (p 330), which he sees as especially important for professionals, experts, and credentialed labour, defining these as occupying "objectively ambiguous class locations" (p 337), and also accepted the concept of "medicated class locations" highlighting gender as an important determinant.

Crompton and Jones (1984) again stress the need to relate occupational function to class, arguing similarly to Carchedi (1977) that some workers face "structural ambiguity" as a result of the conflict between those capitalist and collective worker functions within the same occupation, and over levels of 'control' which, they suggest, relates to the degree of exploitation. However, Crompton and Jones are again only concerned with authority over other workers and do not consider the additional dimension of those workers, concerned with social reproduction, who exercise control over their human products. Such controlling functions relate to their class position by altering relationships with their employer and with other workers, as well as their own self-perception. Further, since such workers are heavily dependent upon the state not only for their work and market situation but for the existence of their product, then the political processes take on an immediacy and importance not found in other sectors.

For Crompton and Jones, white-collar workers do confront the likelihood of a greater centralisation of control and the loss of decision-making functions. As employers need to ensure that employees act according to organisational goals and values, which is seen as especially important in relation to those workers who possess real control through some degree of delegated authority or specialist skills, so they will deploy a range of controlling strategies. These vary and may include offering material rewards and career enhancement, deskilling, dequalification through opening up the market, the creation of organisationally specific qualifications so as to tie, or 'encircle', employees to a particular employer. Again, as in the decentralisation initiatives, employers could also distinguish more clearly between strategic and operational control so as to ensure that major decisions are retained at the centre whilst diverting workers' energy into the day-to-day issues of implementation. Workers also have a range of strategies available with which to respond to such controlling mechanisms, although their ability to lay claim to specialist knowledge is seen as particularly important in how effective they might be (Jamous and Peloille 1970). Human service workers not only have some difficulty in laying claim to specialist knowledge, as recent government ministers have not failed to remind them, but any delegated authority they might possess is not only "on loan" and vulnerable to being taken by their professional management but also by the much more potentially volatile group of elected representatives. Yet equally, such workers have, until recently, been effective in determining both the nature of social needs and how these are best met, possessing a degree of power unacceptable to critics from left and right (Wilding 1982, Friedman 1980).

Crompton and Jones (1984) suggest that all white-collar work should be placed along a continuum, varying in terms of their functional certainty to capital and labour, the degree to which they participate in authority and control, their ability to both conceptualise and implement, and their market and work situations. Thus there will be those with considerable power, autonomy, decision-making, and sometimes skill at one end, and at the other, those who find that at best their skill, power and autonomy are marginal and constantly under threat. However, reality is likely to be more complex than can be contained within any structural model. For those workers who perform functions that serve capital it may indeed be difficult to distinguish between their work and market situation and those of capitalists. No doubt such workers have a clear sense of their interests and how best these can be served. However, even within this group, there will be those who are either less secure, having a greater sense that because they 'serve' so their authority is borrowed and can be taken away, or who do not so closely align themselves with the values of capitalism. Similarly, whilst there are those who might objectively belong to the proletariat, nevertheless reject it at a subjective level because, for example, they see themselves as upwardly mobile, continue to experience some marginal differences in their work situation in relation to other colleagues, or continue to feel a status differential. Even if they recognise their proletarian position they may not wish to pursue their interest through collective action, or if they do, nevertheless see such activity in terms of an instrumentalism or group particularism rather than class consciousness. In addition, it is also the case that sources other than class, however defined, can be significant both in terms of social identification and collective action. Consequently class location may well be mediated by gender, race or ethnic origin, nationality, or cultural life-style and consumption patterns. Indeed in Crompton's more recent work (1993) she argues that "diverse 'images of society' and thus potential motivation to act" (p 203) are likely to be found within an essentially fragmented middle class. As an example of this she highlights the growth and specificity of public sector employment in which employees, especially in human service work, "are more likely to favour 'collectivist' or 'corporatist' modes of macro-economic regulation than those in similar occupations in the private sector" (p 204).

Whatever the outcome of the struggle over autonomy and control, which for some, including public service workers, may never be finally resolved, Crompton and Jones suggest, workers are likely to prefer, "inclusion rather than exposure". Thus they suggest the growth of white-collar trade unionism should be understood as an attempt to protect their relatively advantaged work situations, existing internal labour markets, and members' interests. However, the act of joining a union may well signal a view that their interests are no longer synonymous with those of their employers, leading them to seek alliances with other workers. This may be especially important in human service work, where decision-making and interventions are dominated by non-market criteria and where a significant number of workers with a collectivist philosophy have been recruited. Crompton and Jones rightly argue that there are in fact two aspects to the analysis of white-collar trade unionism: firstly, an explanation at the aggregate level; and secondly, why certain groups in particular occupations, in specific organisations, join unions and what it might mean to them. At the aggregate level, changes in class organisation is a necessary, but insufficient, condition for the overall growth of white-collar unions. On the more specific level, they note, similarly to Carpenter (1988), that, "many features combine and inter-relate to encourage or inhibit unionism" (p 174). However, a decision to join a trade union may not be directly influenced by positional pressures but could rather, as appeared to be so in the Islington study, be experienced as part of an occupational membership (Carpenter et al. 1990). Furthermore, attitudes to trade unionism are not fashioned entirely, in production, but mediated by developments in families, localities, and via ascribed membership of other social categories (Goldthorpe et al. 1969, Nicholson et al. 1981, Carpenter et al. 1987, Campbell 1988, Marshall et al. 1988). Similarly the case study confirms the view that any sociological analysis must take account of the totality of workers' prior and current experiences, their understanding of these and how these relate to their hopes for the future, alongside an analysis of labour processes, and crucially the role of activists within the workplace engaged in the process of constructing class and social relations (Carpenter et al. 1987, Nicholson et al. 1981, Crompton and Jones 1984). Carpenter (1988) neatly summarises the issue thus, "trade unions are not created in a vacuum. Some features of unionism are probably universal: a need shared with others to work in order to live, and to combine with them to overcome individual weakness in the face of a powerful employer ... But the actual circumstances in which these tendencies are made real varies enormously" (p 19) and we might add, as does the nature of the trade unionism that follows.

The character of white-collar unions

What then can we expect of the character of a white-collar union and what does their trade unionism symbolise? There is an underlying tendency in some of the literature to associate trade unionism with a consciousness of 'labour', and membership of the labour movement, in contrast with professional bodies which are associated with a commitment to existing structures and being aligned with management. Indeed Blackburn and Prandy (1965) attempt to offer a theoretical framework to determine the degree of a union's 'unionateness' based on an image of an ideal blue-collar union. They identify seven criteria by which to judge a union's character: (i) whether it declares itself to be a trade union; (ii) whether it affiliates to the TUC; (iii) whether it affiliates to the Labour Party; (iv) whether it is independent of employers for the purpose of negotiation; (v) whether it identifies collective bargaining; (vi) sees protection of members' interests as a major function; (vii) whether it is prepared to be militant. They describe the first four of these as indicating levels of "societal unionateness", and the last three as a measurement of "enterprise unionateness". The overall degree of unionateness is for them a measure of class consciousness and potential for class action. Yet as Beaumont (1992) suggests other independent unions, such as the Royal College of Nursing, are also increasingly "union-like" despite not having adopted the formal requirements within the Blackburn and Prandy framework.

Indeed that has been an increasing overlap between the concerns and responses from both professional associations and trade unions (Carpenter et al. 1990). Moreover there is, in fact, no reason to assume a unity of purpose and perspective within either of these types of collective bodies (Price 1983, Carter 1986). In addition blue-collar unions are themselves more often than not instrumental in approach and it is important to acknowledge the changing social meanings to the criteria used by Blackburn and Prandy. Rather, as Carpenter et al. (1990) argue, union character is better understood both as a dynamic process and one that is the outcome of various complex transactions between dominant coalitions of officials, activists, and ordinary members, operating in a specific politico-socio-economic and occupational environment, that is also related to the union's history. Consequently, it would not be unusual to find within a white-collar trade union demands that: may be disadvantageous for other workers and 'belie the proletarian nature of all trade unionism' (Carter 1986, p 133); attempt to maintain or enhance existing status or material divisions within the labour market (Armstrong 1986); avoid alienating their own members within supervisory or managerial positions (Carter 1986); are a mixture of individualistic and collective actions, determined not by ideology but their efficacy in achieving specific benefits (Mercer and Weir 1972, Price 1980, Crompton and Jones 1984); are confined to a narrower range of issues compared to blue-collar unions identified as requiring collectivist solutions (Mercer and Weir 1972); and which utilise militant tactics in order to maximise personal rewards and ensure possible career progression.

However, it is equally apparent that a number of white-collar workers do have wider ideological beliefs, prior relevant experience, along with skills, attributes and an energetic commitment, that motivate them to an activist role within the union, often securing themselves local leadership roles as stewards (Nicholson et al. 1981), and which also creates a tension between the ideologically committed steward and the more instrumental member. It may well be that the membership will tolerate such ideological stewards providing their own needs are dealt with effectively. Such stewards may also be needed for their vigilance, energy, knowledge, commitment, and willingness to take personal risks on behalf of both individual members and the union as a collective body. Conversely, Carpenter et al. (1987) note that stewards are not themselves devoid of instrumental goals, and that indeed being a steward may lead to additional tensions since the role can open up opportunities for social mobility, a route to management and enhanced status. In periods of low union consciousness with little accountability demanded, stewards can accumulate considerable influence and their views may even be seen as being those of the union. With a relatively passive membership stewards have opportunities to define the union's agenda or determine the 'appropriate' response to management.

Mercer and Weir (1972) thus suggest that white-collar unions will tend in practice to display an ambivalent and shifting blend of attitudes, a combination of individualism, sectional collectivism and societal collectivism. Alternatively, to escape from the more usual dualism between individualism and collectivism, it is possible to identify a number of different types of consciousness, all of which can be present in a union at any one point in time, although the relative influence of each would be expected to vary over time. Thus it would be possible to find:

(i)   Individualistic or particularistic strategies
(ii)   Group particularism e.g. professionalism
(iii)   Group universalism i.e. an occupational consciousness as typically found in traditional protectionist trade unionism
(iv)   Collectivist particularism e.g. a consciousness of gender or race
(v)   Collectivist universalism e.g. a political consciousness of class

Price (1980) similarly concludes that the concept of structural ambiguity is useful for exploring the union character of certain white-collar workers, quoting Roberts et al. (1977) that "White-collar workers are willing to support either individualistic or collective action or a combination of both depending upon the strategy that best fits their situation" (Price, p 172). Price correctly, I believe, suggests there can be no easy equation between union membership and the adoption of a general collectivist philosophy. Instead, it is important to consider, especially given the diversity of the white-collar workforce, the attitudes and strategies of each group in the context of its particular historical development and present circumstances. Furthermore, Price makes the important point that, "collective organisation and individualistic aspirations are fully compatible bedfellows" (p 173). A similar conclusion is reached by Crompton and Jones

(1984, p 203), whilst Mercer and Weir (1972) adopt the more conservative view that white-collar workers offer a limited instrumentalism, "a conditional assent not to the values but to the possible efficacy of trade unions in obtaining tangible benefits for their members" (p 257). A union's character is, therefore, better understood as moving in either direction along a continuum with, at one end, expressions and behaviour reflecting a conscious and explicit politics of class and, at the other, operating in an essentially pragmatic, opportunistic manner based on the current fairly narrow material and sectional demands of their members. Some unions may be more consistently located over time at one point along the continuum, leading to greater confidence in generalising about its character, but its location at any point will depend on a range of factors, some of which will lie beyond the organisation and its members.

In unions such as NALGO, recruiting the full range of white-collar workers, from deskilled proletarianised clerks to managers deeply enmeshed within capitalist functions via those ambiguously located workers, union policies are firstly, likely to reflect the views of its well organised sections, although these may ultimately come to represent those of the majority. Secondly, they are likely to be compromises reflecting the tensions between the different sectional or class interests as well as the different occupational cultures (Crompton and Jones 1984), although again the majority of members may agree on a broadly similar strategy to tackle a common problem even though it may be defined as a problem for different reason or have different consequences. Thirdly, within the public services, whilst the issue of the exercise of control over another worker may be significant, especially since this may involve control over another member of the same union, an equally important area, which raises the union's relationship to the wider labour movement, is that of the relationship between its policies and the service user, over whom the members may exercise considerable control. Finally, individualistic strategies may be amplified for in addition to there being a service ethic, which may inhibit the pursuit of militant action, public service work is also characterised by its individualistic nature, a relatively low level of collective teamwork, a professional faith in one-to-one relationships with a focus on individual change, and a close proximity between the interests of workers and managers in the delivery of services.

Conclusion

This chapter has explored the growth and heterogeneity of white-collar work and the parallel expansion, and growing militancy, in white-collar trade unionism. By acknowledging the heterogeneity of white-collar work it is recognised that different explanations may be necessary for the growth and character of trade unions amongst particular sections of white-collar work. Three distinct categories of workers were identified: those who essentially carry out the functions of capital;   those who effectively occupy proletarian positions; and those who are ambiguously located between them. An examination of the nature of public, or human service work and its principal employer, the state, led to the conclusion that this is a distinct fraction of such ambiguously located workers. Such workers are engaged in the function of social reproduction but also operate with values and processes that are inimical to capitalism. Whilst they may experience considerable autonomy over their work such workers are accountable not only to professional or generic managers but also to the political process and are thus disadvantaged in their efforts to identify or protect a specialised area of knowledge. Again, not only must they confront the controlling strategies of management (both professional and political), but they themselves exercise considerable control over the human product of their labours. No automatic relationship between trade unionism and class consciousness is assumed and although changes within the production process have been identified as being important in the process of unionisation, other social identities outside of production, and the role of key activists within the union have also been seen as important, and which will be evident in the next chapter when the historical development of NALGO is considered. Trade union character is a changing and evolving, multi-faceted phenomenon, that emerges through complex processes. Consequently, in a union such as NALGO, encompassing virtually every category of white-collar work, it is rarely possible to speak of its policies, at either national or branch level, as though they imply a unity of view and purpose. Rather, policy and practice tend to be unevenly developed, and reflect the outcome of conflict and negotiation between competing interest groups within the organisation, who are also likely to have competing views on the nature and purpose of trade unionism itself.

Note

1 Tenant organisations and single parent groups have been known to advise their members not to contact social workers; women's organisations have challenged what they experience as the patriarchal basis of much of social work, especially in relation to such matters as domestic violence, rape, and mental health issues; black organisations have been hostile to the public service response to understanding and meeting the needs of black consumers, particularly over housing, fostering and adoption, black children in care, mental health and justice issues.

2 NALGO: The development of a trade union consciousness

This chapter looks briefly at the current organisation of NALGO before considering its early history as it developed from being a social club for predominantly senior local government officers to an established trade union prepared to engage in the full range of militant industrial action and to adopt confrontational strategies in relation to government policy. The overall approach is influenced by Offe's (1985) three-dimensional analysis of trade unions and interest groups. This focuses on: the individual social actor and his/her relationship to the organisation; the structure, growth and relationships of the organisation itself; and the social system in which it operates. Particular attention is paid to the period between the end of the 1960s and the late 1970s during which time the union experienced a significant growth in its membership as well as launching itself into full-scale strike action, albeit for only one section of its membership   Such changes are then considered within the context of wider political developments. Of particular significance for NALGO's emergent character we highlight: the growing disillusionment over the potential for social democratic reform to tackle persistent social problems; the ideological orientation of a significant section of those entering the welfare professions during this period; the impact of a new form of public sector managerialism; the relative failure to attain full professional status within social work, an influential occupation within NALGO; the impact of the fiscal crisis; and the influence of a growing militancy within the wider labour movement.

The limits of trade unionism

Both classical (Marx, Lenin, Trotsky, Gramsci) and contemporary socialist writers have highlighted the 'limits and possibilities' of trade union action. In contrast the syndicalist tradition has argued that the power of trade unions represent the driving force in the transformation of capitalism by the working class, and the general strike as the ultimate weapon to bring about the downfall of capitalism itself, "the chief agency of class struggle in the present, and ... The embryonic administrative structure of the Socialist Commonwealth" (Hinton 1973, p 102). Such traditions of trade union militancy have remained within the movement through shop stewards movements, rank and file organisations, and the movement for workers control. However the mainstream of socialist thinking has been concerned to highlight the structural limitations of trade unions created in response to, and operating within, capitalism.

Perry Anderson (1967) highlighted five major limitations to trade unionism. Firstly, he notes that trade unions are in fact an essential part of capitalist society. Whilst, on the one hand, they resist the existing unequal distribution of income, they do not challenge the principle of unequal distribution itself. They are, he says, an expression of a socially divided society but not a challenge to that society: they are able to bargain and negotiate but not transform. This follows Marx's comment that, "... trade unions work well as centres of resistance ... They fail generally from limiting themselves to a guerrilla war against the effects of the existing system, instead of simultaneously trying to change it ...." (Marx 1968, p 229). Secondly, Anderson says that trade unions are "a de facto representation of the working class at its workplace ... institutional reflections of their environment" (p 265), in contrast to political parties which seeks a rupture with the environment. Again this follows the classical theorists, Lenin and Gramsci, who contrasted the trade union to the political party, the latter embracing a range of social classes, notably intellectuals and middle class elements, and with a vision that supersedes capitalism. Thus Lenin (1917) argued, similarly to Marx, that trade unionism was structurally limiting in its demands, and that it needed a theoretical injection from revolutionaries who would develop the existing 'working class consciousness' to a 'political consciousness', "able to react to every manifestation of tyranny and oppressions, no matter where it takes place, no matter what stratum or class of the people it affects" (p 99). Anderson's third point is that the main weapon in the trade union's armoury, that of withdrawal of labour, is extremely limited and ineffectual as a political weapon, even though it might be able to extract concessions and reforms. This is contrasted with the need for "an aggressive over participation in the system" (p 226) in order to positively create socialism. Fourthly, he identifies the sectoral nature of trade unionism which generates a corporate rather than socialist consciousness. Finally, Anderson argues that, "trade unions have only a sectoral power potential not a universal one" (p 267), there being no parity of power between 'management' and 'labour'. The former is able to use money the "universally transformable medium of power" to defend and promote its interests whereas labour is untransformable, and can only be withdrawn. Anderson goes on to argue, however, that where there is no political articulation of class conflict through a political party, the basic expression of such conflict, the economic struggle between workers and employers will persist. Trade unions, he says, despite their structural limitations have nonetheless a "creative and irreplaceable role in a socialist movement" (p 273) asserting as they do, an "unbridgeable difference between Capital and Labour" (p 274). Similarly, Allen (1966) reminds us that whilst the prime aim of trade unions is to "protect and improve the living standards of their members", they must also be perceptive and responsive not only to changes in the work situation but also to changes in its environment in general. Thus, whilst a trade union consciousness might best be thought of as instrumental class consciousness they also contain significant numbers who believe, to varying degrees, the trade unions are an expression of class consciousness. There is then a tension, between their short term aims and actions and longer term aims, held by some sections of the movement, to transform capitalism.

More recently, Fairbrother and Waddington (1990) highlight the tension within trade unionism between what they describe as "responsible unionism" and the "practice of collective organisation". For them, "put starkly, the issue for unions is whether to organise and operate in bureaucratically effective ways, or on the basis of collective participation and involvement ... there is a central tension ... between pressures toward hierarchical, accommodative forms of unionism, and workplace-based union activity" (p 16). The former is tied to a perception of unions as part of a corporate machinery, and they thus become concerned with an accommodation with government policies through the regulation of trade union procedures and the stability of the organisation, based on a centralised structure and a representative structure. However, they also note an extension of local bargaining autonomy. Thus, somewhat ironically, national in- itiatives which often focus, for example, on individual recruitment, ultimately rely upon an active collectively-based structure at the local level. Such tensions, are to be found within white-collar trade unions in terms of their actions and the motivations of their members, as they are in manual unions.

Thus within white-collar unions will be found members with sharply contrasting perspectives on the role and potential of trade unions. These will be reflected in a wide range of reasons and motivations given for joining a union, which can be represented along a continuum. At one end are those who feel they have little choice, as with a 'closed shop'. Next are those who join without having given the matter much thought but see membership as part of the package you accept when commencing employment. Then come those who wish to benefit from the services offered by the union, judging it in the way they would for any membership organisation. Next are those who, either reluctantly or more positively, accept the need for the union as an insurance policy that might be necessary in order to defend either their own personal interests, or those of their colleagues. These are followed by those who see the union as the most effective body for the promotion of group interests. Finally, at the other end, are those who join because they see trade unions as part of a universal labour movement, a socialist organisation, which closely relates to their own personal politics. Union policies and character will, as they develop and change, reflect such differences and the influence which any of these competing positions may to able to exercise.

Unions are complex structures, with a life of their own, and their own survival can be a most powerful driving force, and an end in itself. Further, in addition to any ideological differences in the nature of trade unions, they typically contain other internal divisions and interest groups. These can be based on a range of factors including where members are located in the structure (for example, divisions between ordinary lay members, local branch officers, activists, or full-time union employees); identity politics; professional or occupational rivalries; and divisions of social class and status (which can be especially pronounced in a union such as NALGO that recruits at all levels of the public services and across different occupational cultures). Such 'interests' are not simply descriptive categories, but represent the basis on which members might actively mobilise within the union to defend or enhance their position. Union character is not immune from such internal divisions and competing perspectives, but is rather shaped by them along with its relationships with other external bodies, notably management and government most immediately but also other trade unions, and more general economic factors that are likely to impinge upon its members interests. Trade unions then not only have to contend with testing the limits of organisations within capitalism that seek to both secure the best for their members from the existing economic relations, at least as much, as they wish to transform them, but also must balance their own competing internal demands with a view to avoiding, as a minimum criterion, consistently alienating any significant section of the membership.

The organisation of NALGO

NALGO, which recently merged with the other major trade unions within the public services, COHSE and NUPE, to form UNISON, the largest union in the UK, was itself prior to this the fourth largest trade union in Britain and the biggest white-collar union in the world. NALGO was also the primary union for local government white-collar workers, who accounted for two-thirds of its three-quarter million membership. NALGO was an 'open' union, accepting all white-collar workers in the public services (except the civil service), irrespective of grades, although the Federated Union of Managerial and Professional Officers (FUMPO) did emerge to represent the interests of senior staff in local authorities, health authorities and other similar organisations. Nevertheless, the description of NALGO by Nicholson et al. (1981) as "a white-collar microcosm, containing analogues of almost all the administrative and technical specialisms to be found across the range of white-collar employment" (p 48) remained true. NALGO's size and heterogeneity, a problem exacerbated in the new merged union, brought its own problems, for this "makes it more difficult to formulate generally agreed-upon demands to mobilise a common willingness to act" based on an understanding and acceptance of shared collective identities and mutual obligations of solidarity (Offe 1985, p 187). Yet, as Offe notes, the power of the union depends at least upon its perceived sanctioning potential which in turn is partly related to its size and ability to generate a willingness to act. The highly participative relationship between union leaders and members required to bring about such sanctions is, however, undermined by the growth in internal bureaucracy that usually follows from a growth in the membership.

NALGO was organised on a branch structure, involving over 1400 branches, based on a combination of geography and employer, with separate branches existing within each geographic area for local government workers, health service workers and those engaged in the gas industry. The branches sent one delegate to the union's Annual Conference, which constitutionally was the policy-making body. Between the branches and the Annual Conference were 12 District Councils to whom again each branch elected one delegate. These organised separate Service Conditions Committees for each of the organised sectors and elected from within their own membership a National Executive Council (NEC) which ensured that policies were implemented and appropriate full-time officers appointed. In fact, it was the NEC that dominated union policy, "power in the union can and does reside in a handful of senior members of the NEC" (White 1975). Taylor (1978) went further, suggesting that the NEC itself was "dominated by the most senior, long-standing members, and fails to provide a representative cross-section of the membership as a whole" (p 242). Thus there was often a tension between the Annual Conference, which took its direction from the more active sections of the membership, and the conservative NEC, elected by the total membership.

Collective bargaining in local government is still characterised by a high degree of centralisation and institutionalisation. The present Whitley Council system was established in 1946 when several national joint councils, including the Local Authority Administrative, Professional, Technical and Clerical Staff (APTC), were created. Under the Whitley system national negotiations take place over pay levels and the major conditions of service. There are also regional and local structures with 27 Provincial Councils covering service conditions and Joint Consultative Committees for staff and blue-collar workers based in each authority which are, from the employees' side, formally separate from the union organisation. There has, however, been a growing tension between such centralised bargaining and demands from the then NALGO branches for greater self-determination.

Growing into trade unionism

At both national and local levels NALGO's policies were first and foremost concerned with conditions of employment and wage levels. More recently it adopted a wider brief pursuing, for example, a campaigning role in defence of public sector provision, promoting equal opportunities policies, producing guidelines on good practice, for example on sexual harassment at work (the first union to do so) and engaging in wider political issues. This contrasted sharply with its earlier image. Thus, in 1909 Levi Hill, then the union's Assistant Secretary, declared, "anything savouring of trade unionism is nausea to the local government officer and his (sic) association" (Nicholson et al., 1981, p 48). *The Economist*, in 1965, stated "it was the kind of trade union a general secretary must dream about, nearly 400,000 votes solidly for moderation and a near guarantee of no awkward personalities" (quoted in Taylor 1978, p 242). Again in 1975, in "Public Service", the union's newspaper, 'Scorpio' looking back commented, "NALGO itself had an air of destiny: if the Almighty was a card holder in a union then NALGO would be his (sic) ticket. No strikes, no trouble and a quiet fusty-dusty daily round that meant wearing a dark suit from Monday to Friday. The world extended as far as the town hall steps and politics was as welcome as smallpox" (Public Service, May 1975).

Formed in 1905, by a small group of high ranking officers as a local government officers guild, NALGO was concerned, it declared, "to provide the means for social intercourse amongst its members and for their improvement, advancement and recreation" (Taylor 1978, p 241). Its membership was drawn mainly from town clerks, city engineers, and surveyors who occupied most of the official positions and controlled its activities during its formative years. Even quite recently the Birmingham branch was known as the "guild club", and a more radical NUPE branch arose as a direct reaction to its conservative politics. Laffin (1988) argued that NALGO's aim was not to correct any economic injustices or grievances, but rather to develop a national market for career development. Similarly, Price (1983) notes that its emphasis was on professionalism and social benefits based on "a distinctive group consciousness nurtured by the structured and bureaucratic work environment of local government service" (p 158). Their role and status as public servants would, it was believed, be validated by the wider community and from this would emerge an improved reward system. It was a unionism best described, according to Price, as "harmonistic collectivism".

Blyton and Ursell (1982) suggest that it was this perceived community of interest, based on the non-commercial nature of their work together with the relatively secure expectations around career development, which led not only to a common identity of themselves as public servants, but one that over-rode any differences there were in rank and function. Thus despite the heterogeneity and hierarchy within the public services, local government officers still felt able to join together in one union when multi-unions might have been more logical. However, it is equally important to acknowledge, both the need for a strong united union to counter the strength of management, and the encouragement given by management itself for the development of one single union (Blyton and Ursell 1982). Furthermore, other factors such as departmental and service loyalty, and the internal variations within both administrative and direct human service work would have made it quite difficult for workers to unionise according to other criteria such as rank, material reward or even professional specialism.

The public servant identity was moreover sustained by the emphasis given to the administrative responsibilities of those occupying senior grades in local government rather than to their managerial functions (Blyton and Ursell 1982). Similarly, as a greater sense of professional identity across different occupational groups began to emerge, the emphasis shifted to a shared professionalism and it was not until a new neo-Taylorist managerialism began to emerge from the late 1970s that these harmonious relationships were challenged (Newman and Clarke 1994). The initial absence of a substantial negotiating role at a local level further reduced the likelihood of major conflicts of loyalty and interest for those holding senior posts in joining a union in which their subordinate levels were numerically stronger. Instead, conflicts could more comfortably be left to the national negotiators to resolve, or diverted into a debate based around professionalism rather than disputes between workers and management. Equally, the compliance of those occupying the subordinate levels of existing differentials in status and rank, the highly individualised processes for securing rewards, and the secure internal career structure, were all influential in ensuring that they were not prepared to translate such structural conflicts into matters of industrial relations.

It was not until the end of 1920 that NALGO took trade union status, which was accepted only reluctantly in response to falling membership (Volker 1966). Yet, by the end of that year, and in direct response to its new status, its membership rose by 8000 above the previous year and was three times that of the 1918 figure. Trade union status had, until then, been resisted by the membership's desire to preserve strict political neutrality, and by their self-image as public servants accountable to the whole community. Indeed, much of NALGO's behaviour was premised on the view that there was little difference between the interests of local government officers and their employer, although this did not prevent attempts being made after the First World War to introduce the system of 'Whitleyism', which was then rejected by individual local authorities.

The adoption of such a consensual perspective had a powerful influence on NALGO's development, both in respect of the interests of its own members and in its relationship with other trade unions. For example, Taylor (1978) notes that it was not until 1938 that NALGO was even able to gain precise information on what salaries local councils paid their staff, and it was not until 1942 when the wartime Coalition Government established the National Joint Council, making industrial arbitration compulsory, that NALGO began to move forward as a trade union. This was followed in 1946 by the setting up of the national Whitley system for pay determination, reflecting the apparent post-war consensus in which public employers were projected as 'model employers' (Laffin, 1988). It was not until 1964 that NALGO affiliated to the TUC and 1970 when it sanctioned its first-ever strike, involving a mere 18 members.

The issue of TUC affiliation illustrates NALGO'S early approach, taking as it did over 40 years of debate and ballots before a majority for affiliation finally emerged. The issue was first raised in 1921 when it was opposed by the NEC, but it was not until 1942 that the full membership actually voted on it and 1964 when the NEC, spurred on no doubt, by government pay policies and the setting up of the National Economic Development Council, favoured affiliation and advised the membership to vote in favour. Even then, with a 77.7% poll, those in favour (138,120) had only a 19,589 majority. According to Volker (1966), the primary question had always been about the union's political neutrality and the extent to which affiliation meant or implied support for the Labour Party. Additionally, it was also seen as a loss of status as it meant joining an organisation whose membership had been built upon and was identified with manual blue-collar workers. The decision, in the end, was taken not on the emergence of a new political ideology, but pragmatically to strengthen NALGO's bargaining position and gain greater access to political policy-making.

The seeds of militancy

NALGO found itself in the early 1970s not only with an expanding membership, rising from 338,000 in 1964, the year of affiliation, to 690,000 more than double by 1977, but operating in areas of public service provision (notably personal social services, planning and environmental health) in which social reform was high on the agenda (Hall 1978). This permissive and promotional environment which characterised the 1968-1974 period, with its expressed aim of tackling and eradicating social problems, gave radicalised workers permission to adopt critical positions in relation to both those local employers and union colleagues, who did not actively embrace the reforming spirit. Furthermore it allowed them to vigorously pursue their clients' interests regardless of whether or not this consequently placed them in conflict with either another occupation within the public service, or indeed with the policies and practice of their own department. Such a process effected some occupations more than others, with a growing body of radical literature emerging around personal social services, planning and to some extent housing. Equally, the development of alternative organisations, such as NALGO Action Group and parallel bodies such as Case-Con and PHAS (Public Health Advisory Service), emerge from these same areas and play a significant role in the development of radicalism within the union.

New recruits and a high point of social democracy

Many of the newcomers were young graduates schooled in a different political culture during the late 1960s and early 1970s and armed with a growing and wide-ranging academic critique of welfare provision in such areas as poverty, deviance, psychiatry, public planning, education and gender politics. As Hall (1978) remarked 1968 was,

> The year of a remarkable cataclysm ... it was an incomplete and unfinished 'revolution' ... It consisted above all of the attempt to instigate 'revolution from above' - to transmit the spark of rebellion from the 'little mother' of student revolt to the great, inert engine of the labouring masses ... It was an assault on the culture and superstructure of late capitalism mounted by the system's own vanguard - a 'lumpen bourgeoisie': a class fraction without a tangible productive base. (pp 240-241)

Hall goes on to suggest that,

> The social and political polarisation which characterises the next decade began from this point. (p 242)

as "the apprentice managers of the world" trained to fill the intermediary positions, with the crucial role of ensuring the social reproduction of capitalist relations in revolt at the state's "repressive tolerance".

No doubt the motivation for entering local government was, in part, governed not only by a sense of 'service' but also in response to a more basic need for employment, especially given the growing shortage of alternative opportunities for graduates in business and commerce. Yet, in addition, many perceived such openings as an opportunity to practise their politics, which had often been developed in an extra-parliamentary arena that included student politics, national campaigning bodies, pressure groups, community-based campaigning and direct service-providing organisations, or as part of the emerging counter culture (Nuttall 1972). Mays (1967) identified an even earlier change,

> Those coming into social work from the mid-1960s were made of different stuff, being younger, more articulate, more critical, less passive. They cannot be assumed to be so clearly inspired by the strong tradition in the middle classes for what may be termed public service .... (p 204)

Rankin (1970) portrayed the situation as,

> The most vocal and dynamic of the new recruits to social work are anti-professionalism. They do not see themselves as skilled experts dispensing therapy to social misfits, but as community workers where the client is no longer the sick person but the sick society. (p 21).

Simpkin (1983) reinforces this, arguing that the new recruits believed that,

> Social work intervention could in some way be critical in promoting wider change. (p 142).

Social work was not the only occupation to benefit from such recruits as similar changes were taking place in planning, public health, community work and welfare rights. Summing it up, Cowley (1977) stated,

> These professionals do have a liberal humanist ideology which embraces the desire to serve others, and in practice the state offers far more attractive employment to politically conscious young people than does industry and commerce where their involvement in exploiting workers is more direct and obvious. (p 92).

It was as if, as Simpkin (1983) noted,

> A generation already in revolt was to put its standards to the test. (p 136).

All of which led Jack (1988) to despair that,

> Since the early sixties, the social services has been peopled and managed by the products of an education and training system ... which has been dominated by a soft left political ideology. The radical perspective on social welfare replaced the previous liberal, functional view ... in college curricula, and the upheavals of the post-Seebohm reorganisation and the shortage of qualified workers, it occasioned, fostered the colonisation of SSDs and their subsequent management by the graduates. (p 13)

Thus many such recruits were less willing to passively accept established practices and attitudes, were less inclined to a public service model, more willing to identify themselves as workers selling their labour power, and who might well have conflicts of interest both with 'management' and indeed some of their older NALGO colleagues.

Moreover, such recruits were joining the public services at a time of, and often in response to, change and reorganisation carried through in a climate of optimism and a commitment to eradicating social problems. The Seebohm Report (1968), later to be translated into the Local Government Act 1971, brought together the three previously separate departments of child care, welfare and mental health into a generic family-oriented social services. Although subsequently criticised for its centralising and proletarianising features, the Report spoke of the decentralisation of services via local area teams, locating social work intervention in the context of 'the community', and advocated the appointment of 'community development officers', stressing that "a clear responsibility should be placed upon the social services departments for developing conditions favourable to community identity and activity" (para. 483) and, most importantly, acknowledging the basic structure of an unequal society.   Alongside Seebohm there were a number of other 'progressive' pieces of legislation and government reports, including the Skeffington Report (1969) advocating limited public participation in planning; the Children and Young Persons Act (1969); the Fairbairn-Milson Report on Young People (1969); the Chronically Sick and Disabled Persons Act (1971); the Race Relations Act (1965, 1968); the Local Government Act (1966) introducing 'Section 11' funding; the Sexual Offences Act (1967); the Abortion Act (1967); the Divorce Reform Act (1969); the Wootton Report on Drugs (1968), named a "conspiracy of the drugged" by the *Daily Mirror*; the Arts Council's report (1969) recommending the repeal of the Obscenity Law; and the Inner Area Studies (1972).   In addition there were shifts in housing policy away from redevelopment to the preservation of neighbourhoods and existing housing stock.   In all there was a growing focus on social deprivation with a recognition of the need to re-examine the relationship between service provider and the consumer, the targeting of specific disadvantaged groups, and a generalised call for greater public participation in social reproduction, e.g. the Educational Priority Areas (1968), the Urban Programme (1968), and the Community Development Programme (1968).

Hall (1980) describes such reforms as "the legislation of consent ... shifting things into a less rigid, more loose, more permissive social code" (p 2) representing a high point of social democratic reformism and an expanding budget, but also bringing an increase in state regulation in the field of moral conduct.   Further, this 'liberation' was short-lived.   Indeed in 1969 Home Secretary Callaghan was already calling for a "halt to the advancing tide of permissiveness".   Nevertheless the legislation's permissive core offered not only real gains to the progressive middle classes but provided them with the possibility, via employment in the welfare 'consciousness creating' industries, of introducing progressive practice in a liberalising or indeed liberating mission amongst the disadvantaged.   This was also not without Fabian elements of 'saving' or 'reforming' those that were previously 'lost', a tension that has always been part of the social welfare/problem discourse, which places increasing power and influence in the hands of the state welfare agencies.

Nonetheless, such a plethora of state activity gave politicised public service workers hope that there might indeed be sufficient opportunity and even managerial support, to apply their critical perspectives developed both in academia and the radical practical alternatives that had been springing up.   This period of optimism survived until the mid-1970s by which time Crossman had announced, "the party's over", and "the authoritarian backlash" (Hall 1978, p 258) against the 1968-69 cultural revolution and strident political protest, was well set in.   By this time, too, a marxist-feminist critique had been developed of the earlier radical initiatives, along with the emergence of a more sober and popularised analysis of the state (Cockburn 1977; Community Development Project 1974, 1975, 1977a, 1977b) and indeed of public welfare itself (Bailey and Brake 1975).

The rise of public service managerialism

Such reforms had consequences for the management of public service provision and saw the emergence of a new style of local government management. The Bains Report (1972) on local government management modelled on the private sector, advocated the introduction of corporate management that emphasised the need for strategic forward planning and managerial co-ordination, and stressed the need to strengthen the managerial officer group and senior elected members via centralised co-ordination, decision-making and administration. Cockburn (1977) and Howe (1986a) trace the evolution of corporate management through four committees on local government - Maud (1967), Mallaby (1967), Patterson (1973) and Bain (1972), all of which echo the same themes of "integration, control from the top, more efficient use of money and labour, forward planning for a bigger impact on the job in hand" (Cockburn, p 13). Cockburn (1977) described such corporate management as being concerned with,

> The system as a whole, its goals, strategies and growth. It has regard to the pattern of relationships within an organisation to ensure efficient flows of information, to defining channels of responsibility and accountability - for whom you answer and to whom; to the design of decision-processes so that different types of decision are taken at appropriate levels and in appropriate sequences.
> (p 364)

Bennington (1976) saw it as a creaming off of,

> A new, or at least a different 'managerial elite' from among both the officers and elected members ... the onus on reconciling conflicts of view and achieving consensus on issues is pushed down to the third tier ... a filtering device, screening out wild ideas from below, and buffering Chief Officers and Committees from critical or dissident pressures from within departments ... harden the division between policy making and implementation - between those who are incorporated into the 'management' part of the pyramid and those whose work flings them into contact with the outside world. (p 15)

Clapham (1985), however, distinguishes between this version and a second approach which was to be achieved by,

> Less formal, ad hoc working groups of officers and members, constituted in response to particular issues and disbanded when the work was complete ... the matrix approach ... leaving corporate planning much more to the service departments themselves. (p 30)

It was a strategy to technicise and depoliticise issues, an attempt to correct the increasingly recognised dysfunctions of bureaucracy through greater co-ordination and to better manage a declining resource base. However, although corporate management was speedily introduced it was equally a short-lived strategy with few authorities implementing corporate management processes by 1978. Cockburn (1977) locates its emergence as a direct response to the growing fiscal crisis, although at the time of its introduction public expenditure continued to grow,

> On the one hand the growing need to keep down costs, to manage scarce resources as fear grew about the level of public spending. On the other, the apparently undiminishing problem of deprivation, the shame of urban poverty in what was supposed to be a thriving and exemplary capitalist state. (p 65)

Clapham (1985), however, argues that other interests were involved including those who saw corporate planning as a means of addressing social problems. He suggests that Cockburn mistakenly emphasises a one-way relationship between local government and the overall interests of capital, and that powerful interest groups within the local state, acting autonomously, were in fact responsible both for its rapid rise and subsequent demise. In particular, he highlights how it was in the interests of both the chief executives and the political leadership to push for such reforms and, conversely, how resistance from departmental interests and from within local communities to the changed structures and depoliticising tendencies, respectively, brought about its downfall. Further, Clapham adds that whilst corporate planning was one strategic response to the fiscal crisis, it was flawed to the extent it could also result in increased spending. However by the end of the decade the emphasis was more explicitly on controlling and reducing public expenditure thereby requiring other strategies.

The significance of corporate management for public service trade unions was simply in the emphasis it gave to a new managerialism, which was felt throughout the structures, and the increased difficulty for front line workers to influence policy development. For some, especially those in the personal social services, corporate management was simply the generalised expression of a managerialism of the bureaucratisation that had grown within their occupation and was seen as conflicting with their professionalism. Such trends have perhaps been expressed most strongly in relation to social work (Cawson 1982, Black et al. 1983). Jones (1983) notes that,

> Rather than marking a new dawn for social work ... the Seebohm reorganisation has led to many social workers experiencing a marked diminution in their independence and a far greater pressure to meet the requirements of the Department. (p 114)

Satyamurti (1981), in her study of a social services department, found that

> Social workers did not view the organisation outside the area team as an object of loyalty or identification. They viewed it as a source of frustration or, at best, as devoid of meaning ... they felt that no appreciation, sympathy or support came from the management group ... This meant that they could be quite cavalier about whether or not they fulfilled certain organisational requirements. (pp 35-36)

Along with other writers (Lipsky 1974) who have highlighted the policy making role of front line bureaucrats, Satyamurti acknowledges the difficulty of managing such workers given the problems of imposing direct scrutiny of their practice, which is often exacerbated by a lack of clarity over guidelines for practice. Overall though, Satyamurti noted a change on the part of management,

> From seeing the organisation as a social work agency to seeing it as a social welfare or social service agency, standards which derived from professional criteria of good work received less emphasis (p 38).

Indeed, she suggests casework skills, supposedly lying at the heart of social work intervention, were increasingly irrelevant, being "possessed by few and practised by fewer" (p 185). Howe (1986) drew a similar conclusion that work was "increasingly prone to management predetermination" (p 151),

> Managerialism has proved to be pervasive and seems to have reversed many of the hopes of the early supporters of the Seebohm Report. The expectation was that after reorganisation, the welfare tradition offering routine agency services would succumb to the sophisticated skills of the independent and individualised practices of professionals. In the event many would claim that the reverse has happened. (p 152)

Howe argues that the rise of the 'welfare manager' has almost inevitably led to a situation where they attempt to redefine the nature of the work and its setting, extracting "what uncertainty there is in the process" (p 156) in favour of overall rational planning; restructuring the training requirements and the type of worker required; and reshaping the form and style of organisation to that of a mechanistic pyramidal and hierarchical authority structure. All of which, he suggests, has important consequences for how workers perceive themselves and the opportunities for bringing about change. With some justification Howe concludes that,

> The continuation of social work organisations along business management lines, coupled with the field-workers' perceptual shift from independent professional to local government employee, has encouraged many basic grade workers to associate in trade unions ... (pp 156-157)

Public service trade unionism would not, however, have emerged with the same force had it not been for the relative failure of the professionalisation 'project' of key welfare occupational groups. The 'project' not only failed to establish their status as an acknowledged profession, but also to attract a significant number of what were probably the majority of workers, who were more neutral in their position towards trade unionism. As an alternative to trade unionism professionalisation has traditionally been viewed, as Parry and Parry (1976) suggest, as "an occupational strategy which is chiefly directed towards the achievement of upward collective social mobility and, once achieved, it is concerned with the maintenance of superior remuneration and status". Similarly Johnson (1972) sees professionalism as "a peculiar type of occupational control rather than an expression of the inherent nature of particular occupations" (p 45). For Wilding (1982) it is also the desire to have control over their own terms of work and,

> To this end are claims for the exclusion of the uninitiated, control of entry, the licensing of members directed ... The supposed characteristics of professions ... be regarded as links in the chain of argument directed to that end, rather than as inherent and inalienable characteristics of the work of particular occupations - in short as attempts at gaining and justifying power and privilege. (p 6)

However, as Carpenter et al. (1987) point out, it is unlikely that we are here talking about a desire shared by whole occupations but rather segments within them. Consequently others within the occupation with different prior orientations and long-term goals are able to compete for the ideological and strategic ground. Similarly there is evidence of a growing convergence between professional associations and trade unionism, and especially so within human welfare.

Public service workers within welfare capitalism must, however, overcome a number of specific problems if they wish to pursue a strategy of professionalisation. Firstly, given their predominant status as state dependent employees, unlike those more autonomous self-employed professional counterparts, they are weakened by the fact that they are confronted by a customer, who is also their employer, who is both well-organised and operating in a monopoly situation. They are, thus, largely dependent on the state's willingness to determine the client groups, the needs or circumstances to be addressed, the general manner in which they are to be tackled, and their authority to intervene (Johnson 1972). Wilding (1982), in fact, suggests that there is a high level of interest reciprocity between the state and welfare professional groups, but that any successful outcome for the profession can only be achieved at a price, and requires the occupational group to demonstrate both its commitment to dominant values and its ability to manage social problems,

The state needs the profession to perform important social functions; the profession needs the state to enforce licensing and monopoly ... the granting of professional status ... the granting of expert, occupational incorporation. (p 11)

However, the state may also have priorities other than those involving high levels of autonomy, trust and privilege for particular occupational groups. Thus, for example, in managing the fiscal crisis and restructuring welfare, the state has been more concerned with controlling the activities of such welfare occupations, seeking to reduce costs, increase their social control functions, and eliminate any ideological content to their work that might be at variance with it.   Yet some relative autonomy does exist for welfare workers in which this can be challenged for, as already noted, the direct level of state control can never be complete, as this is often simply impractical, and welfare workers can mobilise to assert their own definitions. Moreover, the meeting of social need via collective non-market provision contains the possibility of an alliance with a range of interests that challenge capitalist, patriarchal, and discriminatory social relations. However, this in turn runs the risk of losing any previously acquired trust, and may offer little in return for their investment in such oppositional groups who may well oppose other, especially privileged, aspects of the profession's position.

Further, as Hoggett (1984) notes, where critical forms of theory and practice do develop within the professionalised state apparatus they find themselves in a political struggle with dominant approaches and are likely to be excluded or marginalised, although certain aspects of the critique might well be incorporated or 'recouped' into the dominant explanations or solutions. Moreover, any attempt by welfare professionals to relate to other constituencies not only questions their social legitimation role and mode of intervention, but also undermines the rationale for their own existence. Thus the processes of denying the user-as-subject, deskilling the citizen, family and community, reproducing patterns of dependency and powerlessness, which have been essential both in the management of social need and in the assertion of a professional body of knowledge in the determination of the welfare product, may be difficult to abandon (Wilding 1982, Hoggett 1984). Yet such occupations find it equally difficult to create the necessary social distance between themselves and the service users, or to convince either the state or the public that they do indeed possess skills and knowledge that are in scarce supply, difficult to acquire, and should be highly valued (Johnson 1972, 1977, James and Petoille 1970). Thus as a former Social Services Minister stated,

> The problem child, the alcoholic husband are not suitable subjects for the intervention of the professional social worker. The agent with the natural skills and faculties is the biological mother. We hear a lot today about social work, perhaps the most important social work is motherhood.
> (Patrick Jenkin 1977)

Indeed, much of welfare practice can appear to be not that markedly different from everyday social intercourse thereby making it more difficult to gain recognition as an expert with special competence (Howe 1986). Moreover, as Johnson suggests, the supposed social science base accompanying state mediation tends to result in a situation where welfare practitioners are 'advisors' within the context of political decision-making rather than being in a position to make authoritative and independent pronouncements. Further, establishing a collective identity is itself difficult given intra-occupational conflict and the possibilities for identification with particular local civic and political cultures rather than with a professional community (Johnson 1972, Duncan and Goodwin 1982). Human service occupations are also highly gendered and a strong correlation between the likely success of any professionalisation strategy and the predominance of men within the occupational group has been argued by writers such as Hearn (1987). He suggests that in those occupations such as human service work, where women have played a major role in "the socialisation of emotional experiences", there will be a tendency for men to either seek positions of control or to subordinate such activity to that of other male-dominated professions. Moreover, where women have occupied managerial positions they are nevertheless divided by social class and race from those in subordinate roles. Thus it is only if men occupy both supervisory and practitioner positions within the occupation that professional recognition becomes likely.

Professional bodies out of step

In addition to such structural problems facing the semi-professionals the actual tactics adopted by those in the public service in pursuing professionalisation, at the same time as trade unionism was expanding, were not the most appropriate and have often appeared out of step with the immediate needs and concerns of those in the occupation. Again the cutting edge has been social work where efforts to secure professionalisation were first attempted by the Charity Organisation Society (1869), known affectionately as 'cringe or starve', claiming a scientific understanding of individual poverty, producing its attendant technologies of the file, the visit, the body of knowledge and training.

The contemporary drive toward social work professionalism has necessitated both the rewriting of the COS message in a modern idiom and the acquisition of more 'scientific' knowledge as the basis for power. Thus Parry and Parry (1979) argued that, "the growth of psychiatric social work and the use of psychological theory as the basis for casework strengthened the movement towards professionalism" (p 35). However, even with the establishment of the British Federation of Social Work (1936) there were major problems in trying to develop a coherent approach from the competing range of social work bodies and their dissolution was a complex and lengthy process. It was not until 1970 that the British Association of Social Workers was formed, symbolising the birth of the new profession.

BASW, however, found itself unable to focus exclusively on 'professional' issues but instead was forced to openly compete with NALGO over the representation of the material interests of social workers (Andrews 1978). It also found itself under considerable attack as an elitist organisation by its attempt to restrict membership to qualified workers (Carpenter et al., 1987). When in the mid-1970s, industrial unrest amongst social workers was increasingly evident and NALGO, having already had some success over London weighting, took action over cuts in public expenditure, BASW spoke out against such measures (SWT vol. 8 no. 26, 5.4.77), arguing that social workers could not be represented properly by "a conglomerate trade union". It further questioned the acceptability of social workers being required to take industrial action "on grounds not directly related to the practice of social work". BASW was and remained divided over its attitude to NALGO and social work trade unionism (SWT 9.5.78 articles by Andrews, Lumley and Hill, for competing perspectives; also Hill in SWT 12.9.78). The growing strength of trade unionism was clearly apparent but BASW's desire for professional status, and therefore exclusivity from other workers led to its fateful attempt to achieve this via a new union in opposition to NALGO and, therefore, other public service workers. Its message, that working through NALGO might be acceptable to some in the public services but not to social workers, was misplaced and mistimed as public service workers were increasingly united in adversity, following public expenditure cuts, and social workers were engaged in industrial action that required the support of other colleagues in the public sector. Nevertheless the ill-fated British Union of Social Workers was launched in late 1978 with only 1500 members and BASW opened its doors to non-qualified workers. However BASW's belief in the new union did not run very deep and by the mid 1980s the new union had all but disappeared.

BASW not only misread the mood amongst social workers but failed to see government policy in relation to social work as part of a wider strategy toward all public sector workers. Instead it either preferred, or could not free itself from, the professionalisation project which required it to proclaim its separation and distance from other public service workers. Yet given the state's own priority of curbing the power and autonomy of public service workers, BASW's strategy was unlikely to receive its backing and indeed played into its hands by fragmenting the workforce. BASW failed to recognise the growing separation between managers and fieldworkers on the one hand, and the growing consciousness of mutual self-interest amongst all workers in the personal social services, let alone across occupational and departmental boundaries. Furthermore it failed to respond to the growing body of critical literature about the role and practice of social work and was instead associated with the traditional, but heavily criticised, casework which was also fast disappearing as a practical option for fieldworkers faced with increasing demand from clients with very practical and immediate needs.

Militancy in the wider labour movement, the fiscal crisis and the demise of social democratic reform

The late 1960s and early 1970s was also a period of increasing militancy amongst sections of the working class, and disillusion with labourism. Despite high expectations (Nairn 1965) Wilson had failed to win the support of the trade union movement in his 1964-70 period of government, any vestige of his radical pretensions being removed by his position in the 1965 'red scare' seamen's strike. In the end Wilson had offered little in the way of economic reform to his government's own social base, with the trade unions being perceived as an infinitely more effective instrument for economic leverage (Blackburn 1970).

As a result of strong international competition, rising wage levels, and restricted labour markets, Britain faced an economic crisis as the share of British profits almost halved between 1964 and 1970 (Glyn and Harrison 1980). Similarly, Britain's share in the world export of manufactured goods had halved between 1954 and 1970 and her economic growth rate remained low. The result was a crisis of profitability as the better organised sections of the trade union movement secured increases in line with, or greater than inflation, but intense international competition prevented a simultaneous rise in prices to maintain profit margins. By 1972 unemployment had risen from under 0.5m to beyond the then seemingly unacceptable figure of 1 million, effectively breaking the existing bipartisan goal of full employment. Yet the trade union pressure that had been building up did not subside and, indeed, after 1968 there was a marked increase in strike activity. The number of strikes per year leapt from 2378 to 3906 between 1968 and 1970, and although they dropped to 2228 in 1971 they had again climbed up to 2922 by 1974. Similarly the number of days lost (1000's) jumped from 4690 (1968) to 10,980 (1970) to a peak of 23,909 (1972) involving 1.7m workers (*Yearbook of Labour Statistics*, 1977, ILO). Moreover other groups of previously unorganised workers pressed forward their claims.

Wilson's response was a voluntary, followed by a statutory incomes policy, increases in welfare charges and attempts to control trade union militancy with the weight of the legal system (In Place of Strife, 1969). However attempts to secure the support of the trade union leadership in holding down wage demands only led to increasing hostility amongst rank and file members and further industrial unrest. Legislative efforts also failed, and when workers in the 1970 Ford strike reached a compromise deal, it was followed "by a flood of wage demands, especially in public sector industries which had not so far been in the forefront of the wage struggle, indeed many had not been on strike since 1926" (Barnett 1970). It was, according to Hall (1978), "The revolt of the lower paid (teachers, civil servants, dustmen, hospital ancillary workers), a response to rapid price inflation, rising unemployment and a period of zero growth ..." Gamble (1986) summed up Wilson's 'New Britain' strategy thus, "By 1968 the whole strategy was in ruins and the extent of disenchantment and disillusion throughout the labour movement was intense" (p 168). Disillusionment with the Labour Party as a vehicle for economic and social reform was to continue with the 1974-79 administrations of Wilson (his second) and Callaghan. Thus Gamble (1986), whilst describing Labour's 1973 programme as being "the most left-wing statement the party had adopted since 1945" (p 169) notes that once in office it drifted to "highly orthodox policies ... first package of monetarist measures, including cash limits, monetary targets and round after round of spending cuts ..." (Gamble, p 170).

Sandwiched between the two Wilson governments were the four years of the Heath regime which was characterised by outright rejection of corporatism and open confrontation with the trade union movement. Alongside a general law-and-order campaign (Hall 1978) the trade union movement found itself labelled as extremist and confronting new legislation to control its activities (Industrial Relations Act 1971). However, during 1972 there were even more major industrial struggles which swung decisively in favour of the trade unions. Hall (1978) describes 1972 as,

> The year in which the working class virtually without political leadership of any strategic kind ... took on, defeated and overturned the whole Heath confrontation strategy ... More strike days were lost in that year than in any since 1919, and this included the first miners' strike since the General Strike of 1926. (pp 293-4)

What had sustained the wage militancy during both the Wilson and Heath governments was not the official trade union leadership but the rank and file membership, and principally their shop stewards. Thus between 1950 and the end of the 1960s, 95% of all strikes recorded by the Department of Employment were 'unofficial'. According to Jefferys (1979), "it has been the survival and extension of this work-place based organisation that has enabled the manual working class to retain its sense of common identity and to lock white-collar workers into the same reaction" (p 10). Wilson had earlier described such "unofficial" action as reaching crisis proportions and the Donovan Report (1968) spoke of the "inflated power of work groups and shop stewards" recommending their incorporation into the formal management structure whilst placing the unofficial strike outside the 'protection' of the law.

Following the defeat of Heath in 1974 two important developments took place which related directly to public service workers. Firstly the subsequent Labour Governments of Wilson and Callaghan attempted a return to corporatism, but this failed to stem the tide of wage militancy which, along with the 1973 oil price rise, led to a loan from the International Monetary Fund (IMF), cuts in the social wage and in public spending, and the doomed Social Contract (1978-79). By contrast, expenditure plans for the first part of the 1970s had spoken of growth. The 1971 White Paper advocating a shift toward 'community care' through the work of the new social services departments, had a growth rate of 9.2% for personal social services in 1972/73 and an average of 6.8% after that.

Although this was revised in 1972 to a growth rate of 8.5% for the years up to 1976/7, local authorities increased expenditure in personal social services by a rate of 17.2% in 1972/3 and 18.7% in 1973/4, and expenditure policy debates continued to be dominated by considerations of unmet need (Webb and Weston 1982). However, by 1975 the public expenditure White Paper was projecting an annual growth rate of only 2% for current expenditure up to 1978/79 and a consistent trend downwards in capital expenditure with cuts of 35% in the first years. Gough (1983) points out that after the rapid growth in total social spending in the first half of the 1970s, rising to 28% of the GDP, overall spending over the next four years rose by less than 1%. The picture was, in fact, much worse once the costs of social security and employment services are excluded. Thus housing expenditure was reduced by 13% under Labour, and education by 6%, although personal social services expenditure grew by 8%.

Secondly, although it was the Labour Government which launched the first monetarist policy and introduced the first round of substantial cuts in public expenditure, it was within the Conservative party that there emerged the beginnings of the 'New Right' with its explicit rejection of consensus politics, Keynesian economics and welfare spending, promoting instead greater social discipline, a return to the sovereignty of the market, and attacking the strategy of increasing equality. The welfare "scrounger and layabout" were identified as central to undermining the social fabric and the welfare state and its professionals were seen as destroying personal liberty, individual responsibility and economic growth, all of which was said to sap the collective moral fibre of the nation. Between 1979 and 1983 the Conservatives further reduced expenditure (Gough 1983) making an initial cut of £91m in 1979 from Labour's plans for personal social services (Critical Social Policy 1982). However, the attack on public expenditure was not simply economic but also ideological so that across a whole range of services, policies have been restructured and the role of the public sector white-collar worker has been consistently undermined. Thus since 1979 the policy thrust has been towards the recommodification and residualisation of welfare services through marketisation, privatisation, the dismantling of services, as in the ending of any public sector house building programme, and the erosion of the principles of equality and redistribution.

Alongside this the Conservatives mounted an attack on what they perceived to be bureau-maximising welfare providers in local government. Thus they imposed reduced budgets, financial controls, penalties for 'overspending', restrictions on their ability to raise local taxes, and ultimately abolishing a tier of local government. Whilst such financial restrictions affected all authorities, and occasionally resulted in protests from Conservative-controlled councils, the central state's wrath was directed primarily at what it saw as Labour 'overspenders', and especially those where a left opposition was emerging. In addition, it targeted those welfare professionals who, with their formative grounding in the permissiveness of the 1960s, were seen to be leading the nation into demoralisation, encouraging welfare dependency, and an excess of bureaucracy and over-regulation (Clarke and Langan 1993). Further, through their trade unionism, and monopoly position, such workers were perceived as extracting unjustifiable material rewards, and thereby acting as a drain upon the economy.

The strategy to weaken and undermine the trade unions included excluding them from any dialogue, attacking them ideologically and raising fears of redundancy whilst also reducing career development possibilities through a contraction of the services. Furthermore, with the exception of the "Clegg comparability awards" of 1974-75 and 1979-80, public sector workers' pay fell behind their private sector counterparts (Laffin 1989), and lagged behind relative to average earnings (New Priorities in Public Spending, 1988). Cuts in public expenditure affected not only the levels and quality of service, or public sector wage relativities, but also job losses, worsening working conditions and the slowing down of promotion prospects, all of these being important to a group of aspiring white-collar workers.

O'Connor (1973) argues that the fiscal crisis was a direct cause of the growing politicisation of public sector workers, suggesting that the increased pressure on them would result in the development of alliances with other sectors of organised labour. Likewise, Cousins (1987) concluded that its roots lay in an earlier period and that it was "state intervention to regulate incomes and industrial relations during the 1960s and 1970s which had the most significant impact on work relations and trade unionism in the public service sector" (p 126), as it left them with a strong sense of grievance and injustice over their worsening position and their subsequent industrial action to protect themselves led to further increases in trade union membership, a more militant consciousness, and a growing rank and file organisation. Laffin's (1989) research supports this view, arguing that in a fiscal crisis there is an increased likelihood for organisational control to break down as, "elected and appointed management in local authorities have faced growing resistance, overtly and covertly, from among subordinate officers. Authority and hierarchy no longer appear as compelling as they once were ..." (p 32), making it more difficult to sustain or 'buy' trust as in a period of expansion. However, the attack on public services during the early 1980s was a dominant factor in stimulating the new urban left's strategy to make local government controlled services responsive to need, imaginative in approach, and a political base for developing an alliance of oppositional groups to the New Right's consumerist, and privatising approach, and "its recommodification of social life" (Keane and Offe 1984, p 26). Although Le Grand (1990) argues that the welfare state demonstrated its "robustness" during this period, "Over the 13 years from 1974 to 1987, welfare policy successfully weathered an economic hurricane in the mid-1970s and an ideological blizzard in the 1980s" (p 350), the attack nonetheless left its imprint upon public service workers and managers.

The continued withdrawal of resources from public services over this period, the overall climate of uncertainty around the future of jobs and services, and the growing numbers of those seeking welfare support at a consequence of the government's economic and social policies and demographic changes, along with an increasingly hostile attack on white-collar welfare workers has, no doubt, helped to sustain their militancy and their traditional defensive and reactive trade unionism, making them less receptive to launching a counter attack based on a transformation of practice. Furthermore by the late 1980s the focus for the more radical authorities had shifted yet again to that of their own political survival, leading to more confrontational strategies in their relationship with the trade unions.

NALGO edges leftwards

NALGO's growing militancy can thus be understood by locating it within this wider context: a new generation of policitised members, committed and active in a short intense period of increased social reform, who witnessed a general overall rise in trade union militancy and class conflict, the growth of a national shop steward movement and increased rank and file activity. In addition they were not untouched by the emerging social movements,

A seemingly bewildering and diverse scenario of intense activism, lacking cohesion, theoretical clarity or tactical perspectives ... producing no material political force, though it infiltrated and inflected, permanently, every other radical movement with which it contracted an alliance. (Hall 1978, pp 253-258)

nor by the wider disillusionment, but not irreconcilable break, with Labour as a force for social change as hopes faded that the reforms of the late 1960s would see real progress toward greater social equality and participation in civil society. Instead the mid-1970s marked the beginning of a shift to right-wing authoritarianism and a decline in the social reform project. For public service workers this meant, in particular, cuts in service provision, an increase in managerialism, and a loss in pay differentials and declining conditions of service. Furthermore, faced with such changes, public service workers were unable to turn to professionalism as an alternative strategy to secure their collective occupational interests, although again this strategy was never fully rejected or abandoned, a combination of the traditions of Fabianism and the desire for recognition of the worthiness of their product being too powerful for that. Without these wider social, political and economic events, NALGO would not necessarily have gone down a progressively militant road. Yet whilst much might have been learned from the industrial activity of other workers, the level of class consciousness as opposed to trade union consciousness amongst the white-collar public sector remained low.

Taylor (1978) illustrates NALGO's swing leftwards with reference to its public position on a number of policy and political issues. He cites, as examples, its attack on the 1974 Housing Finance Act; its support for the nationalisation of all development land, increased family allowances, a higher redistributive system of taxation, its backing of the miners in their two strikes of 1972 and 1974, its contribution to a fund for Chilean political refugees and its membership of a campaign opposing the Chilean junta. Other examples could also be cited, such as the 1969 conference decision to impress upon the TUC the need for equal opportunity with equal pay policies, and the support given to positive action over equal rights in 1973; opposition to private medicine and pay beds (1974); support for the Grunwick strike fund and the picketing of Grunwicks; support for imprisoned workers in Poland (1977); and the advice given to members from the 1977 conference that they should not cross picket lines mounted by unions affiliated to the TUC in any officially recognised dispute. This more active and militant trade unionism continued into the 1980s with, for example, a stoppage in support of the Peoples March for Jobs (1981), action against industrial relations legislation, and the establishment of its own political fund (1988). NALGO was also more willing to move into what had previously been thought of as professional matters and, for example, prevented BASW from imposing examinations on social workers in order to become approved social workers under the 1983 Mental Health Act.

In addition, NALGO became increasingly militant in relation to its own members' direct employment interests. Thus in 1970 it established a special strike policy committee and sanctioned its first-ever strike. In 1971 it increased its special reserve fund for strikes and began developing rules and guidelines governing industrial action which were adopted by the NEC in 1975 and further amended in 1977. By 1982 it was publishing its own *Industrial Action Handbook*. Further, there was a steady overall rise both in the number of stoppages and days lost per 1000 workers in local government between 1967 and 1974 (*Department of Employment Gazette* February 1976). Although it is not a unilinear trend, with a significant dip during 1971/72, the overall upward trend is nevertheless undeniable. Thus the NEC's Emergency Committee, which was responsible for considering the initiation of industrial action and for approving such action, faced a significant increase in the number of cases it was being asked to consider between 1971 and 1975, with only eight cases in 1971 compared with 168 in 1975.

During 1972, social work staff were involved in industrial activity over stand-by duty with Manchester, Salford, Chester, Oldham, Warrington and all the London boroughs withdrawing from such work in the October. In 1974 NALGO carried out a determined campaign over the "London weighting allowance" involving a total ban on overtime, refusing to work with agency staff, selective strike action, and with some branches calling for a total strike of all NALGO members (Emergency Committee Minutes, April-June 1974). By 1975, NALGO was not only taking industrial action as part of the TUC response to rising unemployment (November), but an increasing number of branches from across the UK were taking part in protests against public sector cuts, a process which picked up rapidly during 1976 and 1977. In May 1977, 319 branches were fully implementing an overtime ban and a further 221 were liberally interpreting it. However, it should be noted that 483 branches took no action. 1977 also saw a revival of action taken by workers in social service departments over stand-by duties with the withdrawal of the service being a common response in all areas. Tactics included one-day stoppages, overtime bans, a ban on non-contractual overtime, the picketing of all council meetings during budget discussions, non-cooperation with consultants, non-attendance at public meetings on council business, a refusal to perform duties linked to vacant posts, non-cooperation with management, marches and demonstrations, solidarity action with other unions, plus days of action. Such disputes became a common feature throughout 1978 and 1979, affecting both metropolitan and non-metropolitan counties as well as the London boroughs. In addition, there were other, though less widespread, disputes concerning staff accommodation, grading, local reorganisation, the quality of service provision, hours of work, and changes to public policy such as abortion, and privatisation. Whilst workers in social services tended to play a leading role in such industrial activity, culminating in two major actions by field social workers and residential workers, other public service workers including architects, librarians, nursery nurses, recreation workers and housing workers were all involved in specific disputes, and those actions around the cuts in public expenditure involved workers throughout the service. Union activity also increased at both inter-branch level (e.g. the setting up of the Greater London Trade Union Co-ordinating Committee Against Public Expenditure Cuts in 1976) and at national level (e.g. a special conference on expenditure cuts in January 1977 and national one-day actions against cuts and changes in the health services).

Yet such developments need to be kept in perspective, for although the amount of strike pay paid out to members increased considerably so that between October 1983 and June 1984 NALGO's reserve fund fell from £6m to £2.8m, the number of branches in receipt of this increased from only 14 (1981) to 25 (1984). As the Emergency Committee states (July 1984), the amount reflects "the enormous cost of a small number of local disputes" paid out to all branch members involved in protracted disputes. Nevertheless strike action is the ultimate industrial weapon which had not been used before 1970 during the union's first 65 years of existence, and such figures do not reflect the overall level of industrial unrest or the range of tactics utilised by NALGO members. Thus Ingham (1985) demonstrates that working to rule and withdrawal of cooperation were more favoured and widespread forms of action with more incidents being reported in local government than the total figure for all industries. Yet even taking account of all forms of industrial action, Ingham concludes "an authority taken at random would be expected to have less than one local dispute every 2.25 years" (p 11).

The rise of the shop steward system

It was during the late 1970s that NALGO's internal structures became more aligned to traditional trade unionism through the introduction of a shop steward system. This had been recommended by the Working Party on Communications and Membership Participation, set up in 1974 and reporting two years later. Shop stewards, declared the report, would be "the final point of distribution and the first point of reception of members' ideas" (p 5) and were "of crucial importance to the effectiveness of NALGO both now and in the future" (p 12). The report highlighted a new role of direct negotiator for the steward, and pointed to the Sheffield Branch as having a 'model' shop steward structure. Nevertheless, when the guidelines to branches were issued, they emphasised that the new role was primarily to ensure better communication and "not from any feeling that there should be a general move away from the present arrangements for consultation and negotiation to something like the plant bargaining of some of our industrial colleagues" (NALGO 1977). The impact of the steward system was both uneven and slow to take effect. Joyce et al. (1988) interviewed 60 NALGO Branches in 1982 and concluded that the "penetration of the steward system was strongly dependent on the type of local authority on which the branch was based" (p 112). Overall they found that only one-fifth of the local authority branches in England had a steward system although if the system of departmental representatives was included (as allowed for under the original NALGO recommendation) then three-quarters of all branches in England and Wales had shop stewards, the majority of which had been set up between 1978 and 1979.

The arrival of the steward system did not necessarily signal the supremacy of a militant or politically conscious office floor workforce. Ingham (1985) suggests that from his research "there would appear to be no evidence of a positive relationship between the degree of unionisation and the likelihood of overt industrial action" (p 13). Terry (1982) refers to unpublished data, collected by Fryer, which showed that stewards spent most of their time handling individual grievances. Issues concerning the authority as a whole were not regarded as important and there was little concern with what could be called collective matters. Moreover, Nicholson et al. (1981) found that union members with high job status were disproportionately active compared to their lower level counterparts. Indeed, among the stewards themselves those who held higher grade occupations displayed higher rates of contact with their constituents than other stewards, devoting more time to steward duties and speaking out more at union meetings. The consequences of such activity was not uniform, however, as there was no overall shared interest or political perspective among high grade trade union activists. Nevertheless, rank and file workers were continuing, in 1982, to elect higher grade workers to represent their interests, illustrating again the blurring of roles and functions between those in management and those on the front line. This can be partially explained by the relatively short career distance between basic grade positions and those roles carrying some managerial or supervisory responsibilities. Thus, for example, those entering social work in the early 1970s, possibly equipped with a degree, but otherwise with a professional qualification found themselves well placed to rapidly occupy the expanding job opportunities in lower management. Furthermore, developing an interest in trade unionism may also have a degree of self-interest for, as Garrett argues (1980),

> The trade union can, however, be another ladder to success where competition, ambition and individual achievement may get you somewhere. (p 210)

Indeed, activism within NALGO provided a potentially powerful means for upward mobility within local government, offering entry to (some of) the corridors of power and an opportunity to demonstrate those "leadership skills" which management might be very willing to turn to their own advantage. Certainly it is not unusual to discover radical trade unionists occupying both middle and lower middle management positions: a structurally difficult situation that became even more fraught as cuts in public sector funding required them to both manage declining resources, which impinged upon either services and/or jobs, while retaining a trade union perspective.

Nevertheless, irrespective of the political make-up of the local authority, NALGO continued with its industrial militancy during the 1980s and, despite the over-representation of some sections of its membership in such disputes and the undoubted conservatism that applies to large numbers in the union, this has involved workers from all sectors of public service and throughout the UK. It is equally clear that such internal differentiations, whilst still readily apparent, are not as significant as they were in the earlier 1970s, "when newly established social service departments were set apart from other departments as centres of union activism" (Joyce et al. 1988, p 39). Thus in Lewisham in 1988, 1000 NALGO members were out on strike for five weeks over the refusal of the council to provide security screens for staff at its Housing Advice Centre, following increasing concern over violence at work. Similarly, delegates to the 1987 annual conference voted unanimously in favour of a boycott of the Government's Job Training Scheme, and in 1989 NALGO called its first national strike after the employers rejected a 12% pay claim. In a ballot involving 62% of the membership, 59% voted in favour of striking.

In a consultation exercise on the then proposed 'New Union' to be created from the merger of NALGO, NUPE and COHSE, 1000 branches responded, 500 of which were NALGO branches, highlighting a number of general trends (NALGO 1991). Although the summary findings did not distinguish between the responses from the three unions, or represent a statistically representative sample, they nevertheless gave an indication of views and trends in NALGO. On equal opportunities the report noted,

> There was considerable support for measures to ensure equal opportunities and fair representation and the differences were largely ones of emphasis ... one strongly expressed view was for clearly defined links between equal opportunities structures, self-organised groups and service groups at all levels which allow for direct input on service conditions issues affecting women members, black members, lesbian and gay members, and members with disabilities, by those members whenever necessary. (p 2)

Only a minority of the responses were opposed to the whole concept of equal opportunities and these were reported as taking the form that 'all are equal'. The report noted a "strong consensus" that women need to be more directly represented in the negotiating process and having "reserved seats" was one of the ways suggested. Almost all the responses stated that,

> The New Union should have rules to combat sexual discrimination ... a majority of respondents said that black members need to be more directly involved in negotiation ... The majority supported some form of separate organisation for black members ... the overwhelming majority said ... should have rules against race discrimination ... most responses said that a rule against discrimination on the grounds of sexuality was needed ... A large majority said that self-organised structures were needed.

On the question of shop steward organisation the report stated that "the importance attached to developing an effective stewards system ... cannot be overstated. It came through in the answers to practically every question" (p 3). Considerable support was given to ensuring that there was the widest possible lay participation with decision-making structures being as close to the membership as possible and "a large number of ideas were put forward" on how to increase participation with "the largest single call ... to make meetings of members accessible". Alongside this, it is not surprising that, "There was strong support for the idea of making full-time officers accessible and properly accountable, especially to branches and members" (p 4). Finally, on the issue of the relationship between the union and political concerns, the report noted that:

> A wide range of common political interests was identified. They included matters concerning 'citizenship' - civil rights, equality, human rights, environment quality of life - and issues of public policy and provision - poll tax, privatisation, the future of the NHS, etc. (p 7).

In addition, "an overwhelming majority of those responding were sure that these wider political concerns could be integrated into the New Union's normal democratic processes ..." (p 7), although a substantial minority were against the New Union holding any kind of political fund.

However, whilst there is no doubting NALGO's transformation from a conservative social club to a fully-fledged trade union, its future direction is unclear. Whilst NALGO's ability and determination to defend and promote its members' interests may have expanded considerably, the extent to which it identifies these interests being served by promoting those of the service user remains questionable as its relationship to decentralisation demonstrates. As already stated in Chapter One, there is no automatic link between growing industrial militancy and an increased class consciousness. Whilst such a link may have been evident for a significant number of union activists, it is as likely that the driving force behind much of the union's new-found militancy is better understood as a combined protective group consciousness and individual self-interest. Furthermore, we are reminded that whilst tracing clearly discernible overall trends and patterns, the union remains a socially and politically heterogeneous body. Consequently, it is important to acknowledge the uneven development for members in their accepting the necessity of, let alone embracing, the union's high profile militancy.

Acknowledgement, therefore, needs to be made not only of the traditional gap between activists and ordinary members, and the tensions that exist between full-time officials and members or between the different union structures, but also the significant variations in occupational cultures that have emerged, and the relative impact of other competing influences such as professionalism. Some occupations, notably social work, have played a prominent part in shaping the overall patterns and trends in the union and indeed, some writers (Joyce et al. 1988) have suggested that theirs is a qualitatively different form of trade unionism. There is, however, no doubting their impact on the union's affairs and, because of this, a more thorough analysis is provided in the next chapter. However, the study of decentralisation in Islington, and the nature of NALGO's politics in that branch, suggest that whilst considerable differences in orientation continue to persist between occupational or departmental groupings, radicalism is by no means the prerogative of any single grouping, but cuts across functions, grades, traditions and status. It is also processual and is influenced by a range of factors. Yet despite any such internal variations which are not simply a matter of degree but reflect conflicting trade union perspectives, with large sections remaining conservative, there is no doubting the overall changes that have taken place to NALGO's character and which have continued in the new amalgamated public service union "Unison".

3 Social work radicalism

A willingness to engage in industrial militancy has increasingly been a characteristic of all workers within the public sector, but not all sectors or occupational groups have been equally committed. Specific groups of workers have traditionally had more of a relationship to radicalism than others. Field social work stands out as being an occupational group with a highly articulated version of radicalism: a radicalism that focuses not only on the position of the social worker as worker but has also been known for its occasional attempts to explore the possibility of a radical practice (defined in relation to anti-racism, feminism and socialism) in relation to service users. However, social work has not been alone in this respect as others such as planners, teachers and health service workers have also combined notions of traditional trade unionism with a commitment to progressive practice. In Islington, the Social Services and Housing departments were the two most frequently mentioned as having the strongest radical base, whilst conversely a number of occupational groups - engineers, administrative staff, and those in finance - were identified as historically conservative, or reluctant trade unionists.

Given the influential role of this radical trade union tradition within social work in influencing the contemporary character of public service unionism, this chapter examines its emergence, focusing specifically on field social work. In exploring the nature of this radicalism, we highlight the tension between those seeking a strong trade unionism and those who wished to develop a qualitatively different and oppositional day-to-day practice. For the former group, a trade union identity was to be forged via the development of a 'worker' consciousness, the active promotion of member interests, linking up with other trade unionists in both the private and public sector, and working towards the reform of NALGO's structures and practices with a strong emphasis on grass roots activism. Those seeking a new radical practice had a greater focus on the relationship between worker and user, the promotion of new forms of organisational structures, both within and beyond the local authority and through the support of self-help or user-based groups. We also examine two major industrial disputes involving social workers, the 1978/79 fieldworkers' strike and the 1983 residential workers' dispute, exploring both the extent to which these disputes reflected the nature of radicalism within social work, and their relationship to NALGO as a whole.

The emergence of radical social work

Sharron (1980) identifies 1975 as a numerical giant leap forward for trade unionism in social work when, "83,000 people, many of them social workers, joined NALGO, four times the growth rate in any previous year" (p 9). They were to become, he states, "the cutting edge of trade union organisation within NALGO" (p 10). However Simpkin (1989) places the emergence of social work radicalism very firmly in the earlier period of 1968,

> ... the year which saw the spectacular plunge of an intellectual generation into the attempt to dictate its own history ... the most seductive route towards reconciling and implementing sets of often very contradictory principles became participation in public service organisations, joining a state apparatus which was being newly expanded in the optimistic belief that economic growth would finance a philosophy of welfare ... (pp 160-161)

Langan and Lee (1989), reflecting on the defining characteristics of radical social work, note that its,

> Striking features ... are the clarity and simplicity of its basic themes ... One of the most positive features ... from the start was that it put forward a **critique** of existing patterns of social provision ... it questioned conventional practice in terms that pushed the interests of the clients to the fore ... (pp 4-7)

For them radical social work sought to generate a wider awareness of the power that social workers had and, they suggest, its desire to transfer this power to users. However, it is suggested here that this desire to empower service users was never more than a minority tendency within radical social work, and that indeed one of its central weaknesses was its failure to develop ways of working with users as citizens.

Langan and Lee identify three approaches within radical social work: the revolutionary approach with its emphasis on the controlling elements of social work and the need for revolutionary changes in the social and economic order; the reformist approach, prepared to defend any positive features of welfare; and the prefigurative approach, intent on developing transformative practices that would prefigure the future. However they omit the central feature of radical social work in the 1970s which was its essentially workerist strategy: seeing the social worker not as a professional but as an employee, a worker who can only move forward in a trade union firmly rooted in the wider labour movement. It was a strategy that minimised the significance of any 'progressive' work within the occupation, and which, according to Frost and Stein (1989), contained two elements, "a simplistic transfer of trade union ideology from the private sector to the public sector and, second, an over-reliance on all-out industrial action" (p 36). The consequences for practice were, for Pearson (1989),

> That all attempts to ameliorate the effects of poverty ... were to be judged as a 'cool out' and a 'con', as attempts to adjust the client to the system ... The welfare state was a 'safety-valve' that functioned in such a way as to avert protest and the eventually inevitable revolution ... (p 47).

Pearson goes on to argue that radical social work was characterised by an analysis of the welfare state that "acted as a subtly constraining force against human liberty and the possibilities of emancipation" (p 49).

Such an analysis found its most coherent expression through the journal "Case-Con" (1970-1978) which not only acted as essential reading material for radical practitioners and students of social work, but also as an umbrella under which localised groups of radical workers could meet. The broad position adopted by the editorial collective was that the solution to the social problems encountered on a daily basis by social workers, lay not with marginal special programmes or improved services, but firstly with organising within NALGO to improve wages and working conditions, and secondly by uniting with other workers in struggle. Simpkin (1983), representing this position as "revolutionary socialist", suggests that,

> Just as we can begin to understand the demands and organisation of our job only if we analyse it as workers within a capitalist economy, so we can break through both artificial and the more substantive barriers which divide us only by linking up as workers with the labour movement and the organisations of other exploited groups. (p 142)

Again, he states,

> The point of organising together is to assert some choice and control over one's own life and work ... the most important aspect for radicals of being members of NALGO ... is the direct connection they have with other local authority workers. (p 147-48)

Similarly, Bolger et al. (1981) argue that as a federal union, NALGO forces welfare workers to become involved at least with other local authority workers. For them, any form of trade union action must immediately take welfare workers outside of their professional circle of colleagues and allies leaving them no choice but to popularise and deprofessionalise issues in NALGO in order to win wider support. Case-Con further argued that social workers should reject the controlling functions in their work and instead assist their clients in any way possible to gain the material necessities they had a right to. However, this could not be achieved by grass roots action alone but only by organised class struggle and, to quote Simpkin again, "social workers should give priority to advancing that struggle" (p 22).

Such an approach led to a strong emphasis within the radical social work literature on the labour process within social work, an exposure of the limitations of the initiatives and methods of work that figured with increasing prominence in the early 1970s, a rejection of the idea of a transformed relationship under capitalism between user and provider, and a call for militant trade unionism. Whilst the Case-Con editorial recognised both the division between professionalism and trade unionism, and ultimately the need to bring these together, the emphasis within the journal was to attack the former and defend the latter. In Case-Con 2 the editorial argued that the task was,

> As well as developing and refining our theoretical analysis of social work in modern capitalism ... channel the radicalism and socialism of such a large body of social workers to an effective end ... a ginger group within (NALGO) to put our collective views on conditions of work and the wider political issues more strongly. (August 1970)

It recognised that social workers were divided between "the new progressive elements putting all their energies into BASW in its formative year, and the older established social worker pushing demands in NALGO" and that "radicals and socialists" would want to work with both groups.

This dilemma of where to focus attention continued to be raised. In Case-Con 3 an anonymous writer stated,

> Some social workers still hope to change BASW into a trade union, but even if that did happen this would cut social workers off from other employees in social services.

The appropriate union ... is NALGO, but the response (to this) ... is 'that bureaucratic reactionary useless organisation, you must be joking'.
(March 1971)

The article went on to argue that the formation of NALGO Action Group (NAG) held out hope and indicated the way forward, concluding "we must not hive ourselves off as a special elite of public service employees: we must fight for radical policies within NALGO as trade unionists alongside our colleagues" (p 12). In Case-Con 4, Deacon attacked BASW's policies suggesting that an exposé of these was necessary because "many social workers ... still have illusions in traditional professionalism" and the "belief that government might actually listen ... seems to demonstrate a particular type of social work arrogance" (June 1971, p 11). By Case-Con 10 the dilemma had been resolved by an article entitled 'BALLSW' written by 'BASWIT' who attacked BASW's aims as "elitist and anti-democratic ... spreading professional control over ever-widening spheres;" its political interventions were seen as "naive" with "leaden compromises", its struggles as "elephantine". Nevertheless the potential strength of BASW's 10,000 membership was acknowledged and it called for "the building of an alternative, and we are in no doubt that the most urgent priority is to work with NALGO to create the rank and file social work movement called for by the Case-Con conference, whose success will be essential to the demise of the BASW philosophy" (January 1973, p 19).

However, although there was increasing clarity within Case-Con on the need for a trade union rank and file movement, it continued to acknowledge the problem (no. 20, September 1975) of Case-Con's role between the competing perspectives of the "professional view of social work and the radical/revolutionary and trade union perspectives", especially since "in practice many social workers realise that, radical or professional, there is often no difference in the job". What is significant, however, is that, rather than analysing why there might be so little difference, and exploring the possibilities for developing a radical or revolutionary practice, the article concluded with the now familiar refrain,

Case-Con's function must lie in ... providing a forum for isolated individuals and organised groups to meet, to politicise the former, to undermine the professional claptrap that abounds in social work circles and introduce all social workers to rank and file trade union activity.

Thus, even when the magazine did turn its attention to special issues (e.g. on women, gay and lesbian issues, community work and residential care) the central thrust of the articles was to either unmask the repressive role and function of the worker as agent of the oppressive state, or to highlight the inadequacies of any 'progressive' practice. Thus, for example Case-Con 15 (Spring 1974) Women's Issue, had substantive articles on women's role in capitalism as the private reproduction of labour power (Weir), women's reaction to social work values (Garrett), women in NALGO (Stilwell) and sexist ideology in casework (Wilson), but little on how to transform such critical understanding to practice when working as, with, or alongside women. Instead the major concern was the relationship of social workers to NALGO. Similarly, Jones (1983) suggested the need was for a rank and file organisation that would be formed by a critical stance towards the union leadership. Whilst others such as Corrigan and Leonard (1978) criticised such an approach and proposed that despite their imperfections it was enough to work within those institutions created by working class struggle over 100 years, Jones maintained that the role adopted by NALGO leadership during the 1978/79 strike threw doubt on their optimism.

However there were also, during this period, radicals whose primary focus was on how to transform the relationship between worker and client/consumer. Simpkin (1983) identifies these "libertarian socialists" who, "placed a premium on developing new forms of living and personal relationships", suggesting that they "tended to deny they were social workers or controlling agents at all" (p 138). Simpkin identifies Clark and Jaffe (1973) as the best exponents of the libertarian case that "only after an extensive process of personal change is an individual competent to dictate what programs are feasible for large numbers". Simpkin suggests that libertarians were concerned with creating a sharing experience and a collective security and he cites such initiatives as patch systems, welfare rights, and intermediate treatment as examples of attempts to make services relevant. One could add, no doubt, public participation exercises, neigh-bourhood forums, area management, area-based anti-poverty strategies, girls' work, or focusing on the specific needs of black people as similar examples in other areas of welfare. Simpkin correctly highlights the dangers of co-option, the costs of participation and the restrictions of funding within such work, concluding that "working at the grass roots confers authenticity without much corresponding power" (p 141). Despite his stress on the need for such work, Simpkin remains close to the revolutionary socialist viewpoint and his promotion of a joint approach is more a product of how he perceives welfare work under Thatcherism than what was necessary in the 1970s. Yet it is, in fact, somewhat misleading to characterise the libertarian socialist position as being singularly preoccupied with personal change and personal relationships as this ignores its concern with what constitutes radical practice which embraces, but goes beyond personal relationships to include organisational structures and the delivery of services.

Social work radicalism during the 1970s was thus dominated by the revolutionary perspective. Cohen (1975) sees this approach as containing three strands which he describes as "theory, self-help and client co-option". The first emphasises the need for a theoretical understanding of economic and social systems and social welfare's role in relation to these. The second emphasises the need for activism within the labour movement, and the third is to acknowledge the social control function of the worker and to find an alternative. Cohen concludes, however, "there is very little indication ... of how the revolutionary social worker would operate very differently from his (sic) non-revolutionary colleagues" (p 88). Indeed the Case-Con editorial of September 1975 is very explicit on this point;

> Common to both community work and social work is the repressive function they fulfil ... which works to check the realisation of working class action and power ... in practice, and ideologically, social work translates works of class deprivation into individual pathology ... community work, like social work, diverts attention away from political class issues ... collective action is not a radical action in itself, and participation is a reformist blind-alley as it leads to consensus not conflict. (p 2)

Similarly, Clapton (1977) argues that

> By attempting to operate 'radically' from within, the movement has been appropriated as a means of improving and refreshing the social services, instead of questioning their existence and function ... The efforts of politically conscious workers are better employed in relations with fellow workers and arguing for an understanding of the state as it affects its employees rather than dissipating their energies in the search for revolutionary practice. (p 16)

Goldup (1977) likewise suggests, "the challenge radicals in social work present is not primarily on the job. It is in confronting their own status as low level bureaucrats". Even writers such as Simpkin (1985), who recognise the significance of so-called libertarian socialism, nevertheless warned that they "risk irrelevance or a drift into liberalism" (p 133) and argued that workers should unionise,

> Not just for our own protection but to ensure our continued relevance ... essentially we join the union to pursue our own interests, and social workers are at last abandoning earnest self-sacrifice in pursuit of better pay and holidays as well as working conditions which can improve the response to clients' needs.
> (pp 143-45)

Such politics, in a Britain dominated politically since 1979 by a dynamic New Right, have left social work in a vulnerable position. Thus Nellis (1989) concluded,

> The biggest difficulty confronting radical left-wing social workers in the mid 1980s is its failure to spell out what it means to practise socialist social work in a political environment where socialism is in extreme crisis, and unable to offer organisational, and possibly even ideological, support to social work". (p 110)

It was not, however, as though other analyses and strategies were not available, although these probably emerged too late in the 1970s to become influential in the face of the Thatcherite assault. Thus such texts as Corrigan and Leonard (1978), Statham (1978), and Brake and Bailey (1980) argued for a wider approach that, whilst maintaining a trade union politics, expanded it to include the promotion of collective non-hierarchal teamwork, involving users in decision-making, engaging with radical alternatives occurring outside social work practice, promoting decentralised service delivery, and developing ways of working with individuals. Simpkin (1989) felt that differences of emphasis in radical politics had nevertheless been contained by a common unity around cuts, pay and conditions of service, culminating in both the social work strike and the election of Thatcher's first government. Thatcher's election meant that the "development of the critical awareness required to secure and legitimate radical activity became much more crucial; subsequent writing began to build up a more sophisticated integration of theory practice ..." (p 168).

A number of new texts appeared in the early 1980s which begin to posit the notion of democratising practice and empowering the consumer at the centre of their strategies for change (see Sutton et al. 1980; Bolger et al. 1981; Curno et al. 1982; Hearn 1982; Jones 1983; Simpkin 1983). However, the only national development to emerge from radical social work during that period was the growth of "women and social work groups" which in 1979 held the "Feminism and Social Work Practice" conference, and was followed by three further national conferences in 1980, 1981 and 1982. This was to be followed shortly by the emergence of a parallel development based on an 'anti-racist' critique which led to the formation not only of black workers' groups but, on a national level, the emergence in 1983 of the Black Workers Trade Union Solidarity Movement. Much has been said in support of such developments. Simpkin (1989) sees both as "central to the dialectic of individual and collective, giving an essential depth of awareness to any possible renewal of radicalism" (p 169), whereas Hearn (1982) argues for "the centrality of gender and reproduction for an understanding of social work" (p 30). Not surprisingly the Birmingham Women and Social Work Group which began in 1978 argued that the "emerging feminist perspective in social work is crucial for the future of social work services that affect the lives of women" (Brook and Davis 1985, p 115).

By drawing not only from feminism but also from recent developments in the theory of the state (London to Edinburgh Weekend Return Group, 1982), feminist social work argued that women's interaction with the state was contradictory, receiving services that were needed but in a form that was not. Furthermore women social workers shared the oppressive experience of patriarchy just as much as their female clients and, sometimes, dismissing the hopes of their radical male social work colleagues "that the Revolution will liberate them along with the working class" (Birmingham Women and Social Work Group, p 122), the emphasis shifted to developing new ways of working with users. According to Hudson (1989), "a constant thread of both black and white feminist social work perspectives has been a recognition of the capacities and strengths of women" (p 82). This recognition has been applied both to women social workers, especially in their drive for greater acknowledgement, career development, influence and power within both their work organisation and trade union, and to women as clients, particularly in their relationships with men, families and state organisations. However such gender identity politics has also tended to minimise the significance of class politics and consequently played down conflicting interests between women. Moreover, Hudson concludes, despite some recent additions to the feminist social work literature (Hamner and Statham 1988; Dominelli and McLeod 1989) that, "it is difficult to find a collective vision about anti-sexist social work ... their effectiveness in ensuring that feminist principles and ideas are translated into action has been limited" (p 92). A similar process can be seen in the emergence of anti-racist social work which contained a number of threads including a critique of social welfare for its perpetuation of oppression, ideologically and in practice, in relation to black and ethnic minority peoples, a critique of white practitioners in welfare for ignoring the needs of black people, and the assertion of a commonality of interests between black people (see Mitchell and Russell (1969), Parmour (1989) and Nanton (1989) for a critique of such a position).

What is significant for our purposes is to note that by the time radical socialist local authorities were putting forward proposals for decentralised services along with a transformation in the relationship between service provider and user, the most politically developed section amongst public service workers had already rejected or marginalised such strategies, especially when they came from their employers or required alliances with managers and politicians. They also increasingly felt on the defensive from a Thatcher government that was raising fundamental questions about the very need for state social work at all whilst social work itself was increasingly internally fragmented following the emergent feminist and anti-racist critiques.

Social work strikes out

The 1978/79 field social workers strike marked a high point in industrial militancy for NALGO members. Yet it also illustrated the tensions, both within NALGO as a whole and particular occupational groups within it, between radicalised workers and those seeking to pursue the more traditionally conservative approaches of either a group collectivism in their trade unionism, or professionalism. This was the largest strike of social workers, lasting 42 weeks (between August 1978 and June 1979), affecting virtually all parts of the UK. However, in total it involved only just over 2500 workers, a tiny fraction of the 100,000 non-manual social services employees. The dispute was about both the inadequacies of the centralised wage and conditions of service bargaining machinery of Whitleyism, and a straightforward pay dispute. Cooper (1980) highlights the centrality of the salary question for precipitating the strike, illustrating the way in which social workers' pay structures had suffered relative to other, more senior workers, both within their own departments and the comparable field of the probation service, as well as externally with pay awards to other sectors.

Support for local negotiating rights had been building up since 1976 when, following increased duties since reorganisation, the NALGO Annual Conference decided, against the advice of the Executive, on a policy of locally determined agreements for social workers.   Joyce et al. (1988) argue that since other local government officers already had local negotiating machinery, the social work dispute should be understood as being as much about a local demand for change rather than a national union demand, reflecting the increasingly hostile attitude of rank and file social workers to what they saw as the incompetence, lack of determination and duplicity of the national officers of the union. It was, they argue, an attempt by social workers to rid themselves of centralised direction, which was defined as unresponsive, remote, bureaucratic, undemocratic, obstructing the membership and time-wasting. Additionally, local bargaining might free them from some of central government's efforts to hold down pay increases and demonstrate the power and importance of a rank and file movement.

In the early part of 1978 local claims were presented to employers and rejected. In July, NALGO Branches in Tower Hamlets, Newcastle and Sheffield asked the union's Emergency Committee for authority to take industrial action. After an overwhelming ballot in favour, strike action took place on the 14th August in Newcastle and Southwark, to be quickly followed by Tower Hamlets. In all, social workers in 16 local authorities went on strike for an average length of three months, with Tower Hamlets being out for nine months. By the end of the year the strike involved such diverse authorities as Leeds, Cheshire, Strathclyde, Surrey, Sheffield, Kent, Hackney, Northumberland, Liverpool, Gloucestershire, Gateshead, East Sussex, Manchester, Waltham Forest and Islington.   The Emergency Committee set up a special Strike Operations Committee (September 1978) but rejected a proposal that this should be run by striking social workers. It had noted in the August that there were between 35 and 40 claims for local re-grading but argued against a national social work strike on the grounds that the strike fund would be empty within 3.5 weeks. As the strike spread the All London Social Work Action Group was formed, and by September it was writing to NALGO's General Secretary "to use your influence within the NALGO hierarchy to effect a more dynamic and determined leadership" and complaining of an "over-cautious" approach. In the November over 600 social workers occupied NALGO headquarters to prevent union leaders from reaching a solution that did not meet their demands. Considerable hostility toward NALGO's national officers was expressed by the strikers in the social work press (see for example SWT Vol 10 no. 20, 16.1.1979), often stressing their patronising attitude and refusal to meet the strikers (SWT Vol 10 no. 23, 6.2.1979 and Vol 10 no. 24, 13.2.1979).

The strike was never straightforward, with splits in the union over whether such a large amount (over £3m spent on strike pay) should be allocated to one section, and some internal tension resulting from an ambiguity toward social workers by other NALGO members.   Thus as early as September 1978 Newcastle was reporting an anti-strike motion, subsequently defeated, being put at the Branch. Nevertheless this was not a uniform response, for example, the Southwark Branch voted by a 2-1 majority in favour of the strike and resolved, "not to take any action which would weaken the effectiveness of the strike" (NALGO EC minutes, 3.10.1978). However, there was also a clear and important division over whether or not the dispute was primarily about pay (the view ultimately of the national negotiating committee) or about local negotiations (a view held by a number of strikers) (SWT Vol 10 no. 21, 23.1.1979).

In addition local strikes continued long after the employers' offer was accepted and NALGO had instructed all its branches to open negotiations with their authorities (SWT, Vol 10 no. 23, 6.2.1979). This was partly because strikers were not expected to return to work unless meaningful local negotiations were taking place, but also because local employers were being advised by their national negotiators not to negotiate seriously until all strikers in all authorities had returned to work (SWT, 20.2.1979). Yet union support was waning and NALGO's chief national negotiator argued that the union had gone as far as it could and that there was nothing further to be gained other than "the bankruptcy of this union" (SWT Vol 10 no. 23, 6.2.1979). This was also the view adopted by Joyce et al. (1988) who noted that those on strike represented not even half of one per cent of the total membership, yet at one point the strike was costing £0.5m a month.

In January 1979 a new grading system was put forward by the employers at an NJC Joint Working Party and was accepted by NALGO's Local Government Committee. A special national conference of the union then accepted the recommendation despite being rejected by social workers. The official dispute ended in February, but by the middle of March seven branches were still involved in the dispute over the return to work and the last branch to return (Tower Hamlets) did not do so until June. In the end only Islington achieved a local agreement and was the first to return to work having achieved pay increases of up to £900, whilst other workers in areas such as Newcastle returned complaining of increasing pressure from local management. In the middle of March, *Social Work Today* was reporting that only four authorities had in fact resolved the dispute that had formally been ended at the beginning of February (SWT, 13.3.1979). Moreover, when strikers did return they often did so in a mood of bitterness and feeling as though they had been pressured to do so by the union's national emergency committee. Thus one of the local convenors, Graham Burgess from Liverpool, stated, "Just because we are back doesn't mean that we have stopped fighting" (SWT 27.3.1979, p 3). Yet for some it had been a positive experience, for as one Islington activist commented,

On a personal level I gained a lot. There was a feeling of solidarity, strength and power ... a high spirit of achievement and feeling that this was the way to get your management to do the job properly ... the most liberating thing was realising that people could manage without social workers.
(Social worker - female)

A number of writers (Bolger et al. 1981; Jones 1983) have claimed that other gains were achieved through the strike, citing the emergence of groups such as the Leeds Social Workers Action Group, which produced a local workers' plan for social work, subsequently published by NALGO. A similar body in Sheffield launched a local magazine, "Strike News", held work-site fieldworkers meetings, and adopted a similar role to that performed by the All London Social Workers Action Group. Similarly, Jones (1983) identified what for him were three important issues that emerged as a consequence of the strike. Firstly, for many workers this was their first experience of collective action and solidarity leading, he suggests, to more creative relationships and the development of new skills and confidences. Secondly, social workers were able to initiate some alliances with other workers. Thirdly, he argues, it led to "detailed discussions about the manner in which certain positive service aspects were being eroded through cuts" (p 43). However Simpkin (1983) disagreed, recalling that "those of us who had hoped to use the strike to discuss and initiate radically new forms of relationships with client groups were disappointed" (pp 153-54), and he further notes the effect of time on those initial changes in consciousness, "our solidarity as fieldworkers gradually disintegrated and staff turnover eroded group memory. The individualistic processes of social work reasserted themselves, though less comprehensively than before" (p 153).

Brogden and Wright (1979) argued that money and esteem were the key issues at stake (see also SWT Vol 10 no. 3 12.9.1978, pp 7-9). Using data from a questionnaire of 360 social workers they conclude that workers took strike action not so much because they rejected their role, and wanted to transform it, but because "they felt others were rejecting them". In support they quote those involved, "I was frustrated with everything - just felt like a dustbin. Our morale was really low", and "I saw the strike as a reflection of society's evaluation of us". Nevertheless they suggest that there were four major outcomes: a substantially increased sense of unity (mentioned by 90% of their respondents); a heightened understanding of the political dimension to their job (mentioned by over a third of respondents); a deeper commitment to trade unions and their involvement in them despite, they say, "the commonly expressed bitter reactions to their experience of their own union, NALGO"; and a clearer division between themselves and management. Elsewhere (1979) they identify four specific responses by NALGO which caused disillusionment amongst social workers: strike breaking activity by local NALGO members in other occupations; the apparent lack of advice on the actual running of a strike; the supposedly deliberate obstruction by local union officials; and the handling of the strike at national level. They conclude,

> NALGO itself seems headed for continuing conflicts with this previously dormant group of service workers. Put more importantly, for the first time, social workers have come to realise that their own strike was not dissimilar, in origins and in reactions to it, to the simultaneous strikes by grave diggers and ambulancemen (sic). (p 16).

NALGO conducted its own evaluation of the strike which was contained in a draft White Paper entitled 'Industrial Action - An Alternative View' (November 1979). Here it argued that the strike had been "a very emotive issue" both in terms of its financial effect and the general attitude of the membership towards social work, "which was hardly sympathetic and at least misunderstood". It pointed to the conflict between NALGO's National Local Government Committee, which was "from the outset opposed to allowing individual branches to commence industrial action until such time as real negotiations had been exhausted" and its Emergency Committee, which had allowed the Newcastle and Southwark branches to begin action when talks had broken down "at the first stage". Indeed, it places a heavy responsibility on the Emergency Committee whose decision it said,

> Resulted in a protracted dispute with unco-ordinated action against local employers ... unwilling to enter into negotiations and national employers who would not concede the principle of removing the prescribed grade.

The result, it concludes, "was a very difficult dispute which, at the end of the day, produced improvements in social worker salaries but fell far short of the National Council's desire to remove prescribed grades". The report was also at pains to highlight the relatively small number of members involved in the dispute, pointing out that only 45 out of 124 branches with social worker members made a reference either to the Emergency Committee or the Strike Operations Committee. Of these only 28 sought authority for strike action. In 17 cases a sufficient majority was secured "although in some instances the majorities obtained were less than those normally required by the EC for strike action to be approved".

Internal tensions continued, reflected in a motion to the 1980 annual conference from ten branches noting that, "the deficiencies of NALGO's procedures for industrial action as exemplified by the social workers strike did not arise from failings in the procedures ... but primarily from the unwillingness of the majority of social workers to engage in industrial action". It was also noted that social workers had badly misjudged their employers by not anticipating that they "would be willing to allow deprived sections of the community to suffer further deprivation as a consequence of the withdrawal of social services". The 1980 debate was significant not only for acknowledging the gap between the striking social workers and other sections of the union, but also for recognising the shift in the membership's attitude to industrial action.

> No doubt in the early 1970s the possibility of having more than 1000 members on strike would have been regarded as unrealistic but by the latter part of the decade this has happened ... it is not unrealistic to recognise the possibility of some 20,000 being on strike.

Yet the draft White Paper also pointed to some of the intractable problems faced by those setting out on such a course;

> ... consideration needs to be given to the nature of the work undertaken by the majority of members and to the various forms of industrial action open to them and their possible effectiveness ... Not all services ... are of general application ... The community as a whole benefits from the provision of public services but the benefit to various sections or individuals varies enormously according to their circumstances or needs ... stoppages at work do not affect the profit-making ability of the employer ... he is not engaged in this pursuit in local government, health or various other NALGO services. It should be appreciated that many of the problems which NALGO faces in respect of industrial action ... stem from the nature of the service which members are employed to provide.

The residential social work dispute

As we saw in the last chapter, the fieldwork social workers strike was not the only industrial action involving NALGO members during that time. Throughout 1980 industrial disputes continued across the UK over stand-by duty, local reorganisations, the imposition of O&M studies, and most commonly the continuation of cuts in public expenditure, involving NALGO members from all occupational groupings. However, the union's next major dispute involved the residential social workers following the employers' rejection in February 1983 of a pay claim submitted 13 months earlier in January 1982. The National Committee recommended industrial action in April, advising on a work-to-rule but rejecting the suggestion of a residential care admissions ban, fearing that it would not be supported. However this was subsequently overturned by a Delegates Meeting and an admissions and overtime ban were put into effect. This proved ineffective and attempts were made to escalate the action, e.g. a national day of action in October and, in some branches, indefinite strike action. However, only approximately 50% of the social services branches undertook any escalatory action, and by the end of December after losing a national ballot for further action the dispute was over and NALGO defeated.

Again the union launched an inquiry resulting in a report by the National Local Government Committee to the 1985 Local Government Group Annual Meeting (NALGO, 1985). In exploring the reasons for the failure of the action the report highlighted the divided loyalties of residential workers (because of their commitment to their clients), and the insufficient attention given to the industrial strength of residential workers in the face of employer intransigence (p 21). In addition, it also cited the failure to gain support from both non-NALGO and NALGO union members, the difficulty of building up a collective identity in isolated work units and the in-effectiveness of the initial action. Further, the report highlighted the uneven d-evelopment of collective consciousness in the union, noting that, "in many branches even other social services members ignored the dispute and some fieldworkers actively sought to circumvent the effects of the industrial action ... and others were prepared to take far stronger action than the residential workers" (p 22). On the positive side the report noted an increase in residential worker membership, increased union organisation and the emergence of activists in the residential sector.

Perhaps the most significant of the report's 17 recommendations was one recognising the need for branches to form teams of branch officers and activists from the wider membership to visit dispersed work units on a regular basis during a dispute. However, this was nevertheless quite a limited response since here was an opportunity to explore the most appropriate way of engaging members and non-members in union matters at all times regardless of whether or not a dispute was in place. Given that a number of local authorities were simultaneously involved in decentralising a whole range of services this was an important lost opportunity to rethink the whole structure and organisational base of the union in the light of such trends. Similarly, some analysis might have been made of the different material and work situations facing different groups of NALGO members. Residential workers occupy another industrial world to even their fieldwork colleagues with the old titles and associated symbolism of "house parent" being hard to shake off. They often share the same home as their clients, with whom they might have a close living and working relationship, and consequently, as Joyce et al. (1988) point out, "not only is there the problem that they are bringing chaos to the homes of their clients, they are also introducing chaos, in many cases, into their own homes" (p 103). These and similar differences in work and market situation often reflecting class, race and gender divisions, are central to NALGO's membership, yet little attention has been given as to how these differences can be welded together and strategies devised that do not simply reproduce wider societal divisions.

Conclusion

The centrality of radical social work to the development of an industrial militancy in NALGO justifies an exploration of its nature and practice. The tension between a radicalism fashioned from a model of industrial unionism, associated with the traditional working class, and one seeking to promote a progressive welfare practice has been highlighted as particularly important. Whilst never completely resolved it is apparent that it was the former tendency that won at least ideological supremacy although, as can be seen in the case study, workers continue to be sharply aware of the tensions between adopting such a stance and their 'welfare' orientation. It is equally clear that initiatives such as decentralisation, especially those espousing greater democratisation of public services and political life generally, relate more comfortably to those workers wishing to critically examine their own practices, relationships with users, communities or neighbourhoods, and the policies and ideological underpinnings which provide the framework for these. A belief that active engagement in these areas is both an important political project in itself which can make a qualitative difference to both the lives of individual and collective service users, as well as civil and political life in general, even if to do so may involve giving up some of one's own privileges and power as a worker or elected representative, is central to both proponents of decentralisation and sections of the politicised public sector workforce. Overall it was those who held the view that their immediate managers and elected councillors were no more than the equivalent of the traditional manager or owner of capital and labour, and that they themselves were simply workers reproducing capitalist social relations, who appear to have won the ideological argument, and dominated key positions in local branch structures. This has had a considerable effect on the potential success of policies such as decentralisation, particularly when, through lack of experience, increasing pressure from central government, a perceived sense of urgency about succeeding in their policy intentions, and no doubt a fear of losing political office, those same managers and councillors acted in ways that tended to confirm rather than challenge the analysis.

4 Decentralisation and the urban left

By the early 1990s over half the local authorities in the UK had decentralised at least some aspect of their services. This chapter examines the emergence of decentralisation as a key strategy. Although our main interest is on those authorities who were controlled during the 1980s by Labour councillors associated with the urban left, we will look initially at the overall development of the policy, and make some distinctions between different objectives and approaches contained within it. Similarly decentralisation is not without its historical predecessors, and reference is made to where the contemporary initiatives follow or break with the past. From here some examination will be given to the more radical initiatives that have had the democratisation of public services and local political life as a central objective, and thus going well beyond new administrative arrangements that dominate more traditional approaches.

In considering these radical strategies it is important to locate decentralisation within the wider politics of the new urban left, especially since for many authorities it represented the central thrust of their overall programme. The emergence of the urban left, and the social background of those involved, will be traced briefly along with its principal ideas, concerns and proposed strategies. Consideration will then be given to the theory and practice of decentralisation within the broad urban left approach, drawing from a number of authorities both the key aims and objectives and some of the major difficulties they have encountered in the implementation of their ideas.

Decentralisation sweeps all before it

It is estimated that over 61% of all local authorities in the UK now have some form of a decentralised system and a number of writers have also pointed to a wide range of municipal decentralisation in other European countries (Hoggett 1987, Epstein 1990, Burns, Hambleton, Hoggett 1994). This trend has by no means been confined to one political party. Although the majority of those decentralising authorities have been Labour controlled there are examples of both Liberal Social Democratic (Tower Hamlets) and Conservative (Bradford) authorities who have pursued such strategies. Indeed there is no doubting its popularity - a "lemming like pursuit" according to

Beresford and Croft (1986) - and in the assessments of a number of writers, its permanency. Thus, Dale (1987) argues that decentralisation, "represents an important break from the main post-war trends in thinking about social service delivery" (p 152). Similarly, Hoggett, Hambleton and Tolan (1988) argue that, "far from being a passing fad, (it) can be shown to be a deep-seated trend in the development of the social and economic organisation of western democracies which will be of major significance in the 1990s and beyond" (p 2), a view that remained unshaken by the middle of the decade (Burns, Hambleton and Hoggett 1994).

Great claims have been made for decentralisation (Sills, Marsden and Taylor 1986). Hambleton and Hoggett (1984) state that such initiatives, "open up exciting possibilities for making public services more responsive and relevant ... radical forms of decentralisation represent a fundamental challenge to established ways of organising and running public services" (p 1). Wright (1984) equated its popularity with that of the enthusiasm for 'participation' in the 1960s and in another piece (1985) described it as, "a tidal wave of fashion ... which looks like sweeping all before it" (p 12). However, the fact that the idea of decentralisation has been enthusiastically espoused by a wide range of academics, policy makers and elected representatives from across the political spectrum should in itself be a sufficient reason for caution before accepting it as an unchallengeable 'good thing'. Indeed some writers (Peters 1985, Hambleton and Hoggett 1984) have expressed concern that its general popularity concealed major ideological differences so much so that the term had become meaningless. One writer concluded that the label, "may actually obscure initiatives whose essential logic ranges from the centralisation of institutional power to managerialist cost-cutting and rationalisation, from the incorporation of urban social movements within the tentacles of the local state to Eurocommunist and Libertarian Socialist strategies aimed at the transformation of the state, economy and civil society" (Hoggett 1988, p 217). Even more recently we were being warned that decentralisation is but a means to an end and that clarity about objectives is essential (Burns, Hambleton and Hoggett 1994). In fact, when stripped of any contextual meaning decentralisation is no more than a description of the breaking down of larger political and administrative units into smaller ones. In this sense one can agree with a number of writers that decentralisation is politically neutral (Deakin 1984, Conyers 1986). "Localism pure and simple wears no party label" (Deakin 1984, p 21).

This overall popularity for decentralisation has, however, been explained by some as part of a wider post-fordist restructuring of the management of human resources across both the spheres of private production and state welfare (Stoker 1989, Hoggett 1990). Both the left and right, equally critical of state bureaucratic control, are seen as attempting to maximise those opportunities provided by technological and managerial developments although the right's cost reducing agendas and marketisation may be more significant. Cochrane's (1989) view is that decentralisation is but one strategy within the management of change at a local level, a response to an increasingly diversified and fragmented social structure. This is viewed as an extension of local government's important role, emerging from the mid-1970s, of bringing together and managing the relationships between various local interests. In this perspective decentralisation offers a sophisticated form of urban management providing opportunities to engage a wide range of organisations, licensed by the local state, and who might otherwise be excluded from the bargaining process. Within a period of severe financial constraint entwining local interests in the processes of local government is important for state legitimation. Here we are concerned with those strategies, associated with sections of the radical left within the Labour Party, that were seen as central to the creation of a broadly based alliance, mediated by the left-wing of the party, of public sector workers, through their trade unions, and the disadvantaged and marginalised, either as service users or through their collective organisations. This alliance was not only to act as a defence against the attacks from a right-wing central government but would also be the springboard for the promotion of socialist structures and practices (Webber and Shields 1986). Radical decentralisation was the left's response to its own earlier criticisms of welfare organisation and delivery. The proposed restructuring of service delivery and management along with the politicisation of local political life was to be the cement that held the alliance in place. Cochrane and Massey (1989) are, however, doubtful that such efforts can do no more than confirm the essential weakness of local government in the face of capitalist market forces.

The practice of decentralisation

Our principal concern here is with the decentralisation of local government services. From an organisational perspective this involves the creation of sub-units of local government based on neighbourhoods or small areas, from which previously centralised services and resources are to be provided. Within this context the key issues for decentralising authorities identified by a number of writers (Conyers 1986) have been:

(i)   which services to decentralise and how many, whilst some have focused on one service, with housing being a popular choice, others have attempted a multi-service approach;

(ii)   if the strategy is to be multi-service then whether to decentralise all at once or gradually, phased in over a period of time;

(iii)   what criteria to use for the selection of neighbourhoods, e.g. existing ward boundaries or ones subjectively determined by the residents;

(iv)   what should be the size of the neighbourhoods (decentralising authorities have used an average population range of between 7000 and 24,000);

(v)   to what extent should the organisational image be altered by providing purpose built offices;

(vi)   what should be the relationship between those services that are decentralised and those that remain at the centre;

(vii)   to what extent should there be common support services; what management structure should there be in decentralised offices, and how should these relate to departmental management structures, both within the local offices and to the senior levels of management beyond;

(viii) to what extent should the decentralised workers be required to work generically across a range of specialisms or continue working within their traditional occupational roles organised in departments and job descriptions;

(ix)   what decision-making functions can be devolved to the local office;

(x)   what areas of discretion can be left to decentralised front-line workers and to what extent are they expected to take on a wider neighbourhood brief that is likely to involve them in some aspect of community development;

(xi)   what should be the relationship between local offices and other agencies operating in the same area;

(xii)   and what should be the relationship between localised service delivery, responsive to local need, and centrally determined strategic policy decisions.

Whilst these concerns have often been tackled as organisational matters they also inevitably reflect the politics of those involved, highlighting both the political model of public service delivery and the democratic vision of those promoting the strategy. The localisation of local government services is not a new phenomenon. Since the mid-1960s there have been a number of initiatives, albeit somewhat uncoordinated, that have had as their focus the delivery of public services at sub-local government levels. A number of the current initiatives have indeed followed the patterns of their predecessors, and some of these earlier models such as the Newcastle-Upon-Tyne's Priority Area Teams have continued, and are felt to have a number of strengths over the younger versions (Hambleton and Hoggett 1988). Both the Seebohm Report (1968) and the Barclay Report (1982) on personal social services, recommended an area or patch-based approach to service delivery linked to a community development strategy, and many local authorities introduced area teams in response (Means 1984, Hadley, Dale and Sills 1984). Similarly, in housing, area based management policies emerged at the same time, often on the so-called difficult-to-let outer estates. Some, such as the Cowgate Project in Newcastle dealt with a range of housing services including rent collection, repairs, housing transfers and waiting lists, advice and information, and environmental improvement. Such projects also attempted to link up with other public sector and voluntary agencies working in the area including those, such as the police and health services, that went beyond local authority boundaries.

Central government also emphasised the importance of localised decision-making and budgeting and launched it's own 'area-management' trials (Harrop et al. 1978). Although a single service approach tended to dominate such developments a number of authorities attempted to match the growing corporatism in local authorities with a corporate approach at a local level (Hambleton 1987). The inner city strategies, developed in the late 1960s and early 1970s, included a wider community development approach that was geographically focused and concerned with the channelling of resources towards areas of greatest need, improved coordination between all local government departments, and better communication between the authority and its local communities. This emphasis on increased participation in public services, a central feature of social policy during this period, led to the development of more sophisticated consultative mechanisms, including support for neighbourhood councils, the development of area or city-wide consultative bodies, and additional funding to the voluntary sector.

A number of criticisms have been made of these early initiatives, (CDP 1977, Corkey and Craig 1978, Miller 1981, Bridges 1981, Lees and Mayo 1984, Hambleton and Hoggett 1988). Amongst the most significant were that they tended to be: small in scale, and confined to particular areas within a local authority's boundaries; the resources committed to them were generally limited; they tended to be experimental in nature and therefore, were perceived to be outside the mainstream of service delivery, and unable to exert much influence over how major services should be delivered or what the priorities ought to be. Although the marginal nature of the programmes left some room for manoeuvre in style and approach, there was little chance of them making a real impact on the central problems in the areas where they were located. There was also often a lack of coordination between projects, each being initiated by different departments and traditional departmental rivalries remained largely untouched. Most significantly, because they were essentially concerned with an apparent growing disaffection between usually inner city residents and their local authorities, or the management of urban tensions and greater social integration, they tended to be managerially led. More specifically, with a few notable exceptions, they were usually led by officers rather than politicians and where they were single service oriented they were primarily concerned with developing better contact with their particular client group, extending their knowledge of the area, and finding better ways to manage both the overall level of demand and the needs of individual clients. Finally, many of the problems and issues identified, before or during such initiatives, tended to be unrelated to locality either in terms of their causation or solution.

Willmott (1987) may be correct in stating that not much was learned from this earlier round of initiatives or, as Deakin (1984) claims, that the decentralisers of the 1980s closed their ears to the lessons because they might be inconvenient to their project. Indeed on the face of it many of the current initiatives can be seen as continuous with the earlier phase. Thus as Epstein (1990) notes, four-fifths of those authorities that introduced decentralised services during the 1980s did so only in one service activity. Many were also primarily concerned with the management of demand, although this was more in the context of a declining resource base rather than in response to concerns about the inner city. However, a number of the recent initiatives did profess to be qualitatively different from the earlier models. Thus whilst many of the managerial objectives differ little from earlier initiatives (DRIC 1986) a number of authorities introduced a more explicitly political dimension to 1980s style decentralisation. Some writers have described this in general terms as the raising of political consciousness (Hambleton and Hoggett 1985) whilst others have attempted to be more precise. Thus DRIC highlights five political objectives: the mobilisation of public support; defence of local government; to extend decision-making down to the local level; devolve power down the council pyramid; and devolve power to citizens at neighbourhood level (DRIC 1986). This extension of democracy was to be achieved by developing a more direct, or participatory approach, and more specifically, to create a sense of ownership towards public services by both the direct recipients and the general population, at a time when the effectiveness of local government was under attack from central government, and there was increasing centralisation in policy direction. Indeed, decentralisation was seen as a central part of the left's response to such centralising tendencies, "decentralisation aims to rebuild the base of popular support for the local authority against growing central interference in its affairs" (Gregory and Smith 1986, p 101).

Hambleton and Hoggett (1985, 1988), amongst others, argue that there are some common underlying motives behind all the current decentralisation proposals. This they characterise as a response to "bureaucratic paternalism" and a feeling of remoteness towards the existing structures, a sense that public services have been insensitive to user need, that service providers have been unaccountable and increasingly powerful, and a shared dissatisfaction with a "centralised, state run, functionally managed, public service provision". Likewise Gregory and Smith (1986) note that, "departments themselves have grown into massive and bureaucratic organisations ... rigidly divided and non-cooperative at their points of contact with the public" (p 101). Thus, decentralisation in the 1980s, unlike similar ventures in the previous decade, was one response by those committed to public service provision to what was perceived as a crisis of local government. For the political right the crisis was equally apparent, but the solution lay in the introduction of market forces into the workings of local government, and wherever possible the privatisation of such services.

Clearly this dissatisfaction with public services can generate a number of responses, and Dale (1987) identifies three different ideologies operating within the decentralising authorities, which she describes as the pragmatists, the populists, and the local socialists. The pragmatists were essentially concerned with improved efficiency in the management of service delivery, which may involve some resident participation, whilst the populists having a 'bottom-up' perspective to political change and a hostility to concentrations of power wished to see greater devolution to neighbourhood levels. The local socialists, "the most ambitious, but potentially the most ambiguous approach", (p 153) were seen as emphasising new forms of service delivery by transforming relationships between workers, and their relationships with service users, both of which were to be underpinned by a raising of class consciousness and the remobilisation of support for the Labour Party.

Hambleton and Hoggett (1988) develop a useful 'conceptual map' in an effort to explain responses to both the crisis of bureaucratic paternalism in local government and the wider crisis in democracy itself. They begin by identifying two crucial trends in local government during the 1980s affecting all political parties. Firstly, they note the 'unprecedented politicisation' of local government across the whole political spectrum and, secondly, the attack by central government on the efficiency and value of local government as a whole. Local government had such a focus because it was perceived as an alternative power base and source of opposition to central government, from both elected members and white-collar public service unions, but primarily because of its centrality in the implementation of welfare services and its wider role in social legitimation. In addition to those market led solutions, Hambleton and Hoggett identify the emergence of two alternatives. These they describe as consumerist or collectivist solutions, both of which they see as leading to radical changes in the organisation of local government. Consumerist solutions emerge from those who see local government primarily as a "productive and administrative system" (p 18), whereas those promoting collectivist solutions are more focused on it as a political system. Hambleton and Hoggett identify three main elements in the consumerist approach which has a concern for 'quality' in public service provision. These are: firstly, listening to the consumer both directly, in their collectivities - voluntary organisations and user groups - and as individuals, and indirectly by utilising the knowledge of front line workers; secondly, becoming more accessible, both physically and socially to the consumer; and, thirdly, speaking to the consumer. Burns (1989) sees such organisational changes as being centrally concerned with the integration of services, "creating forms of management which can corporatively reflect the neighbourhoods' needs in preference to the professions and new forms of non-specialist, generic, working - so that staff become multi-skilled ... enabling them to reflect the non-departmental needs of the public" (p 9). However, whilst acknowledging that good communication between service users and providers is crucial, Hambleton and Hoggett point to the central weakness of this approach in highlighting its failure to address issues of power and inequality in such relationships, and specifically the issue of consumer choice within the public sector. In addition, they argue that whilst the consumerist approach may improve services for individual users, the approach does not acknowledge the needs of the collective consumer, pointing out that, "many local authority services are provided to groups of consumers and that there are clear limits to any individual approach" (p 24).

In contrast, the collectivist approach to reform, with its emphasis on political processes, is as much about the democratisation of public services and the quality of government as it is about their localisation. Thus, Beresford and Croft (1986) argue that the key issue for them is the development of, "more citizen-based and citizen-controlled services" (p 21). Others make the even stronger claim that, "... We are talking about promoting direct worker/user co-operation and influence; about establishing local control on the streets and estates; about encouraging officers to work as part of a neighbourhood team; about striving towards self-servicing communities which, in time, will evolve into socialist communities" (Davis et al. 1984, p 10). In more measured tones, Hambleton and Hoggett (1987) see the collectivist solution being about the extension of both representative and participatory forms of democracy in relation to either the representation or mobilisation of collectivities rather than individuals. Four possible approaches to the democratisation of public services (p 56), are identified:

- Extend representative democracy
- Extend direct democracy
- Extend consumer democracy
- Infuse representative with direct democracy.

They see the extension of representative democracy as coming primarily through the setting up of area based committees of elected members. Examples of attempts to extend direct democracy might include the funding of community based and voluntary organisations, as in the GLC strategy, and greater user group participation in the management of service provision. Consumer democracy can be widened in ways already identified, but specifically by such things as focusing on consumer advocacy or the extension of consumer rights, greater use of research into consumer need and opinion, and identifying and working with those groups who do not make use of services to which they are entitled. Finally, they see the infusing of representative democracy with direct democracy coming about through the establishment of neighbourhood based committees, comprising not only elected members but also community organisations and under-represented groups. Hambleton and Hoggett see this collectivist approach as libertarian rather than statist in character, and as such is an attack on Labour's centralist tradition.

Having made this distinction between the consumerist and the collectivist approaches a number of qualifying comments are in order. Firstly, as a number of writers (Barker, Hambleton and Hoggett 1988, Conyers 1986) have noted, in practice most of the initiatives included a range of often competing and conflicting objectives. Indeed there are contradictions within the respective models as well as between them, e.g. responding to local need and extending local accountability may clash with targeting resources at previously excluded groups, so that "principled policy formulation at the centre may be undermined by populist action at the front line ..." (Butcher 1986, p 115). Secondly, the majority of decentralising initiatives have been solidly within the consumerist camp, and even those professing the need to democratise have not progressed very far in their efforts, "initiatives aimed at establishing a degree of consumer control over service delivery have nowhere moved beyond the experimental or pilot stage" (Beuret and Stoker 1986, p 5). However, as Hambleton and Hoggett (1988) point out, there is a connection between consumerist and democratisation perspectives in that they bring the individual consumer into some of the decision-making processes, and may thereby empower them. Equally, however, Arnold and Cole (1988) remind us that the consumerist and democratisation strategies may in fact be going in opposite directions, as the former may well conceal a strategy of centralised managerial control, as indeed were the objectives of many of the earlier attempts at localisation and participation. Similarly, Hoggett (1988) warns that without the devolution of power the decentralisation of services may "enhance the productive forces of the public sector but may do so via the centralisation of command" (p 227).

Emergence of the urban left

The proponents of the collectivist solutions, sometimes referred to as "local socialism" (Buddy and Fudge 1984) were part of the broader new 'urban left', a diverse group that emerged in the early 1980s. As Gyford (1985) states, "Neither organisationally nor programmatically is there any one authoritative centre representing the totality of local socialism" (p ix). There was, he says, not a single ideology but, "a syndrome or a set of associated characteristics" (p 18). Goss et al. (1988) agree that it was "a far from homogenous force" but suggest that its class composition was, "predominately middle class and employed within the public sector. Voluntary sector workers, social workers, community workers and local government officers, all saw that a move towards more progressive policies would improve their clients' lives and expand services ..." (p 5). Moreover, a number of writers have indeed questioned the viability of such a diverse group and the social movements with whom they sought an alliance to be able to constitute a force for social change (Bourne 1987, Goss et al. 1988). The emergence of this ill-defined movement has been traced back to the late 1960s (Gyford 1985, Green 1987, and Lansley et al. 1989), with community action, the anti-poverty programmes, single issue campaigns, and the new social movements of feminism and en-vironmentalism, all seen as important influences. From within these there developed a powerful critique of the statist assumptions and practices of the Labour Party and a determination to democratise it (Lansley et al.). Rowbotham (1984), speaking from within the urban left, notes that,

> As the threat to welfare and local community services increased from the mid 1970s, the need for links between grass roots campaigns was recognised ... even this combination in protest was not enough. Power to shape the policies which determined the allocation of resources and the kind of community provision was also necessary. This led partly to the development of proposals from below, partly to a renewal and radicalisation of activity in local government. (p 8)

Yet Livingstone (1987) noted that, such developments were slow to have an impact on mainstream politics stating,

> Like Greenham Common, CND and Greenpeace, the GLC was unmistakably a product of the 1980s, and like them it grew out of the upheavals of the 1960s. The upsurge of the left ... part of an upsurge of creativity which affected the arts, popular culture, lifestyle and sex lives much more than it affected the party politics of the day. Racism, sexism, participation and ecology, issues which appeared on the agenda of the sixties, took over a decade to reach the attention of the political parties. (p 9)

During the latter part of the 1970s many such community and social movement activists, however, had joined and gained prominent positions within the Labour Party, often at the expense of right-wing officials, "to begin a long and determined march through the institutions of local government" (Green 1987, p 206). They had been brought together as much by a sense of dissatisfaction with Labour's post-war legacy (Boddy and Fudge 1984, Campbell and Jacques 1986) as a reaction to the politics of Thatcherism. It was, according to Livingstone (1987), "a generation that grew up with and saw the limitations of a welfare state whose lack of democracy alienated those it was supposed to serve" (p 9) and, "Instead of trying to do everything for people, we broke away from Labour's client approach to politics and enabled some people to begin to do things for themselves" (p 9). The experience many of these activists had in campaigning to defend public services during the late 1970s, and their ultimate failure in building a mass base for this, had left a sense that it was again necessary to demonstrate the desirability of collectively based services. This 'class of 81' was populated by people who had often acquired their ideas and political skills from outside of local government and had a different relationship to the Left which allowed them to work in alliance with a wide range of groups, social movements and political parties. As Livingstone (1987) stated, "I believe that changing society requires an alliance: an alliance between progressive individuals and groups within the apparatus of the state, and the forces for change that exist outside the parliamentary system" (p 8). Similarly, Ward (quoted in Rowbotham 1984) states, "Elected power is not an end in itself, but a resource, to be shared with other groups and movements, and used in alliance with them to achieve social change." Again, 'London Labour Briefing' argued, "Labour councillors need to break out of the confines of council chamber politics and link up with those extra-parliamentary forces ... which alone can provide the forces for a real fight" (quoted in Gyford 1983).

Thus by 1984 there were approximately a dozen major authorities controlled by the urban left who, "set out to control the local state rather than to administer local government" (Green 1987, p 207). Boddy and Fudge (1984) identify four main objectives within this strategy to create a viable socialist model. The first of these is essentially defensive and concerns the protection of existing standards and level of collective services, against concerted efforts by central government to reduce the level of services or remove them from the sphere of public provision. However, this was recognised as being insufficient in itself given the apparent levels of dissatisfaction felt toward such services (Blunkett 1984). Secondly, to demonstrate what socialist models and approaches might look like in practice at a local level, "the local state used as an example of what we could do as a socialist government at a national level" (Blunkett 1981 quoted in Gyford 1985 p 67). The third objective was to shift popular consciousness about what alternatives might be possible, thereby closing the gap between vision and reality. Again, to quote Bunkett (1984), "What we are contemplating ... a vision of the future, involving the use of socialist values in mapping out the new territory opening up before us ... offer people a sight of the world that we would like to see" (p 44). The fourth was to mobilise support around local services and to build alliances, "a coalition of interests", and regenerate flagging interest in the Labour Party, albeit a transformed party, with a view to gaining national power.

The urban left's commitment to the value of local government has been seen by some as a reflection of its limited power base (Stoker 1988). This is supported by Blunkett who maintained that, "Local government is the only place where currently Labour Party representatives are seen to be making decisions about the lives and well-being of ordinary people" (1983 quoted in Green 1988, p 214). Yet for other insiders it was the flexibility of local government in the meeting of need, which could overcome the authoritarian rigidity of the state and socialism's lack of popularity (Rowbotham 1984). Lansley et al. (1989) identify two further reasons for this elevation of local government. Firstly, they point to the critique that had been developed, often by the urban left themselves in their earlier incarnation of community activism, of the way local councils interfered with people's lives but failed to consult them, excluded them from decision-making processes, and ignored the interests of whole sections of the population. This led them to argue that services should be "based locally in manageable neighbourhoods, communally run by elected neighbourhood councils" (see also Weir 1984, p 26). Secondly, such an open and participatory style of government could only be implemented at a local level which could then become a testing ground for a whole range of ideas and quote Blunkett and Jackson approvingly, "A realisation developed in local Labour parties that local government might develop, once again, into the tool for change which had been so effective in the late nineteenth and early twentieth centuries" (Lansley et al. 1989, p 66). Thus, the core components of the urban left's strategy included a desire to devolve control over local government, and to mobilise its potential power to effectively challenge established interests through the use of the resources and delegated moral authority (Stoker 1988). This dual vision of being more open, accessible and representative of previously excluded groups, on the one hand, and determinedly challenging of vested interests, on the other, was attractive to a wide 'rainbow' coalition. Thus local councils could be used, according to Massey et al. (1984), "to illustrate an alternative both to Thatcherism and to Labourism ... based on the feminist, anti-racist, anti-nuclear and more generally socialist ideas emerging throughout the sixties and seventies ... an alliance in which political ... resources and powers are made use of to strengthen, support and give a voice to industrial and extra-parliamentary action" (pp 225-6). This alliance, of the disadvantaged, the previously excluded, the public sector trade unions, and the locally elected representatives was perceived as the new dynamic of social change, replacing, or at least competing with, the traditional working class, which had been largely written-off as fragmented, inert and conservative. Edgar (1987) defends this strategy arguing that such new social forces have "a significantly better track record than campaigns emanating from traditional industrial organisations" and suggesting perhaps prematurely that their successes, "at the vanguard of the radical project" were due to their ability to speak, "not just with a political but also a cultural voice ... reflecting something in the present tense of the real world."

Decentralisation was but one, albeit important, strategy in the urban left's approach. As Hodge (1984), leader of Islington Council stated, "We believe that it's absolutely imperative that these decentralisation proposals are enacted, because it is the one way of building the grass roots support ..." (p 20). Other key elements within their wide ranging programme covered: employment and the development of the local economy based on local skills, socially useful production, and support for the co-operative movement; equal opportunities and anti-discriminatory practice; support for voluntary organisations; the development of cheap and reliable public transport; the expansion of cultural activities; a concern with current policing methods and police accountability; the promotion of citizen rights; and the development of environmentally safe industries. The urban left attempted, although not always successfully, systematically, or consistently, to tackle traditional areas of local government responsibility in new and innovative ways and introduce additional policy areas onto the agenda. In all areas they sought to use their power and resources to promote a collectivist ethos and to meet the needs of previously marginalised groups. For Goss et al. (1988) their politics were, "partly about policies, partly about style", involving a reassertion of political control (p 5), and a shaking up of the bureaucracy. Elected members were increasingly unwilling to act simply on the advice of the officers, but instead expected them to behave far more politically. Blunkett (1981) expressed the general ethos of the approach when he spoke of the need to,

Get people to relate their local community problems to a sense of political purpose ... the people who work for local authorities have got to be committed to a new type of politics. They are not expected to be members of the Labour Party but they should have a commitment not to an isolated individual but to the community itself. These workers should see that they are part of community action, that they are part of the political education with a small 'p'. Then the whole of our services can be thrown behind working people ... to do what they want to do in their way in their community. (pp 95-103)

By 1987 the influence of the urban left philosophy was already on the decline and we were soon to see the birth of a 'new realism'. This marked the end of the language of alliances and democratisation, a withdrawal into a defensive mode of maintaining and supporting current service provision, and making improvements where possible within existing constraints. It also led to a reassessment of some of the tactics adopted with some, such as the Labour Co-Ordinating Committee (1988), scornful of the approach taken during the rate capping campaign, describing it as 'naive' and 'disingenuous'. The priority now for the Labour councils, it was argued, was to show that they could improve service delivery without increasing expenditure or employing more staff.

The defeat of the Labour Party in 1987 had left the local socialists in a depressed state. As Peter Broadbent, Chair of Neighbourhood Services Sub-Committee in Islington stated in interview,

We banked very heavily on a Labour victory for our financial position ... now our policy options are very limited indeed ... I don't think it is entirely desperate.

Islington's leader, Margaret Hodge, in an interview with Wolmar (1987), also stated that they had been looking for a Labour victory,

To a much greater extent than they had previously admitted. Its failure to materialise has made the fence razor sharp. (p 10)

The impact of the defeat was not lost either on officers central to the overall strategy,

Politicians quite clearly banked on a Labour government. They knew they would have real problems and they have ... We're losing staff ... that dominates people's thinking. There's a lot of discussion about closing one or two Neighbourhood Offices. That was a proposition supported by management but the politicians ruled as unacceptable so it's a watering down of them all. We've had to find 10% cuts last year, this year and next too ... the crunch is still to come.
(Assistant Co-ordinator of the Decentralisation Unit, Islington)

As Wolmar (1987) points out the urban left's plan of ignoring the financial constraints in pursuit of expansionist policies was doomed by this election result, and within a year the final loopholes that had allowed local authorities to be creative in their accounting had been closed. Thus it was not long before stories such as that of Manchester cutting the domestic rates by 8%, the first time in 20 years, and freezing their decentralisation programme, became increasingly commonplace. However, whilst the defeat of the Labour Party and the continuing determination of the Conservatives to control spending and restructure local government were major set-backs for the urban left, they should not be allowed to obscure the very real difficulties inherent to the whole project.

Thus Gyford (1986) was already highlighting the dilemma of whether the aim of local socialism was to disperse power or mobilise it for a Labour victory. The former runs the risk of falling outside the socialist vision whilst the latter runs counter to the idea of extending democracy and may not be entirely appealing to a number of groupings.

Gyford argued that it was hoped to resolve this by elevating the role of party activists, whose task it was to win hearts and minds in favour of the urban left's vision. The methods of community development were to be applied but without the central role given to the participants in determining the outcome that is usually associated with the approach. Gyford questions the extent to which the advocates of decentralisation were prepared for what would appear to be a lengthy process of people learning from their own experiences and working out their own destinies.

For Rustin (1984), the urban left over-estimated the representativeness of existing activists, so that they were too often out of step with those outside the movement, a view shared by Campbell (1987) who argued that policy-making in relation to issues such as anti-racism and anti-sexism were not sufficiently shared with local communities but were formulated in the town hall. She, like Gyford, identifies, "a new language (that) is being thrown around as a stick to beat people with, militant moralism, is replacing pluralism, solidarity and consciousness-raising" (p 13). Yet others argue that this is too one-sided pointing out that it is unrealistic to expect a small group of councillors and activists to be able to control the thoughts and activities of such diverse groups (Beuret and Stoker 1986). Nevertheless local groups were under considerable pressure, because of the potential resource pay-off, to get involved and to commit a considerable amount of time and energy to the process, which in turn requires them to defend it. So whilst a too heavy-handed attempt to control neighbourhood groups would simply create sham organisations, it may also inflict considerable damage to already over-stretched groups from which they may not recover. Beuret and Stoker are nonetheless right in suggesting that it is the very diversity and autonomy of the local groups that is the strength of neighbourhood politics. The difficulty is how to live with, and indeed actively seek out, the conflicts between such groups whilst managing and delivering public services. For them, the crunch issue facing the local socialists was how to transfer a philosophy, "born from outside and in opposition to the state, to an operating practice when in positions of authority within the state".

Again although the urban left identified the relationships between the state and service users as often oppressive, hierarchical and stigmatising and insisted that these must be transformed, they in turn largely failed to acknowledge the controlling nature of many of the relationships in capitalist state welfare. Many of the 'services' offered to the user are, in fact, unwelcomed and imposed interventions, which may lead to the removal of civil rights and liberties, and the careful monitoring and correction of 'inappropriate' behaviours. It is in such areas, crucial to the everyday lives of public service users, where there is usually no local democratic mandate for state intervention, no accepted definition of the problem, or explanations of its cause or potential solutions, and where their achievement would be a difficult and complex process. Yet the urban left failed to even embark upon trying to establish a local mandate for its policies and interventions in social life let alone work out how to manage the inevitable conflicts that would result. It too willingly accepted that the rules regarding appropriate behaviour that are enforced by the local state have both widespread support and are appropriate. Further, where it has identified problems in relation to local legitimacy for its interventions, it has been to suggest, as in equal opportunities, that it is the authority that is the progressive element. Whilst interventions concerning the safety of young children, for example, are perhaps not best left to localities to decide, if the intention is to democratise the structures and relationships in the public sector then the values that inform such interventions and the strategies that are used when intervening cannot be excluded from the debate not only at national level but also at the level of the neighbourhood. Indeed to do so largely invalidates the democratisation strategy.

Again the link between the urban left and the traditional labour movement of the trade unions has never been very strong, and when trade union support has been forthcoming it has usually been confined to the public sector. There was a real sense that the urban left had, in fact, written off the trade union movement as another manifestation of a failed post-war project, substantially reduced numerically, fragmented and divided, increasingly marginal, and no longer the basis for a Labour Party victory, let alone a more radical social transformation. Livingstone (1984) criticised his colleagues for what he saw as their 'arrogance' and 'intolerance' towards the trade unions and the belief that the urban left were immune from criticism from this quarter because they were now the radicals. Yet it does seem difficult to envisage the construction of a plan for socialist transformation that does not include a central role for workers and their organisations, unless the originators have not themselves had any involvement in such politics. Similarly it might be argued that there was little understanding of the nature of paid employment itself and its domination by particular relations of production which confront those who wish to convert such labour into a political project with enormous difficulties.

Decentralisation and the urban left

For a significant number of local authorities where the new urban left were either in control or very influential, and especially those at the district level, decentralisation, with the dual strategy of making local authority services more responsive and extending local democracy, was central to the whole local socialism project (McDonnell 1984). It was hoped the policy would involve people, especially those previously excluded social groups, in the decision-making processes of local government; give greater access to knowledge and resources to make participants more powerful; change the locus of decision-making to smaller more easily identifiable neighbourhood units; increase the confidence of ordinary citizens, bringing into political life previously untapped skills and energies; widen the political debate; create the basis for challenging and undermining capitalist relations and structures; transform worker-consumer relations in the public sector and introduce greater worker control. However, as noted earlier decentralisation appealed to a number of groupings within the Labour Party and it was possible to find in cities such as Birmingham the influence of a number of competing political philosophies (Barker, Hambleton and Hoggett 1988). Further, decentralisation was not supported by all sections of the party, especially by those sections of the 'hard left' who saw it as an unnecessary diversion away from campaigning politics, possibly leading to 'do it yourself' cuts, and as failing to acknowledge that the working class would always be prepared to defend state services that were under threat (Lansley et al. 1988). However, for the urban left, committed to a participative democratic path to social change, decentralisation had a vital role to play.

Shield (1982) has no doubt about its potential in relation to the socialist project, "inasmuch as it helps organisationally to lubricate the channels along which we may encourage the devolution of actual control" (p 11) and, in a later piece (1983), puts forward six arguments for the centrality of decentralisation. He argues that: firstly, by improving service delivery decentralisation takes us nearer to the socialist goal of meeting need. Secondly, an increase in participative democracy brought about through decentralisation is, he says, in line with the socialist vision of a "well-informed and energetically participative democracy". Thirdly, local control is advocated not only in response to an immediate concern people have for their locality but is also said to be compatible with the socialist goal of individual power and freedom for all. Fourthly, decentralisation is projected as part of a wider strategy for popular planning so that, "a local ward development campaign ... could be transforming street wisdom into neighbourhood development, while a borough-wide public consultation and worker-participation programme could become the democratic management of the borough's overall popular socialist programme" (p 21). Fifthly, Shield argues that it can restore the flagging reputations of local authorities and generate support for a fight against the government and, finally, by creating "powerful caring neighbourhoods co-ordinated under democratic working-class plans" decentralisation could help to clarify a socialist vision.

Shield was not alone though in attaching to decentralisation such ambitious and far reaching possibilities, as well as playing down some of the tensions and contradictions between and within these. Graham Stringer, leader of Manchester Council, like many of the urban left in local politics highlighted the need to involve people in decision-making, "We want to bring people in and open up the town hall, ask people what they want and involve them in the decision-making process. We want to involve all sorts of different people who are exploited in society and provide support to these people" (*Tribune* 19/7/85). Brian Powell, former leader of Walsall, argued that, "We deprive people of knowledge ... they don't understand how power works. We deprive people ... by placing so many obstacles in people's way, so many diversions and irrelevancies, that people can't find their way through the maze" (pp 14-15). Thus, Walsall's policy document, 'Haul to Democracy' identified one of the basic aims of the decentralised neighbourhood offices as being, "To place in the hands of the local community a resource which they can exploit for the purposes of influencing policy, exploring new ideas and furthering control over their own lives" (Community Action 1984, p 15). Again, as Charles Clark, then Chair of Hackney's Housing Committee stated, "We want to transfer the point at which decisions are taken. The question we have to ask ourselves the whole time is: why cannot this decision be made at the local level?" (quoted in Wintour and reproduced in Stoker 1987). Others, such as Blunkett (then leader of Sheffield) and Green were more cautious stressing the need to make clear distinctions between those decisions which could be devolved to local areas and those more strategic issues which should be retained at the centre, being collective rather than local responsibilities.

Seabrook (1984), himself very sympathetic to decentralisation, agrees with Powell that the neighbourhood offices are not there simply to deliver services but are a means of developing local confidence, drawing out and building upon existing but sometimes hidden skills and strengths, and "reflecting and supporting the values and defences of working class people" (p 71). He quotes Powell, "repairing the damage the system does to people, that's only half the story ... The neighbourhood offices are also to facilitate that self-expression to give people an outlet in the places where they live" (p 71). For Seabrook these offices, by providing a focus in the areas people live, have the potential to raise, "all kinds of questions that have been outlawed in the political debate", concerned with social relations, dependency, solidarity, self-worth and controlling one's life. Corrigan (1979 quoted in Bassett 1984) likewise shares a similar view on the importance of political organisation within the state at its local levels because of its accessibility, arguing that this is, "intelligible to working people both as a target and in terms of having a real effect ... it is in the localities that any real participatory democratic close intrusion into the capitalist state will be made" (p 101). Similarly, bodies such as London Labour Briefing and the Labour Co-Ordinating Committee stressed the potential to transform the producer-consumer relationship but simultaneously introducing more worker participation and other democratic management practices, described in Hackney's post 1982 election document as securing for workers "... the best possible control of each industry or service". Judged by comments from workers quoted in Seabrook's book and from discussions with activists in Islington, many employed in the public sector also shared such high ambitions, and were drawn to work in such authorities. As one former Neighbourhood Officer in Walsall put it,

> ... for the first three and a half years it was great ... a real melting pot of ideas with people with tons of talent who'd never been involved in local government ... it became a magnet for loads of people ... something different happening in local government ... they thought there was going to be more power to the people and all that implied, and there was going to be money to spend and it was going to be controlled by local people. It was going to make services accountable to the councillors, rather than just a committee, and it was going to make councillors accountable, a thorough-going political process from the bottom upwards which was also going to get rid of some defective working practices that had been apparent in local government, and the petty right-wing corruption ... local government was worthwhile, it was worth changing, and it could be changed. (interview)

However, in order to achieve such an ambitious programme radical decentralisers faced a number of hurdles. Firstly, there were those issues internal to the organisation of local government. These concern both the requirements of any organisational restructuring, including everything from the provision of training and support for employees to ensuring clarity of roles, accountability and the division of labour, and in the specific context of decentralisation being clear about the relationship between centralised power, local accountability and territorial and social justice (Stoker 1989, Gyford et al. 1989). Secondly, there are powerful and well entrenched conservative interests at the heart of the cultures of bureaucracy, professionalism, departmentalism and managerialism (Gregory and Smith 1986, Stoker 1987). These must be tackled, and such processes transformed without losing entirely some of the benefits to be found in this form of organisation (Stewart 1984, Pinker 1985, Deakin 1987). Certainly both councillors and workers in Islington expressed the view that a number of key officers leading the negotiations with the unions were themselves actively opposed to the project. Lansley et al. (1989) suggest that a failure to effectively tackle such conservatism was to limit the potential of the radical decentralisers. Equally, the introduction of the user/citizen into the process of defining needs and how these are to be met does not in itself remove this cornerstone of professionalism. Thus Khan's (1989) research on Islington's neighbourhood forums suggests that the centralised departments viewed them as marginal, that the areas of service provision, which had been the main preoccupation of the officers did not always coincide with the priorities of the forum membership and that officers were hesitant about raising matters that might result in the services being criticised. Not only are professionals skilled in the art of managing opinion to more reflect their own interests but within the welfare relationship they have the added advantage of dealing with individuals, many of whom are dependent and vulnerable, rather than collectivities. Even when faced with the latter they can rely on both differences between individuals within a specific category, and differences between categories, to sustain an argument that only they as neutral professionals can effectively mediate such relationships. Additionally, they are sustained in their belief in themselves, their practices and understandings as these are validated not within the context of locality or community pressure, but primarily from their training and education, their associations and their national and international networks. Moreover, persuading community organisations to engage in such initiatives, especially in the context of resource constraint presents its own problems. For many service users and residents it is more important to have an efficient and effective service that meets their needs than it is to engage in debates about structures for decentralised services or to seek greater or different forms of democratic control (Gregory and Smith 1986, Murray 1985). The paradox facing decentralisers and users alike is neatly summarised by Burns (1987),

> It is pointless giving power over to the community until service provision is straightened out and there is something for them to get involved in. The problem of service provision will never be resolved until power is devolved to the local community. (p 12)

Thirdly, there is no doubt that the political and economic climate in which the urban left was operating not only placed limits on what could be done but led a number of authorities to fight shy of decentralisation, believing it was better to defend what was already in place than to attempt an expansionist policy (Beuret and Stoker 1986). Equally, persuading workers that sufficient funds would be available to sustain an ambitious programme was always going to be difficult (Dale 1987) and, as Margaret Hodge acknowledged, attempting to introduce radical changes whilst simultaneously defending local government against central government's attack on its resources was always going to test the urban left's resolve,

> We were into campaigning and opposing ... there was little energy left to do other things we should have been doing ... (quoted in Lansley et al. 1989, p 117)

Others have pointed to the limits of localist politics themselves and the tendency to paint too rosy a picture of local political practices, as a major stumbling block (Cochrane 1986). Indeed, as Canver and Yaylai (1987) have argued in relation to Islington's black and ethnic minority communities, the localist emphasis is not always something that is necessarily shared by all citizens and users. Certainly the neglect of a national strategy and the absence of a national leadership, especially in the context of labourist centralism at the heart of the party, wedded to parliamentary politics, to the virtual exclusion of all other forms of political activity, strongly ambivalent to the autonomy of local government, with its emphasis on universal minimum standards and technocratic solutions to social problems, with ends not means, meant that neither a broad-based programme nor greater democracy could be either taken for granted or be expected to emerge organically (Beuret and Stoker 1986, Hoggett and McGill 1989). Inevitably the reality of the decentralisation programmes was somewhat more mundane than the expressed hopes and objectives of its supporters amongst the new urban left.

Urban left decentralisation in practice

A large number of authorities have been involved in decentralisation programmes yet it was Walsall, an "unlikely location for the New Jerusalem" (Deakin 1984, p 18), and under pressure because of the bi-annual elections for one-third of the council, who began the process in 1981. It decentralised its Housing Department, including the repairs service, into 31 neighbourhood offices, and recruited sympathetically-minded officers to run them, a process that took less than 12 months in all. Walsall's key objectives which were to be replicated elsewhere were: to provide a more responsive service by being more comprehensive, convenient, and informal; offering greater local autonomy; facilitating community development through promoting participation, providing information, and focusing on the area office as a place to influence policy and service delivery; and improving relationships between officers and the public by increasing the role of front-line staff, ensuring they were more sensitive to users' needs, insisting that they take responsibility for their work and placing inter-personal above administrative skills.   The neighbourhood offices were generally open-plan, with some smaller interview rooms, kitchen and toilet facilities.   All staff were expected to respond to anyone needing assistance, there being no receptionists, and the public had access to the computer-based information around housing allocations.   Teams of workers were located in the neighbourhoods to respond to housing repairs and were in touch with the local office.   The offices provided an information service, including welfare rights and were a place for community organisations to meet both socially and informally as well as for their more formal business meetings.

Other authorities followed with similar aims although the more radical agenda has been characterised, in contrast to Walsall, by multi-service decentralisation.   Thus, whilst Manchester's initial 1982 policy spoke of an area based approach to service organisation and provision, the election in 1984 of more left-wing councillors ensured that decentralisation and democratisation were considered as inseparable.   The new plans envisaged the setting up of between 50 and 60 local offices, each covering 7500 to 9000 people, and providing services in housing, personal social services, environmental health, and building and street cleaning.   Similarly Rochdale has had decentralisation on its agenda since 1986 but it was not until 1989 that it became a central concern, embracing the objectives of integrated services at a local level with devolved decision-making (Dobbin and Martin 1989).   The Council's policy document spoke of a 'seamless service' and the establishment of a new Neighbourhood Services Department.   The strategy envisaged 18 local offices, each with a community development role, servicing between 10,000 and 12,000 people.   The familiar themes were stressed including, improving the quality of services, informal settings, one-stop integrated service provision, local budgets, community use of the local offices and the development of local committees.   According to Dobbin and Martin, Chair and Assistant Director of the Neighbourhood Services respectively, "it is the very real threat to local democracy ... that necessitates bold policies designed to get closer to the residents to encourage and enable effective participation ... seek to localise, integrate and empower ..."

Such initiatives have been typical of developments to date, although the majority have paid greater attention to the issues of service delivery and quality of provision rather than an extension of democracy, and most have found that even then progress has been slower than anticipated.   Thus Gregory (1985) (quoted in Beuret and Stoker 1986) after a review of initiatives in London concluded that whilst, "the commitment concerning devolution of influence and control remains on the agenda (it is) as a second stage" (p 8).   Only Walsall managed to successfully implement their policy on the basis of the 'big bang', but then they lost control of the council in 1983 and progress was rapidly halted although not reversed.   Most of the initiatives continue to resemble Beresford's (1985) assessment, "a few hesitant steps forward, rather than the large scale progress that might have been expected" (p 3).   (See Beuret and Stoker (1986), Collingridge (1986), Elcock (1986), for other examples of specific initiatives).

As already indicated the efforts of the urban left to decentralise and democratise have by no means been smooth in their progress, and a number of initiatives have either emerged in a much modified form from what was originally envisaged, or failed to get beyond the drawing board.   One of the early attempts to introduce a radical programme of decentralisation, but which was subsequently abandoned, following massive opposition from the white-collar unions, and replaced by much more modest proposals was in

Hackney. Here the idea had initially been promoted by the local Tenants Federation in conjunction with the manual workers in the Housing Department (Hackney Joint Repairs Report 1980). The council elected in 1982 was staunchly committed to decentralisation and spoke of opening 30 neighbourhood offices with elected neighbourhood committees. It was also determined to have an extensive consultation process, seeing this as part of democratisation philosophy. "The objectives of greatly improved services, of increased participative democracy, and of neighbourhood control, cannot begin to be pursued without the adoption of participative democratic methods of implementation" (Hackney Decentralisation Working Group 21/4/83 quoted in Hoggett, Lawrence and Fudge 1984, p 65). It organised over 100 informal and participative meetings across the borough in a two month period, which culminated in a 'Hackney Goes Local' weekend conference with over 300 groups represented, who were then invited to fill in a blank sheet outlining what services should be decentralised and how the programme should be organised.

According to Shields and Webber (1986), the Hackney initiative represented a "concerted attack upon the administration's departmentalism, managerialism and professionalism, and the reactionary aspects of the town hall trade unions" (p 134). However, other writers (Wintour 1983, Hoggett, Lawrence and Fudge 1984), noted that there were two schools of thought in Hackney - those who were more concerned with improving service quality, Wintour's 'minimalists', and those who saw it as a means of building up a socialist movement and resisting attacks by central government, the 'maximalists'. Certainly, the draft manifesto of the Borough's Local Government Committee (1982) spoke of, "offering the opportunity to people of controlling their services ... an incentive ... to be drawn into politics, a prerequisite for building a wider socialist democracy" (quoted in Hoggett, Lawrence and Fudge 1984, p 63). As with other proposals, Hackney was concerned both with improving the quality of services, by integrating them on a small area basis, and also committed to, "local participative democratic control over these reorganised services, by delegating powers to basic grade local workers, by encouraging worker/user cooperation and by establishing Neighbourhood Committees intended to be locally representative" (Shields and Webber, p 134).

Following the consultative process, the council produced 'Red Print' a weighty document outlining their plans, "the most exciting and radical challenge to traditional local government that a local authority has ever generated" (Shields and Webber 1986, p 138). These included neighbourhood offices encompassing housing, social services and environmental health. Most significantly, they were to be structured on the basis of multi-disciplinary teams which were to cut across existing departmental structures, a model which Islington began to move towards in 1991 nearly six years after launching its initial package. The neighbourhood centres were also to offer a general meeting place for community organisations along with some invaluable resources such as printing facilities. Most crucially, they were to be open during the evening and on Saturdays, and to offer child care facilities. The staff of these local centres were to be accountable to, "a democratically elected body of local representatives, which would play an increasingly important role in controlling the Council's services and resources" (Hackney Red Print quoted in Fudge 1984). Furthermore, the proposed Neighbourhood Committees would all be established as a sub-committee of the Borough's powerful Policy and Resources Committee, and would include "street representatives", ward based interest group representatives, non-voting representatives from the neighbourhood centres and the ward councillors as ex-officio members. These committees were to have responsibility not simply for monitoring or advising on matters related to service delivery but were also to have the power and responsibility for local budgets and the hiring and firing of staff along with other industrial relations matters.

The Council's far-reaching plans, however, met intense opposition from the white-collar unions, especially NALGO, who imposed a ban on any work connected with decentralisation after their 12-point programme, which they insisted be dealt with before decentralisation could go ahead, had apparently fallen on deaf ears. Additionally, there were reservations from the local Tenants Federation, who were more concerned with seeing a substantial improvement to the housing repairs service and whose concerns were limited to the relationship of landlord-tenant than in the greater ambitions of decentralisation. Consequently, 'RedPrint 1' was withdrawn following its rejection by an overwhelming number of the local councillors and by the local Labour Party group and was replaced by a much more modest 'RedPrint 2' in which there was little mention of the extension of democratic control of the services. Gone were the neighbourhood committees and inter-disciplinary teams, and instead the chains of command with the centre were considerably strengthened. Nevertheless, the whole implementation process was virtually brought to a complete standstill by a union boycott so that writing in 1984, Community Action noted that, "... there's scarcely more than a whiff of decentralisation in the borough" (Community Action 1984) and the council were to find themselves embroiled in a conflict between local tenants and their organisations on the one hand and NALGO and NUPE trade unionists on the other, involving the occupation of area housing bases by the tenants and some strong and uncompromising tactics by the workers to have them evicted, which ultimately resulted in the defeat of the Labour leadership.

Conclusion

This chapter has examined the growing popularity of decentralisation throughout local government in the UK. In exploring the often conflicting aims and objectives espoused within decentralisation it has highlighted the distinction between those initiatives that primarily have been concerned with a restructuring of the administrative machinery of local government, so to improve the quality of service provision and ensure better management in circumstances of reduced resources and the changing role of local government, and those whose aim has been to democratise public services and extend local democratic life. It is this second category which has been the main focus of attention, and such initiatives have been examined within the context of the emergence of the diverse but identifiable 'new urban left'. This was seen as offering something resembling a coherent programme, based on their control of the local state, and to be fought for through an alliance of progressive forces within the state, the public sector trade unions, the users of public services, and the extra-parliamentary social movements. More detailed attention has been given, both to the theory and the practice of the urban left's concern with the devolution of power and the extension of democracy contained within its approach to decentralisation.

5 Research methodology

As in the work of Nicholson et al. (1981), my research aim was "of a rich and rounded analysis" (p 44). The overall approach adopted was that of a case-study, and the methods, whilst relying primarily upon qualitative techniques, also included some associated with quantitative research. The case study provided an opportunity to utilise a plurality of methods (Smith and Cartly 1985) in which quantitative and qualitative research can be combined, for as Bryman (1989) argues, "One of the most obvious advantages of deploying the two in tandem is to check the validity of the findings using different approaches to data collection" (p 175). It was felt that a case-study approach with an emphasis on qualitative methods would better capture the views and understandings of public service trade unionists in Islington, the context in which the decentralisation policy was introduced and the six year time span covered in the research. The Islington case study brings together the views of 105 NALGO members, most of whom were active within the Branch. Ninety-six of the cases were employed within the neighbourhood structures. Most of the occupations within the neighbourhood offices are to be found within the sample, and 20 of the 24 offices are covered. The offices covered in the questionnaire provided a geographical spread within the Borough, as well as a cross section of trade union activism, and a representative sample in relation to user demand and satisfaction levels. The majority of those interviewed had demonstrated, through their acceptance of a Neighbourhood Shop Steward role, their commitment to building a trade union structure based on the decentralised organisation. Most had been employed within the Borough throughout the implementation period of decentralisation, and for the majority being a member of NALGO was an automatic extension of their employment within local government.

The London Borough of Islington lies just north of central London, with Haringey to the north, Camden to the west, Hackney to the east and the City of London to the south. Islington has a population of 168,700, which is small relative to other London boroughs, but has an above average population density per hectare. According to a 1987 social survey (Islington 1987), 71% of the population in the borough were white UK; 8.5% were Afro-Caribbean; 7.5% Irish; 4% Cypriot; 3.5% Asian; and 5.5% classified as 'other'. Islington is among the ten most deprived local authority areas in the UK and was designated as an inner city partnership area in 1978. A MORI survey (MORI

1989), notes that out of the 755 wards in the Greater London region in 1981, ranked according to four census indicators of deprivation, the most deprived ward in Islington (Thornhill) was ranked 42nd, and the least deprived (Canonbury West) was ranked 239th. As many as 16 of the 20 wards were ranked among the 100 wards between numbers 72 and 172, and according to MORI, only the borough of Hackney displayed such a high level of concentration. MORI suggests that approximately 33% of the borough's population experiences severe material deprivation. Over half of the borough's homes are rented from the Council, which according to a Policy Studies Institute report (1986) was the fourth highest proportion of council-owned property in inner London, whilst a further 19% rent from either housing associations or private landlords. The PSI report also noted that some 9000 households were on the Council's general waiting list, equivalent to over 20% of the total permanent housing stock. A further 8000 households were reported as being on the transfer list. Less than one third of Islington's households either own outright or have a mortgage on a house or flat. The borough has lower than average annual incomes per household in comparison with the whole of Greater London and above average unemployment.

Islington has two Parliamentary constituencies, both of which are represented by the Labour Party. Fifty-two borough councillors, who stand for election every four years, represent the borough's 20 wards. In the May 1990 local elections, Labour won all but three of the seats. However, the 1994 elections produced a setback for Labour, with the Liberal Democrats gaining 11 seats and the Tories one, with Labour holding 40. In 1990, and before the educational services in the borough previously undertaken by ILEA were transferred to it, the Borough was spending approximately £190m per annum, or £1535 per adult. The MORI survey discovered that 44% of Islington's residents were satisfied with the way the Council was running the Borough, which compared well with other inner city local authorities surveyed by MORI, although it did note that those who were experiencing relatively high material deprivation were less satisfied with the Council than were those who were better off.

Partly with a view to improving service provision and partly to extend the level of democratic control over services, the Council elected in 1982 introduced the decentralisation policy, involving the relocation of housing, an associated repair team, non-residential social services, environmental health, welfare rights, and community development, into 24 neighbourhood offices, serving an average population of 6500, in neighbourhoods that, as far as possible, were to reflect community perceptions. In addition, each office was to provide a range of community facilities and resources to be made available to local neighbourhood community organisations. The first four of these were opened in March 1985 and the last one in March 1987. It was intended that workers in the neighbourhood offices would function in multi-service generic teams, and that old departmental boundaries would evaporate. Alongside each of the 24 neighbourhood offices there was to be an equivalent Neighbourhood Forum, comprising local councillors, service users, representatives from neighbourhood based community and voluntary organisations, and staff employed in the local neighbourhood office. The main purposes of these Forums were: to deliberate on the priority of work of the staff of their neighbourhood office; to monitor and make recommendations on the quality and level of service being provided in the neighbourhood, either through the neighbourhood office or otherwise; to draw up plans for local projects, the expenditure for which would be met from a local budget; and to comment on Council plans for the neighbourhood. Ultimately, it was the Council's intention to devolve local budgets down to the neighbourhood level and to give increasing powers to the Forums. The full cost of the programme has never been formally stated, although the capital cost was around £10m as many of the 24 neighbourhood offices were purpose built, at an average cost of £450,000. The London Borough of Islington was chosen as a case study as this represented the most sophisticated of the decentralisation initiatives. The democratisation of services was central to the process, and thus the policy was neither simply an administrative or managerialist restructuring. Islington's was also one of the first multi-service decentralisation initiatives to be launched successfully. Furthermore, it has withstood the difficulties of the initial implementation period and is now well established. Finally, public service trade unionism within the Borough had a reputation of being well organised, vibrant, radical, and, moreover, had been active in the 1982 local election, which brought the radical councillors into office.

The case study is based on a combination of interviews and questionnaire returns, totalling 105 cases, of NALGO members in the borough. A central aim of the research was to allow the subjects to speak for themselves, as this not only adds to the richness of the findings but is felt to be the most effective and powerful way of illustrating important points, and to ensure a balance in relation to occupations, gender, hierarchical position and 'race'. The primary method utilised was that of semi-structured interviews, each lasting a minimum of 90 minutes, and some for two and a half hours. Forty-three current and former NALGO shop stewards working in Islington's neighbourhood offices were interviewed, between October 1988 and April 1989. Some preliminary interviews had been conducted in the Spring of 1988 with three Neighbourhood Officers, but these do not form part of the interview sample. In addition to the in-depth interviews, a questionnaire (the complete schedule can be found in Appendix 3) was circulated to NALGO members in six of the 24 neighbourhood offices and amongst those Branch Executive members who were not employed within the neighbourhood structure. The objectives in undertaking the questionnaire were to get beyond the union activists at the neighbourhood level to the broader membership so as to both deepen the level of understanding and to make a comparison between the views of the currently more passive membership with the more active; to increase the sample of NALGO activists from which to draw conclusions; to include those occupational groups who were not appearing in significant numbers amongst the activists; and to look in more detail at a representative sample of neighbourhood offices. The questionnaire was carried out after the majority of interviews had been conducted, at the end of February and beginning of March 1989, thereby enabling the inclusion of questions related to the initial interview findings. The questionnaire was distributed in two stages, in four offices in the first stage and the remaining two in the second. Sixty-two detailed questionnaire returns, completed in late February and early March 1989, were received from a self-administered questionnaire, using a 25% stratified sample from amongst the neighbourhood offices (see Appendix 1 for the basis on which they were selected for the questionnaire). Fifty-one of the questionnaires were completed by NALGO members working in six of the 24 neighbourhood offices, a 25.5% return rate on the 200 questionnaires distributed, and nine were completed by members of the Branch Executive, who were not employed in the neighbourhood structures.

Amongst those responding to the questionnaire there was an equal balance between men and women, of which just under half were less than 30 years old, over two-thirds lived outside the Borough, 60% had completed their education to degree level. Overall, 225 questionnaires were distributed, which produced a return rate of 27.5%. The 200 questionnaires distributed within the neighbourhood offices represented a 25% sample of NALGO members working in the decentralised structures (i.e. of the 1000 decentralised posts, 800 were NALGO members). A combination of the interviews undertaken and the questionnaires returned produced a 12% sample of NALGO members in the neighbourhood offices.   The intention was to interview Branch activists who identified the new neighbourhood office structure as a basis for trade union organisation, and to match these, via the questionnaire, with the views of ordinary, and essentially non-active members.   However, the vast majority of respondents were, in fact, active within the union.   Those who did classify themselves as ordinary members were either quite active in some organised way within the union, or acknowledged particular areas of interest within the union's activity.   In addition, with the two albeit important exceptions of defining the appropriate boundaries of trade union activity and the extent to which they saw their trade unionism as an extension of a wider belief system, the views of these ordinary members were not significantly different from those of their colleagues who had some experience of formal union positions.   Any differences that did emerge were relative rather than substantive, and despite their more pragmatic and traditional approach to trade unionism, which was by no means completely absent from the activists, these ordinary members showed themselves to be involved in the union, to value their membership for the collective support and protection it brought, and to see their membership as a link with a wider labour movement.

On reflection, this absence of 'passive' members is perhaps best explained by the length of the questionnaire, the fact that I was dependent, both for its distribution and collection, on the Neighbourhood Office Shop Stewards, which may have resulted in a less than efficient, even selective, system of distribution, or may have inhibited their return, although envelopes were supplied and confidentiality assured, and also possibly plain indifference.   Nevertheless, the questionnaire not only widened the data base but also assisted in the process of validating the interviews.   In addition, semi-structured interviews were carried out with senior managers and elected members, including those who had been centrally concerned with the decentralisation initiative and the negotiations with the trade unions.   Access was also given to interviews with senior stakeholders, conducted by colleagues at the School for Advanced Urban Studies.   This helped to gain a broader, and richer picture, by being able to move between different points of view, of the thinking and events around the decentralisation policy, as well as providing competing perspectives, and also verifying views expressed by the trade unionists.   In addition to the interviews and questionnaire with the primary participants within the union (see Appendix 1 for a detailed breakdown of the interviewees), further material was gained via analysis of relevant documentation, minutes of meetings and reports from the Authority, supplied through its Decentralisation Unit, and from NALGO, accessed via the union's national headquarters and at the branch level in Islington.   This was done partly to get a better understanding of the relationship between events unfolding in Islington and similar developments in other branches across the country.   Furthermore, it was a way of gaining access to branch policy in the very early years of the decentralisation initiative and in respect of other aspects of industrial relations.   The Authority's material not only highlighted alternative explanations, but also provided some relevant factual material which was then used in the semi-structured interviews as a means of challenging views expressed by the participants, or using them as a probe for more in-depth discussion.

Although white-collar trade unionists represent only one of the important 'stakeholders' in the policy initiative, they were seen as both significant, given not only the power they could exercise in determining the relative success of the policy, but also their assigned strategic role in promoting a competing definition of public services to that of the new right, and as a relatively neglected stakeholder in the evaluation of the impact of the policy.   The intention was to convey a sense of a process, unfolding over time, tracing events and focusing on, as stated by Bryman (1989), "what prompted it, what people thought of it, how they reacted to it, how it developed, its outcome, and what people thought of the outcome" (p 137) and, "not to infer the findings from a sample to a population, but to engender patterns and linkages of theoretical importance" (p 173). The purpose as Burgelman (1985) states, "is primarily to generate new insights that are useful for building theory" (Burgelman p 42). In this instance the insights were to be directed at the nature of contemporary public service white-collar trade unionism, the relationship between such workers and their welfare product, and the issues involved in initiating and managing organisational change in the public sector.

The interview sample:

The intention was to interview all the then current Neighbourhood Office Shop Stewards and, in addition, former Neighbourhood Office Shop Stewards, current Departmental Representatives and members of the self-organised groups. The focus was on those NALGO activists working in the neighbourhood offices, and within these, those activists who had identified the new workplace as the setting on which to build a trade union structure, and had sought a trade union position within the new structures, rather than continuing to focus on the older departmental system. The assumption was that these Neighbourhood Shop Stewards were perhaps more likely to have either seen the potential importance of the decentralised structures, or to be more directly grappling with the problems associated with the new policy, both from the point of view of conditions of service and service delivery, as well as attempting to develop a neighbourhood based trade unionism. However, not all the offices had workplace stewards in post, or only had one such steward, either because the numbers working in the office were so small as to only generate one stewards position or, more usually, only one of the two available posts had been filled. In both such instances attempts were made to identify and interview other activists who were either former Neighbourhood Office Shop Stewards, or current or former Departmental Representatives. Interviewing Departmental Representatives gave a better picture of both the range of neighbourhood offices and of the three departments within each office although again there was a high vacancy rate amongst such representatives. The small number of such interviews though could not be interpreted as being representative of either the departmental stewards overall nor of such stewards within any one department, but must be read as the views of individual activists within the neighbourhood offices. In addition, interviews were conducted with a small number of those working from the neighbourhood offices and were active in one of the union's self-organised Groups, or who had been active in NALGO or directly involved in the negotiations around decentralisation during the period of its introduction 1982-85. Such interviews add to our overall understanding since the main intention was to bring together a sense of the trade union experience from within a focus of the neighbourhood workplace.

An initial list of Neighbourhood Office Shop Stewards was supplied by the Branch Office, who were happy to co-operate with the research. However, the names supplied did not reflect the current occupancy of shop steward positions in the neighbourhood offices and the list had to be supplemented by a telephone check with every office plus additional names given by NALGO representatives who knew of those activists that had previously held office. In addition, a letter of introduction outlining the research project was sent to every neighbourhood office and the Branch Executive in the hope of trawling any stewards who had been missed. Gathering potential interviewees in this manner cannot guarantee that all those who might want to be interviewed are identified and are able to make themselves known although there was a "snowballing" effect as the research progressed. All but one of the interviews took place at the interviewee's place of work, with each interview lasting, on average between one and one-and-a-half hours, although some were extended to over two hours. All the interviews were tape recorded, with the permission of the interviewee, and were subsequently transcribed in full. The majority of interviews were conducted on a one-to-one basis although there was one occasion when a group of three were interviewed together and another occasion when two people were interviewed together. In both instances all the participants were asked the same questions, the major difference between the single and multi-person interviews being that the latter did inevitably generate some discussion on the individual responses of those participating which resulted in the development and expansion of themes and did not appear to inhibit or stifle comment. These multi-person interviews arose, not by research design, but in response to the availability of the interviewees and in some respects they were preferable to the single person interview as they facilitated a more discursive, reflective approach more conducive to extrapolating the finer details and complexities of the situation than was sometimes the case in the single more formally structured interviews.

Some difficulties were experienced as a consequence of interviewing people at their place of work, and often during working hours. In some cases there were no facilities available that were really suitable for a quiet reflective interview undisturbed by external noise or interruptions, either because they were being used for other purposes or they simply did not exist. Some interviews were conducted at the desk of the interviewee amongst the desks of other workers and prone to telephone, colleague, or consumer interruptions, as well as background noise and occasionally having to change the location mid-way through the interview.   Some of the interviews took place during the interviewee's lunch break and although away from their desk nevertheless had to be carried out amidst the soup making and sandwich activities of colleagues seeking a respite from their duties.   More generally interviews were conducted in either the neighbourhood office interview rooms or the staff-cum-community room. Responsibility for organising the physical space was left to the interviewee, as was ensuring their availability during working hours when this was the chosen time, which was done through the use of flexi-time, lunch breaks, meeting towards the end of normal working hours or through obtaining line management permission to be interviewed during working hours. As they were being interviewed as trade unionists, rather than Islington Borough Council employees, permission to interview was not sought from the Authority although contact was made with the Borough's Decentralisation Unit informing them of the general aims and objectives of the research, the timing of the interviews, and seeking their co-operation.

The research focuses on the perspectives of the subjects of research, reproducing a faithful recording of what people have said and their verbatim comments are a central feature. In addition, we wish to convey a strong sense of the context in which the research is conducted as this adds to our understanding of the processes or issues under study, but also acknowledgement that the context has to some extent been constructed, and is maintained by those participants within it. Thus the study was concerned to convey a sense of how the relationships between the trade unionists and other stakeholders were unfolding and, in particular, to get a better sense of the working situation of the participants. This was done by: exploring the historical development of public service trade unionism and the growing industrial militancy within it; looking specifically at industrial conflicts within the Borough of Islington; giving some detailed consideration to the policy background and locating it within the context of the politics of the new urban left; giving consideration to Islington's own approach to decentralisation and where the politics of the Borough stood in relation to the urban left strategy; and attempting to gain a sense of life in the new neighbourhood offices, although in this respect my observations were unstructured and unstrategic, arising from visits to a large number of the 24 offices for the primary purpose of conducting interviews, and was supplementary to the interview material. Equally it is important to emphasise that what was under study was part of a continuing process, and this is done through linking the new policy proposal with existing relationships between the stakeholders, the tracing of events as the policy initiative unfolded, identifying crucial stages in the process, and making an assessment of future developments. However, because the decentralisation policy is itself still unfolding and developing, the study cannot be seen as the examination of a finished process, although the important phases of the early implementation are covered.

The research posed a number of difficulties, including that of access, "what it is desirable or possible to investigate, and by which methods, is constrained by the access opportunities available to the researcher, research resources, and the special characteristics of the setting in which the research takes place" (Nicholson et al. 1981, p 45). Although the NALGO Islington Branch was sympathetic to the proposal and agreed, through the Branch Executive, to both co-operate and to inform the membership about the project, I did not have direct access to important information. This was not withheld, but simply did not exist, and reflected the low level of organisational infrastructural support at the union branch level where the essentially lay members are expected to play an equal role in negotiating both service delivery issues and member interests but with few resources to do so. Such material included: a list of NALGO members in the neighbourhood offices, a list of either departmental or neighbourhood office shop stewards, and a record of those who had been centrally involved when the policy was first introduced. Consequently I was dependent upon the memories of key union actors and on building a network tree as one contact led to another. The absence of a neighbourhood office membership list also prevented direct personal contact when seeking to administer the questionnaire. Individual shop stewards were reluctant to produce lists of members in their 'shop', and indeed were not always able to be exact about the number of members. They preferred rather to act in the gate-keeping role when it came to passing on information about the research or distributing questionnaires. One consequence of this, apart from having to rely upon the stewards' efficiency and diligence, was that the process of following up non-respondents was virtually impossible. Interestingly, stewards displayed little reluctance to pass on the names of other stewards. All those activists who were contacted directly to request an interview responded positively and only a very small minority appeared guarded in the interviews.

A further problem was that a number of those who were active around decentralisation during the first phase of planning and implementation (1982-1985) had changed their employment and could not be traced as not surprisingly the union did not keep such records. Similarly, many of the existing activists were relatively new to the Authority and had not experienced the full implementation process. Their views were, nevertheless, important because many had moved to the Authority either specifically because they were in sympathy with the decentralisation strategy, or because of what they knew of the Authority's overall political approach. However, despite some activists leaving the Authority and others joining, this was through a process of 'natural' change, spread out over time, and there was never a decisive break between an 'old' and a 'new' guard. Therefore, although not everyone had been with the Authority throughout the six year period under discussion there was a sufficient sense of continuity.

The six year focus also produced a further problem in that the research was significantly dependent upon people's recollections. However, with the help of prompts from Branch documents, it was surprising how much detailed information the participants could recall and indeed how immediate the issues were. In addition, the research could not confine itself strictly to the focus of public service trade unionism and decentralisation. Other important events had occurred during this period involving the trade unions and their employers both in the traditional areas of industrial relations and in the wider political arena. These, more recent, events may well have influenced how the participants responded to particular questions and topics, so that they were reacting not because of something directly related to decentralisation but other mediating factors. However, this interweaving of influences not only seems unavoidable, given the time span and the nature of the subject, but is also a realistic reflection of how trade union politics are formed and actions are determined.

Finally, time and available resources prevented the study of a second case which may not only have enhanced the generalizability of results but also tested out the 'London factor'. Local politics are always to some extent influenced by local factors and the politics of the new urban left in London may well have been quite distinctive from their counterparts elsewhere. However, the research does both attempt to take account, through the available literature, of comparable processes elsewhere, and to concentrate on factors that are not specific to London. It nevertheless remains that the London factor cannot be disregarded. For example, the rate-capping campaign, which was especially prominent in London, and its defeat, was seen in Islington as highlighting the failure of the members' political will and credibility, and symbolising a political style that may well be seen as ruinous of the Labour Party by many left-Labour authorities outside of the metropolis. Indeed such reservations were also to be found within the capital and within Islington. In fact there is little to suggest that the central concerns of the NALGO trade unionists in Islington over the implementation of the decentralisation programme were not shared by the colleagues in other authorities outside of London.

6 Industrial militancy in Islington

This chapter examines the relationship between NALGO's organisation, policy and practice in Islington Borough Council and those developments, outlined earlier, in the union at large. Initially the focus is on the Branch organisation, paying particular attention to the impact of the revised structure, introduced following the Borough's decentralisation policy, and specifically the extent to which union activists and office holders experienced this as facilitating union organisation. The growth and development of industrial militancy and political activity in the Branch is then traced, paying some attention to early disputes in the 1970s but primarily examining the major disputes that occurred during the period since the election of a new radical "urban left" Labour administration in 1982, and the subsequent introduction of the decentralisation initiative. NALGO's response to this specific policy will be covered in subsequent chapters.

A central feature of this chapter is to demonstrate the changing and increasing nature of militancy in the Islington NALGO Branch, a branch considered both by its own members, and also by the union at national level, to be worthy of the label "militant". However, within this broad definition, union politics are shown to vary and change according to occupation, department, grade, and in a decentralised structure, physical location. It is further suggested that the particular political style of the Branch and the domination in certain important Branch structures by different political groupings not only resulted in a more overtly militant position but also explains in part the low levels of participation in union life by other sections of the workforce, some of whom being the very workers the Branch's policies were intended to support. Finally, we explore the relationship between militancy in the Branch and the degree to which the Borough's policies and reputation had attracted to its employment a number of workers across a range of occupational groups who brought with them their previous experience in either political activity or active trade unionism.

The structure of NALGO in Islington Borough Council

Our focus within NALGO is primarily at the branch level where there exists a range of representational structures that can be based on workplace, department, job specialism or interest group, each of which is co-ordinated by a shop steward structure, with the Branch Executive having overall responsibility for all branch matters. However, a modified union structure emerged within Islington as a consequence of the Borough's decentralisation policy. Prior to this the NALGO Branch was organised primarily around departmentally-based shop steward committees, with other 'shops' based either on occupationally defined "sections" or geographically based workplaces. However, this emphasis on the service departments was no longer appropriate given the quite different working conditions and problems in the neighbourhood offices in comparison with those still centrally located where strong coterminosity between departmental membership and geographic location remained. In addition the 24 multi-service neighbourhood offices began to transform the departmental structures and their inter-relationships. As a consequence a new "neighbourhood office shop" was created to represent all NALGO members in the decentralised offices, each with one or two shop stewards, determined according to union membership size per office. However, this workplace shop steward organisation continued to be paralleled by a departmental system of service stewards, who were organised both in the neighbourhood offices and the centralised departments, and another steward structure based on specific occupational roles, usually where the role might be located within a number of geographical sites, but never in such numbers in any one site as to be able to have sufficient "voice". Neighbourhood office interests were represented, therefore, within a total of five shop stewards' committees: housing, social services, chief executives, environmental health and an overall neighbourhood office committee. The neighbourhood office committee elected one steward for every 24 union members, whilst the traditional service delivery committees continued to elect stewards on a job description basis. Each departmental stewards' committee continued to negotiate separately with the centralised management structure of their own departments, with each one having its own arrangements for doing so. The neighbourhood office stewards from all 24 offices met together on a regular basis in the Neighbourhood Office Shop Stewards' Committee and all negotiations with the Authority that related to NALGO members in the decentralised offices were reported on at this committee. This also elected from amongst its members neighbourhood office representation on the Branch Executive Committee. In addition, there was a Neighbourhood Services Joint Management Staff Committee which was seen as a major avenue of information between the Neighbourhood Office Shop Stewards Committee and the various departmental managements. Beyond that, there were branch-wide "interest groups", including one each for black workers, women workers, Irish workers and gay and lesbian workers, all of which have representation on the Branch Executive.

One consequence of this complex structure was that an individual member working within a neighbourhood office could belong to a number of "shops", each with their own demands in terms of time, energy and focus, plus creating a degree of confusion over role division and a sense of fragmentation. Thus, for example, a female Afro-Caribbean Housing Advice Worker working from within a neighbourhood office would simultaneously belong to her neighbourhood office shop, her housing department shop and her housing advisory shop. In addition, she could also be a member of all, or any one of, the branch-wide interest groups for women, black workers and gay and lesbian workers. To further complicate matters she might find that whilst her neighbourhood office steward was located within her workplace, her housing steward might be based in the centralised housing department office, whilst the housing advisory steward might be based in a different neighbourhood office. Finally, the representation from the interest groups might be neither from housing nor from a decentralised office. Within such a structure identifying how and where to pursue one's interests is no easy task and sustaining the level of interest and attention within whatever union 'shop' was chosen would demand considerable energy and commitment.

The system was not, then, without its difficulties. Thus a report in March 1986 by the Branch Secretary noted that,

> Our experience so far ... has been that while major issues ... tended to unify members, it has been more difficult to maintain unity amongst the different groups of workers where issues affecting specific groups have arisen ...

A later report from the Branch (December 1988), based on discussions at the Neighbourhood Office Shop Stewards Committee, concluded that,

> At present the structure is not working efficiently. There is no co-ordination or liaison between the departmental committees, consequently stewards and members are often unaware of who is negotiating with management and what decisions have been taken.

Furthermore, it stated, "some of the stewards' committees which are supposed to represent the membership in neighbourhood offices simply do not operate effectively." The report recommended that the Neighbourhood Office Shop Stewards Committee should become more central and take a co-ordinating role in an attempt to bring about better communication between sections in the Branch, convey a more unified view to management, and create a stronger voice for the neighbourhood offices. This was a view shared by a number of the shop stewards interviewed,

> Decentralisation makes it difficult to organise ... 24 offices plus centralised offices. Keeping everyone informed ... mobilising support over what happens in one office ... 24 individual offices with their own characteristics related to their specific area ... Decentralisation sections you off and isolates you. In a central office if something goes wrong everyone is there and people would support you. Here, you can lend support but you are much more vulnerable.
> (Housing Advisory Worker - female)

Another felt even more strongly about the changes,

> What's happened to the union since decentralisation is that it's been decimated. It's totally and utterly wrecked the union because the whole way of organising has been fundamentally altered ... a lot of people previously active have lost contact, because it's difficult to know where to go.
> (Community Worker - male)

Whilst this was perhaps not representative of all the stewards, it was, nevertheless, common for them to talk of a process of fragmentation, isolation, confusion, poor communication and overall weakness within the Branch, points more fully developed in Chapter Ten but which are illustrated here,

> We're very scattered and union membership is very devalued at the present time.
> (Administrative Worker - female)

> I would say that everything you do (in the union) is ten times more difficult once you've been decentralised because of the structures. You've been used to having strong departmental lines, then they're all broken up ... you still have the departmental lines but they're not cohesive so it's much more difficult to achieve things.
> (Principal Housing Advisory Officer - female)

> Decentralisation has had a very negative effect in the union's organisation. It made it a lot weaker, made it fragment into lots of departmental shops and job description shops ... very poor attendance at meetings. Not every job description has a steward but most of them have. Not all departmental stewards are based in the N.O.
> (Welfare Rights Worker - female)

Clearly not all these feelings, which are representative of the stewards interviewed, relate solely to NALGO's new Branch structure. Nevertheless, the overwhelming feeling was that whilst a decentralised structure creates additional problems, to which we shall return, the Branch had been unable to respond effectively and its structures were, if anything, exacerbating the difficulties.

Gaining confidence in the 1970s

NALGO Islington has a militant reputation, and it is not surprising to find this militancy emerge in parallel to, although sometimes ahead of national developments within the union. The first shop steward organisation was established in the Borough's library service in 1969 following a grading dispute, which "transformed a branch previously dominated by relatively senior officers and which was very quiet" (Branch Secretary interview). A number of small, but significant, actions took place as the mid-1970s approached. In September 1973 an unofficial strike, by the Essex Road Social Services team, broke out over unsatisfactory standards of accommodation, and was subsequently supported by the NALGO's national Emergency Committee. This was, according to Garrett (1973), "history-making, precedent-setting stuff". Reflecting on the action, supported by 90% of fieldwork staff, Garrett highlights the novelty of the situation and the inexperience of the participants,

> Being on strike was a new experience, and for most an uncomfortable one ... They quickly felt vulnerable and relatively isolated on the picket lines. Neither the team, the Department nor the Branch was as prepared as it might have been. It was a surprise ... when a postman asked if they wanted him to honour the picket line ... (p 11).

Garrett saw the strike as not simply about the situation facing those social workers, but as "action on behalf of all Islington workers in unsuitable illegal conditions" (p 11).

In the 1974 "London weighting dispute", Islington was the first to take branch action, and in the following year it joined in the national half-day TUC stoppage against unemployment and public spending cuts, as well as supporting short stoppages by its housing workers over working conditions, unfilled vacancies and the freezing of posts. Social workers were also further involved in an eight-week strike which closed down other services as a result of picketing (Case Con no. 16 summer 1974). However the inexperience of the branch was also evident as it fell foul of the union's Emergency Committee for not properly informing it of its proposals or following the procedures for industrial action (Emergency Committee Minutes, 1974).

In 1977 the Borough's Social Services Department was involved in another dispute, concerning alleged discrimination over the job application of a previous union activist seeking re-employment. Again this brought a rebuke from NALGO's General Secretary which ended the potential dispute (Emergency Committee 1977). However, in the same year the branch did take strike action over the "intransigent attitude of the employing authority" in relation to poor office accommodation (September) and an earlier threat from members in the Housing Department of joint industrial action with colleagues in

MATSA, again over unsatisfactory working conditions, was only called off after management agreed to improve the accommodation. Similarly, during the 1978/79 national social workers' strike, the branch played an active role and, indeed, managed to produce the only satisfactory outcome, in the form of a locally negotiated settlement. Thus, throughout the 1970s the NALGO Islington Branch was engaged in both a number of local disputes and in any regional or national initiative co-ordinated by the union. During this period it not only flexed its militant muscles but tested and learned about a range of trade union tactics as well as coming to terms with what it meant to be part of a larger union structure.

All change on the Council and in the union

1982 was quite a significant year for a substantial section of NALGO members in Islington who actively campaigned against the election of SDP candidates in the local election after they had crossed the floor from the Labour Party. A number of stewards interviewed supported the views put forward by this former steward,

> The council in '82 got in as a result of the support of the workers ... I don't think they were arguing for a Labour victory but certainly against the SDP. What is true is that a number wore two hats, being a NALGO activist and also in the Labour Party.
> (Social Worker - male)

Others also commented on the mutual support between public service workers and Labour's "new left", many of whom were themselves former public employees. Prior to the election, conflict with the SDP councillors had already resulted in a number of disputes which began with two strikes in early 1982 (February and March). The first, a two-day strike in the housing department and then a one-day strike of the whole branch, were given retrospective approval by the national Emergency Committee. The third occurred in March when there was a two-week strike in the housing department. Figures sent to the Emergency Committee showed three Branch ballots, all of which produced heavy votes in favour of strike action (e.g. 767 for an indefinite strike, 167 against). Indeed, over the three ballots the numbers in favour of the strike continued to rise. Yet, despite this support, the Emergency Committee terminated the strike on the twelfth day. This was followed by a short strike over the closing of a children's home. This dispute produced a split within the union with the then established Branch officers, based in the libraries service and belonging to the Communist Party, recommending a return to work. Although this strategy was defeated by the Branch, it was only by a small majority, and consequently the Emergency Committee refused to support the strike whilst the Branch remained so divided. As a result a united left opposition ousted the Branch Secretary and his supporters and returned a new Branch leadership which remained more or less intact for the rest of the decade.

1982-4 marked a period of relatively good relationships with the newly-elected Council. Labour had swept the board in the April elections, taking all but one seat. Consequently and almost inadvertently, this thrust into the limelight a number of younger, radical, but inexperienced councillors. This was also the period of initial planning around the then proposed decentralisation strategy to which we shall return later. At this point, however, some of the other major disputes in the Borough are highlighted. These occurred in parallel to NALGO action over decentralisation, and helped shape the union's response to the Council's strategy and practice.

The children's day centre dispute

The first major dispute of 1984 began in April, over a pay claim for nursery workers in the children's day centres, and involved a 17-week strike. A pay claim had been made in October 1983 but had been held over until the January 1984 meeting of the local Joint Staff Committee. NALGO felt that the Authority had given little thought to the claim and that the declared proposal to refer it to the Social Services Committee would not only cause further delay but was also side-stepping the negotiating machinery as the union had no negotiating role in that committee. A further unproductive meeting was held in April, and this was followed by a Branch meeting vote on strike action in which 301 voted in favour and nobody against. The strike involved 500 NALGO members, lasted three months and cost the union £294,966. It was not until the end of July, following a ballot (narrowly won) and indefinite strike action by social services field services, architects, housing (transfers), computer operations and adult day care, that a settlement was reached. The dispute raised strong feelings about the then still relatively young management that flew the red flag from the town hall. One activist at the time recalled that it was,

> Quite an eye opener ... just in terms of seeing what was involved, trying to keep the whole thing going, wishing it would end ... and also an eye opener for Labour Party members in terms of seeing what a pragmatically oriented Labour council would do ... I was surprised at the general treatment we got, especially the council propaganda 'trading in misconceptions', quickly turning the blame on the workers, attempting to frustrate our efforts to attend council meetings. It took people by surprise that this very prominent left-wing council with the red flag flying over the council chamber which always prided itself and publicised its good practice, and when an important and low paid part of the workforce is told to forget it ...

However, the dispute was seen as a partial victory for NALGO, as the Branch Secretary commented, "The final offer from the council is worth approximately £300,000. This has to be set against an initial offer of around £15,000 before the members came out on strike, and the total financial implication of the claim of £780,000" (NALGO Islington, 1984).

The racism dispute

In 1985 the Branch was involved both in a major local dispute, which involved 500 members and caught the attention of the national weekly journals and, along with other NALGO members elsewhere, the campaign against rate capping. Both experiences were to have major consequences for the Branch both internally and in its relationships with the Authority.

The local dispute, which occurred in August, over a case of racial harassment which was "hailed as a pioneering anti-racist action ... threw up a lot of worrying problems, (yet) failed to win widespread support ..." (Wolmar, 1985). Strike action took place over five weeks in response, according to the Branch, to "the Council's failure to adequately deal with racism and racial harassment and its threat of disciplinary action against NALGO members wishing to operate an anti-racist policy in the neighbourhood offices" (NALGO Islington, 1985). A report to the union's Emergency Committee (August 1985) spoke of 18 months of active harassment in the Rent Accounts Section of the Borough's Housing Department, and other forms of harassment which it suggested went back over three and a half years. A report to the local Joint Trade Union Committee spoke of exclusion from social events, ashtrays being emptied on desks, derogatory remarks, vocal support for the National Front, materials necessary for work being kept from black workers, unnecessary checking up on work, allegations about dishonesty and verbal intimidation.

According to the Branch, efforts had been made during 1984 to get management to take the issue seriously following a complaint made to shop stewards in the January against three workers in the Housing Department (NALGO Islington, 1985). One had been redeployed, initially with the union's agreement, which was later regretted, and the other two faced informal disciplinary action. In November 1984 the issue was again raised with the Chair of Personnel as it was felt that insufficient action had been taken, but after a number of informal meetings a separate investigation was rejected by the Council. NALGO, which had set up a Racial Harassment Working Party in the October to review its own policies and attitudes around racial harassment, continued pressing for disciplinary action. Five members of staff were eventually formally charged with racial harassment but at their hearing in April were given the lowest in the prescribed list of penalties in the staff code.

NALGO remained particularly concerned on two accounts: that another union, MATSA, had represented one of those accused despite an apparent verbal assurance that it would not, and that the outcome did not appear to equate with Labour's 1982 Manifesto. This had stated, "Labour would treat very seriously any grievance against a council employee connected with racial discrimination. Racism will be considered 'gross misconduct' which could lead to dismissal". According to the Branch Secretary, the Branch had placed, "quite frankly too much trust in management (and the Council at a later stage) carrying out the Equal Opportunities Employment Policy effectively. We were not adequately prepared for the delays imposed on us by management ..." (NALGO Islington, 1985). A Branch meeting in June voted, "with two votes against and nine abstentions at a meeting of over 300 members", that those guilty of harassment should not work with the public and that if they continued to do so union members would refuse to co-operate with them. In July, the neighbourhood office to which one of the guilty had been redeployed declared it was willing to lift the non-co-operation policy providing that the person gave an assurance on her future conduct and agreed that her past action had been discriminatory. When she rejected this the NALGO staff at the neighbourhood office walked out. This was followed by a meeting of members in the then 13 neighbourhood offices who voted by 107 votes to five with 14 abstentions to support strike action and the picketing of the neighbourhood office. Official national backing for the strike came seven days later.

The strike lasted five weeks but although some concessions were made, NALGO failed to achieve its objectives. Wolmar put this failure down to both the "lack of any support from any other town hall union ... MATSA, the white-collar section of GMBATU ... threatened industrial action if she were moved (from the redeployed post)" and some lack of conviction by many NALGO members (Wolmar, 1985). Yet the strike did raise the profile on racism and, according to Wolmar, challenged both the Council and the unions' efforts to date, "to create an atmosphere of positive anti-racism" (p 17). Strong feelings persist about this dispute. One former steward stated,

> From the outside it seemed absurd ... a turning point in Islington ... I didn't think it was the right strategy to go out on. A lot of people seemed to come out not because of the issue but because they were genuinely fed up but that's the wrong way to get people out ... you have to have a clear strategy.

Another questioned both the strategy and motivation behind the dispute,

> The neighbourhood offices were reluctant to involve the centralised sections ... they didn't even tell the central stewards for a week. Lots either resigned, became inactive or drifted to other unions because it was badly organised. It felt as though it was only a neighbourhood issue. A lot of the old union guard had been promoted to neighbourhood offices and this was their last battle. Many of these got promoted into management.
> (Housing Lettings Officer - male)

The drift to other unions following the dispute and a belief that that the dispute had been badly handled was confirmed by a number of stewards. Doubts were expressed about the original allegations; the strategy of focusing on one individual; and the lost time and inaction by NALGO during the first year. In addition there was a major internal Branch dispute during the strike, involving members in the libraries, who threatened a mass resignation and would not support the dispute because of the Branch's alleged mishandlings, its failure to follow procedure, and ignoring an earlier report. In relation to this last point, one Branch Executive member argued that although the report, which was from the libraries, was "well argued, reasonable and detailed, it was nevertheless seen as a 'betrayal'". She highlighted a number of problems: the report had been leaked to councillors before going to the Branch Executive; it was never sent to the strike committee; it had come from a centralised department that had no involvement in the neighbourhood offices; and it was seen as coming from the old branch leadership with the purpose of discrediting the present Branch Secretary. Yet despite this it caused some damage as it was never answered properly as far as many ordinary members were concerned, and a number of members from the libraries were subsequently elected into key posts in the branch.

Opposition was not confined to the libraries and members continued to drift to MATSA, especially within the Housing Department. As one former steward commented,

> What you had were a number of traditional union members who didn't feel they could leave the trade union movement but couldn't agree with what NALGO was doing.
> (Principal Advisory Officer - female)

However it was not all negative for, despite "the horrible atmosphere in central Housing" the same worker noted,

> It served a positive purpose ... it was a way of building a lot of support in the neighbourhood office that perhaps wouldn't have happened without it.

Yet, one must question whether such ends justified the means, for not only did the Branch lose a number of members, appear divided over an important issue and fail to reach agreement with the Authority on how to proceed in such cases, it is hard to see how the experience can have helped the offenders to change their behaviour and thinking, except out of fear. Indeed, one Branch Executive member, expressing the views of a number of colleagues, highlighted the main problems of organising in what was a relatively new and highly sensitive area, and how such incidents do not fade easily from the collective memory but rather can leave deep and bitter feelings and divisions,

> People didn't understand the issue. It was really one of principle about having direct contact with the public but it got personalised. It brought up lots of feelings ... the union wasn't particularly sensitive in terms of its own policies and strategies, for

example having two white men interviewing the woman on her attitudes to anti-racist training. People were just throwing the word 'racist' around, creating a lot of bitterness. People who wanted to defend her in any shape or form felt they were under attack. Others were very self-righteous ... A lot of damage was done to the union, people have retreated, there is a fear about taking up such issues.
(Housing Co-operatives Officer - female)

Rate-capping

1985 was also the year of the rate-capping campaign which was not an industrial dispute but on the contrary was meant to be a joint trade union - local authority campaign against central government's policies. However the outcome, which was seen as most unsatisfactory by a number of NALGO activists, further soured relationships between the Branch and the Authority, and strengthened the view that the Council's radical politics were more concerned with rhetorical posturing than meaningful action. NALGO felt "let down" according to the Branch Secretary. The Council was seen as having "chickened out" in June 1985, when it set a rate, despite a period between autumn 1984 and summer 1985 of joint campaigning. Consequently,

Since then there has been a lot of cynicism on our side about joint campaigning ... As soon as the Authority begins to implement Tory policies they will come into conflict ... They'll be seen by the workforce as the agent that is cutting their jobs and working conditions. I did not see the government going ahead to surcharge and disqualify all the London borough councillors. Therefore, the anti-rate capping campaign ... provided real opportunities for a tripartite alliance based on a resistance to proceed with Thatcherite policies ...
(Branch Secretary - male)

A number of stewards representing a wide range of political backgrounds expressed similar views. Typical of such comments were,

A lot of the demoralisation around in public sector unions is because councillors have led them up the hill and down again ... The Labour Party has a responsibility to lead (against the Tories) and basically they've capitulated.
(Housing Advisory Worker - male)

Rate-capping had the support of the workers but the council let it go. They came into office to fight and retain services. You either fight or get out. Now it will end up as the workers against the council instead of us together against the government. The council hasn't got the bottle ... backing down all over.
(Occupational Therapist - female)

They gave up and decided to make the best of a bad situation by staying in office and doing what they could. The alternative would have been to refuse to make the cuts ... This would have forced a crisis and if it had been repeated elsewhere ... provided an opportunity to get rid of Thatcher. I don't think it matters if cuts are made by a Tory or Labour council.
(Housing Benefit Officer - female)

The union responded well on rate-capping. It was terrible though because it was dragged along on the coat-tails of the Labour Party ... That was so winnable ... 40 councils not making a rate if the GLC hadn't collapsed ... I've never seen a campaign that was capable of being expanded, during the dark days of Thatcherism.

Millions of people upset. A political movement waiting to be tapped and sadly it wasn't ... If you're talking about local democracy rate-capping was the issue ... the moment has gone. Now people don't see any solution because they think the leadership is going to cop out ... to move rightwards. People who claim to represent them have never done anything for them, or if they have they can't bloody remember it. When was the last time they effectively opposed something or proposed something that actually leads to something better ...
(Senior Estates Manager - male)

Some stewards made the direct connection between the rate-capping campaign and the parallel discussions taking place around decentralisation. The sense of disappointment and cynicism over the councillors' actions on rate-capping only made the union more suspicious about their statements on decentralisation. Some were equally bitter towards their own leadership, remembering how the opposition to decentralisation in the early part of 1985, which saw the policy voted down three times in Branch meetings, had been tempered following an,

Impassioned speech by the Branch Secretary, who warned that rate-capping would follow if the vote went against decentralisation.
(Lettings Officer - male)

The union leadership were all bought out. They were all Labour Party members, didn't like the contradiction and didn't like being reminded of it ... it was railroaded through at an AGM. Social Services and Housing both voted twice and rejected it by a massive majority ...
(Senior Estates Manager - male)

Locked out

1987 saw two further industrial disputes, both involving lock-outs: firstly the Housing Advisory Workers and then the Home Care Organisers. The Housing Advisory Workers had submitted a regrading claim in February 1986 which was rejected in May. A local appeal was heard in the November and a new offer rejected in the following month. A work to contract had begun in the September, which was intensified in January 1987. In the February the management declared the Advisory Workers were in fundamental breach of contract, refused to negotiate, and suspended a NALGO member at the beginning of March, which was to be followed by the suspension of other workers a few days later. Two one-day strikes followed, one in the neighbourhood offices and one Branch-wide, but without any response from the Authority. The suspended workers were locked out for 16 weeks and in the end the dispute had to be dealt with by the regional Whitley Council which supported the claim, regrading the Advisory Workers and back-dating it to the beginning of the dispute. For one worker involved there were two lessons to learn,

If public sector unions withdraw labour the employers save money. The union should expand its range of tactics to avoid members being isolated ... I felt let down by the fact that the Neighbourhood Housing Officer didn't support us ... they had to suspend us personally and they could have resisted that. Now you think it's not worth trying to get their support.
(Principal Housing Advisory Officer - female)

In September 1987 it was the turn of the Home Care Organisers to find themselves locked out of their office as a result of a dispute about cover arrangements and the absence of clerical support after the Organisers had been decentralised. Prior to decentralisation there were almost three Home Care Organisers who would provide cover for each other. This would be lost on the move to neighbourhood offices. The Organisers and the Home Carers protested by putting up a picket on their central office on the day of removal. The removal workers refused to cross the picket lines and the Organisers were suspended. However they carried on working (without pay) from their central office for the next three days. The management then gained entry to the office one night, removed all the files and equipment and locked the Organisers out for a further two weeks. In the end the strain of their new-found militancy took its toll and the Organisers gradually returned to work. As one of them put it,

> Numbers dwindled down, leaving only eight out of 24 and after two weeks people couldn't take the strain so we had to go back although we're still in dispute. We got a lot of support from the Branch. We lost because we weren't strong enough.
> (Home Care Organiser - female)

Such disputes during the 1980s not only engaged the unions membership in issues that went beyond traditional bread and butter trade unionism into political campaigning but were also influential in shaping the branch's perceptions of the urban left leadership in the Authority. Such experiences both generated a cynicism towards Authority pronouncements and also provided a rationale for not critically reflecting on their own practices as welfare providers.

Factors shaping attitudes to trade unionism

Whilst the production process remains a focal point for the creation of an interest in trade unionism, the Islington research confirmed the importance of factors external to the workplace. Thus, out of the current or former shop stewards interviewed, 80% mentioned such external factors as reasons for joining NALGO. A not insignificant number, 37.5%, saw their membership as part of a wider commitment to trade unionism and socialist politics. Typical comments from this latter group included,

> It's basically a working class organisation. Society is made up of various power groups and when you're at the bottom of the heap the only thing you can join is the trade union movement.
> (Community Worker - male)

> I joined NALGO immediately. I'm a socialist. I think every employee should be in a union.
> (Housing Advisory Worker - female)

> Trade unionism is the most relevant form of political action. It's a way of expressing political commitment ....
> (Social Worker - male)

> I believe in trade unionism and the principles behind it. I believe it is the only organisation that will represent my ideas and my interests.
> (Housing Advisory Worker - female)

A small group of stewards (7%) mentioned their involvement in the Labour Party specifically,

I've always been a member of a trade union because I'm a Labour Party member and that's one of the rules anyway.
(Administrative Worker - female)

Of those who referred to other important influences, 10% mentioned their general background, education and involvement in community based politics,

I got my views from growing up, university, life in general. My parents weren't very political.
(Social Worker - female)

17.5% mentioned the importance of family background as being essential to creating a set of values and beliefs that lead to trade unionism,

It was never a question of not joining one. It was the way I was brought up ... grew up with labour ideas and one of those being in trade unionism ....
(Housing Advisory Worker - female)

I come from a working class, Irish Catholic background which had a big bearing on my involvement in politics and trade unionism. There were few job opportunities ... I joined a union at 16 ... it's your only stand to be heard and be voiced as workers in society.
(Housing Advisory Worker - male)

I'm from a working class background. My father was a T & G Shop Steward in the 60's ...
(Housing Advisory Worker - male)

My father was a strong union member in the South Wales mines. I picked some of that up ... it's important to be a trade union member and part of the labour movement.
(Social Worker - male)

20% of the stewards also mentioned work related concerns as being paramount to their joining citing, job protection, security, strength, solidarity, and the need to have a voice as reasons,

I joined for strength and support, not to be victimised and isolated as an individual.
(Estate Manager - male)

To be able to have a say and not be just a pawn.
(Occupational Therapist - female)

You need a union to protect yourself ... some people aren't very confident and a group defends them. We should have a closed shop.
(Housing Benefits Officer - female)

The union is there to put over the members' viewpoint.
(Home Care Organiser - female)

In addition, the opportunity to promote specific policies and the nature of the job was highlighted in the following way,

I don't know how I could do my job and not be in the union. The union is all about people's rights ... I don't think I could advise others to get their rights without fighting for my own ...
(Welfare Rights Worker - female)

Carpenter et al. (1990) also remind us that the decision to join a trade union may not necessarily be directly influenced by positional pressures because joining the trade union can be, "part of the process of occupational socialisation". Bamber (1986), in a study of the Steel Industry Management Association, identifies three types of motivation for joining a union:
(i) group motives (i.e. a general preference for collective representation);
(ii) instrumental motives (e.g. job insecurity, concern with wages and conditions); and
(iii) external motives (such as employer policies, colleague influence and union pressure).
The great majority (50%), identified the first, citing unity as strength, a moral obligation to be a union member and the stronger bargaining position of a group as reasons for joining. A further 22% identified instrumental motives whilst 28% chose external factors. As in the Islington research, Bamber often found it difficult to distinguish between group and instrumental reasons as these often represent a distinction between means and end.

In the questionnaire to NALGO members in neighbourhood offices (Table 6.1, Appendix 2), respondents were asked, "What was the most important influence in shaping your attitudes to trade unionism?" The results showed that whilst 34% mentioned the changing nature of work (government and management policies, management behaviours and working conditions), 66% mentioned non-work related factors with family, politics, friendships and education dominating. However, asking respondents what they felt had been most influential does not do justice to either the complexity of the process, or to the range of influences on their trade unionism. In a more detailed question, respondents were asked to indicate whether or not they had been influenced by a range of variables which covered: (i) family and friends, (ii) work and market situation, (iii) government policies, (iv) other external influences, (v) the union itself, and (vi) their profession. What emerges is the importance of both the work/market situation and a number of specific external influences in shaping their trade union attitudes.

By far the biggest single factor identified was the policies pursued by central government in relation to public services, with 90% of the respondents stating that these had influenced them, 56% saying that it had been very influential. This is not surprising given that in answer to another question, 86% of the respondents agreed (83% of them strongly) with the statement that, "The policies of the present government are a direct threat to local government services and workers". Furthermore, 86% of the respondents agreed with the view (52% of them strongly) that, "State provided services are an effective way of meeting social need". These workers not only saw the government as a threat to their work and the services they provide, but also placed a high value on those services. In addition, these were workers who felt that their skills and contribution were undervalued, so that 86% agreed (56% strongly) with the statement that, "The skills of public service workers need to be more fully acknowledged", with only one person disagreeing. Similarly, 69% agreed (44% strongly) with the statement that, "Public service workers are professionals and should be recognised as such".

Other external factors also appeared very influential. Thus, 77% of the respondents said that other trade unionists had been influential and it is also worth noting that elsewhere, 59% of the respondents had highlighted the influence of their friends. Thus 31% stated that they had a significant number of friends who were active trade unionists, whilst for 29% of the respondents this applied for most of their friends. For the majority, these were friends who did not work for the Authority. Thus, 54% said that very few friends worked for the Authority, 9% said that none did, whilst 27% said a significant number did, and only 2% said that most did. Again it is significant that 79% of the respondents indicated that either a significant number or most of their friends outside work shared their political views. Such non-work friendships were clearly seen as important with 56% stating that these had been influential (19% very influential).

Another influence was the general economic climate, with 75% of the respondents stating that this had influenced their attitudes to unionism, 73% stating that the high levels of unemployment had been important. In addition, 69% said they had been influenced by their education. In respect of other external factors - a political party, gender, the media, ethnic origin - respondents tended to be equally split with approximately half being influenced and half not. A smaller number (33%) had been influenced as a result of their membership of a pressure group, but this may be linked to the fact that only 13% currently belonged to a national pressure group, 29% to a national campaigning group, and 9% to a local community action group.

In contrast, few of the respondents appear to have been influenced by their immediate family. Thus, 56% and 59% stated that their father and mother respectively had not been at all influential in their attitudes to trade unionism. Only 13% had been very influenced by their father and a mere 6% by their mother. However, in answer to another question, only 17% of the respondents stated that their father had been an active and politically committed trade union member, whilst this was the case for only 9% in relation to their mothers. Eight per cent described their fathers as, "Generally active but non-political", and 6% said they were "Not active except on special issues", a description applied to 13% of the mothers. In contrast, 36% of fathers and 48% of mothers were described as "Never a member of a trade union", whilst 9% of fathers and 9% of mothers were said to be either reluctant or indifferent members. Eleven per cent did not know anything of their father's trade unionism and similarly 9% were unaware of their mother's position.

Not surprisingly a substantial number (59%) of the respondents declared that they were influenced in their attitudes by the policies of their own trade union. This was in sharp contrast to the lack of influence from their profession. Thus, 54% stated that their professional training had not at all been influential, although 36% had been influenced, but even more powerfully, 71% of the respondents said that their membership of a professional organisation had not been influential.

It should not, however, be forgotten that in addition to these external characteristics, and the importance of the union itself in influencing attitudes, respondents were also strongly influenced by their market and work situation. This is clearly shown in Table 6.2 where working conditions, pay levels, work colleagues, and their role in the Authority were all influential. Thus both the motivating drive to join a trade union and the influences on workers' attitudes as trade unionists are complex and wide ranging. Carpenter et al. (1990) suggest that in their study, the union orientation for social workers was a balance between defending their work and market situation, responding to client needs (all their fieldworkers are reported as having a high degree of commitment to the service and to client needs), personal aspirations, and external commitments such as family, social groups or politics. Whilst a consistently high proportion of the respondents in Islington were influenced by their work and market situation, equally powerful were other factors such as, the union itself and aspects external to the work place, some of which will, however, have a direct bearing on their working situation. In particular, for those human service workers directly dependent on the state for their market position, their working situation and the quality, indeed existence, of their product, the political sphere necessarily takes on an importance not found in other sectors, except perhaps on those occasions when government imposes a policy that impinges on their market or work situation. However, when such situations do arise, as with an incomes policy, they have tended to be short term and apply uniformly to all workers. Public service workers must constantly be aware of the significance of government.

Becoming a shop steward

There are two powerful images of the process by which shop stewards are elected. One is of the politically committed, well organised group who work hard to get their people elected, and if necessary, are prepared to bully and harass. This process is said to be facilitated by an apathetic workforce which allows anyone who stands for the post to secure it. The implication here is that the steward does not fully represent the membership: their activism is out of place and not desired by the broad and moderate membership. The second image is that of the lively and keenly contested branch election, reflecting the high levels of activism within the union. Clearly there are tensions between the activism of the steward, many of whom will be more than willing to have an official role within the union, and the broad membership (Nicholson et al. 1981). Yet the process by which stewards come to occupy the post does seem to be more complex than is suggested by either image. In Islington, there was a problem of not enough people coming forward for shop steward positions, but many of those who did end up in the role had been approached and persuaded to take it on. Their qualities were recognised, and the membership prepared to accept them, especially given the additional work that would be required to fulfil the role, which they were willing to do. However, there were other occasions when nobody appeared willing to come forward until finally someone acknowledged the importance of the task. Thus, of the 43 stewards interviewed, 48% stated that they had taken the job either because nobody else was prepared to do it, they were filling an empty space, and/or because they were encouraged to stand and were elected without opposition. Typical of the comments were,

Most people get into it by default. The last steward resigned, so I became a steward in default of anyone else wanting to do it.
(Social Worker - male)

Nobody else wanted it but then I thought that the Neighbourhood Office Shop Steward was important.
(Advisory Officer - female)

... partly because I'd had the experience, and other people knew I had when they approached me, and I felt I should use my experience.
(Welfare Rights Officer - female)

A shop AGM was called, a couple of months after I joined. The steward resigned. There was nobody else .... For a couple of months it was vacant. I agreed although I had no experience. I had another meeting recently and I carried on because no one else was interested.
(Welfare Rights Officer - male)

The previous steward went on maternity leave. I was just coming back. There was no one else. I was always interested in becoming steward ....
(Occupational Therapist - female)

I was active in the union and friendly with the shop steward, who got a semi-management job, asked me to take over ... there was nobody else.
(Housing Advisory Worker - female)

People asked me. It needed to be done.
(Administrative Officer - female)

My turn had come. Clearly someone needed to do it. I don't think I would say I had a natural inclination to be a union officer.
(Environmental Health Officer - male)

What emerges from these comments is the inter-relationship between the absence of people coming forward, somebody being encouraged to stand because of the skills and qualities they possessed, or were thought to possess, and their feeling that the job should be done, or they would like to do it. People do not come forward themselves but recognise the importance of these stressful and demanding roles and encourage others. Such a process challenges both the image of the strongly contested elections for union posts and its mirror image of the determined, power seeking, shop steward. Thus,

One or two suggested I do it. There was never a lot of competition. I thought it would enhance the interest at work.
(Estates Manager - male)

Hew Beynon (1973), in his study of trade unionism at a Ford motor plant, reached similar conclusions. He found that the vast majority of stewards had no intention of becoming active when they joined the plant. "Few pushed themselves forward. Their qualities were noted by their mates and by other stewards. They were approached and cajoled" (p 196). He argues that, "activism is, above all else, a social process, and talk of personality types directs attention away from this. Men (sic) who become stewards have to recognise the potential in themselves and to have it recognised by others" (p 192).

On becoming a steward one does not have a free hand, even with the most passive of memberships, being ultimately limited by what the membership will agree to do. Nevertheless, stewards do have privileged access to management, which involves engaging in various relationships of formality and informality. The role will involve them in consultation exercises, negotiation, the exchange of information and being party to personal revelations and gossip. Various kinds of informal contact may well be cultivated by management both to anticipate and head-off potential trouble and ideally to incorporate the stewards within the managerial framework. Where such organisational informality exists it can be extremely difficult for stewards to avoid entirely as it can be a valuable source of information and an opportunity for themselves to be influential in avoiding conflict. The dilemma for the steward is how to conduct such relationships in a manner that does not result in the abandonment of the members interests, or which neglects their representative role, but yet allows them some freedom to manoeuvre, or make decisions, for which they are then accountable. Ironically, stewards may want to be made to be more accountable whilst the membership may be happy to allow them greater freedom to take initiatives. However, it would again be mistaken to assume that periods of relative membership passivity will continue indefinitely and that the membership will be untouched by changes either within their workplace or external to it.

Islington's militancy: its uneven development

Islington NALGO's militancy is apparent not only by tracing its recent history, but also in the views expressed by its current members. Of the 43 activists interviewed, 17 of the women and 16 of the men described the Branch in terms of being 'militant', 'socialist', 'left of Labour', and 'militant relative to the union as a whole'. However, variations between departments are evident with recent events suggesting a decline in militancy and, as indicated below, an acknowledged widening gap between activists and the overall membership,

> Very much on the left of the union nationally ... some of the most left politics in the union ... on the poll tax one of only three branches in the country that has a non-compliance policy ... historically good policy on cuts and other issues. On paper, policy is very good although in terms of actual action that doesn't mean that it is particularly true ... true of all public sector branches ... local authorities had such a bashing ... fairly low in confidence.
> (Housing Advisory Worker - male)

> I got the very clear message at the national conference that the Islington Branch is certainly on the left of NALGO.
> (Housing Advisory Worker - male)

> Clearly it's to the left of the council ... but we don't flex our muscles very much these days.
> (Environmental Health Officer - male)

> Reliably left - sometimes too left ... a lot of posturing ... the core group of people are Labour left, probably far left.
> (Housing Benefits Officer - female)

> The EC is very left-wing but the Branch as a whole is wishy-washy.
> (Library Assistant - female)

> ... quite militant. Very successful over equal opportunities. A lot of people are aware of the organisation that goes into NALGO ... the Branch is obviously pretty left-wing.
> (Welfare Rights Officer - male)

Trade union militancy within the Branch has not however been experienced uniformly by all departments or occupational groupings and nor does it necessarily remain a permanent feature of any department although reputations can be long-lasting. Particular departments were perceived by the shop stewards as having a much longer pedigree in radicalism whilst others were equally clearly identified as conservative or hesitant in their political engagement. For example, the great majority of those interviewed identified social services as traditionally the strongest department, with housing identified either as currently equal first choice or, more usually, close second. In addition the past strength of the libraries department, which had dominated the Branch officer positions during the 1970s, was frequently acknowledged. On the other hand, other departments, notably the engineers, finance and (in the neighbourhood offices) the chief executives, were seen as the traditionally weaker sections. Such views on the overall strength of departments are reflected in the following,

> Prior to decentralisation social services carried NALGO. They were the strong shop ... if you got their support you were halfway there ... You can still rely on them to

be there or thereabouts at the time of a dispute even though they don't take such a great part as they did.
(Environmental Health Officer - male)

Social services seem to be the backbone of NALGO in Islington ... especially in this office. They'll turn up for meetings and get involved in issues. Interestingly they're the most middle class, very well educated, articulate, and in a sense that goes together.
(Estate Manager - male)

There are great traditions in terms of organisation and activity. Social services have a better tradition than say housing as do libraries ... but that is changing.
(Improvements Officer - male)

Disputes still centre around social services and housing and people in those sections are prepared to take up issues by the very nature of the people in those jobs ... so although you don't have the same cohesion now in social services it is still those departments where issues emerge.
(Housing Advisory Worker - female)

There's quite a lot of activity in housing ... it tends to go in waves ... libraries seem to have a strong union. They fight very strongly whenever closure is threatened and get out a lot of material.
(Welfare Rights Officer - female)

Such strong and relatively consistent trade union radicalism was not always welcomed, especially if it sometimes left other workers feeling worse off. For example, the relative strength of both social services and housing at the time of the decentralisation reorganisation had enabled them to achieve better terms: a point not lost on other sections but one which was as likely to generate negative feelings towards these union sections as it would towards management. As one experienced steward stated,

The older departments got better deals especially on grading. The chief executives were at the bottom. There was no regrading of administrative workers ... It was annoying to find some with better working conditions ... it left some resentment especially since the Branch hasn't tried to generalise these privileges.
(Assistant Neighbourhood Officer Chief Executive)

Similarly, another commented,

Social services came in (to the NO) six months late. Antagonisms arose as a result. We saw them as obstructive ... they were historically strong and had the power to stay out ... the Branch bowed to their strength ... the racial harassment strike threw up organisational problems on the need to set up N.O. shops. Social services wanted to keep their structures ... kept throwing spanners in the works ... bloody nuisance ... they still wanted to report back to the department.
(Housing Co-op Worker - female)

Activists in social services recognised the problem and the potential damage caused to relationships with other trade unionists. As one social worker, reflecting on the period of decentralisation into neighbourhood offices commented,

We felt we were on our own ... We should have all gone in together. We would have stayed much more solid. The union would have been more solid with less opportunity to split us off ... ramifications in our office that have continued even

until now ... we're always considered a bit precious, a bit prissy, a bit separate, always unco-operative. We got left the pokey little hole in the corner to sit in.
(Social Worker - female)

Others confirmed the continuing inter-departmental tensions which affect trade union work as well as occupational tasks,

There's not much inter-departmental co-operation ... In most offices there's a lot of conflict ... social services don't give us in housing the support we need ... in relation to clients we have in common. We can see how social workers are also in a difficult position ... confidentiality is stronger ...
(Housing Advisory Worker - female)

Activists identified a range of barriers between social services and other departments including: the stress of confidentiality; the social work jargon; the constant demand and expectation that they are always available; the nature of their work; and their late arrival into the neighbourhood offices. All of these resulted in "an arch of filing cabinets to fence us in".

The explanations offered for such departmental variation were generally rooted in the nature of the work, the people drawn to it or, as in the quote above, the educational and class backgrounds. Others mentioned the apparently greater need for trade unionism as a consequence of the work being undertaken,

More are involved in face to face contact or are on the receiving end of bad planning and lack of resources.
(Lettings Officer - male)

Social work makes you more aware.
(Housing Advisory Worker - male)

The kind of jobs we do you have to have certain attitudes to do the job successfully - advisory workers are generally more aware.
(Housing Advisory Worker - female)

Social services are quite vulnerable without union membership because their job is quite politically difficult and they need the protection.
(Administrative Worker - female)

Explanations for the relatively low level of trade union involvement of other departments, such as chief executives employing a majority of low paid, female, and black workers, highlighted a range of factors. Clearly there was felt to be an issue around the self perception of such workers,

They feel very much as office workers without any particular discipline of their own ... they haven't got any power.
(Principal Housing Advisory Worker - female)

The workers feel less powerful, less able to influence things - I don't exactly understand it myself because I don't feel that way.
(Administrative Officer - female)

... in a way it's because they take the brunt of work from all the other departments and the brunt of reception work. They're quite an oppressed section of workers as well as being the lowest paid.
(Welfare Rights Officer - female)

Conversely, certain perceptions of NALGO can be seen as off-putting to these workers,

> It is very difficult to get new members to join because NALGO is perceived as always going out on strike ... It is not seen in the positive light of what you can achieve ...
> (Administrative Officer - female)

This view was often linked to a general lack of awareness about the benefits of trade unions,

> ... you've got a lot of admin staff ... low paid, inexperienced in trade unions and not aware of what trade unions can achieve ... what can be done if you all work together ...
> (Welfare Rights Officer - female)

> Mainly young black women with little trade union experience.
> (Welfare Rights Officer - male)

Others felt that NALGO itself had neither properly addressed the immediate concerns of the administrative workers, nor fully acknowledged the greater material costs incurred by these workers in taking industrial action,

> Branch officers tend not to respond to sections that are either weak or not toeing the Branch line. More could be done ... workers like them throughout the country are excluded from the union ... more needs to be done at grass-roots level otherwise it's just the union imposing things from the top.
> (Housing Advisory Worker - female)

> Union meetings are dominated by white middle-class men talking with amazing zeal about strike days when it makes no impact at all on their incomes ... the complacency and ease with which they talk about taking industrial action alienates lower paid staff ... not in that position.
> (Estate Manager - male)

> ... the cost of taking industrial action ... is obviously much greater. I think the image of the union needs to be changed where the first thing you do is stick your hand up and we're all out on strike.
> (Estate Manager - male)

The relative newness of the chief executive's department was also a factor in its union character alongside the disparate departmental background of those employed therein and the continuing occupational variations. Yet it was also suggested that a new consciousness might be emerging amongst this group of workers,

> A new department, represents lower paid workers, mainly women and it's one of the biggest challenges facing NALGO.
> (Improvements Officer - male)

> A lot of people in chief executives are from other backgrounds and haven't had that cohesion that characterised other departments ... they didn't have a department of their own.
> (Housing Advisory Officer - female)

> The old admin workers were never well organised.
> (Estate Manager - female)

I can't really represent that section even though we're based in it: the three specialist

posts of community worker, welfare rights officer and environmental health officer
were just tagged on the end ...
(Welfare Rights Officer - male)

The Chief Executives shop is emerging now after three and a half years.
(Assistant Neighbourhood Officer - male)

Finally, the low level of NALGO membership amongst the Neighbourhood Officers in
chief executives, and the consequent lack of encouragement from them to basic grade
workers to join the union, or to have time off for union matters, was also a significant
factor. Rather it was felt that the chief executives tended to be more hierarchically
organised and managerialist, making it more difficult for workers in a small office and
having personal relationships with their line managers to gain confidence and engage in
union politics. Recent changes to introduce a generic career grade were seen as
strengthening this process,

In chief executives the two managers ... neither in NALGO, one was but resigned.
There are other members that are in NALGO ... they may be members but when it
comes to doing anything, expressing anything they're very intimidated by their
position because their managers are not in NALGO. There's a lot of fear around
about jobs and job security. They can be militant if they don't get on with their line
manager. For instance in this office a lot of the admin workers get on well with
their line manager, and she's not in NALGO, and that often comes in the way of
being active. They feel that if they're not there she'll have to do it.
(Welfare Rights Officer - female)

The career grade means you can shove 'em around at will and do anything.
Promotion and advancement is now dependent on line management.
(Community Worker - male)

... it reintroduces the likelihood of discrimination.
(Administrative Officer - female)

Some do well financially but in actual fact only a certain number in any section can
be promoted and there are restrictions on how many can be promoted in any one
year.
(Administrative Officer - female)

Such departmental distinctions do not, however, reflect the full complexity of the
situation. Firstly, whilst there may be some sections with stronger traditions of
militancy, this is by no means a fixed once-and-for-all situation. Trade union
consciousness and engagement amongst different groups of workers, even with the same
employer, changes over time according to shifting circumstances. Thus in Islington it
was felt strongly that decentralisation had completely de-stabilised traditional
departmental trade union patterns. Secondly, differences were noted between
neighbourhood based workers and those centrally located, both across the Authority in
general and within specific departments. Thirdly, within any one department it is
possible that groups of workers occupying particular occupational roles will be identified
as being more involved in union politics. Fourthly, there are other groups, such as
women or black workers, who can get beyond departmental and occupational barriers
and see their interest as being more effectively represented via the politics of identity.
Fifthly, workers also came together around their membership of a political party, and
finally one needs in all instances to distinguish between the activists from any grouping
and the general membership.

As indicated earlier, decentralisation had a major impact on NALGO's organisational ability and as with other major organisational changes it had disrupted traditional patterns and relationships. One worker described it as,

A massive dislocation which we're still not coming to grips with.
(Improvements Officer - male)

Decentralisation almost pulled the rug out from under the feet of the union.   Social Worker - male)

A number of those interviewed identified the housing advisory workers as a strong occupational grouping, a view reinforced by the relatively large numbers of neighbourhood office shop stewards from this grouping,

One of the strongest sections ... They started the strike around racial harassment and then after their 14 week lock-out were still going strong.
(Occupational Therapist - female)

A very closely knit group prior to decentralisation and they appear to have kept it like that.
(Estate Manager - male)

Similarly the perceived overall strength of social services was modified by a more focused analysis,

Social services had a reputation which was more to do with field social work rather than those in administration or residential work.
(Neighbourhood Officer Chief Executives - male)

Social services are strong in the neighbourhoods but centrally there is very little organisation and you can almost guarantee they would cross the picket lines.
(Estate Manager - female)

Others questioned the perception of unified departments in other ways,

Housing is mixed. There is a division between younger people new to Islington and the old school who've worked here for many years and are dead against many things Islington stands for including equal opportunities.
(Estate Manager - male)

A number of NALGO members had come together as a result of a shared politics of identity, pressing for particular interests that bore little or no relation to either departmental or occupational structures. Known in Islington as the 'self-organised groups' these had formed around women workers, black workers, gay and lesbian workers, and Irish workers. Again such groups varied in strength and vitality over time. Commenting on the 'Black Workers Group', one black interviewee noted,

It's been in existence for six years. I don't think they've got that much input into what the union does. There are lots of groups ... some more influential than others but the black workers has not been - for example Islington removing its commitment to positive action in recruitment.
(Administrative Worker - female)

Another commented similarly, but noting a shift over time,

The best organised used to be the black members but recently they seem to be less so. Again a reflection that people in those groups do feel powerless, that they can't

achieve very much ... the self-organised groups haven't got involved in the campaign against the dropping of positive action.
(Housing Advisory Worker - female)

The importance of key people in sustaining such groups was identified by one black worker,

A lot of black workers who started at that time have actually left ... very let down by what has happened with decentralisation ... peed off with Islington.
(Community Worker - male)

Not too dissimilar were those comments made by women involved in the 'Women in NALGO' Group, although one felt positive,

There's quite a lot of strength and activity of women workers.
(Welfare Rights Officer - female)

More typical was the view expressed by one of the women Branch Executive members,

The problem is, it doesn't really function well unless there is a real issue to get stuck into ... yet the women's officer post in the Equal Opportunities Unit was cut or not filled and there is still massive discrimination in employment and promotion. There are only about eight women on the EC out of 30-35.
(Library Assistant - female)

Some of those involved in the 'Irish Workers Group' spoke more optimistically although it is noticeable that this was the one group that had both multi-union membership and crossed the manual/non-manual divide,

It goes beyond NALGO, although NALGO dominates. Nevertheless there are manual workers involved. It's used as a support group, consciousness raising. There's evidence of front line discrimination and a lack of knowledge of the position of Irish people. NALGO hasn't addressed these issues yet.
(Housing Advisory Worker - female)

According to the Branch Secretary the self-organised groups, whilst they "fluctuate in terms of numbers involved ... are starting to have an effect on how the Branch works and have developed issues such as racism and sexism". Yet the discussion on the significance of such groups in relation to the Branch also spotlighted the tensions between Branch Officers and the broad union membership. This relationship should not, however, be thought of as one-sided. One woman worker, describing an incident of pornographic material coming into the libraries, contrasted the position of the library 'old guard' who,

Couldn't see the issue and weren't willing to do anything ... or didn't think it was important,

with the immediately supportive response from the Branch Officers and the Executive Committee who were 'overwhelmingly in favour' of action. She felt that,

If any of the self-organised groups took an issue to the EC it would be supported but as soon as you move away from there it is disastrous. Others are just apathetic.
(Assistant Librarian - female)

Others were more critical of the way such groups came into existence as a consequence of a 'symbolic top-down politically correct approach', and the lack of a thorough-going policy in the Branch,

It was the EC who passed a motion in favour of setting up self-organised groups and named black workers as one of these ... there was never a groundswell of support from the bottom ... Branch officers haven't come to terms with the position of black workers: how to provide support for black workers who are harassed. Things are done on an ad hoc basis. The Branch doesn't really take much notice of self-organised groups but the groups are useful to the Branch because they can be given all the really difficult sensitive issues. Every time there's an issue of race people say let's talk to the BWG but never consult at any other time.
(Community Worker - male)

The Branch only pays lip service ... there is the overwhelming feeling that they should meet but their meetings tend to be badly attended ...
(Housing Advisory Worker - female)

The differences between the membership and the elected officers and activists were noted by a number of those interviewed in relation to Branch politics overall,

Once you get away from the EC and into the membership NALGO is basically a conservative union with a small c.
(Estate Manager - male)

NALGO's politics are hard to assess. There is a large amount of apathy in the Branch as a whole which is reflected in the low levels of turn-out at Branch meetings ... We've got a problem of a lack of stewards throughout, right across the Borough. There is a tendency for the activists to be a lot more left-wing than the membership. We come along with policy proposals which the membership doesn't necessarily disagree with but isn't prepared to act upon.
(Improvement Officer - male)

The Branch seems to take up the issues but at the end of the day most things collapse because members haven't got the will to take it further.
(Environmental Health Officer - male)

A number felt that responsibility for this state of affairs must in large part rest with the activists,

The problem is that the Branch doesn't necessarily involve the members in discussing the way forward in general. It does it very thoroughly with specific issues but doesn't have general discussions. The issues of the moment take precedence over the anticipation of problems ... large numbers have left NALGO for other unions. There was not enough of a response to those who don't want to take strike action, instead they said they were better off without them. By writing people off you reinforce the barriers that put them off in the first place. The role of leadership is not to stand on its dignity.
(Lettings Officer - male)

I'd suggest in some ways that Islington NALGO does have some things in common with the Borough ... both are concerned with what they're doing, particularly with image, not so much with getting things done but being seen to be involved ... always been an element of being very with it, up to date or even if you like, trendy ... always a problem with too much rhetoric, too much posturing, too much emphasis on showing off their position ... Although it's good to have this ... there's a conflict between them and those who aren't always aware of the issues that affect services or with the ordinary members. The union hasn't gone far in terms say of getting

more black stewards on the Executive ... *Guardian* reading types ... they're all graduates ... people much more given to giving good statements about combating racism ...
(Estate Manager - male)

A soft left Branch that thought it was hard left ... big city politics ... extremely patronising. An extremely trendy way of looking at left issues without dealing with the membership ... I think that's actually driven away a lot of members ... they've idealised what they want, structured it 'out there' and have not built anything to lead people ...
(Senior Estate Manager - male)

Large numbers didn't go to meetings. They're intimidated and feel it's always the same people, same rhetoric, same words, same big dialogue all the time ...
(Housing Advisory Officer - female)

Identity via membership of political parties was also an important factor within the Branch although there were conflicting views as to which parties were most significant numerically, strategically, and most influential in relation to the Branch membership. Of all the groups mentioned the Socialist Workers Party was most frequently cited with 40% of those interviewed acknowledging the influence of the party within the Branch leadership whilst a further 25% mentioned the role played by other organised groups,

Certain caucus groups, the SWP spring to mind, but I don't know how much influence they have. At any Branch meeting they are visible by their oral input. They're quite good orators. They're used to that sort of platform ... quite well organised. Having said that people know who they are and sometimes, even if they have a valid point, because they cried wolf once too often, they could turn people off ...
(Estate Manager - male)

Left wing groups are fairly well represented, especially the SWP.
(Occupational Therapist - female)

At shop stewards meetings SWP seem to have a strong hold ... members don't want their policies of 'all out indefinite action and bring down the council, bring down Thatcher'. They're out on a limb, not in touch with reality.
(Field Social Worker - female)

The SWP are over heavily represented in the shops. Not necessarily in terms of numbers but in terms of the power they can wield. It would seem like a deliberate policy to move in on the union.
(Social Worker - male)

Others were less certain of who was most influential,

Difficult to say ... there are political influences within the Branch but I don't see any one dominating ... the broad left is probably controlling the Branch ... people who've come up through the 70's ... who reacted against the old style CP left.
(Improvement Officer - male)

There are active factions which seem to counter each other.
(Administrative Officer - female)

Loosely speaking, it's Labour left although no particular faction dominates ... The

Branch EC is a much more mixed bunch with right-wing Labour, CP members through to Trotskyist organisations. No particular group ...
(Housing Advisory Worker - male)

In the old days it was the broad left. The SWP had a strong influence, the CP had a base, up to 81/82 it might be seen as controlling the union. Now the broad left have power. There is no clear line. A lot of people are in the Labour Party.
(Social Worker - male)

Pretty heavily influenced by left of Labour Party but in the past year that influence has diminished slightly and there has been a slight movement to the right.
(Principal Advisory Officer - female)

What we have then is a complex and uneven picture of trade union consciousness and activity across the Authority. There are certainly traditions of trade union radicalism within certain departments, but these are not fixed, their strength fluctuating over time, being vulnerable to organisational change, as well as pressures within the environment beyond the immediate workplace. Similarly, other departments do not stand still but find themselves drawn into industrial militancy again for a variety of reasons. Neither are departments homogenous but consist of a number of occupational groupings and these too have their own relationship to radicalism. Place of work can also be significant both in terms of reinforcing traditional patterns or bringing workers closer together in spite of such departmental or occupational traditions. Clearly NALGO's ability to do this in Islington's neighbourhood offices is quite crucial for its future development. Furthermore, workers are able to form interest groups that cut across occupational, departmental and workplace loyalties. In Islington such groups emerged both around political parties and a politics based on social identity. Occasionally membership of such groups might coincide with an occupational grouping so that it is difficult to determine which is in the driving seat. Thus, in Islington a significant number of Housing Advisory workers belonged to the SWP. However, only a relatively slight change in the personnel of such a small occupational group could have a significant impact on its role in Branch politics. It is important to recognise that not only is the strength and vitality of these different groups rising and falling over time and in relation to specific issues, but that the Branch should be seen not simply as a body whose members organised in different sub-groups take it in turn to occupy the leading role according to need and resources. Rather these are competing interest blocs within the same organisation, which overall is officially committed to the mutual benefit of all its members, yet whose militancy may be a source of resentment to some and whose actions may be an attempt to secure a particular political style or strategy not shared by the other blocs.

Finally, the point stressed by many of those interviewed is the divide across the Authority between the activists and the general membership. This is something which must be taken into account in any assessment of Branch militancy, but equally it cannot be properly assessed simply by taking a snapshot of union activity at any single moment, nor without relating union involvement to the wider environment in which it is operating. As one steward, aware of changing circumstances stated,

I don't know about the future ... it's not a good climate for unions. People are getting more and more squeezed financially ... thinking ... will I have a job next week, next year ... It would have to be a very good cause, people will no longer just put their hand up and go out on strike ... the better members of staff are leaving ... vacancies are not being filled, more pressure of work ... morale is very low ...

outside pressures beyond the control of the council ... we're all asking for the same
... the room for manoeuvre is shrinking.
(Estate Manager - male)

How are such overall levels of militancy within the Islington Branch to be explained?
Clearly local working conditions and national disputes have been significant, as have
management responses to particular situations and their approaches to organisational
change. However, what is equally striking is the number of those interviewed who
identified Islington as a relatively good employer, who made a positive decision to work
for the Borough and who brought with them an existing political understanding and
active engagement in political and trade union activity.

Perhaps not surprisingly, people tended to give a number of reasons for joining
Islington. Some of these were inevitably very practical, although they were often linked
to more political or ideological motivations. Practical reasons tended to focus on it
being the only job on offer, a move to a better job in terms of wages and/or working
conditions, or it being close to home,

I liked Islington's philosophy and ideas. Its decentralisation politics appealed to me.
It was also convenient: I live in the borough and am a single parent.
(Social Worker - female)

I knew a lot about Islington ... I was born here ... worked here ... knew the political
scene with my dad being a member of the Labour Party in Hornsey ... In comparison
with other London boroughs it's still got a lot going for it ... the decision making
process here ... is fairly democratic ... I knew some of the trade unionists ...
(Senior Estate Manager - male)

However, what is more striking are those who had a positive image of the Borough, or
of particular policies, who stated a preference for working in a progressive authority,
one with good employment practices,

I was impressed with Islington's political situation ... Historically it always had a
fairly progressive, militant, fairly radical reputation ... also attracted to the concept
of a small area team ... I was offered one in Hackney and turned it down.
(Social Worker - female)

... had a very good reputation for training and as a good place to work. It was a
committed department, highly interventionist.
(Environmental Health Officer - male)

Specific policies that tended to attract people were, equally, decentralisation and equal
opportunities,

When the whole idea of decentralisation was discussed it looked really exciting. For
the first time it looked as though users of services could actually control the services.
It sounded really dynamic, really interesting.
(Community Worker - male)

It seemed to be a very progressive borough and to have equal opportunities at the
forefront of its policies.
(Estate Manager - male)

Others indicated that they were looking for a Labour controlled authority and that
Islington, amongst others, fitted that description whilst perhaps offering something else
as well,

I knew a lot about the Borough having lived here for ten years. I preferred to work for a Labour left authority but under no illusions as to the reality ... although I wouldn't be working here if the Council didn't have an EO policy because I'm a registered blind person.
(Housing Advisory Worker - male)

I wanted to work for a Labour council. I was interested in ensuring it was as fair as it could be: could deliver a good service and had no great resistance to unionism.
(Occupational Therapist - female)

In addition what is also striking is the number of activists who came to the Borough with either previous trade union experience or involvement in politics, either in a political party or community-based politics. Indeed, a number of those interviewed felt that Islington had actively gone out to attract and recruit such people but many now felt disillusioned and disappointed by what they saw as the Borough's failure to live up to its reputation or pursue its policies appropriately. Thus Islington NALGO included a significant group of experienced, politically conscious and active workers attracted to, and welcomed by, the Borough, who subsequently found themselves at odds with their employer over the latter's perceived inability to live up to its reputation, to defend and promote its publicly espoused policies and its failure to manage organisational change.

Conclusion

The growth of industrial militancy in Islington NALGO illustrated in this chapter is, not surprisingly, a reflection in part of those changes taking place within the union nationally. Yet it is also in some degree an atypical Branch if Ingham's (1985) calculations on the regularity of industrial disputes in local government are accepted. Islington NALGO's militant reputation is deserved but it is also illustrative of wider trends showing how all sections of workers throughout the local authority's services were drawn into industrial action. Yet equally it demonstrates the complexity of the union, the different motivations, competing interests and conflicting politics within it. Militancy may have been a more frequent response in some departments, occupations, or localities but nearly all workers have been concerned about traditional trade union bread and butter issues of pay, working conditions, and experiences or perceptions of management.   The Islington NALGO Branch has also moved, albeit slowly and sometimes painfully, into other areas of concern, as illustrated by the 'racism' dispute and the rate-capping campaign, which are more political and reflect a changing set of union concerns and practices, and which explicitly highlight conflicts between union members, as well as in relation to management.
  Such developments vividly highlight both the uneven development of industrial militancy within the union and the still deeply held conservatism amongst significant sections of the union's membership, as well as its lack of experience and organisational failings in trying to mount and sustain such efforts. The increasingly negative reaction to the Authority's handling of industrial disputes cannot be divorced from the union's response to the decentralisation initiative occurring simultaneously. What we find in Islington, is the gradual emergence during the late 1970s, and especially the 1980s, of an industrial climate (itself a reflection in part of the national political climate) which is increasingly unconducive to the successful implementation of a radical initiative designed in some sense to offer an alternative vision to that propounded by New Right policies in the delivery of public services. However, this was not yet the case as late as 1982

when decentralisation was first introduced. Indeed there was a period of two years during which time relationships between union and employer were comparatively positive. By the mid 1980s attitudes and perceptions had again changed due to the management's handling of a series of disputes; the influential role played by politically experienced and committed members who had been drawn to the Borough, and indeed welcomed by it, but who became increasingly disappointed with this and other politically similar authorities' unwillingness to pursue particular strategies and tactics thought to be appropriate by the activists; the union's inability to break free from traditional trade unionism; and the significantly reduced amount of manoeuvrability open to both the Authority and the union. We shall return to these issues after first looking at the decentralisation strategy and the overall approach of the new urban left.

7 Decentralisation in Islington

The last chapter examined the development of the urban left, the place of decentralisation within this broad strategy, and the relative progress made in implementing the programme. We shall now go on to explore in some detail the decentralisation initiative in the London Borough of Islington, a Borough controlled politically after 1982 by Labour Party Bennite councillors. However, something first needs to be said about the emergence of the urban left in the Borough before examining the decentralisation proposals and describing the implementation process. The major objectives within the policy and their relationship to other similar initiatives are also explored. The process of negotiating with the workforce is examined and the major areas of conflict with NALGO identified. Consideration is then given to some of the initial evaluative work that has been carried out on the development of the policy within the Borough. Finally, we consider some of the shifts in emphasis that began to emerge from 1987 following the defeat of the Labour Party in the general election of that year, the earlier defeat of the rate-capping campaign, and the abolition of the GLC and the metropolitan county councils.

The Borough of Islington

The London Borough of Islington lies just north of central London, with Haringey to the north, Camden to the west, Hackney to the east and the City of London to the south. Its population of 165,000 is small relative to other London boroughs, and is in slight decline (1991 Census), but its population density per hectare remains the highest in the capital. The population is multi-racial with 71% of the population described as white UK, 10.6% Afro-Caribbean, 5.8% Asian, 4% Cypriot, and 7.5% Irish. Within the borough the majority of the black and ethnic minorities live within the central and northern wards whilst a traditional white working class dominate the southern areas. Islington has two Parliamentary constituencies, both of which are held by the Labour Party. Fifty-two Borough councillors, who stand for election every four years, represent the 20 wards in the Borough. In the May 1990 local elections, Labour won all but three of the seats.

Islington is among the ten most deprived local authority areas in the UK ranked by the Department of the Environment using 1981 Census data, and was designated as an inner city partnership area in 1978. According to a 1989 MORI survey (MORI 1989), of the 755 wards in the Greater London region in 1981, ranked according to four census indicators of deprivation, the most deprived ward in Islington (Thornhill) was ranked 42nd, whilst the least deprived (Canonbury West) was ranked 239th. As many as 16 of the Borough's 20 wards were ranked among the 100 wards between numbers 72 and 172, and according to MORI, only the Borough of Hackney displayed such a concentration of deprivation. MORI suggests that approximately 33% of the Borough's population experiences severe material deprivation.

Over half of the Borough's homes are rented from the Council, which according to a Policy Studies Institute report (1986) was the fourth highest proportion of council-owned property in inner London, whilst a further 19% rent from either housing associations or private landlords. The PSI report also noted that some 9000 households were on the Council's general waiting list, equivalent to over 20% of the total permanent housing stock. A further 8000 households were reported as being on the transfer list. Less than one third of Islington's households either own outright or have a mortgage on a house or flat. Unemployment in the Borough, in the late 1980s was close to 20%, although this did decline to 11% (March 1990), and it has lower average annual incomes per household in comparison with the whole of Greater London.

The Authority has a reputation of providing good quality services and in 1990, before the educational services in the Borough, previously undertaken by ILEA, were transferred to it, was spending approximately £190m per annum, or £1,535 per adult. Moreover, the 1989 MORI survey discovered that 44% of Islington's residents were satisfied with the way the Council was running the Borough, which compared well with other inner city local authorities, although it did note that those who experienced relatively high material deprivation were less satisfied with the Council than were those who were better off.

The decentralisation initiative

The Labour Party's local election manifesto of that year outlined a strategy which closely fitted the emergent urban left analysis and programmatic response. The decentralisation and the democratisation of public services were seen as an important element to the Borough's approach, within a general commitment of opposition to Thatcher government. Islington's decentralisation policy was and remains one of the most extensive and radical of all the multi-service decentralisation schemes (Heery, 1984; Burns, Hambleton and Hoggett, 1994). Hoggett saw it as, "the most radical in terms of its scope, scale and complexity ... closest to what I would see as a real socialist experiment within British local government" (Hoggett 1988, pp 226-227). The new Labour Council elected in 1982 introduced the decentralisation policy both to improve service provision and to extend the level of democratic control over services. The approach, which was to emerge during that first year in office, involved the decentralisation of housing services, non-residential social services, environmental health, welfare rights, and community development, along with an associated repair team. These were relocated into 24 neighbourhood offices, each serving an average population of 6500, in neighbourhoods that reflected, as far as possible, local community perceptions. Each office was also to provide a range of community facilities and resources to be made available to local neighbourhood community organisations.

The first four of these neighbourhood offices were opened in March 1985 and the last one in March 1987. It was intended that as far as possible workers in the neighbourhood offices would function in multi-service generic teams, and that old departmental boundaries would evaporate, although to date this has yet to be fully realised. The full cost of the decentralisation programme has never been explicitly stated although the capital cost was around £10m, as many of the 24 neighbourhood offices were purpose built, each costing on average some £450,000.

Alongside each of the 24 neighbourhood offices there was to be an equivalent Neighbourhood Forum, comprising local councillors, service users, representatives from neighbourhood based community and voluntary organisations and staff employed in the local Neighbourhood Office. The Forums were seen as the means for the extension of local democracy. Their main purposes were identified as: deliberating on the priority of work for staff within their neighbourhood office; monitoring and making recommendations on the quality and level of service being provided in the neighbourhood, either through the neighbourhood office or otherwise; drawing up plans for local projects, the expenditure for which would be met from a local budget; and commenting on Council plans for the neighbourhood. Ultimately, it was the Council's intention to devolve local budgets down to the neighbourhood level and to give increasing powers to the Forums.

The roots of the policy: ideological or pragmatic?

The Islington Labour Party's concern with both localisation and public participation go back to the 1970s, long before the urban left began to influence strategic thinking, even though Smith (1980) notes the existence of a "new guard" of young middle class members having an edge within the local party by 1971. Such early initiatives were somewhat limited. They were usually concerned with only one service activity, often social services or housing. The participation strategies tended to be restricted to consultation, "the participation by the public in the discussions that lead to council decisions". However, the main achievement, according to Smith, was a much strengthened voluntary and community groups sector, supported and developed by the Council's grant-aid programme, often in order to provide direct services, and the Authority's recruitment of community workers (Smith 1981). In some ways this can be seen as preparing the way for what was to come in the 1980s for without this ground clearing exercise, and the strengthening of the middle class groups in the local political culture, the urban left may have found it considerably more difficult to establish their dominance in a borough that historically was a traditional working class stronghold.

Labour's control of the Borough was interrupted at the end of the decade by the defection of a number of right-wing councillors to the Social Democratic Party. Yet when, in 1982, the voters were given their first opportunity to indicate their reactions to these developments, and their experience of the SDP in office, they evicted every one of them and returned another Labour administration with 51 out of 52 seats. The new Council whilst sympathetic to the politics of the urban left, was also one that was very inexperienced in public office. Its approach, according to its leader Margaret Hodge, was to be in sharp contrast to earlier Labour "Tammary Hall" style administrations which were noted for their "low rates, low spending, and low rents", had a loathing for the voluntary sector, and were "exceedingly racist", especially in housing policies, which were "deliberately framed to exclude Blacks" (interview 1991).

The urban left had gradually acquired a dominant position within the Borough.

Initially, the defeat of the Party in 1968 provided the opportunity for "new young professionals to grasp control. There was a massive amount of talent in the early 1970s" (Hodge 1991). This group was viewed by the indigenous white working class as "outsiders", with no working class links or local traditions, and it was this conflict between the young professionals and the working class which, according to Hodge, led to the right-wing defection to the SDP who took many white working class votes with them. Although Hodge felt that this working class support had largely returned by the end of the decade there remained, "a strong tenants movement in parts of the Borough that is anti the Labour leadership". By the end of the decade Hodge and the Labour leadership were to make an explicit attempt to mobilise support from this sector against those previously identified as allies within the overall urban left strategy.

The 74-page election Manifesto of the incoming 1982 Council spoke of a new relationship between the electorate and council and firm opposition to the Conservative government. It stated that,

> Decision-making must be based on discussions across the Borough ... There is a need to give fresh impetus to breaking down the bureaucratic isolation of much of the Council's activity. Involving more people will lead to services that more closely reflect needs, are better run, and have stronger support in the community (p 1).

It went on to stress the need for improved relations with the trade unions and then identified decentralisation, although the details were suitably ambiguous, as a key strategy in its approach. It proclaimed that,

> Effective involvement of the community at large cannot be secured if the great majority of decisions are taken centrally. All service departments must be decentralised with local area teams or local facilities under a substantial degree of local management. The role of the Council will be to set the overall framework in terms of minimum standards, finance, responsibilities as employer and co-ordination (p 2).

It is, however, of some note that in Islington the desire to extend and devolve decision-making was more pragmatically motivated than in some other authorities. In Islington it was the relationship between greater user and citizen participation, and more effective service delivery, that was crucial rather than a commitment to the extension of citizen democracy per se. As Hodge (1988) stated,

> There are ideological reasons for undertaking decentralisation. In the Islington context these are important but secondary ... Our motives were highly pragmatic, concerned with the efficiency and co-ordination of the services we provide ... to overcome the anonymity of services, to change them in a more sensitive and personalised direction (p 32).

Thus whilst believing that local government was in crisis (Hodge, p 29), the primary task in local government was to "reclaim the legitimacy that such an institution had in the past", a slightly different emphasis from having a vision of a future socialist local democracy. The key task was to create a sense of solidarity around a number of policy areas, and based on opposition to Thatcherism, across the borough. However, in a subsequent interview Hodge argued that decentralisation was nevertheless, "a focus for change" although one that was, "different from ... the 1970s which was about spending more" (1991). She also maintained that in the early discussions on decentralisation, "it was far more about empowerment than about service delivery". However, it was the pragmatic approach that was shared by the Assistant Decentralisation Co-Ordinator who stated,

> It's absolutely pointless doing it if you didn't demonstrably improve the service to
> the public. They could be consulted, it could be perfectly democratic but if they're
> lousy services ... there is no point in doing it.

Similarly, a paper written by the then Co-Ordinator of the Unit, Liz Du Parq (1987),
stressed the relatively conservative objectives in decentralisation: greater physical and
social accessibility, co-ordinated and integrated services, and greater accountability of
services and service providers to representative neighbourhood forums, who control
resource allocation and influence service delivery. Such ambitions are indeed radical in
comparison with what was common practice in local government, and in relation to all
state provided services. Nevertheless, it still remains a circumscribed agenda, and one
that does not envisage a transformation of political relationships, or a bringing onto the
agenda issues that had been previously suppressed. They were radical proposals but
within a familiar pattern. Nevertheless, the extension of democratic forms always has
its risks and need to be managed by those wishing to control events. It is, therefore,
perhaps of no small significance that, for example, the issue of non-collection of the Poll
Tax was never a topic for discussion within the Forums. Similarly, in a review of the
Forums in 1990, the different constituencies comprising the Forums were kept apart for
the purposes of the evaluation (Islington 1990).

The policy process

Islington Labour Party began the process of devising its decentralisation strategy before
its election in 1982, and two small working groups with a focus on the manifesto made
some preliminary investigations into progress in other authorities, which included a day
trip to Walsall. One of the participants in the manifesto group and beneficiary of the
day's outing, Maurice Barnes, was to become the moving force behind the
decentralisation policy, even though he was opposed initially by Hodge and the more
senior councillors, and only won the lead role position by one vote out of some 90.
Hodge stated in interview that she felt it was "wrong for someone coming out of a local
government officer job" to have such a post, and was uncertain whether Barnes "had a
clear political direction ... he was far more about managing" (Hodge 1991).

Following the election of the new leadership, the Labour Party, with just ten of their
51 councillors having served on the Council before, and some such as the Chair of
Planning having, in his words, been "elected by accident", immediately had the powerful
Policy and Resources Committee establish a sub-committee on decentralisation. This
was chaired by Barnes and comprised committed back benchers, and the chairs of main
service committees. In addition, they set up a Decentralisation Officer Working Group
(May 1982), led by the Director of Recreation with hand-picked individuals making up
the membership. The third element of the strategy was to establish a Decentralisation
Working Party within the local Labour Party, comprising one representative from each
ward. Barnes was to use this as a means of communication with the wards and hoped
that the party would be able to bring the three powerful forces of councillors, senior
officers and trade unions together.

The officers involved in the planning process were given 50% of their time to work
on the decentralisation proposals, and one day a week was given over to strategic
meetings. They were soon to second on a full-time basis two senior officers, one each
from Housing and Social Services, and recruited four Neighbourhood Support Workers.

No minutes were kept of their weekly meetings for according to the Chair, "if we were to work as a team everyone had to trust each other, and if we decided on something then we weren't going to be caught up by the exact wording ..." (interview). They worked to a tight time-table as fundamental decisions of principle had to be ready by September 1982,

> The time-table was quite clear, we had to have every office in place by the time of the next election and there would be no pilot schemes.
> (Interview: Chair of Working Group and subsequently Chair of Neighbourhood Service Unit).

The aim was to have the first neighbourhood offices open by June 1984, following an extensive consultation process in early 1983. However, unlike Hackney there was to be no blank sheet to be filled in. Barnes stated in interview that he was "horrified" by what he saw of the consultation process in the neighbouring borough. Islington would consult on the basis of a clear view of how many offices they wanted, which services were to be included, and the basis of the neighbourhood boundaries.

In October 1982 the Borough published, "Decentralisation - the Brief for Consultation" in which they put forward for consultation three possible levels for the number of offices: 34-36, 22-24, and ten. It also listed the services to be decentralised which covered: housing, environmental health (part), welfare rights, community work, social services (field and domiciliary), along with administrative support. At the end of the consultation process, in April 1983, the Council decided that it would proceed with the same services plus the area repair services. It agreed to have between 23-25 offices which would be opened on a phased basis, the first four to be ready by June 1984. Subject to a management review of the initial phase, they would then establish the organisational and staffing levels for the remaining offices. Consultation with the public took the form of public meetings, "nearly 100 public meetings were held in three months" (Islington 1986), and via the Council's bulletin, "Neighbourhood News" which was produced regularly and distributed widely throughout the borough. For the workforce, there were both workplace meetings and formal negotiations with the trade unions. The latter was initially via the Joint Trade Union Committee (JTUC), but following the first management services report in December 1983, 'Decentralisation One', on organisational and staffing proposals for the first four offices, this changed to negotiation with the separate unions. Conflicts and tensions were almost immediately apparent and the whole negotiation process took two and a half years before it could be said to have moved into a more stable set of relationships characteristic of employee-employer bargaining.

Opposition from NALGO

From the outset NALGO felt pressurised and complained about the short time, initially 15 days, which was later extended by a further 15, by which the Council expected a reasoned response. NALGO viewed the initial report, 'Decentralisation One' as, 'inadequate in all respects' (NALGO 1986, p 2), and embarked upon its own consultation process with its membership, as well as requesting clarification and further information from the management. It was not until April 1984 that formal negotiations on the report began. NALGO raised a number of concerns which included: the absence of any receptionists in the proposals; the level of administrative support; the high property ratios for estate managers; the small numbers of social workers to be located in each office, which they said would lead to inadequate duty services; and a lack of supervisory staff. At subsequent meetings the Authority made some concessions around the receptionists and administrative support and pressed NALGO to agree to the advertising of 16 senior posts for the first four offices, which the union refused to give.

In the event, the Authority decided to proceed with the appointments of all posts, which then became the subject of an official national boycott by NALGO. The union also registered an official dispute with the Greater London Whitley Council over an alleged breach of agreements by the Council on decentralisation, some procedural agreements, and equal opportunities policies. Tension was further increased when the Council Working Party accepted all 65 of the recommendations of the management review report, whereas NALGO challenged 40 of these. It was not until September 1984 that the boycott on the posts was lifted following intervention by the Whitley Council, which as far as NALGO was concerned (NALGO 1986) had been generally favourable to them,

We had achieved better staffing arrangements in Housing, Housing Benefits and Environmental Health, with much improved job descriptions (p 3).

NALGO nevertheless felt there remained, "substantial areas of difference especially in Social Services" both in relation to philosophy of approach and the proposed number of workers.

In November 1984 the Branch AGM agreed that the Authority's proposals on Social Services were unacceptable, but that the four offices could proceed without social services staff if that was necessary. This was ultimately what happened, as negotiations on the position of social services took a further six months. These resulted in increased staffing levels in both basic grade and senior social work staff. However, the outcome left other workers feeling that social services had secured the best deal, and created a sense of resentment, not only because of their better material position but also because they were seen by some as setting themselves apart from the other workers, and joining the neighbourhood staff only after some of the initial opening problems had been tackled.

Negotiations with NALGO continued into the second phase of implementation, and it is clear that both sides used the decentralisation policy to extract as much as they could from the other in relation to a whole series of only indirectly related matters (a point acknowledged in Islington's "Going Local" booklet, p.8). Thus, Barnes stated that the Council refused to expand under-fives provision until the decentralisation agreement with the unions had been reached, describing this as "a useful bargaining counter" (interview with colleague). The union also felt that the Council employed a similar tactic in 1985 over their claims on the extension of equal opportunities provision. For their part, NALGO closed the Neighbourhood Offices for five weeks with strike action immediately after the opening of the second phase of the implementation process, in July 1985, over a dispute on the implementation of the equal opportunities policy. On the other hand, a motion to boycott all work on the decentralisation initiative during a strike over the pay and conditions of the council's nursery workers, was rejected by the Branch Executive, although this may have been more tactical than a matter of principle.

Maurice Barnes (Community Action 1984), reflecting on this period of negotiation with the unions regretted NALGO's traditional stance of neutrality towards the policy objectives, reacting solely to the practicalities of the proposals. In interview with a colleague he stated that it was right that a number of concessions had been made, particularly around the increase in social work staffing, although acknowledged that the major concession had been to maintain specialisms rather than the preferred strategy of greater genericism. The Assistant Co-Ordinator for the Decentralisation Unit felt somewhat stronger arguing that,

... people were dressing up their own professional arguments and issues in trade union terms, making them trade union issues when they really weren't ... very little to do with terms and conditions but with professional issues ... very much finding reasons to resist it.
(interview)

The Borough's own booklet, 'Going Local' commented that, "The essential conservatism of local government professionals had to be recognised" (p 7), a comment echoed by Hodge (1988) who stated,

The greatest resistance from our trade unions came from social services ... partly to do with their professionalism ... see themselves as slightly superior ... even the most radical local government officers are afraid of change (p 33).

Heery (1984) writing before the first neighbourhood offices were opened felt that NALGO had been "wary and defensive" (p 58) which was he felt, a disappointing response for a Council who, he believed, wanted to draw the unions "into open-ended and informal discussions on how best decentralisation could be affected ... keen to hold workplace meetings ... (and) hoped to replace the conventional adversarial system of industrial relations with a more altruistic relation between employer and trade union." Heery, amongst others, felt that the problem lay with the unions who,

Refused to countenance such a change in the nature of industrial relations ... insisted that all discussions ... be conducted within formal meetings headed by senior trade union representatives ... (were) keen to bargain over the proposals ... (and) extract concessions (p 58).

NALGO nevertheless believed there were a number of substantial aspects of the policy that required further consideration. These included: the potential deterioration in working conditions; the consequences of increased workloads without a concomitant increase in the workforce; the impact of flexible working; the implications of greater direct public control at the neighbourhood level; and the need to be clear about lines of accountability. Whilst writers such as Heery do not suggest that it is unreasonable for a trade union to raise such matters in the interests of its members, they nevertheless see the unions as a hindrance and obstacle to the development of such progressive policies. Thus for Heery,

In Islington, the trade unions, in acting vigorously to defend their members' interests, have operated as a rather conservative force ... the corporate interests of local government workers may well frustrate and stand in the way of radical reform even when the changes proposed lie in the interest of the wider working class (p 60).

Clearly, there is always a tension with any policy proposal that promises a new set of relationships or structures, but where the parties are required to negotiate that change using what are felt to be outmoded or faulty mechanisms and processes. This is so even when the outcome is felt desirable by all concerned which was not necessarily the case with decentralisation. In addition to an appropriate amount of time and a suitable setting, to have any opportunity of success, a reflective consciousness of the process being undertaken is required, along with a vision of the desired future state, as much as a concern for the detailed content of any proposal. The pressure felt by the young council for a speedy implementation and the genuine anxiety within the union were not, however, conducive to establishing the right setting for such a change despite both sides sharing many of the desired outcomes.

Putting the neighbourhood structures in place

Islington managed to stick very closely to its original time-table for localisation, so much so that by the 1986 elections all but two of the proposed offices were functioning and the final office opened in March 1987, "a remarkable achievement by any standard" (Hambleton 1989). The Assistant Co-Ordinator for the Decentralisation Unit acknowledged that it had indeed been a speedy implementation process resulting in, "loads of problems to be sorted out, teething problems and raggy edges. ..." However, this had been both deliberate and in some respects worthwhile for as he stated,

> Quite deliberate, whilst we've got the money, the political backing ... look at all the other authorities trying to do it by producing 100 page reports and getting nowhere.

What emerged was a dual strategy, which combined the localisation of services with some extension of neighbourhood democracy, and which was in reality to be implemented in broadly three over-lapping phases, although this had not been planned as such at the outset. However, little had been achieved by 1986 in relation to the extension of local democracy, or even more generic working, and whilst Islington had engaged in substantial negotiations with the unions major conflicts remained.

The policy adopted by the Authority was to create 24 multi-service neighbourhood offices, 16 of which were to be purpose built, whilst the remaining eight were rehabilitations of existing Council offices, producing an overall capital expenditure bill of £10 million. Each neighbourhood office was to serve an average population of 6500 and, according to 'Going Local' (p 3) each area had "similar characteristics, particularly the type of housing, the range of ethnic minorities and levels of affluence." However, the MORI research study (MORI 1988) into the Borough highlighted significant differences between the designated neighbourhoods, particularly in relation to housing tenure, the black and ethnic characteristics, income levels and economic activity rates.

In each of the offices there would be the full range of services for each of the decentralised services. Initially, services continued to be managed by the departmental line manager with a Neighbourhood Officer being appointed for Social Services, Housing and Chief Executives. The latter had responsibility for community work, welfare rights and the administrative workers, who were to provide the administrative back-up for all the service providers in the neighbourhood office. A receptionist was appointed for each office although other workers from the Chief Executives, but not the other service departments, also undertook reception duties. As well as providing accommodation and appropriate space for the various professional and administrative staff, the neighbourhood offices were designed to offer waiting areas for the public, areas for children to play, vending machines, public telephones, public toilets, meeting rooms for community use and access to a variety of reprographic materials. There was also to be a secure cash office at which one could pay one's rent, other bills and even at one stage cash cheques. It was envisaged that each office would be, "administratively self-sufficient and capable of dealing locally with requests for housing repairs, rent payments, administration of housing benefits, lettings and transfers and welfare benefits advice" (Going Local, p 27). To do this each office was equipped with its own computer processing terminal feeding into a centrally based mainframe.

In order to deliver this structure, and as a result of the negotiations with the trade unions, the Authority stated that 12 new posts were created to provide welfare rights advice, the community development section was increased, and 16 additional area improvement officers were appointed along with 20 extra housing advisory staff, 25 estate managers, 30 new social workers and 60 administrative staff. According to the Assistant Decentralisation Co-Ordinator, "a lot of people did well ... we've had a slow climb up the salary scales". Going Local (Islington 1986) mentioned in passing (p 10) that as much as £500,000 could have been saved if they had decided to open 22 rather than 24 offices and "this might not have seriously affected service provision", a comment which takes on greater importance in 1990 when, as a result of expenditure cuts, it was proposed that the Neighbourhood Offices be reduced to 20.

The layout and design, especially of those purpose-built offices were meant to be bright, lively, cheerful and welcoming. This was to be done not only through the use of modern comfortable furniture and fittings, including a profusion of plants and greenery, but also by way of the open-plan design so that there would be no physical barriers between the public and the staff and no obvious distinctions, barriers or demarcations between different groups of workers. From my own visits to the different offices it is possible to say that first impressions would suggest that much of this was achieved, so much so that it was difficult in some instances to distinguish users from workers, as it was to physically distinguish, through those obvious hallmarks of status dress and style, the various grades of seniority amongst the workforce. For Hoggett (1988),

> For those of us with a thorough grounding in the traditional assumptions of local government the experience of wandering around one of these new offices is positively breathtaking (p 227).

As will be seen in Chapter Eight, a more detailed inspection reveals the persistence of more familiar differentials and categorisations. Nevertheless, the aim, as stated in 'Going Local', was

> When designing the buildings to ensure that the finish was of a high standard to make them comfortable and welcoming to the public, and that the furnishings and colour schemes created a warm and friendly environment (p 11).

It was intended then that the offices would not only be within walking distance for everyone in the borough (it is estimated that no one has more than a ten minute walk to their local office), but that they would come to be seen as, "an integral part of the life of the area they serve ... community resources" (Islington 1986, p 3). The first four offices were opened in early 1985, with the majority following later that year, and the final grouping coming in 1986. During this period (1982-87) the central objective had been to re-organise and improve the service provision, localising both services and workers. Little emerged from the objective to extend local democracy, although the Authority had declared its intention to establish 24 Neighbourhood Forums in parallel with each of the offices.

In 1984 the Council produced a consultation paper, 'Setting Up Advisory Councils in Decentralised Areas'. This reaffirmed their desire to see greater local participation at the neighbourhood level but continued to speak cautiously about the establishment of "a variety of advisory forums, some of which, in time, could evolve into decision-making Neighbourhood Councils". Following consultation in each of the 24 areas on how such ideas might be developed, a local conference was organised in October 1985, attended by approximately 300 people, at which the issue of participatory tokenism was raised and the Council began to acknowledge the need to devolve decision-making downwards if they were to convince existing community organisations that there was some point to their involvement in this process.

Extending local democracy

Following the conference, the Decentralisation Co-Ordination Unit, itself set up in August 1985, developed a set of guidelines and model constitution for the proposed Forums. The Guidelines stated that the

> Forums will be an essential element in the decentralisation programme as a means of devolving power as well as services. Their primary purpose will be to enable local people to express their views to the Council and to other authorities and organisations. They should encourage people to feel more responsible for their neighbourhoods (p 2).

The paper outlined the power of the Forums to spend money on local environmental improvements and the communal areas of council estates; submit proposals for additions to the rolling programmes of Partnership expenditure; give their views to the relevant Council committee about other spending, the need for capital projects, and local revenue allocations; decide on how Council-run community resources in the area should be used; speak for the local neighbourhood on any aspect of Council policy; and build links with bodies outside the Council, so as to influence their policies and practices.

Ward councillors were to be non-voting members of the Forum and any but the most junior workers in the immediate Neighbourhood Office were excluded from membership. The guidelines encouraged involvement, in a non-voting capacity, of those who worked but did not live in the neighbourhood, and laid down criteria for the designation of 'recognised' bona fide community organisation. These required them to be based in the neighbourhood, agree to the Authority's Equal Opportunities Policy, be non-profit making, non-political, demonstrate that regularly advertised meetings were held, and have at least ten members. Borough-wide groups were required to themselves de-centralise, adopting the same criteria as other local groups, if they wished to be part of the Forum structure, otherwise they would be invited to attend neighbourhood Forum meetings as and when a relevant item appeared on the agenda.

In addition, the guidelines, in an attempt to legislate for the participation of previously under-represented groups set aside two reserved places for the following categories: young people under 21; ethnic minorities; people with disabilities; women with caring responsibilities; and people of pensionable age. The process by which these "sections" were to be represented was to be left to each Forum. Three methods of selection for the membership are possible - election, nominations from local groups, or a mixture of both. The majority of Forums have section "representatives", nominated group members, elected individuals, ward members, plus any co-opted members. The Council must agree to the adopted constitution of any Forum before it can be recognised and local consultations are required before the establishment of a Forum. In the case of the Gillespie Neighbourhood Forum, approved in 1988, the constitution took account of there being 25 elected individuals from the neighbourhood, with each elected person representing approximately 200 electors organised on a street or council estate basis; 17 section representatives (two people each from the young people's section, people of pensionable age, and women with caring responsibilities, three people with disabilities, and eight from the black and ethnic minorities section); along with a variable number of group members.

Islington's Labour Party Manifesto for the 1986 local election underlined the Party's commitment to the Forums stating that,

> Neighbourhood Forums will be the bodies responsible for deciding on and monitoring the structure and delivery of services to all sections of the community in the local neighbourhood area ... The 1986-90 Labour Council will make every effort to encourage local people to participate
> (quoted in Hambleton 1989, p 29).

The first meeting of a Forum took place in July 1986 and 23 were reported to be meeting regularly by December 1990. However, a review of their progress, carried out by the Borough, in May 1989, identified four major weaknesses to their operation. Firstly, it was acknowledged, and my own research confirmed this, that many officers did not take Forums seriously. Secondly, there was felt a need that Forums should have a say in local staffing matters, something which my research found trade unionists to be strongly against. Thirdly, the relationships with the Direct Labour Organisation were felt to be problematic. Fourthly, the absence of decentralised area budgets and area based budgetary information, severely restricted the powers of the Forums.

Islington's attempts to extend representative and direct democracy represented one of the most sophisticated efforts of the new urban left to draw in new constituencies, service users and local citizens into the decision-making processes of the local state. Consequently, their efforts have highlighted some of the difficulties involved in attempting to apply the theory of democratisation. Khan's research (1989) suggested that Islington's Forums had so far failed to secure a position of significant influence, partly because centralised departments saw them as marginal, and elected members demonstrated a reluctance to reconsider matters of policy that had been referred to them by the Forums. He also notes that the areas of service provision, which had been the main preoccupation of the officers, had not always coincided with the priorities of the Forum membership, and that conversely officers have been hesitant about raising matters that may result in the services being criticised. Additionally, he found that the Forums had had only limited success in attracting sufficient levels of interest from the five designated sections, with no Forum having achieved the minimum of two representatives from all sections. Where people had come forward, Khan suggests, they have represented a narrow banding in relation to social class, employment, and age, and that a large percentage were already, "established activists" (p 13).

Khan's research would further suggest that, to date, the Forums have been plagued by all the old organisational problems in such matters as being overly formalised, dominated by a small number of vocal people, and having little direction in their discussions which tended to focus on a narrow range of issues. Taylor's work (1986) with the Newcastle and Sheffield Tenants Federations seems to bear this out. She comments that, "There seems to be little understanding of how to involve tenants in local authority processes" (p 129). The tenants interviewed complained of decision-making processes being inaccessible and incomprehensible, agendas and papers being unavailable or presented too late for adequate preparation, whilst experienced public speakers, usually from the council, dominated the discussion, using a language that was difficult to grasp. Khan does point to some examples of what he describes as 'progressive forums', which included the use of translators, social evenings for specific ethnic groups, organised creches or babysitting, Chairs being elected on a rotating basis, agendas being more open, separate sub-groups being organised within individual Forums, and the attempts by some to establish power bases independent of the authority. More specifically, Canver and Yaylali (1987) argue that the relationship between the Islington Forums and the black and ethnic minority organisations was not always clear, as the latter did not see themselves as being primarily neighbourhood based, nor did they always operate on a membership basis, and often had a "more casual and temporary contact with members of their community" (p 7). Thus the Forum structures appeared both less relevant and did not meet their needs. They conclude that whilst the major decisions continued to be made centrally, it was inevitable that community groups sought to have a say in those central bodies and therefore had less time for work in specific localities. At an Islington conference in December 1986 on, 'Decentralisation: Black Needs, Black Concerns', similar points were made and it was recommended that the Borough establish district committees, made up of several Forums and concerned with wider issues that cut across the neighbourhood boundaries, which would then feed directly into the Neighbourhood Services Sub-Committee. Given the current developments to strengthen the role of that body, the need for community based structures that transcend the limitations of geography seems even more pressing. The Conference Report went on to argue that the Forum constitution simply mirrored the Council structure which might place some white groups at an advantage and may not be seen as appropriate to some black groups. In addition some basic needs had been neglected, such as the provision of interpreters or papers written in a variety of languages, or the possibility that the use of the electoral register as a criteria for voting rights may exclude a number of black people who were nevertheless resident in the borough.

A second survey (Islington 1991) carried out in June 1990, however, spoke of "impressive" results that demonstrated, "how successful the Forums have been in attracting and retaining a large number of people on a regular basis" (p 1). It noted that 667 people were members of Forums, 558 of whom regularly attended meetings. However, whilst there was found to be an equal proportion of men and women attending, the figures for black and ethnic minority members showed that they were half as likely to attend Forum meetings as white UK members. Young people were also significantly under-represented whilst conversely there was an over-representation from people in the 40 to 60 age range and in the over 60 category.

These results reflect quite an achievement both in securing a better representative fit with the local population, and one considerably better than that found amongst elected local government members, as well as extending the number of people who are involved over a lengthy period of time in local affairs (Burns, Hambleton, Hoggett, 1994). Nevertheless, in an interview (1989), the former Chairperson of the Neighbourhood Services Sub-Committee acknowledged that they had not proceeded far enough in relation to extending local democracy,

> That's the one we haven't grasped, the most crucial issue that we haven't resolved ... We fudged it and the fudge is about a divergence between socialists who are essentially centralists and those who are localists, and we haven't resolved it in the Party and in the group.

Similarly, the Assistant Co-Ordinator for Decentralisation commented that in order to move forward in this area,

> You've got to dismantle the present political and committee structure on which reputations and power bases are made. People don't want to give that up.

The dawning of a new realism

Thus the period 1986-89 can be seen as the second phase of the decentralisation policy in Islington where the emphasis was on developing neighbourhood democracy. A third phase, began to emerge in 1989 with the Borough's service quality programme, and notable changes were introduced in 1990 following the local elections in which Labour won all but three seats.

The newly elected Labour Group moved rapidly to introduce some significant changes to the internal organisational structures of the neighbourhood offices, including the requirement that officers attend Forum meetings. A new single Neighbourhood Services structure replaced the previously separate Housing, Social Services and Chief Executives departments. Each neighbourhood office is now managed by a generalist neighbourhood manager who is to be responsible for all the services provided from the office, for working with the local Forums and for the drawing-up of Neighbourhood Action Plans. Although it was agreed to retain the 24 offices, 16 were brought together for purposes of management. Parallel changes took place at the committee level with the formation of a new Neighbourhood Services Committee. Since 1992, two Forum chairs have been co-opted, as non-voting members, onto the Committee. In addition, regular meetings take place between all the Forum chairs and the chair of the Neighbourhood Services Committee.

Some writers have seen these developments as an extension to the already bold strategy to extend local democracy, and a re-establishment of the momentum following a falling off of political enthusiasm in the late 1980s (Burns, Hambleton, Hoggett, 1994). No doubt such changes, which are considerable when compared with the structure of other authorities, do reflect a genuine commitment on the part of elected members and some officers to widen the democratic base across the Borough and devolve more power to influence decisions down to the neighbourhood level. However, the specific form of these have taken can only be fully understood by taking account of political developments both within the Authority and at the national level.

It is, however, important to acknowledge that Islington has regularly attempted to monitor its success in improving services following decentralisation. Thus in 1987 MORI carried out a study on service provision and living standards in Islington (MORI 1988). This noted that 44% of the Borough's residents were satisfied with the way the Council was running the Borough, although almost a third were dissatisfied, and those residents experiencing relatively high material deprivation, and therefore more likely to be using the services of the neighbourhood offices, were less satisfied than were their better-off counterparts. Seventy-one per cent of residents knew the location of their nearest neighbourhood office. However, 16% did not know the location and a further 13% were thought by the researchers to have given incorrect answers. Given the amount of publicity around the neighbourhood offices and the close proximity of residents to them, it was somewhat alarming that nearly 30% either acknowledged they did not know the location or gave incorrect locations.

Just over half (53%) of the Borough's residents had used a neighbourhood office at some point, although the usage rate varied from 35% to 65%. The vast majority (80%) were satisfied with the treatment they had received when visiting, although in five of the offices the dissatisfaction rate rose to one in five. Significantly, the main criticisms identified were the negative attitudes or inefficiency of the staff and the slow speed of service. Further, the satisfaction rate dropped to 60% when they considered the result of their contact. The main reason for dissatisfaction was the absence of anything being done (over 51% of the dissatisfied identified this), followed by a slow response or long delay (29%). Both may be explained by either an absence of resources, or considerable pressure on existing resources, as well as possibly suggesting serious inefficiency. It is interesting, however, that some 25% additionally specified inefficiencies in the treatment they received suggesting that the other figure related to resourcing problems. Margaret

Hodge, however, chose to interpret the MORI research as meaning that Islington workers were "nice but inefficient" (1989) and who were "unable to deliver a high quality service". She went on to suggest that elected members shared some of the responsibility for this by failing to challenge the conservative professionalism of the staff, and not sufficiently acknowledging the conflict of interests between the workers, on the one hand, and the councillors and consumers on the other. She felt that the unions, "treat us as they would Fords", stating, "we are confused by calling on workers to produce things on behalf of consumers".

Some of the subsequent changes can be directly related to Hodge's assessment of the staff and the Authority's relations with the unions. The solution she declared was threefold: to open up the institutions to real democratic control; to devolve power, in the form of local budgets and staffing, and thereby create the active not the passive consumer; and to get the worth of public services back on the political agenda. The Borough had already been forced to make cuts in their spending and this she stated had "been easier because so many more people have been involved in the decision-making". The Borough would in future judge its effectiveness by focusing on the outputs of services and therefore a new style of manager would be needed, who would have a greater concern for "consumer interests not the producer's". Again she emphasised the lack of coterminosity between the interests of the consumer and the worker, and complained of the way NALGO had attempted to use its influence in the Labour Party as a bargaining mechanism rather than using the legitimate collective bargaining procedures. The Borough, she stated, must change its relationship with the trade unions as, "they want services for jobs, we want them for needs".

This then marked a quite specific interpretation of the way to further extend local democracy. What is offered is an appeal to the consumer to see the staff/unions as the obstacle to change, and an alliance with the elected members as the solution. There was to be no more talk of a rainbow alliance of councillors, workers, citizens, community organisations and consumer groups. Hodge, in interview (1991), acknowledged that this was an appeal to a particular consumer, the traditional working class. The new focus was a way of relating back to a lost working class. NALGO had indeed bargained long and hard, and had certainly demonstrated resistance to change some practices that were not always easy to defend. However, more significant, was the fact that the urban left strategy had suffered a major set back, following the defeat of the left-wing local authorities over rate capping in 1985, the abolition of the GLC and metropolitan county councils, the defeat of the Labour Party in the general election of 1987, and with the elimination of those opportunities for further internal creative accountancy within individual authorities.

The defeat of the Labour Party was understood by local politicians such as Hodge, as highlighting the gap between what she described as "the ultra-leftists" and the local working class, who were she said, "nowhere to be seen on the rate-capping marches ... there was a completely false sense of support from the community." The whole rate-capping experience had been for Hodge, "a blistering experience" (1991). The 'new realists' now emerged, with Hodge as one of the leading proponents, determined to stay in office to frustrate Conservative Government policy, a dented shield the symbol of defiance, protecting the weak against the ravages of Thatcherism. For Hodge, "The days of flying banners from town hall windows and hoisting up red flags on the roof are over" (quoted in Wolmar 1987). Outright defiance of the government was no longer an option,

> ... defiance today would be hopeless. We would never manage to extract any
> concessions out of the government and it would result in the government taking

control of local services
(quoted in Wolmar 1987).

Labour authorities would have to face up to cutting back on services and jobs and if a choice had to be made then services would take precedence.

We ... have to accept that the 'agenda' will be dominated by the Government ... [and] work within a tight and worsening legal framework with necessarily limited resources
(quoted in Stoker 1988, p 214).

Hodge was clear in her assessment of where the priorities lay,

Where a conflict of interest arises, the services must take precedence over trade union interests, or even jobs. Without the support of the people for whom we provide services, we shall not be able to protect any jobs
(Hodge 1987 quoted in Stoker 1988, p 256).

The traditional pattern of incrementalism was, she argued, a thing of the past, and in its place she placed a zero budget, a blank sheet with everything having to be re-evaluated and justified. Yet the dented shield strategy would only be effective if the perceived power blocks within the organisation, the trade unions and some sections of management, could be weakened or silenced. Part of this was to draw the community activists and consumer groups into a collusive relationship with the Council either in the sense of agreeing to cuts in particular areas, despite hostility from the unions, or themselves taking on more direct service delivery. More generally, Hodge and the Council leadership would turn their attention to that relatively neglected category within the urban left strategy, but Labour's traditional base within the Borough, the white working class, a move which was also to require some changes of emphasis in relation to specific policy objectives.

Thus the changes to the decentralisation strategy from 1989 do not simply reflect a desire to further extend local democracy or improve services. They also arise from a calculated assessment of what was needed to bind together a different political formation that would enable the Authority to survive in changed political circumstances and where they were under greater financial pressure. For this project to succeed both the unions had to be better managed and further inroads made into the traditions of departmentalism. A situation in which the unions, and individual members of staff, were potentially more accountable to, and under greater pressure from, the neighbourhood forums, along with both a tougher and more unified management, and closer ties between forum representatives, senior officers, and elected members, appeared to have the greatest potential to achieve this.

In addition, community organisations needed to be both encouraged, where necessary, to restructure and re-orient themselves towards a strictly micro neighbourhood focus, in line with the Authority's policy, and to see themselves more as partners, rather than outside or oppositional. The issue is not whether a number of political interest groups, in the form of state workers, professionals, trade unionists, senior managers, elected members, service users, neighbourhood groups, and local citizens, each with sometimes overlapping, sometimes different, and sometimes conflictual interests, can sit together and work their way through a situation confronting them. The key question is what follows when the lead player, in the shape of the local state, orchestrates the gameboard and rules of play. Just as it is difficult for citizens organised collectively to extract rights, resources, or recognition, from a reluctant or hostile state, so it is equally difficult for radicals within the state, whether elected or employed, to hand over power or create new partnerships where there is no external autonomous groundswell of activity demanding and pressing for this from the state. It is only when each is aware of themselves, and their collective interests, that they can bargain and negotiate with others equally aware but both committed to transforming the existing relationships. Whilst this is not an argument for doing nothing until the perfect moment is upon us, it is an argument for acknowledgment of how difficult it is likely to be, especially for those with power and resources, to manage the consequent tensions in the absence of the such circumstances.

Conclusion

This chapter has offered an analysis of Islington's attempt to implement a programme of radical decentralisation, in which three distinct phases have been identified. The difficulties experienced by the Authority, and indeed in most of the other authorities with radical reform programmes, in negotiating the policy changes with the white-collar union NALGO were highlighted. It has been argued that NALGO's persistence at the negotiation table, combined with political changes at the national level that adversely affected the urban left strategy, led to a closer identification between the Borough's political leadership and the more traditional interest groups. These had not previously been a central part in the new left strategy, and had not always supported the new Labour council elected in 1982 in Islington, but belonged more to the traditions of Labourism. By the end of the decade, the Labour leadership felt it was able to consolidate its position, whilst retaining its decentralisation policy, only by introducing further extensions to the policy, building a new alliance with the traditional white working class consumer, and isolating the white-collar union, as the main point of resistance pursuing only narrowly sectional interests.

8 Trade unions and decentralisation

This chapter explores the views of NALGO activists in Islington towards both the principle of the decentralisation programme, as adopted by the Authority, and their experience of it in practice during the first four years of operation. NALGO members were questioned about the potential impact of decentralisation in relation to service delivery, working conditions and the labour process, the extension of democracy and the advancement of socialist practice. The activists were then asked to consider their experience of the policy as implemented by the Borough evaluating the extent to which it had, within the first four years, been able to realise its potential. Again the focus was on service delivery, relationships with service users and colleagues, the level of resourcing, working conditions and job satisfaction, and the experiences of management. In the two subsequent chapters further consideration will be given to the views of the activists on the elected members within the Borough, a large section of whom were identified with the urban left, and then to their perceptions of the impact of decentralisation on the union itself. Overall the intention in these three chapters is to let the respondents tell the story in their own words with only few critical comments or reflections being included. These will be the subject of the remaining chapters.

The Initial NALGO Branch Position on Decentralisation

The Branch position on decentralisation is a simple one, we are neither in favour nor against decentralisation of services. What we are in favour of seeing are improved, effective, and responsive services and when reorganisation results from these criteria being met then our priority is to maintain and improve our members' jobs, working conditions, service conditions and general interests.
(Islington NALGO March 1984, quoted in E. Roberts, Assistant Branch Secretary, Branch Decentralisation Paper 20/2/86)

Thus NALGO Islington laid out its opening position on decentralisation following publication of the Management Service's first report, 'Decentralisation 1', issued in December 1983, and immediately prior to the commencement of formal negotiations with the Management Services Working Group in April 1984. The position adopted not only advanced the traditional stance that a trade union's primary function is to protect and extend its members interests, but also chose to perceive decentralisation as a technical organisational reform. Whilst arguing for "improved, effective and responsive services" it chose to remain neutral on whether there was likely to be a direct connection between these goals and the structures, methods, processes, and relationships in service delivery which were at the heart of the decentralisation strategy. On reflection, Roberts (1986) suggests that this may not have been a sufficient response and that the Branch should either have fully engaged with the consultation process or stated its total opposition to it. Similarly, the Branch Secretary in interview stated that,

> In retrospect that was probably wrong. We didn't have many models to work on and some of the things didn't occur to us until later ...

When asked in the questionnaire to state their feelings on the appropriateness or otherwise of that initial position, 64% of respondents felt that it had been appropriate whilst 35% thought not. However, when asked to clarify their understanding of the Branch's stance wide variations were apparent. A number (28%) spoke of union confusion and wariness, whilst others (32%) felt the union had been against the proposal either in principle or over the way it was to be implemented. A smaller minority (25%) believed that the union had supported, if somewhat hesitantly, the Authority's initiative. Only a very small number (11%) agreed with Roberts that the response had been too reactive, with limited planning and forethought. Thus, the Branch's dual but ambiguous position of neutrality on the policy and defence of members' interests, offering little in the way of leadership or guidance on the specific proposals, had led not surprisingly to wide and conflicting interpretations amongst the membership.

The potential of decentralisation

When questioned about their own views on the principle and objectives of decentralisation the activists interviewed tended towards a positive view even though their comments were often qualified. Their direct experience of decentralisation, the political context in which it had been introduced, and their perceptions of the elected members who were responsible for its introduction all influenced the level of their support. Activists were able to make the distinction between decentralisation as a policy intention and the reality as they saw it. A number of respondents were openly in favour of the initiative,

> As a strategy, it is so much better than the older style centralised, depersonalised system when people went to the office and never saw the same person. It's done a lot to make the Council appear a lot more human to the tenants.
> (Improvements Officer - male)

> When the whole idea of decentralisation was discussed ... it looked really exciting. For the first time it looked as though users of services could actually control those services. It sounded really dynamic, really interesting.
> (Community Worker - male)

The majority, however, could only give qualified support, citing as major reasons for caution: the lack of existing resources and possible further reductions; the hostility of central government; the Borough's inability to meet the raised expectations of service users; and the absence of real links within the neighbourhoods. Such views are illustrated in the following comments,

> A good idea in theory but there must be more money to back it up ... So you're there on the spot with the people you're working with, you can get close to the people and identify needs, but if you don't have the resources people like receptionists get a lot of flack.
> (Occupational Therapist - female)

> If there were the resources then this is the way to work.
> (Estate Manager - female)

> In theory I thought it was a good idea, but I was worried about the Council doing it at a time of recession with a Tory government in power. I didn't believe that the resources would be there.
> (Administrative Worker - female)

> Decentralisation is about improving services and contains within it a glimmer of what services might look like. It's a socialist strategy, but a strategy taking place in the context of cuts. In theory it's a brilliant idea ... but without the resources available to deliver it ... my job hasn't changed at all ... I tell people the same except worse ...
> (Housing Advisory Worker - female)

> Decentralisation with adequate resources and with developed links with the community ... I would generally support. The problem comes when most local authorities are trying to decentralise with insufficient resources and without those links in the community being in existence and having to artificially create them.
> (Branch Secretary - male)

> We were the only people at one stage arguing from a service delivery point of view ... I couldn't disagree with the concept of localised services ... absolutely right ... but not in a cut throat, cut rate way ... The councillors were not at all interested in service provision. It was an atheoretical political concept that was 'right on'.
> (Senior Social Worker - male)

These activists could also identify specific potential benefits of a decentralisation policy even though the emphasis tended to be on greater accessibility to existing services rather than identifying possibilities for a different form of service delivery. Thus it was seen primarily as reforming and relocating the organisation in order to get closer to the user, but this did not imply a transformation of the worker-user relationship, nor any extension to the democratic processes in the public sector. Access to the worker was, nevertheless, felt by most people as being one of the principal benefits of the policy with 85% of the respondents in the questionnaire (Table 8.1) agreeing that consumers had greater access. A smaller, but significant number (53%), felt that decentralisation could lead to users having a better understanding of why certain decisions concerning themselves had been taken, with only 16% disagreeing. Fewer respondents felt that the policy could lead to either a greater understanding of the problems facing the Authority or give consumers a greater say in policy delivery. Thus, whilst 43% felt that a better understanding of the Authority's difficulties would result, 23% disagreed and 24% were unsure. Similarly, 42% felt that users would have a better understanding of the workers' position but 31% disagreed and 16% were uncertain. Again the majority felt that decentralisation could lead to users having a voice in the way services were delivered (55%), having more power in the delivery of services (53%), or feeling more that the services belonged to them (50%). However, some caution is required since the responses of the five respondents (8%) occupying middle management positions always tended to reflect positive views on the policy's potential. One striking feature of these responses to the potential impact on the consumer is that more doubt is expressed about the consumers' understanding of the worker than with any other area: whatever the benefits, the position of the worker vis-à-vis the consumer may not improve.

Transforming the work culture

A strong thread permeating the arguments of the advocates of decentralisation has been that an improvement in service delivery will in part be brought about through a transformation of the public service work culture. Departmentalism, a conservative professionalism and extended managerial hierarchies have all been identified as impeding effectively co-ordinated services. Thus the then Assistant Co-Ordinator to the Decentralisation Unit spoke in terms of,

> You'll never get a service if the departments work on their own and don't take account of other departments ... for the benefit of the punter and not for the benefit of their own perspective ... Departmentalism and professional prejudice have got to be overcome ... in the sense that they as professionals always know best when clearly they don't.

Respondents were asked for their views on the extent to which the neighbourhood office structure, with its closer proximity of previously separate and sometimes hostile occupational groups, had changed patterns of working relationships. Those answering the questionnaire, whilst with considerable hesitancy and uncertainty, indicated that *in theory* the decentralisation strategy could facilitate such change. The results, shown in Table 8.2, point to the possibility of closer co-operation between colleagues across departmental and professional boundaries although somewhat less agreement over its potential to affect relationships with users, change managerial styles, or create a better working environment. Some caution is again necessary since all the five middle management respondents not surprisingly tended to be positive in their responses. Their responses do not however remove the sense that the strategy could lead to better working relationships between colleagues, managers and users. Thus 75% of respondents saw decentralisation as having the potential to dissolve departmental boundaries, whilst a similar 76% felt it could enable workers to share knowledge and skills, and 85% agreed that it could help colleagues to better understand each others' work, although only 48% felt that it might help to break down professionalism. However, on this last point it should be noted that there was insufficient evidence to indicate whether respondents thought that such a development to be positive or negative. From the interview material it was evident that 'being professional' as opposed to 'professionalism' as a particular occupational strategy, was a highly valued concept. Whilst a majority (51%) agreed that decentralisation had the potential to challenge a top-down approach to service delivery (and 50% saw the possibility of it leading to a more participatory and democratic welfare service) it was noticeable and somewhat contradictory that a smaller number (40%) thought that it could improve relationships between workers and users, and 42% felt it could lead to a better working environment.

In addition to seeing decentralisation as a strategy with the potential to make service delivery more effective, respondents were in no doubt that there was a need to radically alter the way services were being delivered. Nobody disagreed with this and 82% either strongly agreed or agreed that radical changes were necessary. Furthermore when asked if there was a need to substantially improve the quality of the relationship between service provider and service user a resounding 91% agreed with only one person disagreeing. Such a response could, however, be interpreted as the expression of a socially desirable, rather than essential, outcome. Interestingly, respondents did not share the view, often expressed in the literature by those critical of decentralisation that it could in theory reduce access to centralised resources or undermine the operation of authority wide policies. On the contrary, there was a majority who did not feel that the initiative would necessarily adversely affect either centralised co-ordination (52%), access to resources (62%), or undermine other important policies that might need centralised monitoring (51%) (Table 8.3).

Socialist principles

In the more radical versions, decentralisation was never simply a more efficient and effective organisational structure. Rather it was seen as embodying principles and practices that were socialist and democratic in nature, and consequently revitalising, what was felt to be a decreasing level of commitment to the public sector, and indeed providing the launch pad for a campaign against Thatcherism. The respondents here, however, were more pragmatic in their assessment of its potential (Table 8.4) with mixed reactions to the likelihood that it could help create a positive attitude toward the public sector and less certainty about its long term politising potential. However there was some support (47%), for the idea that it could help to mobilise people against the more short-term attacks on local government. Nevertheless a large majority (64%) could see nothing new in the idea of decentralisation and could not accept that it contained any potential for bringing about substantial social change (55%). Nearly half (49%) did feel that it might help to recapture some lost confidence in the public sector, although respondents were divided over whether it would enable workers to defend and revitalise the public sector with 38% believing that it could whilst 40% disagreed.

Clearly, holding such views, which suggest that the potential political implications were either not accepted or misunderstood, would have some important consequences when deciding how much personal energy and commitment to give to those aspects of the initiative that require a change in working relationships and practices. Being more accessible could mean nothing more or less than a physical relocation. However, it is perhaps significant that respondents were divided over the connection between the decentralisation strategy and the wider political movements for change. Thus whilst 42% disagreed that the strategy was 'misplaced' in the absence of a mass socialist movement, 36% supported this view, and 22% remained unsure. Clearly, the decentralisation of services is a legitimate organisational strategy within its own terms but an explicitly politicised version is perhaps better evaluated in the context of other developments. The differences in the respondents' perceptions may well reflect the extent to which they saw it primarily as either a political or organisational intervention. Overall what emerges from these results is that decentralisation contains within it the possibility to strengthen those defending a heavily criticised public sector because it actually offers a better service delivery, and this is sufficient in itself without having to advocate it because of its wider political implications.

Improving the provider-user relationship

Finally in this section it should be noted that when asked whether or not they thought that the proponents of decentralisation in Islington were genuinely committed to improving the quality of the relationship between service provider and service user a majority, 75%, felt this was the case. However, the meaning given to improving service provision was not clear, as was indicated by one of the Neighbourhood Shop Stewards who stated that although he initially felt that a number of councillors had been genuine in their wish to improve services, others had been more cynical seeing the policy as a means of disguising cuts in services. The confusion centred on the belief by some councillors that you could indeed do both: improve services and reduce the size of the workforce by making everyone more 'flexible' and productive.

Decentralisation in practice: The Islington experience
Improvements in service provision

In reviewing the range of attitudes amongst the NALGO activists over the potential offered by decentralisation, it is clear that as an idea it did not immediately generate hostile opposition. Instead there was qualified support as activists could see the possibilities for improved service delivery that might result but were concerned that insufficient resources would be forthcoming to ensure success. However, it is equally clear that respondents were divided over whether decentralisation was also being initiated as a political strategy designed to both effectively engage and empower service users and local residents by opening up new structures for democratic participation and transform the relationships between service provider and service user. It is striking that from amongst a group of active trade unionists, many of whom identified themselves with radical or socialist politics and who actively supported the election of the urban left councillors, so few saw their own work in political terms.

When attention is turned to their actual experience of the decentralisation policy and its impact, respondents were much less positive and for many little of the potential had been realised. When asked to make an overall judgment on whether decentralisation had in practice led to a general improvement in service provision, in the areas of greater efficiency, improved quality, an increase in the level of service, or an improvement in the relationship with users, respondents tended to be divided and cautious in their assessments (Table 8.5). Thus, whilst between 36%-40% felt that some improvement had taken place in each of these areas, between 40%-45% felt that things had either stayed the same or even deteriorated. Furthermore when asked to indicate who they thought had most benefitted from decentralisation, a significant majority suggested either elected members or senior management as the main beneficiaries, with very few identifying the direct service user, who nevertheless appeared to do better than the professional workers, second bottom only to their manual worker colleagues. This did not, in fact, mean that workers were unable to identify any specific benefits from the policy. Rather what emerges is that many of the service delivery improvements promised by the advocates of decentralisation were acknowledged as having materialised, at least to some extent. However, the wider political potential with the attempted democratisation of public services was not felt to have been developed, after nearly four years of the initial implementation.

Increased consumer accessibility

Many of the activists interviewed identified greater access for the consumer as a positive outcome. Typical of such comments were,

> For the people using the service its had some very positive results. For example, it was very bad that people living in the north of the Borough had to travel to the centre by bus to see a social worker, pay the rent, or go to the rates office. Now they just have to go to the end of the road for all these services. That's good.
> (Welfare Rights Worker - female)

> It's much easier for clients to pop into the office where a number of problems can be dealt with.
> (Housing Advisory Worker - female)

> The patch is on the doorstep. For most people we're only five to ten minutes away at the most. The old notion of going up to the council has changed.
> (Estate Manager - male)

Apart from a shorter travel time, this closer proximity brought other benefits, including a more personalised service and some opportunities to discuss service delivery issues, as shown by the following comments,

> It makes the service more realistic and more human. People can actually see who deals with the issues. It has given residents more knowledge about how the departments work.
> (Social Worker - male)

> People get to know you much better - as a person rather than a council worker.
> (Estate Manager - male)

> Being more accessible means that there is at least a limited possibility of involvement by local people to discuss services that are offered.
> (Housing Advisory Officer - male)

A number also felt that the closer contact had benefits for themselves as workers in respect of their personal relationships with consumers, their ability to make better and more personally sensitive decisions, and their increasing job satisfaction.

> Being close to the community you're working with is good for tenants and workers. I'm immediately accessible. We're working in the same environment in which they're living. A lot of tenants mistake me for a tenant: that's good. They don't see me as someone who descends upon them from outside as an alien. There's more chance of you getting to hear about situations people are facing. It's probably better being told 'no' by someone you know than taking two buses and seeing a shit in a suit.
> (Estate Manager - female)

> You get a more rounded idea of what people want and need. They're not always able to spell out what they need. People see you differently as a result of being around, but that can mean more demands and so work builds up.
> (Occupational Therapist - female)

> My job's better. I've got a small patch, I can spend more time with people and they don't have to go so far. I'm in touch with other relevant workers.
> (Housing Advisory Worker - female)

You can develop much better relationships. Officers are more able to be discerning in the allocation of increasingly scarce resources.
(Estate Manager - male)

I find I can communicate better and get points across. You can each identify with each other - similar lives, similar needs.
(Social Worker - female)

Improved relationships with colleagues

For a number of workers, decentralisation led to an improvement in their effectiveness by bringing them into closer and better relationships with other colleagues, although this was by no means a universal view and many qualified their positive experience by pointing to the specificity of their situation,

My personal experience has been a particularly positive one and I make no bones about it. People here were much more receptive to looking at new ways of working in contrast to the old centralised office.
(Estate Manager - male)

There is much better liaison between different departments with colleagues just sitting next to you. People do talk to each other and we do have a much better understanding of each other's jobs and roles and how Council policy applies differently across different departments.
(Housing Advisory Worker - female)

As a worker, it's good because I do have the other departments on hand. ... (Social Worker - female)

I am fairly lucky to end up in this office ... it will often come down to who is your Neighbourhood Officer ... they have a tremendous influence over how the office works and your working conditions.
(Community Worker - male)

I work in two offices - in one I feel communication has improved across departments whilst in the other it has totally failed. This is entirely due to bad management in the latter. The potential is there for flexibility, generic work, integration, but the current atmosphere of demoralisation and cuts militates against good working practices.
(Welfare Rights Officer - female)

These positive comments about closer proximity, although they no doubt reflect real feelings and experiences, are nevertheless somewhat misleading as they do not represent the overall position of all those either interviewed or completing the questionnaire. Indeed, with few exceptions, they do not represent the overall position of the individual respondents quoted. Thus from a wide range of potential areas of improvement only one, albeit important, comment received significant support. This was to acknowledge that decentralisation had offered new opportunities for working with both the individual consumer and community groups: a view shared by 51% of the respondents. However, the views of one of the interviewees were not unusual,

I do struggle sometimes to find something positive ...
(Social Worker - male)

Indeed with almost every positive change identified, respondents were anxious to point to its flip side. Very few of those interviewed were satisfied enough to leave a positive outcome stand without qualification. Thus, whilst *accessibility to the user* was identified by a significant number as being a positive outcome of the decentralisation process respondents were equally conscious of the negative aspects of this change. It was not then infrequent for them to speak of: there being too many neighbourhood offices; workers from specific occupational groups being spread too thinly across the borough to be able to offer a comprehensive and reliable service; being unable to provide and apply their specialist knowledge or keep-up with developments; finding themselves left without cover, feeling isolated and without support; their work not being properly understood, especially where they had new or generic line managers; the large number of offices leading to wide variations in the interpretation of policy; the open plan design leaving workers feeling too vulnerable to angry and frustrated users; and there simply not being enough workers to cope with this greater proximity.

The following comments from activists are typical of the feeling that consumer proximity had its down-side. Each of their major concerns are taken in turn and the workers' own comments are used to illustrate the points.

Too thinly spread:

Because of the number of offices every single department is spread very thinly so you get a lot of problems such as no cover for estate managers, no cover for advisory workers and a big problem for reception with only one full-time receptionist. Now you get lots of odd bods on reception.
(Social Worker - male)

Twenty-four offices is completely off the wall. Even the councillors would agree with that now. You've got neighbourhood offices in sight of each other. Going back, if someone came in to the central office if it was an emergency it was very rare that someone was not available and an officer would go out to deal with it wherever it was. Now they would have to leave a message. ... We worked on a district basis and worked closely together. That can't happen now. We're clustered but disparate. We've lost the supportive atmosphere of small team work ... consequently you're more likely to play safe ... less likely to get the right information and do the job properly.
(Environmental Health Officer - male)

A lack of cover:

We don't have a lot of flexibility. The numbers of Home Carers fluctuates - new jobs, sickness, holiday leave - and we don't get a replacement. It's different from the old system where people could be shuffled round ... the job is more stressful. For instance, when you go on leave for two weeks you have to forward plan for those weeks. Well a lot can go wrong in two weeks and so you can never get the job out of your mind. People contact me at home whilst I'm on holiday to sort things out. That would never have happened in the centralised office because there was always someone there to cover.
(Home Care Organiser - female)

Community social work has all but disappeared as management priority is given to maintaining an all day duty service with inadequate staffing.
(Branch Secretary - male, in Branch paper 'Decentralisation' 13/3/86)

A sense of isolation:

People feel isolated, vulnerable, highly dependent on local management to avoid being totally swamped.
(Estate Manager - male)

If there were enough staff, enough resources it would be okay ... in my job I just feel isolated so much of the time. A lot depends on your Neighbourhood Officer ... mine doesn't know much about advisory work. There's the whole security thing ... many incidents aren't heard about outside the office in which it takes place.
(Housing Advisory Worker - female)

It can be very isolating. I can rely on my old network ... but if you're new then its very difficult. There has been no centrally organised training. Your bosses don't know the work either. People are getting frustrated with people not knowing their jobs. There are high vacancy rates and so work builds up in those offices ...
(Lettings Officer - male)

Variations in practice:

There are wide variations between the 24 offices just within housing advisory: a variation in service provision and how certain cases are dealt with ... which can't be explained by the specific needs of the locality. For example, the current interpretation of intentional homelessness.
(Housing Advisory Worker - male)

There are variations between how long each office responds to situations and how the work is organised. I really don't like doing reception and in other offices welfare rights workers don't do it. There should be more uniformity. Equal Opportunities is practised in different ways in different offices. You get interviewed by different people with different styles asking different questions with different ideas of what's a leading question.
(Welfare Rights Worker - female)

Not enough workers:

We had some knowledge of what it would be like in a local office. ... We were always worried that they would put too few social workers in each office ... you need a minimum of eight and then it might work ... the social work service in this area has fallen apart.
(Administrative Worker - female)

The policy had the potential for worker job enhancement - knowing what others did, more team work, knowledge of wider issues - but also led to more pressure because there were fewer people. Smaller teams meant more time spent on face to face work, covering for each other, and therefore less time on developmental work. Indeed much of the community based social work was abandoned. It also led to splits and resentments in the workforce. ...
(Housing Benefits Officer - male)

Combined with the now increasing staff turnover rate it is leading to the unviability of many teams.
(Senior Social Worker - male)

Loss of specialist knowledge:

In central housing we saw a wider section of the population, there was a greater exchange of ideas, information etc. We also had specialist skills ... now its less possible to keep in touch with changes in legislation and policy in specific areas. ·
(Housing Advisory Worker - female)

Inexperienced managers:

Now in terms of support ... I have practically no support in my job. My line manager has practically no experience of welfare benefits. I'm not the only one, various others feel they are more isolated than they would be in a centralised office.
(Welfare Rights Worker - female)

In some cases it led to the recruitment of staff at a senior level who did not have the skills and the knowledge to carry out the role.
(Improvement Officer - female)

For a number of workers, the knock-on effects of such stress related factors as lack of cover and feeling isolated, inclined them towards playing it safe in their judgments about appropriate intervention. What was not clear, however, was whether workers would have preferred the old system rather than the new one or whether a decentralised structure was preferable despite its shortcomings. Thus, a consistently expressed view was that services were now spread too thinly but this would need to be balanced against the former structures becoming so large that people no longer could identify with them. Similarly, the often expressed feeling that there was too much local variation should be placed against the extent to which standardisation is firstly possible and secondly, and more importantly, desirable. Indeed, the bureaucratic standardisation of response to human need continues to be strongly criticised by radical practitioners in the public sector. Nevertheless, the overwhelming impression given by the majority of respondents was that the corrective measures taken against the old bureaucracies had gone too far, to the point where new structures were equally dysfunctional. Thus, for example, social work practice in the new neighbourhood approach was seen as increasingly reactive whereas paradoxically the Borough had previously built up a reputation for pro-active community based social work.

Too close for comfort:

Such comments on the drawbacks of closer proximity to the service user and resident, especially in a period of resource constraint, led a significant proportion of workers to conclude that they were perhaps too exposed and vulnerable to physical and mental abuse whilst conversely the level of managerial accountability to the user appeared not to have significantly increased. Such views come across clearly in the following comments,

Workers are very exposed to the public. If they can't accept that you can't achieve things people can see you're there and come in and shout.
(Improvement Officer - male)

For over two years we've been asking for a door with press buttons that only the staff can use, we're still waiting. Reception staff are very vulnerable, cashiers are very vulnerable ... it's only a matter of time before we have screens and we're closed in again.
(Social Worker - female)

It can be very stressful. There is no relaxed space; nowhere to go for a quiet room, nowhere to write-up cases. You always feel a bit vulnerable. It's quite dangerous ... all sorts of people around ... general increase in violence.
(Welfare Rights Worker - male)

The neighbourhoods are very small so you often get caught out when you're not on duty. Sometimes you want to be able to pack yourself away from it and you can't, partly because of the way the office is laid out and partly because roles get confused. If you have two jobs like being welfare rights officer and on the reception (it) can be very confusing. You get a lot of flack, people want to speak to you now and get very angry. They get annoyed the most when they want to see someone and are told they're not on duty but they have seen them in the office.
(Welfare Rights Worker - female)

These views, which were supported in the questionnaire returns (Table 8.6), demonstrate general agreement on the increased vulnerability and pressure that was experienced. However, respondents did not agree that decentralisation had necessarily required them to get too close to the user (only 24% felt this), but rather suggested that the problems arose primarily from the increased user expectations, insufficient resources, and a failure of management to take responsibility. An overwhelming majority of front line workers felt that they were the ones in the firing line of any user or resident discontent and that local and senior management were no more accountable now to either the workers or the user than under the old centralised system.

Thus 75% of respondents to the questionnaire indicated that the Authority was making workers more accountable to service users but was itself no more accountable to either front line workers or service users. Instead an overwhelming 100% of respondents felt that workers had been left in the firing line of user dissatisfaction. Moreover, 79% felt the policy was based on an idealised vision of the service user and consequently had placed workers under increased personal risk. Following a rape and serious assault of an officer in a NO, the then Branch Secretary summed up the union's position on personal safety thus,

NALGO clearly would not wish to see security counters, grilles, etc as the norm in worker/user contact ... but there is little security at the entry point ... It is relatively easy for anyone to wander into the office. There has been a considerable level of abuse and assault of staff in the offices which requires different security arrangements.
(Branch Secretary in NALGO paper 'Decentralisation' 13/3/86)

False promises and high expectations

As already indicated, the lack of resources to meet the increased level of demand was felt to be a major stumbling block to the practice of decentralisation and it was often so great as to question the viability of the whole project. Respondents contrasted the perceived lack of resources with the messages given to the public about improved services, and highlighted what they saw as a gap between the policy as image and style, with its actual content. Activists emphasised that no matter how nice were the offices or friendly the workers, that's not what brings people to the Authority. Rather they come because they need something and if their needs are not met then they won't be satisfied with just the image. A smaller group not only felt the strategy to be unviable without adequate resources but saw it as a conscious response for dealing with cuts in the resource level,

> People's expectations are up; there is greater use of the service due to its locality focus, yet it is more and more difficult to keep on saying 'no' as the cuts have been getting tighter and tighter. We're talking about a political climate where the Council has to cut its financial input but has much wider service contact. We are offering an inferior service because we're just responding to crises. We're too stretched with too few numbers. Instead of people being empowered to solve their own problems, or with the assistance from the Council, what has happened is we can't offer assistance until it reaches crisis point. There is no preventive work. The emphasis is on keeping the front door open and the duty service operating whereas in the past the emphasis was on getting out into the community as much as possible.
> (Social Worker - male)

> By making services much more accessible, demand was sharply increased beyond the Council's estimates.
> (Neighbourhood Officer - male)

> People don't come in because you're nice to them or it's friendly. They come because they need something or want something, and if ... they're not getting what they need or what they want, or better than before, then you quickly become 'the Council' again. It has so far depended so much on the goodwill of the workers. I haven't heard people say it's worse but not many are saying it's better.
> (Estate Manager - male)

> People require more and better services than local authorities have ever provided ... No matter how accessible or sympathetic workers are you cannot compensate for massive under resourcing.
> (Housing Advisory Worker - female)

Again the questionnaire (Table 8.7) confirmed this picture with substantial majorities identifying the lack of resources as a major problem, a view shared by the neighbourhood office managers. A significant 64% felt that the implementation of the strategy had been impractical during a period of resource constraint. Equally though, it was perceived as making more sense as a political strategy in that 58% felt it had temporarily shifted public attention away from the Authority's inability to provide real services or to cover up inadequate service provision (54%).

Moreover, there was the view of a not insubstantial 48% (with 23% not knowing) that not only did a reduction in the resource base make it more difficult to implement a decentralisation policy but that the policy itself was in fact devised for coping with this reality. A similar percentage (48%) believed that the policy was, 'the first step towards staff cuts', with only 23% disagreeing, whilst 29% did not know. However, these responses do appear to conflict with the more substantial majority (81%) who believed that the proponents of decentralisation genuinely wanted to see an improvement in the quality of relationship between service provider and service user, part of which must involve a material improvement in service delivery. Nevertheless, it does not rule out the view that the policy intention had indeed altered within the first four years. This would indeed correspond to the impression given by a number of those interviewed that the defeat over rate-capping had marked a turning point in the Authority's direction.

Working conditions

One of the most strongly voiced complaints about the actual experience of decentralisation concerned the deterioration in working conditions, which again for many was a disappointment following raised expectations. In the questionnaire, 63% of the respondents who answered agreed with the statement that, 'It has produced a deterioration in working conditions,' with only 21% disagreeing. The Borough's purpose built neighbourhood offices came in for widespread criticism, and were generally referred to as the 'pizza huts'. Respondents not only highlighted the general deterioration, in comparison with what they had been led to believe it would be like, but pinpointed specific aspects, notably:

- noise and other distractions;
- a lack of essential requirements to successfully undertake the work, such as interview rooms and desk space;
- the overall size of the working area;
- the lack of comfort;
- the absence of space for supervision or private work;
- a sense of personal exposure, not just in relation to personal safety but more a sense of being constantly in the public glare with few or no lines of demarcation between themselves as employees and the service users.

As in other aspects, there is also a sense of an inadequate managerial response to employee concerns, as indicated by the following comments organised around the various concerns,

Overall inadequacies:

I thought it was going to be nice ... open plan, nice plants around, nice decor, but you have no privacy, you can hear everybody's telephone conversations, you can't open the windows because of the noise, the smog coming in. A lot of the information we have is confidential, yet next to the files are notice boards that are accessible to the public.
(Social Worker - female)

We need bigger offices, better buildings, more facilities ... the level of noise and things going on ... trying to prepare a case for a tribunal with one person screaming in your ear about rent arrears, another having an argument with the cashier ... the design of the building ... it was a rushed job ... pushed through despite a lot of opposition from the union ... there's a lot of resentment because of that.
(Welfare Rights Worker - male)

Noise and distractions:

The open plan is okay - people can see us working and that's good - but it's a very noisy environment and there are big variations in temperature in the building. It was cramped until they built the extension.
(Housing Advisory Worker - female)

The absence of essential requirements:

On the surface the building is okay, but it's not. There's a lack of interview space: we have three rooms for 40 staff. The building is too small. It's extremely noisy.

There is no quiet room for writing a report, you have to request to go home which is most unsatisfactory. Sometimes it feels very scary. There is tension, upset and stress all around ...
(Social Worker - male)

There are major problems in an open plan office space with little or no space specifically for interviews etc. Users of services have no confidentiality for discussion ... There is too much noise/distraction for those members wishing to write up cases, notes etc. in relative peace.
(Branch Secretary - male: NALGO Paper, 'Decentralisation' 13/3/86)

I'm in a converted, not a new, office. We still have problems with noise, with lighting, with ventilation, you can't open the windows downstairs. There's not enough room, people are sharing desks. We can't have a community meeting in the community room because it's too far away from the door. The disabled toilets are on the third floor! They didn't talk to anyone before they went ahead and built the offices.
(Community Worker - male)

Lack of comfort:

Because of the numbers expected to work in the NO and the space available we end up with overcrowding. They just didn't do their homework. These specifically designed offices generate a lot of stress. When the council became aware of this they sent us off to stress courses!
(Housing Advisory Worker - male)

Absence of private space:

There's a lack of confidentiality. The rent queue is a filing cabinet away. There is no private space, if you're upset you can only go to the loo. There is no supervision space. Some things don't get dealt with as they should because people don't have the brain space to think things through. It's a busy, busy duty day, it's murder. There are high noise levels with high stress levels as a result.
(Social Worker - female)

Personal exposure:

Initially, working conditions were better because it was a brand new office but it has proved to be too small, overcrowded, very untidy, impossible to keep tidy. We share the toilets with the general public ... we didn't think it right to have separate toilets, but now they're getting increasingly filthy. There isn't any privacy for staff because every area is used by the public ... you never get two minutes away from the public, you're always on display.
(Administrative Worker - female)

These comments, expressed by workers across the full range of services and duties undertaken by basic grade staff, paint a picture of serious inadequacies in basic working conditions. Such deficiencies are likely to lead to inefficiency, high levels of stress, sickness and absenteeism, tension between workers, and between them and service users, and poor morale. They are also likely to contribute to how workers' feel about their work and the level of satisfaction they are able to derive from it, issues that were addressed in the questionnaire. Clearly, working conditions alone do not necessarily play a major role in job satisfaction but they are connected, and when linked to having to respond to increased demand with fewer resources we see how on balance respondents were dissatisfied and under pressure. For the majority, job satisfaction had not increased and few had found it an enriching experience.

However the respondents were divided (Table 8.8) over whether long-term developmental work had been adversely affected, with 42% believing that this was the case against 23% who did not, whilst 35% did not know. Overall, decentralisation was experienced by the majority as meaning more work and responsibility but with fewer people, less time, little power, and insufficient rewards. Thus only 21% felt that the policy initiative had led to a greater sense of job satisfaction, with 66% disagreeing, although slightly more (25%) felt that it had led to an enrichment of the daily work. A substantial 77% felt that their power as workers had not increased as a result of decentralisation. 66% believed that they had more work but fewer people available to carry it out, whilst 80% saw it as giving them new responsibilities but insufficient rewards to go with these. Consequently, 60% said they had been left with less time in which to undertake complex tasks. However, respondents did not feel that their skill level, or professionalism had been adversely affected by decentralisation with only 30% and 24%, respectively, agreeing that this had occurred, as illustrated by the following table, but a larger group (41%) did feel that they had lost some autonomy.

Departmentalism

Although Islington's decentralisation strategy brought together a number of key departments the problems of departmentalism continued. Workers from a number of the neighbourhood offices described how new physical walls had been built using filing cabinets and other furniture to separate the departments. It was noticeable that in this initial period of implementation neither the management, with their clearly distinguishable departmental line management structures, nor NALGO, with its dual system of shop steward representation, had demonstrated a positive commitment to tackling this issue. Thus a substantial majority of respondents in the questionnaire agreed that decentralisation had, 'failed to deal with conflicts between departments'. The Assistant Co-ordinator for the Decentralisation Unit stated that there were,

> ... unrealistic expectations about generic working in the NO. But you can't blame the workforce for that because they're still working in a departmental structure.

Much seemed to rest on the particular personalities in the offices, and workers often took their cues from the interaction of the local management team. Nevertheless, there was a sense in which the apparently different orientations to service delivery in each of the major occupational groups, their differential ability to protect themselves from consumer pressure, and industrial action at the very beginning of the implementation process when the first offices were opening all continued to separate and divide occupational groups, although as has already been seen many felt very positive towards the idea of inter-departmental team work. However, in practice this might simply reflect the extent to which a small number of individuals are willing and able to co-operate together. As one worker expressed it,

> Decentralisation brings in another dimension: it demands that you get on with other departments, and if you don't you have problems because you're actually talking about individuals rather than groups. Individuals make quite a difference.
> (Environmental Health Officer - male)

More generally people pointed to the continuing divide based on the old departmental structures,

> There are problems about isolation and communication between different sections within a decentralised office. Some have physical barriers, some have mental divisions ... there is a tendency for people to hand work over to you rather than work alongside you, which is what should be happening.
> (Welfare Rights Worker - female)

> ... close proximity has confirmed negative stereotypes. There are different orientations from different professions.
> (Estate Manager - male)

> They've kept the departmental divide and not broken down the power pyramids ... not changed the management structures.
> (Senior Estates Manager - male)

Industrial conflict at the time when the first neighbourhood offices were opening had not helped in what in any case would have been a difficult period of adjustment as departments with different histories and cultures attempted to accommodate one another. One worker explained the background and the contrasting occupational cultures of two major service providers,

> We started with the strike about racism in the Housing Department. It was a neighbourhood office strike and not a full Branch strike. We'd been in here a week when we went on strike. That lasted for about five weeks. When we came to work there were a number of scabs who had been coming to work ... there were inevitably some difficulties and conflicts. That distorted what in some ways would have been expected in a new office. The most serious difficulties were around relationship between people ... In addition what also did eventually emerge were differences between the two major departments, Social Services and Housing, over their different needs, priorities, and service provision ... even today that still causes some difficulty. Housing has a history of reluctant service provision ... trying to restrict the officers in relation to their role with members of the public ... they see themselves not as providers of a service as such, or being there to help the public whereas Social Services have this much more ... there isn't a community of interest between them.
> (Welfare Rights Officer - male)

Again pressure on resources and differential opportunities to shield oneself from user demands that cannot be satisfied reinforced status differences between departments,

> There have been constant disputes and conflicts over reception duty. As reception workers, they would like to see themselves in the role of funnelling people to appropriate services. In fact, a lot of their time is spent acting as a barrier ... because of that it tends to be those staff who take the brunt of tenant anger and frustration, who take the abusive 'phone calls and who are threatened with violence ... that causes a certain amount of resentment.
> (Welfare Rights Officer - male)

Departmentalism was also recognised by leading councillors and managers as a continuing problem although they did not always see it from the same perspective. Thus the then Chairperson of the Planning Committee and a central figure in the Decentralisation Sub-Committee stated in interview that,

Social workers tend to argue that they are the only ones who can do certain things which has led to problems. They lack the desire to be integrated.

Personalities, historical practices and professional relationships are no doubt important factors in the maintenance of departmentalism. However, whilst all the formal decision-making structures, including the Council committees, reflected the old departmental divisions it was not unreasonable to find workers continuing to think and practice in their known patterns. Nevertheless, in the Authority's one major attempt to tackle this issue during these early years through the introduction of generic clerical workers, there was strong trade union resistance,

> NALGO spent two years opposing generic work. We were told that everyone would get regraded, pay increases, and that new staff would be recruited. We agreed the job description in order to get the low paid staff upgraded and in order to get some extra staff into reception ... The result has greatly demoralised people.
> (Administrative Worker - female)

It was not until 1991, following the election of a new Labour council in the local elections of the previous year, that departmentalisation was centrally addressed. A new Neighbourhood Services Department was created which brought together the former departments of social services, housing, and the chief executives. A new general manager was appointed for each neighbourhood office and a year later the Authority, whilst agreeing to keep the 24 officers, reduced the number of neighbourhood officers to 16 by allocating two offices to eight managers and leaving the remaining eight to manage single offices (Burns, Hambleton and Hoggett, 1994).

Decentralisation as a strategy for managerial control

The advocates of decentralisation have argued that the new structures improve service delivery by giving the consumer greater access and influence, and by allowing workers greater flexibility in their responses and increased opportunities to be more sensitive to local need. Others have suggested that in fact decentralisation brings greater managerial control and has little to do with either the democratisation of public services or possibilities for developing an alliance with local politicians. It was this sense of increased managerial power, either actual or potential, that came across in the questionnaire (Table 8.10). Of those answering, 55% indicated that the policy had increased managerial control and agreed that it had been more to do with managerialism than democratisation, whilst 62% felt that in practice the policy had not led to any new opportunities for working with elected members. One worker expressed his view thus,

> When I was in W... I thought Islington was quite revolutionary, but by the time I came here I knew it wasn't. It was a means of dealing with scarce resources in a much more effective way, it was just juggling ... I still feel it is a more effective way of providing the service. I just don't have any of the political theories that underlie it.
> (Senior Estate Manager - male)

Finally, respondents were asked for their overall reflections on their experience of decentralisation. What emerged was that, in the present political context, the strategy was felt to be too ambitious, although workers were divided over whether services had been decentralised far enough. Furthermore, it was felt that experience has shown it to be insufficiently thought through, and moreover, that it had had a detrimental effect on other important policy areas. The then Branch Secretary summed up NALGO's position by stating that,

> Decentralisation in Islington is far from a success. The council rhetoric has hidden severe problems of under-resourcing and under-staffing, and a severe reduction in service levels in some areas.
> (Branch Secretary - male in NALGO paper 'Decentralisation' 13/3/86)

However, that opinion was divided (Table 8.11) so that whilst a majority (54%) believed that it had been too ambitious in the context of a central government intent on trying to destroy the powers of local authorities, (48%) thought it had not gone far enough in the decentralisation of services. Similarly, whilst (42%) saw it as vague and half-baked, nearly a third (32%) did not believe it had undermined good practice in other policy areas.

Perceptions of management in the period of decentralisation

Respondents were asked to reflect upon their perceptions and experiences of their management in the period since decentralisation. A number of themes emerged in the accounts given by those interviewed. Firstly, workers made a distinction between their local managers, based in the neighbourhood offices, and senior management, who were based centrally and were generally seen as distant and hostile. Secondly, with respect to local managers, respondents made distinctions that were based more on the individual performance of the manager, believing that how they responded to and negotiated their relationships with senior managers were crucial to relationships on the ground. Many of those interviewed detected a change in the attitude and behaviour of their local managers, in response to pressure from above, towards a more confrontational style and a greater determination to be in control. However, others also noted the unevenness of this process and the tendency for local management to be characterised rather by inconsistency and uncertainty. Attitudes to senior management were generally negative with workers expressing doubt over their commitment to decentralisation as a strategy for improving service delivery but rather seeing it as an opportunity to weaken and undermine the trade unions. A number saw decentralisation as a strengthening of central management,

> I think management has been strengthened by decentralisation ... it hasn't strengthened elected members or local democracy. The members are under pressure but there are still those in post who have the same ideas they had ten years ago ... who have ideas about how to make the cuts, decentralisation hasn't changed them ...
> (Senior Estate Manager - male)

> Decentralisation seemed to be a political weapon by management ... an instrument to break up the union power bases and disperse them, very much like a building site effect ... it's hard to get any coherence. Management used that as a ploy.
> (Estate Manager - male)

> Their (senior management) motivation at the early part seemed to be about defending their empires and, covertly at least, there was an antipathy toward decentralisation. Sometimes in our more paranoid moments we tend to think that some of managements' proposals around decentralisation were designed to cause conflict ...
> (Branch Secretary - male)

The relationship between the self-preservation of senior managers and the decentralisation policy was also brought out in the following quote,

> I know there is a core of top managers in centralised departments ... when a manager's job in a central department is at risk managers at that level will block progress in decentralisation to protect that post.
> (Housing Advisory Worker - male)

Others saw senior managers as attempting to make the most out of what was an inevitable process of change,

> When I came it seemed that all management had accepted that decentralisation was going to happen and their sole priority was to make sure that it did and to stampede over the union and any obstacles in the way.
> (Estate Manager - male)

There was also a feeling that insufficient attention and thought had been given to how the policy was to be implemented. The increasing distance between senior management and those on the front line of service delivery only exacerbated the problem especially in relation to giving feedback to senior managers,

> They didn't think the issues through at all. They thought these offices would just become part of the community and the workers would be part of that. When that didn't happen they just blamed us.
> (Improvements Officer - male)

> It was poorly done in terms of quality ... some of the arrangements for workers were badly handled ... little evidence that management had thought things through ... it was just a matter of getting people into the office and making sure the work is done without thinking of efficiency ... A lot was botched up, arbitrary decisions were taken.
> (Estate Manager - male)

Again there was a strong feeling that senior management was out of touch with the day to day experience of front line workers and that decentralisation had not made them any more accountable to either the service user or the workforce,

> It might be useful if management came and worked in a neighbourhood office for a few days to see what it is really like, they just don't know. It's a common experience for management to be divorced from what's happening on the ground.
> (Administrative Officer - female)

> Management and staff centrally have no contact with the public but we're with them all the time ... Having a high profile is beneficial for the management but as workers on the front line we have to cover up for management about what is happening to services.
> (Housing Advisory Worker - male)

> I certainly don't think the management is any more accountable to staff. We are further away from the managers who make the decisions. I have seen the Director of Housing once in four years. We just don't see these people. They don't come to talk to us.
> (Improvement Officer - male)

As indicated, respondents recognised the need to distinguish between different levels of management and evaluate these separately. However, they also saw how more junior managers negotiated their relationships with their seniors as being of crucial importance. Whilst this might be mediated by individual personalities, personal politics, or a greater understanding of the day to day realities of service delivery and working conditions, ultimately it was the pressure from above that determined management worker relationships in the neighbourhood offices. A number of those interviewed could identify changing patterns in their relations with local managers as the latter strove for greater control in the face of restricted resources or sought some alternative way to manage the pressure. Clearly the specific resolution of the senior - local management relationship had a direct bearing on the daily work experience of front line staff,

> There is a gap between management in this office and management centrally which can lead to problems in operation.
> (Housing Advisory Officer - male)

> The thing is that there are so many different levels of management ... they take orders from the Chief Officers ... Here and there you have managers who might be front line managers who do see themselves as trade unionists and will be more sympathetic and liberal minded. They tend to vacillate all over the place.
> (Housing Advisory Worker - female)

> There's a lot of tension between local management and people in the centralised departments.
> (Welfare Rights Worker - female)

The way individual managers reacted to downward pressure was nevertheless seen as important for relationships in the local offices,

> Management varies according to personalities and beliefs. They have people above them laying down policies and guidelines but they also have to manage their own staff. Above the neighbourhood level it confirms all your worst fears about management, they go along with all the worst tactics.
> (Housing Benefits Officer - female)

> There's no overall management policy. Management responses depends on the departmental manager. Some will organise departmental meetings and strategies whilst others will be oblivious to the risks for individual members of staff.
> (Housing Advisory Worker - female)

The attempt by some individual managers to maintain positive working relationships in often adverse circumstances was acknowledged by a number of respondents. The following comments were fairly typical,

> They are sensitive by and large ... but sometimes the response rate is slower than you would ideally want. They should have thought about a lot of things beforehand.
> (Administrative Officer - female)

> Our Neighbourhood Officer has a strong commitment to decentralisation and does take health and safety issues and grievances very seriously as we raise them, but he feels under a lot of constraint in terms of what he can do and doesn't feel able to pressurise central management. So although he's sympathetic he's not very consistent.
> (Housing Advisory Worker - male)

Others were seen as less supportive and less deserving of the workers' trust,

> I've managed to negotiate some things but he's conscious of his deadlines, of

services he wants to provide. If he felt he could get away with not giving us things he would do so.
(Housing Advisory Worker - female)

... monitoring telephone calls from the office ... initially installed without any agreement between NALGO and the Council. The local manager felt he couldn't act as a NALGO member. Generally speaking the managers have acted more as managers than trade unionists. It is very rare for NALGO neighbourhood officers to attend shop meetings.
(Welfare Rights Worker - male)

The management just doesn't see why they should have to deal with consumers who are potentially violent just because they're management. Their view is that it's part of our job. Workers have been threatened with disciplinary action because they wouldn't go on their own to see people who they had good reason to believe would be violent.
(Welfare Rights Worker - male)

Although the respondents were able to identify examples of what, for them, was good managerial practice, especially amongst the management at neighbourhood office level, there was also a sense in which this more local management was bowing to central pressure. The managerial climate had for many respondents swung decisively towards a more confrontational style as local managers struggled to juggle the competing demands of central directives, consumer expectations, a lower resource base and a dissatisfied workforce. Overall it was felt that the changing climate was producing a new style of management prepared to assert its authority and push for new working practices,

Management is bringing in more and more draconian measures e.g. the new sickness regulations ... Local management are trying to see how far they can go.
(Lettings Officer - male)

There's a changing face of management ... non-union management, people who have come up the ladder. They are bowing to Tory pressure. They have deserted the manifesto ... not just in this borough ... but I was hoping because of their reputation they would have made a stronger stand ... they may have thought decentralisation was the answer to service delivery, but when mistakes were identified rather than admitting their errors they continued to insist that they were right and assert the managerial prerogative to manage.
(Housing Advisory Worker - male)

In the questionnaire (Table 8.12), respondents were asked a number of questions relating to their perception and experience of management. What emerged was a negative picture that viewed management as distant and hostile to the workforce, and one questioning their sincerity about certain policy goals. However, this left workers with perhaps a realistic but not unduly pessimistic view about participating in the decision-making processes. Three questions were asked that focused on the workers general relationship to management, the responses to which suggested a certain confidence in their ability to effectively engage with management. The great majority (87%) were fairly clear that management was not always deserving of their trust. Furthermore 70% were confident that attempting to understand a situation from management's point of view would not place themselves in a disadvantaged position. Workers, however, remained divided (48%) over whether they could participate in managerial decision making without confusing roles or resulting in management being more likely to get their way. Nevertheless a sizeable minority (38%), were prepared to question the long held assumption that management has the right to manage. The answers to three further questions (Table 8.13) suggested that workers were well aware that their engagement in the management process would not necessarily be welcomed. Firstly (54%) felt that there was insufficient access to management whilst (87%) agreed that management did not like to have their authority challenged and (71%) disagreed with the statement that management were open to criticism or were welcoming of new ideas.

In addition, little faith was expressed in management's good intentions towards either the needs of the workforce or their representative organisations (Table 8.14). Very large majorities expressed a traditional employer-employee relationship that had little in the way of trust or co-operation. Rather management was experienced (85%) as quick to attack the workforce when resources were scarce by either cutting numbers or undermining existing arrangements made by staff. A substantial 75% felt that management was not committed to an equal relationship with the union but instead was seen as wanting to minimise its influence (72%) and as failing to properly recognise and address the needs of the workforce (54%). Again, 71% did not feel that management gave proper recognition to their responsibilities towards the workforce.

Finally, respondents did not express (Table 8.15) any confidence in management's commitment to supporting good practice in some key policy areas, especially equal opportunities and improving the position of the low-paid, which had appeared in the local Labour Party election manifesto. Indeed, few respondents had much faith in management's overall commitment to the provision of high quality services. Only 28% of respondents saw the provision of high quality service as management's first commitment whilst a mere 13% felt that management was committed to equal opportunities with 64% disagreeing. Again, 78% did not believe that management was committed to improving the position of the low paid, with only 4% believing that they were.

To some extent these replies may reflect more general views held on the relationship between workers and management. However, the experiences of their current management, as outlined above, do appear, with some individual exceptions at an immediate local level, to reinforce any pre-existing negative attitudes that workers may have brought with them. Furthermore, their views found some support with the Assistant Decentralisation Unit Co-ordinator who noted that,

> The NO management teams had been a major problem ... a fair number of staff had been moved into NO management who didn't want to know anything about decentralisation. They were happy working their patch but that was all.

Conclusion

This chapter has attempted to capture the views, feelings and experiences of Islington NALGO activists and members to the decentralisation policy. Views were sought on the principle of decentralisation and the theoretical possibilities contained within it, not only for improved service delivery but also for the development of a new politics at the local level and the democratisation of public services. Respondents were then asked to reflect on their actual experience of the Borough's attempt to implement the strategy, identifying both positive and negative features. To begin with, it is worth acknowledging that most respondents could identify the need for radical changes in the public sector. Further, the potential and actual benefits of a decentralised service to themselves and the service user, especially in relation to service delivery issues and particularly increased accessibility to services, were also acknowledged. However, few could see significant wider political changes emerging.

Overall, despite any positive experiences in practice, decentralisation for the majority was felt to have left them as workers in a significantly poorer position than previously. Thus they found themselves sometimes working in unacceptable conditions, struggling to meet increased expectations with fewer resources, and feeling exposed, vulnerable and unappreciated, a buffer zone between dissatisfied users and management. This divide that was felt to exist between service providers and users was indeed something that was powerfully expressed by a number of activists. In part this was, no doubt, a realistic assessment of the potential physical danger from a number of service users, as well as conflicting perceptions arising from different interests. However, such views also raise the question of whether the explanation for such conflicts and tensions is also to be found elsewhere. It is here suggested, and is discussed in more detail later, that in relation to the union's position vis-à-vis the extension of local democracy that such conflicts are, in fact, inherent in a professionalised relationship where workers perceive themselves and their judgments as superior to those of the service user and especially where the latter has only a weak or non-existent countervailing power base by which to hold the worker to account. So long as welfare provision is premised on such relationships of user inferiority, which need not be the same as dependency, then it seems inevitable that there will be conflicts between workers attempting to impose definitions and solutions on to situations and users resisting this process.

For many activists decentralisation seemed to be more a strategy for coping with a declining resource base than one that would lead to better services and a transformed public sector. This focus on the absence of resources is something to which we shall return as it is not always a concern that necessarily directly reflects current actual resourcing levels. However, it may well reflect the fact that as servicing additional resources became more of a problem towards the latter part of the decade, management realised that the new decentralised structures could indeed, if necessary, be used to cope with the budgetary changes. Overall, the respondents assessed the costs and risks for them as workers as simply too great. Decentralisation in the current context of an overall restructuring of welfare, and a central government particularly hostile to local government, felt more like a do-it-yourself cuts exercise as workers faced ever tighter centrally determined budgets. The welfare task was felt to be one that was increasingly that of both managing demand at the local level and the subsequent consumer dissatisfaction and frustration. Given that decentralisation brought with it a greater personal dimension to the management-worker relationships, although again only at the local neighbourhood level, effective managers were able to gain more local control by extracting some sympathy from the workers, a sense that at least in the manager was someone who was reasonable and doing their best in the circumstances. In addition, workers themselves were more likely in these personalised settings, where there is close proximity, increasing pressure, and some broad identification with the service user, to operate a system of self-regulated 'over-work'. Furthermore it was found to be more difficult to organise together as workers given the relatively small numbers in each office, the large number and variety of occupational roles to be found there, and the pressure that was on the individual worker to get on with the job and often having to do this on their own. This also made it difficult for workers to properly compare their specific circumstances to those of other workers and left them feeling vulnerable to management cutting their particular job and thus less protected than before. Yet conversely, running through many of the responses was a sense that whilst these activists espoused the need for change and expressed a commitment to many of the ideals behind the decentralisation initiative they were themselves, in practice, reluctant to accept specific weaknesses or failings, or had at least reached the point when the accumulation of grievances had led to an overall rejection of the policy and possibilities for change. This same degree of intolerance towards flaws in the programme comes across again in the next chapter which examines the experiences of the activists in relation to their new urban left employers.

9   The urban left in practice

The previous chapter considered the responses of Islington NALGO activists to both the theory of decentralisation and their experience of it in the Borough during the first four years of implementation. Attention is now turned to their perceptions and experiences of the elected members. These were councillors elected in 1982, many for the first time, who approached their task with an espoused commitment and determination not only to improve the quality of service delivery but also to use their elected position to explicitly politicise local government rather than seeing it simply as an administrative task. These were councillors who were either adherents of the new urban left or had been influenced by it, and to publicly symbolise this the Red Flag hung from the town hall.

Central to their approach was the desire to extend and strengthen local democracy, drawing in to the local decision-making processes service users and local citizens, and particularly those who had been previously excluded. Specifically the elected members wished to transform the public sector by empowering users and citizens to take greater control over the nature of the services and the way these were delivered. They wanted to give full recognition to those social groups who they saw as oppressed and to those social movements that had arisen in response. In particular they believed that by using the local authority as a launch-pad, a new socialist alliance between themselves, as elected representatives, community based groups, service users and public sector trade unions could be forged capable of initiating radical social change. Yet they also faced a central government determined to roll-back the state, primarily by removing or circumscribing local government powers and responsibilities and introducing market principles into service provision and management, whilst they themselves often had little or no experience of running local government or managing a large and powerful workforce. What they did want, however, was to move away from the traditional bureaucratic and paternalistic patterns of local government relationships in respect of both service users and their labour relations.

Here we consider the experiences of NALGO activists within the Authority examining the extent to which they felt the elected councillors were able to carry out their intentions. In the interviews and questionnaire with current and former shop stewards a range of topics were identified and are dealt with here, the most significant ones being:

the initial motivation behind the decentralisation policy; the attitudes of the members towards the workforce; the quality of day to day contact with councillors; and the extent to which member accountability towards the local electorate had altered since decentralisation. However, perhaps the two issues raised by most of the interviewees and the ones that appeared to cause the greatest concern were firstly, the overall state of industrial relations, and secondly the perceived commitment to and performance by councillors in a number of other policy areas and at both local and national levels.

It was clear from the interviews that the activists' understanding and experience of the elected members in these areas, often unrelated to decentralisation, had a powerful bearing on the extent to which they were likely to give support to the decentralisation initiative. The introduction of any path-breaking policy, especially one involving major organisational changes of the scale in Islington will almost inevitably include unintended consequences that require cooperation and support between parties who may otherwise have competing, as well as shared, interests. The extent to which NALGO activists in Islington were prepared to offer such support was heavily influenced by what they saw as a lack of political commitment in other equally important policy fields along with their experience of the local politicians acting in their role as employer.

Clearly elected members faced a difficult task. Firstly, there was already an existing industrial relations tradition within Islington that was known and understood by the union and personnel managers alike. Secondly, their strategy was to engage the union in a political dialogue yet this was a complex, diverse and multi-interest organisation whose common identity had been forged around the members' mutual interests at work. Thirdly, the dialogue to persuade the union to change its primary focus to one that was explicitly political had to be conducted through the somewhat inappropriate industrial relations machinery. It is therefore likely that any required shift in consciousness and practice would only come about if the wider socio-political context was also more politicized with other social forces putting pressure on unions and managers to look at the issues through different lenses. Whilst there were some positive omens in the early part of the decade these were all but extinguished by 1987. Even so, operating effectively within the more politicized climate of the early eighties would itself require considerable skill and acumen and would be a testing period.

Member Motivation:

A number of those interviewed expressed some cynicism about the original motivations of the proponents of decentralisation and the extent to which the ruling group on the Council fully understood and supported the policy,

> I was cynical about the councillors' original motivations. Decentralisation is a good idea but I was not convinced that the primary intention was to create a better service. Rather it was about the credibility and power of the Authority. Services may in fact suffer as a result of the Council's obsession with decentralisation as a flagship.
> (Social Worker - male)

> There was a strong feeling originally that one of the Council's intentions was to break down the strength of the trade union via decentralisation.
> (Housing Advisory Worker - female)

This view was supported in the questionnaire with 58% of the respondents believing that the elected members were intent on weakening the union's position at the time decentralisation was introduced,

They had very fixed ideas ... just pushed these through. Some people felt he (the lead councillor) had been given it just because there was a chance that he might just fail. Others felt he was strong and would push it through. Yet he was a very new councillor and so they couldn't foresee that he wouldn't be sufficiently strong ... so the other view has to be considered.
(Environmental Health Officer - male)

It was very much Islington all over. They had to be the borough that was doing the most radical thing. They wanted to attract a lot of publicity and weren't really concerned with the issues behind the policy such as making the services better. Decentralisation became the thing and still is the thing that Islington wanted to be associated with.
(Estate Manager - male)

No doubt such views would be challenged by those actively involved in the policy making process. Councillors could certainly point to Islington's earlier efforts to localise services in the field of personal social services, and also to their commitment to involving the local electorate through their participation programme during the mid-1970s (Smith 1981). Thus, in an interview with a colleague[1] the lead councillor in the decentralisation initiative, who had himself been employed as a social worker in one of the Borough's area social services offices, pointed to the strength of a community development approach during the 1970s, the locally organised campaigns to resist attempts by the SDP (who were the majority party between 1981 and 1982) to centralise services, the vitality of the community sector and the close ties which many of those elected in 1982 had with community-based politics. Similarly the Chair of the Planning Committee and, since 1985, a key member of the Decentralisation Sub-Committee (now Neighbourhood Services Sub-Committee) argued,

Although the policy sprang from this London-wide initiative, Islington's approach was different ... a sense that we'd already gone a long way in that approach ... that we could build on what was already there. There was an expectation that in Islington people would be consulted about the services and would be involved in the decision making.

Whilst such factors would suggest that the ideas and approaches contained within the decentralisation strategy were not entirely without local roots there is nevertheless some support for the reservations expressed by NALGO members. Thus the Assistant Decentralisation Coordinator stated that,

Members were not either fully committed or fully aware of the implications ... a handful of councillors pushed it through. They thought that once they got the 24 offices built and staffed that was it done, what next, whereas that was really only the beginning.

Similarly, the Director of Recreation, and the Chairperson of the original Officers' Working Group, noted how the decentralisation initiative had not been discussed much before the May '82 election. He identified three initial aims of the strategy: firstly, that it should 'be radical'; secondly, that services should improve as a result; and thirdly, that the power of the professionals should be, 'smashed or broken up'. In addition, he stated that although public involvement was seen as an important issue it was, 'soon not seen as a priority.' The '82 Manifesto had only three lines on decentralisation, it was there only as 'a concept' according to a leading voice on the Council, who had been involved in the pre-election manifesto group, and who highlighted a day trip to Walsall by 15 of the candidates in that May election, to see what progress had been made there with the decentralisation of housing services, as an important part of the growing commitment to the policy.

Again whilst there may well have been an earlier tradition to draw upon, the new ruling party did not have any collective working experience to guide them. It was a largely inexperienced group that took office in May '82 with approximately 30 of the 52 Labour elected councillors being new to local government politics, according to the Chair of Planning who was himself, 'elected by accident'. Indeed, according to another prominent councillor, "lots of people didn't even know each other". The new Council was also not in agreement on who was most suited to take the lead role on decentralisation, with the victor securing the decision by one vote out of some 90 votes cast, and against the wishes of the Council Leader and the more experienced councillors. Such a situation led, according to the Chair of Planning, to one where,

> The perception by Chief and Senior officers that these people were young and radical but won't do the business. When we kept on they got suddenly aghast by it.

A view echoed in the following comment,

> People said, here's yet another reorganisation, lots of noise and lots of fuss, but at the end of the day nothing will happen.
> (Assistant Co-ordinator Decentralisation Unit)

Finally, the same interviewee questioned the members' level of commitment which he felt had 'definitely waned' and compared the position at the end of the decade to the early enthusiasms,

> When it was originally being done there was the Decentralisation Sub-Committee ... composed of chairs of committees and committed back benchers ... very powerful and influential ... it has been replaced by the Neighbourhood Services Sub-Committee which ... hasn't had a very high profile or committed chairing ... it's a backwater, it has no business, nothing happens at it any more ... we haven't got political direction ... it's slipped to the backs of people's minds. They don't want to know about the problems with decentralisation.

Islington's Labour councillors were not so vulnerable to local election swings as their colleagues in such areas as Walsall, and consequently have had considerably more time to nurture their policy through. Yet initial doubts about member motivation to the policy goals remained and, indeed, widened as the political climate grew more difficult and councillors were faced with more testing moments.

Councillor Attitudes to the Workforce

> One of the problems with politicians is that they are highly motivated. We know what we want to deliver and why we want it. You can assume that some of the workforce are motivated but some of them just want to draw their pay cheque and you can't motivate them.
> (Former Chairperson Islington Planning Committee)

Strong feelings were expressed by a number of the activists about how they experienced the elected members in their dealings with the workforce. In particular respondents highlighted what they felt to be the councillors' failure to listen to the union's positive contributions on the strategy. This went alongside what was felt to be a general air of disrespectfulness towards them, and a failure to thoroughly tackle the more difficult areas of welfare provision such as mental health and child abuse. This failure to be realistic about some of the welfare relationships had, they felt, left workers exposed and unable to operate effectively. A number of the respondents felt that the councillors were straight forwardly anti-worker and anti-union. Typical of such views were,

> Had the Council listened to its workforce at the beginning it would have had a much better provision but they just thought we were arguing for ourselves rather than from a service point of view but that wasn't the case. They didn't listen and they don't now.
> (Housing Advisory Worker - female)

> Councillors had no regard for the fact that the total exposure of social workers would lead to a poorer service. They didn't want to consider the difficult areas of work such as child abuse, mental health sectioning, or other threatening behaviour.
> (Social Worker - female)

> They see officers as being paid too much, being off sick too much, and not as under pressure or stressed. They're quite happy to cut white-collar staff. They think we're well off compared with others in the borough and that we don't live here.
> (Housing Improvements Officer - male)

> I'll never forget when I went to a meeting with members ... they were talking about two NO being robbed ... they were not concerned that people had struggled to keep the offices running ... it didn't matter that you'd just been robbed or had a shotgun put up to your face. There was no sympathy or concern about how did the staff cope or anything ... simply keep the offices open.
> (Home Care Organiser - female)

Such views were confirmed in the questionnaire when in answer to the question of whether councillors are sensitive and responsive to the needs of the workforce, 75% of respondents said they were not. Similarly, when asked if decentralisation had offered new hope of working with elected members, only 12.5% felt that it had whilst 66% disagreed. When asked to comment on the attitude of the Borough during the actual period when decentralisation was introduced similar views were expressed. Thus only 19% felt that the Authority had been sensitive to the day-to-day needs of its workforce. Similarly a resounding 90% felt that insufficient training had been offered to help workers cope with the new conditions. Whilst this may not be unusual in a borough with a reputation of only using its training resources for its blue-collar workers, it is nevertheless a further indication of an unsupportive stance towards in this case those white-collar workers in the neighbourhood offices. Further there was also a strong feeling, expressed by 68% of respondents that the Authority had failed to make the process of policy implemention democratic.

Contact With Members

Inevitably, the amount of regular day to day contact basic grade workers have with elected members varies enormously according to their function, occupation, geographic location, and the propensity of individual councillors to directly intervene at the neighbourhood office level. For some there was little in the way of direct contact,

> Generally speaking staff in the Chief Executives don't have much direct contact because we're not providing a direct service ... from what I can see they don't

influence the running of the service. Their most significant role is in the handling of individual complaints.
(Welfare Rights Worker - male)

There's not that much contact. Occasionally there are letters of complaint. They seem to get their information about what is happening to the services and workers from the press.
(Housing Benefits Officer - female)

Others were more conscious of the intervening hand of the local councillor,

There is a tendency to intervene in individual cases rather than sticking to policy. The classic is housing transfers. This individual lobbying seems to have increased a lot since decentralisation. It's very bad practice for councillors to get involved in individual cases.
(Housing Improvement Officer - male)

We have a couple of councillors who wander in and out at will. If someone comes to them with a problem they believe it should be dealt with absolutely immediately and that workers should be there in the office at all times to deal with it. They accept that people are out doing things but nevertheless you should be there! However, there are councillors that empathise with different sections of the workforce and different things they do.
(Welfare Rights Worker - female)

It was not that the respondents felt elected members had no right to be involved in policy implementation (Table 9.1), which a clear majority (72%) acknowledged. Yet respondents wanted to distinguish between the legitimate role of the elected member in policy implementation and the manner in which this is carried out. Thus 53% of respondents were clear that they did not agree with intervention in the detail of service delivery. Respondents were more divided over whether or not they perceived councillors as amateurs who should leave questions of practice to the professionals, with 35% believing this to be the case, whilst 49% disagreed. As one worker put it,

Their pressure can be used subjectively.
(Principal Housing Advisory Worker - female)

Again on the issue of greater member accountability to the electorate, which along with worker accountability was a significant element to the rationale for decentralisation, the feeling was that not only had this not materialised but that it had, in some cases, declined. Many respondents felt sharply aggrieved that they as front-line staff were exposed to public anger not only for an increasingly inadequately resourced service but also for complaints that should more correctly be directed at elected members,

It's only the front line workers who are more accountable. I take the can daily for the sins of the councillors. We take the kick-back from the tenants as the services are not delivered or decline .... I don't think there is a worker in this Borough who wouldn't say they are becoming the brunt for those higher ups who sit in their offices and ivory towers and don't think about the consequences of their decisions.
(Housing Advisory Worker - male)

What has happened is that workers have been asked to take the flack locally instead of councillors, who continue to meet centrally. In the past councillors got the flack whilst workers were based centrally!
(Lettings Officer - male)

Similarly, in the questionnaire when asked whether they thought councillors were in touch with the needs and wishes of the consumer, something one could expect to see as a consequence of increased accountability, 61% thought not, with only 27% feeling that they were.

Councillors As Employers: Attitudes to Trade Unions

Perhaps one of the major concerns expressed was what they felt to be the councillors' negative attitudes and poor practices in matters of industrial relations. There was a strongly held view that the white-collar workers, and NALGO in particular, had been labelled as 'naughty children' who must be taught a lesson having spoilt the carefully laid plans of 'the grown-ups'. For the workers, the public image of the progressive councillor was not how they experienced it in practice. Here there was a sense that basic procedures had been ignored, that their opinions went unheard, and that councillors were too ready to resort to punitive measures as soon as things did not run smoothly for them,

> Hodge is on record as saying they don't give a damn about the workforce ... I think they see NALGO as wanting to obstruct ... They never seem to take on other unions.
> (Environmental Health Officer - male)

> Any council that is prepared to lock you out and suspend you for refusing to do work that is not part of your job description cannot be said to be an employer who is supportive of trade unions.
> (Housing Advisory Worker - female)

> The Council's position has often been very reactionary. It's a lot to do with the flexing of muscles - we run the Council, we're in charge - they've got to be seen as controlling the union. The watershed issue was that of racism. On the surface they remain progressive but in practice it hasn't been like that ... Now they just want to stay in control and are happy to use hostile forces against progressive sections within the union.
> (Social Worker - male)

Some referred to what they saw as a rapidly deteriorating relationship with the Council,

> With the councillors it's a bit of a strange relationship. Certainly if you take up till the '87 general election, when this Council amongst others made somewhat of a U-turn, up 'till then there were some issues that we agreed on and some that we did not. Some we would campaign together on and some not. Clearly there are tensions and these have been exacerbated over the last year. There are also tensions to do with employer-employee industrial relations issues, some of which can't be reduced to political differences, but are conflicts which the employer has been unable to resolve. For example, the Children's Day Centre strike in 1984, there were no political differences ... but when it came to our pay claim they just rejected it out of hand and it took 15 weeks of strike action by our members in the Centres and supportive action in the last month to get a significantly better offer. ... I also get the feeling that what is involved in these things is a desire by the employer not to have to lose face and an assumption that the trade union members won't do what they threaten.
> (Branch Secretary - male)

In the light of such comments it is revealing that one of the leading councillors felt that they were doing rather better as managers after 1987, clearly indicating a change of policy and practice in the role of being the employer to one which had a distinctly old feel about it,

> We learned a lot between '82 and '86 about not managing. I think it's unacceptable for councillors to interfere with management ... After '86 we wanted our management to manage ... After the '87 policy review we picked up a whole lot of policy issues ...
> (Chairperson Neighbourhood Services Sub-Committee)

Similar views emerge from the questionnaire when respondents were asked about the way in which Islington had introduced the decentralisation policy. These show (Table 9.2) both a low level of trust towards the elected members and a highly critical assessment of the Council's behaviour in the process. Respondents described the councillors as authoritarian and inexperienced, ignoring normal industrial relations procedures, incompetent, having little respect for the workers, being unwilling to listen, inconsistent in their approach, misleading and impatient when confronting difficulties.

Thus elected members were seen by 46%, with only 17% disagreeing, as inexperienced employers who ignored normal industrial relations. Some 59% viewed the Authority as incompetent and displaying undue haste in how it had introduced such a far-reaching change. It was felt by an overwhelming 81% that the elected members held an idealised view of the community whilst also perceiving the union to be resistant to change. In its dealings with the unions, 62% stated that the Authority had been unwilling to listen to union advice, had shown little respect for the union's negotiators (57%) and, for a minority (38%), that it had ignored the union's willingness to co-operate. Moreover 63% felt that the Authority became frustrated at what they perceived as slow progress whilst 46% felt that it acted in a high-handed and authoritarian way as soon as it encountered any resistance. Indeed, some 27% went on to state that the Authority had deliberately communicated false information about the union's position. Similar opinions were expressed when asked to judge their current experience. Thus for a large number of respondents there was no sense of the councillors taking a positive or sympathetic position towards the union. Rather (Table 9.3), the Authority was seen as not being committed to proper consultation with the union (64%) unresponsive and insensitive to union ideas (61%), and with members primarily interested in personal power and careers (51%).

Respondents to the questionnaire were also asked for any comments they had on what was currently wrong with industrial relations in the Borough. Thirty-nine included written comments. Of these 23 related to the Council as employer and spoke without exception of a lack of understanding, a lack of respect and inappropriate behaviour by elected members, and outright hostility towards the unions. Typical of such comments were:

> At present there is a lack of understanding as to the stressful nature of a front-line position.

> The Council too often does things without negotiation at all.

> Authority's dictatorial attitude towards implementing its policies without due regard for workers' concerns and standards of service.

> The majority of union members are cynical about the Authority's sincerity and are

not able to trust them, as they have broken so many promises and agreements. Industrial relations rely to some extent on a degree of trust and respect. This Authority is adopting Tory tactics of bully the unions, not what you'd expect from a supposedly socialist council.

Again when asked to reflect on the way the Council had introduced the decentralisation strategy a number of respondents included written comments, the majority of which focused on how the Council might have reduced the level of industrial conflict through improved relationships with the union. The concern was again on the felt lack of consultation, the need for better planning, and greater awareness of what such a policy change would involve for those who were expected to implement it, both in terms of the resources necessary to do the job and the likely increased levels of stress that would result. The following comments sum up the views expressed,

> There should have been more consultation, especially after the initial first phase, instead of pushing ahead they should have learnt from their initial mistakes and not repeated them.

> Better planning of the implementation, i.e. better training, changed procedures, changes in central departments, and a better forecast of staff requirements.

Ironically, the views and feelings expressed by these more active members of NALGO do get some support from some of the key chief officers and councillors involved in the negotiations on decentralisation. Thus in terms of the Council's general approach towards NALGO, the Chair of Planning and member of the Neighbourhood Sub-Committee noted on reflection that,

> Up to '86 it was the Personnel Committee that was dealing with it, and it was done very much from the personnel perspective. The guy who was in charge was not in favour of decentralisation ... he didn't think through what he was doing ... he just did it. He was the employer and they were the union.

Furthermore, he could see that this attitude was still in evidence but with specific, albeit difficult to recognise, target groups in mind,

> There is a bit of the Council taking on the union. There are councillors who say, 'this is a bloody stupid issue which we've got to win'. They (the union) know that we will go for them in a fairly draconian way if they try things on ... There is a desire to ensure that the SWP strength doesn't increase any more ... there may be a sense in which that's the underlying agenda.

Similarly, the Director of the Neighbourhood Services Unit felt that,

> Maybe we should have talked more about the way the offices would work, rather than concentrating so much on the numbers of staff ... more able to respond to people's fears which were undoubtedly that they didn't know they were going to be able to cope ... you've got to be able to show people you know they will be able to cope, that you've thought of these things.

Nevertheless, he maintained that they had got "one thing right" in their dealings with NALGO,

> We produced pressure all the time simply through the building programme. The union was aware that (elected) members could say we have these new buildings and we can't fill them because of you.

On the question of whether the policy had been sufficiently thought through, there was again some confirmation from the management's side. The Chair of the Neighbourhood Services unit again,

> The union ... demanded higher numbers than we'd anticipated. Again over the position of the receptionists, the professionals and the unions joined forces and insisted on there being one. I don't think councillors sufficiently anticipated such levels of resistance ... We should have given people more choice about what jobs they could have and where they could be.

And from the Chair of Planning,

> The genericism approach happened by accident ...

Both indicated that the relationships between elected members and NALGO had deteriorated,

> The councillors' overall stance vis-à-vis the unions underwent quite a profound change between 1982-86. They came in as councillors critical of officers for their treatment of the unions, sympathetic to the unions and feeling the unions would be co-operative: By the end of that period in '86 they had begun to realise that the unions were out to gain things for their members, not for the public.
> (Director, Neighbourhood Services Unit)

> We've virtually lost or revised any notion of an alliance ... being in power makes you realise that vested interests, especially the workforce, are more entrenched, and although you want to carry them with you it's understood that an alliance with the workers won't work ... I don't think that a lot of the workforce were as open to that alliance as they were perceived to be.
> (Chair, Planning Committee)

What was most strikingly different about the account given by some of the key participants from the Council's side was that, despite a number of outstanding problems with the workforce, industrial relations were nevertheless quite satisfactory, the only exception being in relation to that group of workers usually referred to as 'the Trots'. However, overall the union was presented in a very respectful light, a tough opponent, but one who could be expected to behave in a responsible manner in a bargaining context where some things were lost and some gained. On the other hand, this did not mean that the management were not committed to eradicating those aspects of work culture, amongst both workers and professional management, which they felt to be unacceptable. So whilst NALGO was seen as responsible,

> They negotiated very well and very hard which is no more than you would expect ... always been very reasonable ... We have a blow up every year or 18 months ... In the main the workforce recognise that we negotiate reasonably and fairly ... I don't think relationships are that bad ... Enough of us are committed trade unionists to believe that it's worth trying to sustain that relationship.
> (Chair, Planning Committee)

Nevertheless the same person felt that management needed to be tougher,

> The managerial climate has been quite bad for some years ... getting people to produce more and not allowing people to get away with skiving ... we're tightening up now ... There are changes that have to occur in working culture ...

Such a contrast in the analysis of the current state of relationships between elected members and NALGO as perceived by these senior officers and elected members and the majority of the activists, can perhaps be explained by the relative weakness in the union. This was how the Assistant Decentralisation Co-ordinator saw things,

> NALGO's pretty marginalised ... it hasn't changed its structures ... they fudged it ... not in a strong position ... not a major threat to the politicians. They're carrying out the cuts and getting a token protest at the committee that decides on them but there's nothing else.

In such circumstances councillors and management can afford to believe that the union is very reasonable and manageable.

Union views on the authority's practice in other policy areas

The climate of industrial relations within the local state is not something that takes place in isolation from the wider political context. Those interviewed were acutely aware of the Council's performance in a range of policy areas some of which were more localised in nature whilst others were part of a political conflict involving central government and taking place on a national stage. Equally, respondents were aware of the local impact of decisions taken by central government, and of the constraints these placed upon the Authority's area of manoeuvrability. However, this did not mean that they were prepared to accept the Authority simply abandoning its professed policy objectives under the weight of opposition from the central state. Indeed, how the Authority responded to the attempts to undermine its power and autonomy played a significant part in how activists assessed its credibility and to what extent they would support its policies.

Union activists viewed the decentralisation programme not simply as a single policy issue but as part of a wider package presented by the Labour group in the early eighties. This included a firm stand against the government's attempts to reduce public expenditure, a commitment to rigorously pursue equal opportunities and anti-discriminatory policies, an intention to improve the position of the low-paid, and a general desire to develop socialist strategies. Many activists felt that the Authority had either failed to carry out such manifesto statements or had buckled under when faced with determined central government opposition. The Council's perceived failure in these areas left many respondents questioning its commitment and adversely affected their willingness to make concessions or alter established patterns of work to support decentralisation. Respondents expressed feelings of bitterness and a sense of being let down over what they saw as the Authority's failure to persist with their opposition to the government, believing that opportunities had been there, but not taken, for the Council to effectively mobilise both the workforce and a range of community-based organisations to mount a successful challenge to central government.

Thus, on the broad question of public expenditure cuts activists complained about the Authority's unwillingness to resist, its compliance in their implementation, and a lost opportunity to mobilise resistance,

> There's a lot of anger and frustration about the lack of any co-ordinated attempt by the Council to have a strategy around rates and cuts in services, especially since many of the councillors were elected on a 'no cuts' platform.
> (Social Worker - male)

> I have a little sympathy with the Council over cuts, but not much ... I think that the areas they chose to cut are some of the most sensitive and do provide a service to

people ... An alliance is unthinkable now. It probably was just a red herring to lead the union up the garden path ...
(Social Worker - female)

... As socialists you have a choice about whether or not you fight the cuts. They should either resign or fight. I'm not suggesting it's easy but they should build an alliance of resistance.
(Housing Advisory Worker - female)

Thus, in response to the question, "what would have been the most important thing that could have been done by the Authority to influence you in favour of decentralisation", 25% identified being more vigorous in pursuing a campaign of resistance to central government as the most important thing, whilst a further 67% stated they would have been strongly influenced by this.

On equal opportunities, despite acknowledging some positive aspects, the Council's level of commitment was again questioned along with its willingness to press on against potential opponents,

On the whole Islington's attitude to EO and women workers is better than other places. It has been wavering a lot recently ... They're backing off from equal opportunities ... just adopting a populist position as soon as people start complaining.
(Library Assistant - female)

Many NALGO members believe that the Council's commitment (to EO) is only paying lip service and that it is not prepared to risk electoral unpopularity through a rigorous enforcement of its policies or a challenge to deeply held discriminatory attitudes and long standing practices.
(Branch Secretary - male)

Again the Authority was seen as unable to maintain a consistent policy of opposition and failing to manage the pressure from central government. Instead they were perceived as lacking in foresight, indecisive, inconsistent and increasingly hard line,

The Council is more image than reality. They're coming up with more and more controversial policies. Some of it's because they're forced to, but some of it is because of bad policies, a lack of foresight, a lack of future planning. You can't blame the Tories for everything. One year they're saying they are right behind you and there will be no cuts and the next they're on the opposite side.
(Housing Advisory Worker - female)

The councillors have got more hardline. We actually thought they were going to resign and leave it to the Tories to sort out the mess they'd created ... a good idea if perhaps unrealistic.
(Administrative Worker - female)

Had they adopted a different approach ... we would be in a very different political climate now. The consequences have been quite dire. For the first time the Council is talking about redundancy ... a real clamp down in areas like sickness and absenteeism ... without any consultation with the union ... a lot more stringent with who we can help ...
(Housing Advisory Worker - female)

Equally there was little feeling that the elected members had been true to their politics,

I don't believe they are trying to protect services. They want to defend their image.

(Community Worker - male)

Most of them are careerists. They were elected on basically a socialist manifesto to protect services, to project jobs, 'Islington cares', but basically they're implementing cuts.
(Welfare Rights Worker - female)

Finally, there was a strong feeling that the Authority's expectations and perceptions of the union were unrealistic and lacking in sympathy,

The image of NALGO is of a white-collar union that doesn't really work and certainly isn't working class. Because of our defensiveness they think we're only interested in our jobs. The argument we've got to get over is that without jobs services go.
(Estate Manager - female)

I've heard Hodge say we should be working together and that we're making matters worse by taking industrial action and not finding ways round the problem ... basically making an attack on us for not pulling our weight ... It depends on what you're asking people to do for this 'greater good'.
(Welfare Rights Worker - female)

Similarly, in the questionnaire, 68% agreed with the statement that, "elected members failed to equally pursue their manifesto policies in other key areas". This sense of a failure to demonstrate a commitment to manifesto policies, especially when faced with conflict either from central government (over the rates) or from within the workforce (over the racism strike), led many respondents to conclude that the elected members had failed a particularly significant litmus test. Their policies were felt to operate only at the level of rhetoric, more concerned with immediate electoral gains, or holding on to power, than those of a clear sighted political body. If this was the case then support for decentralisation could neither be enthusiastic nor wholehearted.

However, this analysis needs to be set against the national context where other authorities were also finding it increasingly difficult to sustain any effective campaign of resistance. Indeed, individual left-wing councils were, by the mid-1980s experiencing considerable difficulties in formulating a united policy of opposition and this was proving to be virtually impossible on a national basis, or between a number of authorities, despite some brief moments of optimism. Furthermore, such efforts were not helped by the failure of the Labour Party nationally to help formulate such a policy, other than urging everyone to vote for them, or to offer active support to the radical local authorities. In such circumstances the ability of individual councils to pursue radical policies or go it alone against central government is negligible. Yet despite this Islington was able during the early part of the decade to continue increasing its expenditure on local services. Those cuts that had been made were mainly (75%) in the capital programme, or if in areas of revenue they represented a halt to new developments rather than the removal of existing services. However the psychology of 'cuts' clearly acted as a powerful factor in the activists' assessment of the feasibility and priority of decentralisation: 'more' rather than 'different' was their predominant concern.

Public service workers were of course working with service users whose overall personal and material circumstances had in all likelihood been in sharp decline, brought about not so much through the removal of local authority services but rather through reductions in state benefits, rising costs, growing unemployment and an advancing age profile. Any increases in local government revenue expenditure had been insufficient to compensate for such overall decline. In addition, such increases may only have acted as compensation, or replacement, for earlier reductions over what had been by 1982 a seven year period. Further, the welfare state has been concerned as much about managing need as in meeting it, and so any declared intention to move towards the latter must imply considerably more resources as well as changes to practice. Moreover, it was not surprising, given central government's hostile pronouncements on the welfare state, to find public service workers believing themselves to be under a state of siege and arguing that they were already operating at maximum output and efficiency. Thus, a wide range of NALGO activists in Islington remained convinced that the Borough had not been as determined as it might have been despite the taxing circumstances. Moreover, they detected a noticeable change in behaviour and attitude by the Council towards the union as their own opposition to central government petered out.

Despite this, however, this had not been the starting point for most of the respondents who were quite clear that trade unions and elected members should work together both in a general sense and specifically, as the most effective way of defeating the Conservative government. Thus 71% responded positively to the question, "It is important that unions and elected members work together". Similarly, 75% agreed that, "councillors, trade unions and community organisations all working together is the best way to defeat central government's attack on public services". Again there was little support for the view that since councillors had such short political lives there was little point in attempting to develop such links. Thus 73% disagreed with the statement that, "councillors come and go so there is no point in developing links with them". Finally, although the numbers in favour dropped considerably there remained a significant proportion who felt that in order to bring about such an alliance trade unions should change past attitudes and practices. Thus, 44% agreed with the statement that, "trade unions should be prepared to modify past attitudes and practices to elected members in order to produce a more positive relationship". However, the gap between the expressed desires or commitments of these activists and their practice is noticeable.

To some extent one would not expect trade union activists to speak against the idea of working with radical left-wing councillors who have been democratically elected, or to be unwilling to alter unacceptable practices either in the union or in their professional roles. After all in many cases they themselves would have often spoken against, and indeed built their local support and reputation, precisely on their opposition to such practices. However, there was little evidence presented of a real shift in actual behaviour by many activists that might have been illustrative of their commitment. Nevertheless, it is in the context of such positive views on the desirability and potential of close cooperation between trade unionists and elected members, and bearing in mind that many of these activists had been drawn to work in Islington precisely because of the Borough's stated political objectives, that their sense of disappointment and frustration at what they perceived as a failure to pursue these same policies should be understood.

Decentralisation and the extension of democracy

The establishment of the Neighbourhood Forums, one for each neighbourhood office, had been a central part of the Authority's long term strategy. Not only would services be more accessible and of a better quality but users and local residents would be able to engage in dialogue with their local service providers, helping to some extent to determine the nature and level of service provision. As we saw earlier, the Neighbourhood Forums were the least developed aspect of the initiative and their lack of impact on the immediate service providers in the neighbourhood offices was apparent.

Very few of those interviewed had actually been to their local Forum, and more significantly, could see little point in doing so. Most viewed the Forums with considerable scepticism, believing them to be unrepresentative; dominated by a handful of self-seeking people; a talking shop without much influence; only adding to raised but unrealistic expectations around service provision, and thereby producing more dissatisfied users; an opportunity for local councillors to extend their local base, sometimes at the expense of the union; and an inappropriate body to have any direct control over prioritising work or employing staff should this develop. Overall, there was very little sense that union members would be able to influence the development of the Forums or that it was even worth trying. Even the Forums' advocates recognised that they had yet to realise their potential. Thus the Chair of the Neighbourhood Services Sub-Committee stated that they were, "the crucial issue we haven't yet grasped, the most crucial one that has yet to be resolved," and that he felt the attempt to extend democracy had to date been a "fudge" which reflected an unresolved issue between centralists and localists within the Labour Party.

Respondents in the questionnaire were, in fact, very much in support of the democratisation of public services and an increase in consumer power. Thus, 80% agreed that, 'new strategies are needed that give more power to the consumer of public services', with only one respondent disagreeing. Similarly, although with a slightly reduced majority, 63% agreed that, 'public services need to be democratised'. Again then there was a disparity between what the activists felt to be necessary and appropriate and what they saw as the current reality in the Borough,

> The Forums are a good idea in theory but unless you can deliver the goods it's a bit of a mess really because people get more frustrated.
> (Housing Advisory Worker - female)

A significant number viewed the Forums both as unrepresentative and to some extent reactionary, whilst simultaneously undermining more longstanding local groups, although those too came in for criticism,

> Forums are talking shops for people who like the sound of their own voice and don't represent anyone ...
> (Housing Improvements Officer - male)

> Decentralisation has also undermined existing community-based structures and created artificial Forums ...
> (Housing Advisory Worker - female)

> Our Forum ... very reactionary ... does not appear to me to be representative of the patch. It certainly doesn't have much understanding of people on low pay, on benefits, in arrears ... just not very representative.
> (Welfare Rights Worker - female)

> There is also a problem with existing neighbourhood groups. Some ... are permanently bureaucratised and not actually democratic organisations. There are some that are just run by two people who see it as their personal property ... to some extent the Forum structure has been grafted on to inadequate community organisations, although this is not true in all areas.
> (Branch Secretary - male)

On the question of the effectiveness of the Forums respondents did not feel that they had much real power and that they were easily manipulated,

The Forums don't address real issues but focus on things like how often are the streets swept. The decentralisation of power which is the important thing has never really taken place.
(Housing Advisory Worker - female)

Forums are just a facade, nothing of any importance goes on there. The Neighbourhood Officer for Chief Executives once assured me that he could get any decision he wanted out of the Forum. It's going through the motions ... a great big show ... using the Forums to increase Labour Party support.
(Estate Manager - male)

Others questioned the whole concept both from the standpoint of being an employee, not wishing to see the contractual relationship with the employer placed in the hands of the Forum, and from the perspective of the need for a strong and powerful centre,

As an employee of the Council I would be very reluctant to have anyone else determining how I worked, how I provide the service, or my conditions of service. I have a relationship to my employer and it is to that employer that I'm obliged to provide 35 hours a week work.
(Welfare Rights Worker - male)

I'm not sure that they're even a good idea ... in some ways it is better to establish a really strong central forum involving local groups rather than these very local forums that don't have much clout anyway.
(Estate Manager - male)

For NALGO the issue of local control is more complex than the setting up of relatively unaccountable local bodies ... There is considerable disbenefit to council workers to have no common conditions of work ... While services must be made more accountable, it is not necessarily a more accountable and democratic model to give neighbourhood organisations little real control over overall budgets but with a great deal of power to interfere in workers' conditions.
(Branch Secretary - male, quoted in NALGO Branch paper 'Decentralisation' 13/3/86).

We have seen how the then newly elected Islington Council in 1982 spoke of a rainbow alliance which was to form a vanguard of opposition to the Conservative Government. It was to be an alliance which, through the promotion of good practice, would revitalize the apparent sense of disillusionment with collective welfare provision. Such an alliance, involving trade unions primarily concerned with defending their members' interests, the Council under increasing pressure to extract greater productivity from the workforce, and community and user groups often very critical of service delivery models and the apparent privileges of those who provided them, was always going to be difficult. It was a strategy, ultimately dependent upon a swift Labour victory in the general election, that assumed local authorities would continue to pursue and pay for progressive policies, utilising every financial tactic available to them, in the expectation that once elected a Labour government would replenish their empty coffers. Although the demise of the strategy can be seen from 1985 onwards, it lay in ruins by 1988 following the defeat of the Labour Party in the general election in the previous year and the collapse of the most resistant local councils over rate capping and the closing down by central government of all the creative avenues for raising additional resources.

When interviewed at the end of the decade activists in Islington indicated that the possibilities of any form of political alliance with elected members had been conditional upon both an assessment of their performance during this difficult period, and their own sense of NALGO's organisational capabilities. On both counts activists felt wholly pessimistic about the prospects for joint work, a feeling compounded by a sense that NALGO's current weaknesses had to some extent been brought about by the Authority's policies and practices. Many of those interviewed, as illustrated below, felt that NALGO was in no position to be actively involved in any alliance as it too was facing considerable internal problems in relation to a declining active membership, ever increasing demands on it in a rapidly changing situation, a widening gap between activists and the majority of ordinary members, and a general decline in morale amongst the membership along with a growing reluctance to take industrial action, or at least the kind of action traditionally adopted by branch activists,

> NALGO is in the process of retreat and union involvement is diminishing. People see it as a lost cause. They see the power of the union being eroded and as that process evolves so it feeds upon itself ... there is probably a core of committed trade unionists who are prepared to attend meetings ... There is a shift to seeing the union as being more about protection than political expression.
> (Social Worker - male)

> The majority are not interested in being active: their membership is nominal. Trade unionism is a mass movement, and if you can't raise 200-300 people out of 2000 for a Branch meeting that must say something. The power of the union is changing. The unions have received pretty much of a buffeting.
> (Social Worker - male)

> A hard core are always proposing one day strikes but the majority are fed up with this approach. People are leaving the Branch and new people aren't joining. There is no strategy to encourage people to join. Everyone is disillusioned.
> (Welfare Rights Worker - female)

However, for many of the respondents, the real problem with building an alliance, and a major factor in the demoralisation of the Branch, was the politics of the elected members. As we have seen, it was not that respondents were opposed to the principle of an alliance with progressive politicians but rather that the union members were disappointed by the strategies pursued by the Authority in the face of central government hostility,

> When I came here I thought there was an alliance, that's why I came ... I don't think the union would ever say they had an alliance. I only have one to the extent that I work for them ... they are doing things that could have been avoided ...
> (Welfare Rights Worker - female)

> These aren't new socialists. Look at their policies ...
> (Assistant Neighbourhood Officer - male)

> I don't think there ought to be anything like a formal alliance because you can't trust the Council ... you cannot trust them about equal opportunities, to serve the public and increase services, because these are not their priorities. These are just concepts they like to bandy around ... NALGO is right to retain a discreet distance from the Council and now with the cuts any such alliance is just out of the question.
> (Environmental Health Worker - male)

The financial difficulties facing the Authority after 1987 and their reactions to these again sharply reinforced the traditional relationships between trade union and employer,

When you see an employer making cuts I don't see any need for an alliance at all ... doesn't matter who is cutting your job ... the basic job of the trade union is to defend its members' rights and wherever an attack comes from the union shouldn't just roll over and take it.
(Improvement Officer - male)

I don't see any alliance ... two opposing bodies ... this Council doesn't seem too concerned with fighting the government, and the union is concerned with defending jobs and conditions then there won't be an alliance.
(Administrative Worker - female)

The role of NALGO isn't and never has been to think out managements' problems for them ... It's not the role of the union to cut services or go along with job losses ... At some point in the future people will be saying what were the unions doing? Were they saying reluctantly that cuts had to be made because it's the Tories fault or were they saying we know what the problems are and we won't collude with cuts?
(Environmental Health Worker - male)

Such conflicting roles meant that at best the union's relationship with the Council would be both variable and fraught,

I'll fight them all the way over cuts but support them if they're threatened with surcharge.
(Housing Advisory Worker - male)

Prerequisites for a successful alliance

In the questionnaire, when asked to indicate the extent to which the adoption of certain behaviours and attitudes by the Authority may have influenced them in a positive way towards the decentralisation policy respondents were able to indicate some clear priorities. They were asked to consider matters relating to: broad features of the work situation; the policy planning process; the necessary features of a re-organised structure to implement the proposed policy; the process by which the policy could be implemented, with a distinction being made between those more formalised aspects to do with management-trade union relationships and the needs of individual workers caught up in the process; the relationship between this specific policy proposal and the Authority's behaviour in respect of other equally important aspects of their programme; the Authority's relationship to the wider political climate in which it was operating; and the extent to which the Authority could facilitate the union's external relationships with consumers and community-based organisations. The detailed responses are provided in the Tables (9.4-9.10) but a summary is offered here.

Although there was inevitably some overlap in the ranking between these broad categories respondents nevertheless give a good indication of their priorities. Thus it would seem clear that employers seeking to introduce major new policy initiatives, especially those involving widespread organisational change, need to pay due regard to a range of industrial relations matters on outstanding grievances: 95% of respondents declared that improvements in these areas would have influenced their support for decentralisation. Although such concerns may be unconnected with the policy initiative they might well be highlighted by the proposed changes. For example, the anticipated enhanced role of the administrative staff under the decentralised structures, coupled with the Authority's earlier statements on low pay, and the need for appropriate training to more effectively implement the new policy, may well have brought these more general and long-standing concerns to the top of the respondents' priorities. Those issues connected with the implementation of the decentralisation policy appear to be marginally less important, yet once respondents began to focus down in this area they were able to identify a range of priorities, both in the process of change and what they felt to be important about any new structure if the policy was to be successful. Thus in relation to the process of organisational change, respondents identified aspects of the Authority - trade union relationship, negotiating processes and regard for the needs of individual employees as being of great importance. The Authority's external relationships and its willingness to locate and be self-critical of decentralisation within this wider context was also felt to be important. Thus although relationships, structures and policies internal to the Authority are generally identified as being of greater priority, these external relationships were nevertheless identified by over 50% of the respondents as being significant in their response to the policy initiative.

Finally, a small number of respondents said they would have been influenced in their attitude to decentralisation had the Authority offered opportunities to meet with consumers. The relatively low level of priority given to this might be explained by a desire to leave the union to resolve its own relationships with other bodies but evidence elsewhere suggests that this cannot be the full explanation. Rather it reinforces a view, explored elsewhere, that the union whilst paying lip service to improving or developing relationships with consumers and community organisations had done little to apply these in practice and appeared negative toward initiatives that could lead it in this direction.

Within each of the categories, respondents indicated a clear order of priority distinguishing between those features which were felt to be essential in any change process and those which were more marginal, although still very welcome. These are set out below with the numbers who indicated that they would have been influenced by each factor given in brackets.

1 Broad industrial relations:

Improvements to the career structure of lower paid workers (48)
Improved training opportunities (47)
Improved working conditions (47)

2 The implementation process:

(a) Formal Relations with the Trade Union

Joint union-management timetable for implementing the change (43)
Regular well-publicised meetings with union members at all levels (43)
In-depth response to union concerns about the proposals (41)
Positive response to accumulated union grievances (39)
Provided union with additional resources to better participate (36)
Greater respect to Shop Stewards (28)

(b) Relations with Individual Staff Members

Greater thought to needs and aptitudes of individuals in fitting people into new jobs (42)
Greater acknowledgement of the stress caused by such major changes (42)
Demonstrated more concern for staff feelings about the changes (38)
Opportunities for any disgruntled group of staff to air their views (35)

3 Aspects of the proposed new structure:

A more accountable management (43)
Energetic and well organised programme for filling vacancies (43)
Programme of regrading and upgrading of posts (42)
Growth in staff establishment (41)
Broader and flatter management structure (29)
A lump sum payment as compensation for changes in working conditions (27)

4 The policy making process:

Actively sought your views (36)
Long period of consultation prior to any policy formulation (33)
More attention to the difference between consultation about ideas and policies (33)

5 The policy context:

Maintaining an active commitment to other major policy areas in the manifesto (36)
Been more vigorous in pursuing a campaign of resistance against central government
(34) Acknowledged limitations of the decentralisation policy as a political strategy (33)

6 Facilitating trade union links with other bodies:

Provided opportunities for unions to meet with community organisations (29)
Provided opportunities for unions to meet with consumers (28)

Clearly one cannot assume that the specific priorities identified here would be the same for other workers in other local authorities at other times, or even for these workers at other times. This is obviously an empirical question. However, it does suggest that workers have both an overall ranking of concerns that cut across broad areas and also have a sense of priority in relation to each category, each of which help to shape their reactions to specific policy initiatives. A further key consideration which has been omitted so far is the impact on the life and structure of NALGO itself. Not surprisingly, trade unionists are interested in the potential effect any change in policy might have on their own representative organisations, and this is explored in the next chapter. However, before moving to consider this, some reflection on the respondents' reactions to their experiences of the policy on more broadly occupational concerns is appropriate.

Islington began its decentralisation programme with some considerable advantages over other authorities attempting similar major innovations. The Council elected in 1982, not only came in with a radical manifesto but did so with some considerable support from its own public sector workforce who had campaigned for a Labour victory over the Social Democratic Party. It continued to attract to it experienced workers who felt they shared a similar set of political objectives and who expressed a desire to work in partnership with the elected members. A number of people had been drawn to the Borough specifically because of the decentralisation strategy and they thereby added their weight to those already employed there who also supported the proposals. Yet their overall experience of working for the Borough between 1982 and 1989 was rarely positive. They had been prepared to back the decentralisation strategy, but not at any price. Inevitably they were concerned, as workers, about their conditions of work, their relations with their employers and managers and the extent to which they felt they were given adequate support to carry out their work. They could also see the need for changing the way services were delivered and for ensuring that public services were made more accountable, but again they would always attempt to balance these considerations with the costs involved in such a process. Similarly, whilst they could see the advantages decentralisation had in fact brought to the service user they would not be blinded to its deficiencies. However, as already indicated, the union perceptions outlined here would not only be challenged by senior officers and elected members but also the position adopted by many activists did not always coincide with other evidence.

Thus one of the recurring criticisms of the Authority was that it had attempted to implement this far reaching policy without the resources to support it and at a time of resource restraint and cuts. Certainly such comments reflect the wider climate in public service provision, especially at the level of rhetoric but also for certain services at the point of actual production. Yet such comments must also be reviewed in the context of Islington's own budgetary situation. As was suggested earlier, between 1982 and 1986 Islington's expenditure in fact continued to rise and many of NALGO's membership benefitted from this directly through regrading and upgrading. Yet what we can perhaps see in such union responses is the belief that no significant improvements can be made to services without a substantial injection of additional funding. To admit to anything else would to some extent be to accept part of the right-wing criticism levied at the public sector. Public service workers must, therefore, present their case from a starting point of assumed optimum efficiency within the existing resources available, and a recognition of how much more could be done to meet need with more resources. Such an argument is not only tied to a sense of having to defend oneself within a hostile environment but is also rooted in the nature of public services. There will always be a tension between the level of resources and increasing human need, expectations, and demands, and consequently resource arguments will never be far away from discussions about service delivery. The process of negotiating over what can be achieved within existing resource levels, identifying what might be done with additional resources, and securing agreement on the allocation of any additions is inevitably conflictual, involving a range of stakeholders, and must ultimately be resolved in the political process, in which the respective roles of the participants as elected members, service providers, service users, and the electorate, will need some clarification. Certainly in Islington the view of the Council may well have been reflected in the comment by the then Chairperson of Planning that,

... we were still growing. Our resources grew all the way between '82 and '86. So in a sense the resources were there, but also I think there were some unreal expectations in the workforce about how much resources they could actually get ....

Or again in the words of the Assistant Decentralisation Co-ordinator,

The Council gave on so many things. There were loads of opportunities for promotion and regrading. NALGO came out of it very well but still resisted ... social services did really well with increased staffing levels and more senior posts created ...

However, this early financial flushness and a desire to do things whilst the going was good, plus a hope that a Labour Government would soon be returned which would be willing to bail them out of any financial problems that did emerge, had other consequences for the workforce. Firstly, there was the accusation that these new and inexperienced councillors were undertaking such a major change in service delivery without giving it sufficient thought. Secondly, there was the feeling that by 1987, with the failure of the Labour Party to gain office nationally and the defeat of Labour local authorities over rate-capping, the whole climate in Islington changed. Given the initial high expectations both about the possibilities for local strategies and the campaign against central government policies, Margaret Hodge's subsequent adoption of Kinnock's symbol of the dented shield was seen as a betrayal.

> Better a dented shield than no shield at all. Better a Labour Council doing its best to help than Government placement extending the full force of Government policy
> …
> (N. Kinnock 1985 Labour Party Local Government Conference)

Maintaining a principled position, even if this meant resignation from office, was felt by many to be a more desirable outcome.

Conclusion

This chapter has focused on the behaviour and attitudes of the left Labour councillors in Islington, during the first four years of the decentralisation programme, as experienced by active trade unionists within the local NALGO Branch. Such an exploration is important given the continuing frequency of industrial relations disputes, especially within the decentralised neighbourhood offices, in an Authority where the political leadership was firmly in the hands of the urban left who aspired, at least initially, to the creation of a new progressive alliance. An important, though not the sole, strategy to bringing about such an alliance was the decentralisation policy. However, we have seen, having examined trade union views in relation to a number of important features of their relationship with the elected members, that not only did such an alliance not materialise but that much of the initial goodwill, on both sides, had dissolved by the mid-1980s. Certainly many of the activists found it increasingly difficult to identify any distinctive aspect of the Islington councillors that marked them off from other employers in their behaviour and attitudes to their workforce.

It has also been argued that, in addition to the merits or otherwise of any specific policy, the attitudes and responses of activists within NALGO are governed to some considerable extent by their overall assessment of the councillors' ability to successfully manage the central aspects of their political programme. No doubt the importance given to this overall performance is to be explained, in part, by the fact that the programme was made explicit, to the extent that a number of workers had applied to work for the Authority because of it, and that there were high hopes and expectations of what could be achieved. However, there is perhaps a more general lesson here for those embarking on radical policy initiatives. Yet a further recurring feature of the comments from the NALGO members is the gap between what they say they believe in, and wish to see, and the extent to which they themselves seem to be prepared to engage politically in order to achieve these objectives. Whilst their critical analysis of the shortcomings of the elected members is often consistent across a range of issues, it is one which allows little room for flaws or mistakes: a position that can only be sustained by retaining a distance between themselves and those they criticise. This is not to suggest that the criticisms of the Authority, found across virtually the full range of occupations within the neighbourhood offices, and from workers holding a variety of political perspectives, were not without foundation, or even fully justified. Perhaps this is especially true in the areas of industrial relations, the general position adopted by the Council vis-à-vis NALGO, and their inability to carry more union support through the policy implementation process. Similarly in the apparent lack of respect for the complexities of some of the welfare relationships, and the difficulties of being a front-line worker during a period when many service users are experiencing a decline in living standards, which whilst it may be beyond the ability of the local authority to do much about nevertheless becomes part of the welfare relationship that cannot simply be ignored by welfare workers. Yet this apparent reluctance by the union activists to commit themselves to, and take some responsibility for, a joint piece of work that is outside the traditional trade union role does, notwithstanding occasional exceptions, appear to be a feature of public service trade union militancy, a theme which was developed earlier and to which we shall return in Chapter Twelve.

Note

1. I am grateful to Robin Hambleton for access to this information.

10 Union structures and politics

The previous two chapters considered the views of NALGO activists within Islington on the Authority's policy of decentralisation. They explored the implementation of the policy and impact on their working conditions, relationships and practices; their ability to deliver an effective service; the potential for expanding local democracy and the desirability of doing so; and their experience of both their professional management and of the elected members, especially in the context of the political strategy of the new urban left. This chapter concludes this section by examining the way decentralisation was seen to impact upon NALGO itself, its structures, and the ability of activists to organise at the Branch level. Further, it considers the extent to which activists felt that there was a need for the Branch to change its orientation to a more pro-active position in relation to service delivery issues. It explores the degree to which union members experienced a conflict of loyalty and role between their active trade unionism, and a willingness to undertake any form of industrial action, and that of most effectively meeting the needs of service users, many of whom being the most vulnerable and disadvantaged. It is suggested that the way in which a policy measure effects trade union structures and practices is an important component in any overall assessment by union activists, not least of all in the extent to which weaknesses in their own organisation are subsequently identified and addressed.

A number of activists were indeed found to be critical of what was perceived to be a failure by the Branch to respond speedily and effectively to the organisational restructuring brought about by the introduction of the 24 neighbourhood offices. Decentralisation had almost inevitably called into question NALGO's own existing structure which had been based largely on departmental representation with some additional special interest groups. The organisational changes introduced by the Borough merited a similarly swift response from NALGO and it was felt by a number of those interviewed that the union had been slow to identify the need for such change or was indeed resistant to it. In addition, many felt that decentralisation had posed a number of problems for the communication systems within the union and the extent to which it could organise effectively. Indeed some agreed that the Union's collective identity had been threatened by decentralisation, and that a new form of public service trade unionism was now desirable.

The structure of NALGO in Islington

Islington's decentralised structures were poised to transform the traditional relationship between service departments and the occupational groupings within them. They also had a parallel effect on NALGO itself since traditionally it too had been organised along departmental lines. Old departmental loyalties had been reproduced in the union and indeed departments, or occupational segments within them, were often identified with a particular set of union politics. Workers had not only seen their colleagues as sharing an occupational role, but also a common relation to the union, and a sense of sharing a union history, but one which was not necessarily the same as that experienced by their union colleagues with whom they were now working alongside and sharing the same working conditions. Indeed, the response to the decentralisation proposal itself had varied across departments and such differential attitudes and behaviours continued to influence relationships between NALGO members in the neighbourhood offices. In addition, relationships between those working in the decentralised offices and those who remained centrally based were not easy.

At the neighbourhood level, NALGO's uncertainty about how best to respond, or indeed the extent to which it could respond effectively, resulted in a dual system of organisation. This attempted to leave the departmentally based system of representation intact but additionally created a shop steward structure based on the neighbourhood offices. A number of activists felt uneasy about the union's new structure, and expressed concern over a range of issues, including the feeling that old departmental tensions had not been resolved; that there remained a sense of ambiguity about abandoning the old structures, even though it could be seen to be failing, for fear of losing colleague support which historically had been based on occupational specialisms rather than geographical location; that previously powerful departments might be weakened; and that neighbourhood-based union meetings were too wide-ranging to appeal to members' immediate, although narrowly defined, interests. Equally, however, the need for effective union co-ordination within a decentralised structure was also recognised. Such points are illustrated by the following comments:

> We've got all the NO stewards and they meet together. That's good because they have different jobs and work in different places so you get to hear what's happening. But then we also have departmental shops and there you get the divisions again ... there are still tensions between groups of workers and they don't have much to do with each other even though they are in the same office. They see each other and speak to each other but in terms of really cooperating they don't.
> (Welfare Rights Worker - female)

> We have set up a two-streamed system, where we have workplace shops and occupational shops. The structure is an attempt to get over departmental barriers but at the same time we have four departmental shop stewards committees which differ enormously.
> (Improvements Officer - male)

> There is a reluctance to breaking up the old departmental structures but with good reason. How can someone like me in Environmental Health get support from other departments over matters that concern environmental health specifically?
> (Environmental Health Worker - male)

Decentralisation presented the issue of how power was to be transformed. A lot of departments were weak and some were strong. It was felt better to break up the

strong ones to hopefully lift the weaker ones. In reality the strong ones became weak. In the past Social Services were always fairly well organised with 100% membership but this is no longer the case.
(Social Worker - male)

The reality is that within trade unions there has to be an element of self interest that gets people there ... you look after other people because if you need it you'll get looked after too. The bulk of your agenda has to focus on your department and your needs ... the grass roots ... that's where the whole ethos of trade unionism begins and you have to keep kindling that. Now the issues seem terribly remote ... the guts have been knocked out of the structure and out of peoples' motivation.
(Social Worker - female)

Responsibility for the poor state of NALGO's organisation was not, however, laid entirely at the door of decentralisation. When asked to identify what was wrong with industrial relations in Islington, 28% of the respondents were critical of the Branch for being unrepresentative, pursuing unrealistic policies in the current political climate, and alienating the ordinary member. However, it is probably not insignificant that the majority of such comments came from middle managers based in the neighbourhood offices. The overall feeling to be expressed by those interviewed was that decentralisation had a major impact on effective communication within the union and subsequently on its ability to organise. Points that had previously been raised in relation to service delivery, were now examined from the perspective of the union activist in relation to union structures and organisational capability. Similarly, the problems previously encountered by service users, in the old centralised structures, of having to travel from their neighbourhoods to a centralised service point were now being experienced by the workers in relation to their trade union activities.

Local variations amongst the offices were also seen as a major problem,

When we were centralised a problem for one was quite clearly a problem for all. Now local variations mean that this is not the case and even within offices there are different practices in the different departments which results in different responses to people's difficulties. There is an even greater departmental parochialism.
(Housing Advisory Worker - female)

Closely linked to this was a sense that there was insufficient centralised planning, coordination and the monitoring of union practice,

There is no one central core generating enthusiasm and ideas to the majority of the union's members who are passive.
(Administrative Worker - female)

Moreover, decentralisation was felt to have isolated and fragmented the union,

In terms of the Union, decentralisation has had the effect of atomising people ... it's hard to get any solidarity, people experience themselves as working in isolation. The Council is a massive employer and with 2500 NALGO members and 36 in this shop yet they experience it as an organisation of 36 not 2500 ... and numbers gives confidence.
(Housing Advisory Worker - male)

The smaller units leave people isolated. There has been a lot of recruitment ... everything was new and there were no established practices of trade unionism
(Social Worker - male)

The number of local offices was felt to have posed a number of significant problems for Nalgo,

> You can't underestimate the impact of these 24 NO. Firstly, there is the proximity problem. Secondly, because we're in such small units it's much harder to say I'm going to the Branch meeting because you know you are leaving nobody behind. Thirdly, people have become parochial, narrowed down by these offices.
> (Social Worker - female)

Increasing workloads resulting from rising user expectations and the level of demand also reduced the amount of time and energy available for trade unionism,

> Everyone is under increasing pressure in their own section. People may be aware of the pressure others are under but it's hard to look beyond their own job or sector: it takes something big to happen for people to get behind an issue. It's harder to get to meetings, harder to get facility time ...
> (Housing Benefits Worker - female)

Union morale

Such difficulties of isolation, and creating effective union structures, co-ordination, and organisation of Branch-wide concerns, were also having an effect on union morale and a number of respondents felt that NALGO was no longer the force it had been prior to decentralisation,

> They're attacking a lot of people at the same time and people acquiesce ... there is no solidarity or comradeship between different groups ... people's belief in the power of the union has declined.
> (Housing Advisory Worker - female)

Members were perceived as less willing to take part in industrial action,

> People don't seem to have the good fight in them any more.
> (Home Care Organiser - female)

or to participate in union meetings,

> When I joined the Borough everyone was on strike around racism. I was impressed that the union had taken such a stand over what was an important issue. I felt the union was quite strong ... but over the past few years lots of people have got demoralised which shows in people not going to Branch meetings.
> (Social Worker - female)

or to see the union as a relevant force in relation to policy issues,

> In many respects the 1982 decisions were made and endorsed by the trade unions, they had an important influence whereas now people don't see unions as relevant. There has certainly been a massive toning down of its relevance and importance to the operation of social service policy. ...
> (Social Worker - male)

The Role of public service trade unionism

NALGO's present predicament led a number of respondents to reflect both on the union's initial position to the Authority's proposal to decentralise and to the more general issue of whether trade unions should be more proactive in terms of policy making. Opinion was divided on both whether or not NALGO should have taken a tougher position to either resist the proposal or support it, and whether or not the Branch's essentially reactive stance was appropriate. For some, the union had not been sufficiently strong in resisting the proposal,

> My limited experience is that the Council got a very good deal out of NALGO, walked all over them in fact. Alright some got better working conditions and more jobs were created out of decentralisation ... NALGO had this fairly open policy which meant it was fairly impossible to challenge what was happening.
> (Improvement Officer - male)

> Whilst it might have seemed a good idea at the time, NALGO should have been more resistant. The union takes the view that there was little they could have done other than get the best for the membership because the Council was so committed and there was so little opposition from the other unions. Yet a lot of people are unhappy in the neighbourhood setting and would rather be back where they were.
> (Housing Advisory Worker - male)

However, in the main respondents felt that NALGO should have adopted a more positive role, fully engaging in the policy discussions,

> With hindsight we neither supported it nor opposed it. We should have done one or the other ... Mind you we didn't have much to go on, the only other experience was in Walsall, which was the same with the management. Maybe we didn't put in enough effort. A lot of members thought it would never happen or never be fully implemented and therefore didn't treat it seriously. Consequently, the union's resources have been terribly stretched.
> (Assistant Neighbourhood Officer, Chief Executives - male)

> The Union should have met with the Council to talk about service delivery and policy issues. These are clearly connected to working conditions.
> (Occupational Therapist - female)

> The Union failed to look at decentralisation as a whole and say how members might benefit overall.
> (Housing Co-Ops Officer - female)

Some also recognised that what was being offered was a new relationship, which the union could not quite believe or trust, and consequently may have missed out on a useful opportunity,

> I disliked the complete non-cooperation policy. It was clearly such a big thing for them politically that we weren't going to resist it entirely and therefore had to get in and start arguing with them. Normally in trade union negotiations you operate on a conflictual model ... here they were saying, 'what do you want' and we were thinking what's going on here, and then feeling why should we have to pluck the figures from thin air based simply on what we know from the job. We got into a real corner over it ... We were caught on the hop initially.
> (Social Worker - female)

Such views were broadly consistent with those of the then Branch Secretary who was centrally involved in the initial negotiations. Looking back he could both reflect upon what might have been and also how difficult it was for the Branch to make the necessary adjustments to its traditional approach to industrial relations,

> In retrospect, if we had been more positive in saying 'yes we think decentralisation is a good idea but think there should be ten or 12 offices' and negotiated around that then we wouldn't have had some of the problems we've had since in terms of disputes ... which have really been the cause of deteriorating relationships with the Council ... It's always difficult for a trade union to make proposals at an early stage because they can be misused by the management or the employer to stitch you up. That was the fear at the time. But clearly, in retrospect we could have pointed to some of the ridiculous things that have happened like there being two NO that you can almost see one from the other ... We saw as our first priorities both to protect our members' interests and to ensure that services were not harmed as a result of decentralisation. That became the major issue and others slipped away. We never got back into discussion of, if you like, an overall concept, an overall theory, or the way in which that concept could be realised. You can say it was a mistake but you can also see reasons for it.
> (Branch Secretary - male)

Inevitably, such reflections on NALGO's initial position led workers to discuss the wider issue of the role of trade unions in relation to policy measures and whether or not the more usual reactive approach was any longer appropriate. A number of those interviewed felt that there was much to be gained by adopting a more proactive role despite some of the consequent difficulties of doing so. Not least of the reasons for doing so was the recognition of the general tension in bureaucracy between hierarchy and expertise,

> There is a need to change our traditional position of waiting for the policy to emerge before making any comment but there are tensions. For one thing it would involve us in a lot more work which we might not be able to do. However, it isn't good enough for the union to say we're not going to have decentralisation because it means changes in our jobs. The union has got to look at it in a constructive way but at the same time it has to safeguard its members from what management wants us to do because management hasn't any conception of what the job on the ground is like.
> (Housing Improvement Officer - male)

Others made the link between the union's role in policy making with the immediate material needs of many of the workers,

> I'd love it if that was the case ... the problem is that if people in the union don't feel as though they can defend themselves they are not going to feel that they can be involved in service delivery ... although a lot of Council staff ... the vast majority are low paid ... all of those are consumers of the Council and in that sense have a very real interest in the quality of the service.
> (Housing Advisory Worker - male)

Some, though, believed that although the union did have a role in policy making the price of attempting to fulfil this was too high, especially in a period of recession,

> A situation where unions are presenting their own policies is more likely to come about as a result of or part of some industrial action. Worker and community plans based on need are needed but the time, energy and resources required to produce

these are not available. You also know that you won't see them materialise ... and they are likely to be used against you as a job or service cutting exercise. The union is ready to restructure and tackle members who aren't willing to change but only in the context of growth, or if the action is likely to be successful. You can't persuade people when the outcomes aren't feasible.
(Housing Benefits Worker - male)

Over decentralisation we didn't really project an alternative strategy. We were bogged down with the minutiae of a whole series of issues, and we had only a limited number of activists. I think we should have done it though, it's important and we might have gained more understanding from users and the community.
(Branch Secretary - male)

Most of those in favour of such a development did, however, identify a number of difficulties in pursuing it successfully, and indeed noted that the Branch had made some attempts to be proactive but that these had not been positively received by the Authority,

We do have some areas where we're still creating policy, mainly national issues. Locally as a trade union it's quite difficult to get support for something that is not reactive. It's difficult because the first dispute we had was when NALGO demanded the Council toughened up the implementation of its EO policy. We were on strike for six weeks although it didn't work.
(Administrative Worker - female)

Most people do think we should have a role in putting forward policies because they want to deliver a service, and at various times we attempt to make our voice heard about service provision or improving it. But often our voice is ignored by Council. To listen to us would mean resource implications or it would be politically unacceptable.
(Estate Manager - female)

Some remained convinced that the traditional approach was the most appropriate,

I don't think it's a situation where the union can make the running, it has to be reactive. It's not the union's job ... they are in terms of jobs generally conservative ... they can only react to changes in working practices ... it's inevitable.
(Housing Improvement Officer - male)

The union shouldn't be proactive because the (Council) members are there to instigate the policy and NALGO is there to respond. It can become dangerous if these roles are blurred ... dangers of the Branch Officers becoming unrepresentative of the Branch. However at the moment, everything is happening too late, it's just reacting and never doing things properly.
(Principal Advisory Worker - female)

This last comment raises perhaps the most powerful argument against public service trade unions adopting a more proactive role in policy making areas. Not only would such a role raise questions about the union's relationship to the democratic processes, however flawed they might be, it also highlights the potential difficulties in relation to accountability within the union itself. It is doubtful that the union as a whole is currently structured in a way that would enable it to formulate, express and advocate for a particular policy. Without such structures the potential for the views of its Officers to be seen as unrepresentative of the union as a whole must remain considerable. However, it is clear from Table 10.1 that respondents were dissatisfied with the traditional role of the union and saw it having a legitimate right to enter into the arena of policy discussion. Thus a clear majority did not want NALGO to confine itself to issues of wages and service conditions. Rather they wanted it to engage in questions of service delivery irrespective of whether there was a direct connection with the level of jobs. Further a majority (66%) felt that the political beliefs of union members should be brought into the work place and a substantial majority (77%) disagreed with the view that the unions had no role to play in producing guidelines on how services should be provided or that it could only do so when members' job security was under threat (89%). Again 68% rejected the idea that the Branch should confine itself to defending jobs and pay levels, whilst a slightly reduced majority (58%) did not agree to confining union activities to improving pay and conditions of service, and a substantial 77% further rejected the idea that a public service union should 'stick to bread and butter issues' of industrial relations. However, it was also clear that for the majority there was no expressed wish to challenge the historical role of the professional local government officer implementing the policies of the democratically elected councillors, with 66% agreeing that, 'local authority workers have a duty to carry out policies on which councillors are elected', whilst only 23% disagreed.

Conflicts of interests between public service trade unionism and service delivery

If public sector unions are to take a more dynamic role in the area of policy making it will be necessary for them to address the issue of their relationships with those who consume public services. Public service workers do not stand in the same relationship to their product as workers in either the manufacturing or private service sectors. Public service workers are essentially concerned both with the meeting of human need and with social reproduction and legitimation. This requires them to engage with people over values, attitudes and behaviours. It was, therefore, particularly important to discover the extent to which trade union activists perceived themselves as being in a contradictory or problematical role in both meeting consumer need and engaging in trade union activity. Amongst those interviewed there was some considerable disagreement in this area. On the one hand, there were those who either felt there was no tension between their interests as workers and those of the consumers, or felt that any such conflicts arose primarily in situations of industrial action and could be resolved through a process of explaining the cause of that action. On the other hand, there were those who believed that there were real conflicts of interest, and that there was a need to develop more extensive relationships with consumers. This latter group tended to be critical of the union's efforts to date in this respect and were concerned about the personal dilemmas resulting from such unresolved conflicts.

For the majority, however, either there was no conflict of interest or if one did arise during industrial action, then an explanation from the picket line or information sent to local community groups about the origins of the dispute would constitute a sufficient response,

> Good service delivery for workers means good service delivery for customers, they are inextricably linked. In a way cuts hit council workers before consumers because we're under pressure to make up the shortfall by working harder ... which is impossible really ... leads to serious problems of stress. Working with the public is really stressful.
> (Housing Advisory Worker - male)

The more successful we are at defending our jobs so we're defending their services. That's the bottom line ... What's good for us is good for the community. I really do believe that. I was surprised at the level of support we got on the picket line ... some got really nasty but there is quite a lot of anti-Tory feeling at the moment. They've got to understand why we're doing it.
(Welfare Rights Worker - male)

Taking industrial action will lead to better services ... there might be short term costs but long term gains. We are trying to preserve jobs and services which is in the interests of the consumer. When we have had disputes most people have supported us, they don't want the cuts either. There are, however, still a large number of people who think we get paid for being on strike.
(Administrative Worker - female)

Withdrawing our labour is not a contradiction although we need to explain our position ... I don't feel mine is a life and death situation which is my bottom line.
(Occupational Therapist - female)

No, there is no tension. The pickets explain the action. During the lock-out the public quickly grasped the issues ... when we've had action the public have supported us.
(Lettings Officer - male)

A number of those who adopted this position also emphasised that industrial action is not something that is undertaken lightly, and that there can be considerable costs involved in doing so, both financial and in respect of creating additional work,

No one wants to go on strike ... you lose money ... particularly people who work in the public services ... we always arrange emergency cover. But people go on strike when they feel pushed to the limit.
(Housing Advisory Worker - male)

I don't think trade unions go out on strike just because people fancy it ... it's a myth ... most people simply can't afford it and this is probably more true in the public sector
(Improvements Officer - male)

We don't relish the thought of losing a day's pay ... a lot of us are single parents, have children, high mortgages, but we feel strongly enough to forgo a days pay. People will listen to that and say okay.
(Housing Advisory Worker - male)

Similarly, in the questionnaire, respondents did not feel that their right to take industrial action should be limited by their relationship with service users, notwithstanding that they would want to both minimise the impact of any action on service users and work with them during the industrial action. Otherwise, as Table 10.2 demonstrates, there was a substantial majority (75%) in favour of the union taking any form of industrial action in pursuit of their interests and a stronger belief (79%) that a decision to take strike action should not be influenced by the potential impact on service users. However, because a majority (59%) also felt that the impact on the consumer should be minimised one could, therefore, conclude that strike action was seen as being a measure to be adopted only when other strategies with less of an impact had been unsuccessful. Whilst the vast majority (86%) agreed the union should attempt to work with service users when involved in an industrial dispute, some of the above quotations would suggest that for many this meant 'explaining' the union's position rather than working co-operatively, or entering into dialogue with service users.

Other activists acknowledged what for them were tensions and contradictions between trade union action and consumer interests. Some felt they had accountability to the service users who were often vulnerable and without a voice,

> It's full of contradictions ... I wish there could be more work done with consumers. It's particularly difficult when working with some groups such as the homeless who don't have a voice ...
> (Principal Housing Advisory Worker - female)

> There is always a tension ... especially for social workers because it's a front line service. I didn't want to take strike action and voted against it in the Day Care strike. I wasn't convinced that the damage done to working parents, mainly single working class women was worth it.
> (Social Worker - male)

> If you take action you know you are accountable to the people who pay for the services ... There is conflict over taking action over pay against people in desperate need for housing ... you need to be aware of the implications.
> (Housing Benefits Worker - female)

> In this kind of industry which is working with people you can't talk about the rights of workers without talking about the rights of service users. You can't do that. People do emphasise service users' issues in Branch meetings and do try to make links ... any successful action in local government must make those links.
> (Housing Advisory Worker - female)

> There is a tension ... there were homeless people who were not being seen ... didn't please me ... I want to help people but I also need to protect my sanity and restrict my hours and other things.
> (Estate Manager - female)

For these workers there was a clearly perceived need to change the relationship with consumers and a feeling that not enough progress had been made in this direction,

> In the industrial sector there is a direct relationship between the industrial power of the workers and the profits of the employer. It is very clear and explicit. Industrial action in the public sector is totally different. There are very few areas where you hit the pockets of the local authority. Most action will in fact hit the users and therefore the effect on the employer is indirect, through either user support for the action or antipathy toward the authority. ... What is absolutely clear is the need for discussion between public sector trade unions and the users not only about policy but also about tactics and strategies so that when action is contemplated it is something that the users know about and support.
> (Branch Secretary - male)

> The eternal conundrum! The contradictions affect everyone ... We've never got away from traditional union action that you don't do certain things, that's what industrial action has meant ... we've got a long way to go in changing that climate ... in the anti-cuts policy we had to push quite hard just to change the wording to make it clear that you had to go out to talk to the tenants. We're a long way away from a situation where we're sitting down as trade unionists with tenants and they're talking

about our issues and we're talking about their issues.
(Improvements Officer - male)

I don't think there really has been much effort to contact local groups ... it's always time, putting yourself out to a large extent. On the other hand there should be more leadership taken by the Branch. You don't feel as though you have the backing or encouragement.
(Welfare Rights Worker - female)

We must have joint work, although I wouldn't say that you can't do anything until you have it, but we must work towards it. The union is slowly learning this.
(Housing Benefits Officer - male)

This sense that only limited progress in this area has been made to date is given further support in the questionnaire where those respondents who strongly agreed that public service unions should attempt to work with consumers when undertaking industrial action, were asked to identify what they personally had done to carry this out. Most had confined themselves to explaining their actions to consumers, usually when engaged on picket duty, but some had also spoken at tenants' and community meetings or gone onto the housing estates. Others had focused on the printing and distribution of information leaflets and posters. Only one respondent mentioned attempting to form a joint trade union and community campaign over the issues.

Conclusion

This chapter has looked at the impact of decentralisation on the structures and politics of the Islington NALGO Branch, as perceived by the Branch activists. It has been suggested that the Authority's policy initiative was a cause for concern amongst local white-collar trade unionists not only because of its impact in the area of service delivery, working conditions, and the maintenance of other important policy objectives, but also in relation to the union's own structures and practices. Further, it was felt by the majority of respondents that NALGO had failed to recognise rapidly enough the implications for its own organisation of the decentralised structures, and was indeed left with an organisational form that was unable to respond effectively to the changes taking place. In addition, many of the policy outcomes that had been identified as problematic from a service delivery point of view were also identified as creating parallel difficulties for the union members. As a consequence, morale was low amongst those members of the Branch who had been decentralised and participation levels were declining, with activists finding it difficult to encourage members to overcome the practical difficulties that had been created in participating in union business at a very basic level, following re-organisation. Yet NALGO members were themselves reluctant to break-up their old structure, even though it was based on an outdated departmental model because not only was this familiar but also, for many, a form of comraderie and strength and had been created through it. Indeed for some a particular style of trade unionism was associated with their department. Nevertheless, decentralisation was creating a number of problems for the union, not least of which was how to broaden members' horizons so that interests other than those immediately and directly affecting them could be acknowledged and responded to.

It has further been argued that, on reflection, a significant number felt that the union should have made a positive commitment to engaging with the Authority over the policy initiative from the outset, and in doing so would have avoided a number of the problems now facing them. This had also caused reflection on the broader issue of the approach of public service trade unions toward service related matters and it was clear that the great majority did not want the union to be confined to the limited role of defending and promoting the material interests of its members, but felt that it should fully engage with the Authority on matters of service delivery. Despite this, however, the majority of respondents continued to maintain the view that there was no potential contradiction between meeting service user needs and the union actively pursuing its more traditional concerns, and in so doing being prepared to undertake all forms of industrial action. Although the majority felt that it was important to work with the service user, especially in situations of industrial conflict, the meaning of this joint work was rather limited, and to date little had been done to apply or promote the concept. Ultimately, the majority felt that any industrial action would not be taken lightly, that there were considerable costs involved for those that did so, and that improved conditions for service providers would ultimately have a trickle down effect to provide service users with a better service. Although this was assumed to be the case there was little evidence to suggest that the Islington Branch activists had done much to confirm that service users agreed with the analysis or to demonstrate that this was indeed the outcome. The Borough's decentralisation policy clearly had significant consequences for NALGO as a union, and it remains to be seen whether or not as UNISON it will be able to make sufficient and appropriate changes to meet the challenges or whether the questions around the general role of the union will be pursued within the Branch. The following two chapters will give some further thought to the union's reactions to decentralisation, attempt to assess the industrial relations conflict in those authorities where the new urban left has been influential, and consider possible courses of action for public service trade unions in the future.

11 Reflections on trade union action

The purpose of this chapter is to summarise the main issues raised by the Islington NALGO activists and members to the Authority's policy of decentralising services and introducing greater democratisation into service delivery and local welfare politics. This will be done by firstly identifying the factors that appear to be important in the determination of trade union responses to the introduction of the new policy. It will be argued that trade union responses are determined not by any single factor, but rather through consideration of a number of issues which are viewed both in their own terms and are also weighed against each other so as to enable 'on balance' judgements to be made. Secondly, consideration will be given to whether or not Islington NALGO's response to the decentralisation initiative was in any sense typical of other Branches of the union. Finally, a brief comparison will be made between the white-collar union reaction and that of public sector blue-collar workers.

Decentralisation through trade union eyes

The Islington case study suggests that a multiple of variables helped shape the responses of public service trade unionists to decentralisation and other major policy initiatives. The majority of activists demonstrated an awareness of the political complexities involved, although they were also prepared to take decisions that reflected their sectional interests, and at the expense of other stakeholders. However, reactions to new policy initiatives are not a once-and-for-all affair, but develop and change over time as each of the key determining variables unfolds, and the relative importance of each shifts in relation to the others. Four over-riding variables in the evaluation of the policy proposal can be identified through the case study, although it is clear that not all of these are either valued by all activists, or that they are all given the same weighting in terms of their importance both in relation to themselves and other variables.

Further, it is suggested that the respondents' reactions need to be placed in the context of their initial expectations of working for a radical local authority and the extent to which these had been, or would be, realised. It was evident that a considerable number of the activists in Islington NALGO either came to work for the Authority specifically because of its espoused political programme, or were already working there and had helped to put the left-wing Labour group in office through an active campaign during the 1982 election. Many activists either shared the politics of the newly elected councillors or felt a high level of sympathy for their approach. The extent to which they felt that their expectations were realised in the subsequent years, and the degree to which they believed the responsibility for any shortcomings rested with the elected members was an important benchmark against which judgements were made on decentralisation.

In addition, another contextual factor was the extent to which the respondents positively identified with professional welfare practice and its assumptions about the superiority of professional knowledge over that of the service user, and the inevitability, if not desirability, of the welfare professional having to mediate between competing welfare publics, to separate the deserving from the undeserving, and to impose where necessary a more elevated and caring set of values to those that it was felt would be found amongst their clients. Greater democratisation within a decentralised setting challenges these long-established principles of social welfare, and any desire to uphold them had implications for how workers perceived the usefulness of decentralisation. Finally, a fifth variable is added to explain the form of the trade unionism adopted in response to a negatively evaluated policy. This relates to the influence of important segments within the union, especially important in a federal union such as NALGO, and what they bring to the process in terms of the occupational work cultures, or the dominant politics within the occupation, which may or may not be associated with a political party. The five major variables mentioned to varying degrees in evaluating the policy initiative by a considerable number of the respondents were:

(i)   their reaction to the policy proposal itself, i.e. did it appear in principle to offer desirable outcomes;

(ii)   what impact might the policy have, and subsequently in its implementation, was it having on their work and market situation;

(iii)   what impact might the policy have, and again subsequently was it having, on consumers and users;

(iv)   what was their experience of the elected members and managers in pursuing the broader political strategy during both the policy making and implementation stages;

(v) how union members perceived the relationship between themselves as unionists and their professional welfare roles and the extent to which this conflicted with expectations around behaviour in relation to new policy initiatives.

Each of these variables, with the exception of the desirability of the policy objectives and principles, contain a number of discrete elements and raise questions about the nature of public service trade unionism and its relationship to service delivery. What they highlight is that whilst public service workers consider changes in the work place in relation to the potential impact on the labour process, they will have additional concerns arising from the nature of their work and their relationship to it. Thus, because many are committed to collectively provided public services based on need, and to their human product, they are necessarily concerned, in a way that other white-collar workers may not be, in the detailed nature of any new policy, its impact on the service user, and the resultant quality of service delivery, along with managements' approach to other valued policies.

Public sector trade union evaluations of decentralisation as a policy initiative and its implications for public sector trade unions:

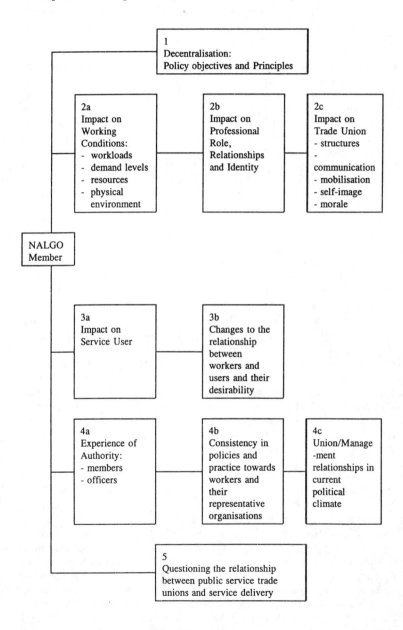

The impact on working conditions

As we have seen, the impact of decentralisation on working conditions figured significantly for many respondents. Activists were typically concerned with a variety of factors including, changes to workloads and their ability to effectively meet any increase in demand, produced by heightened expectations, which in turn was felt to have been consciously generated by the Authority's election promises and subsequent publicity. Related to this was a concern with the level of resources that would be available to meet this demand. Furthermore, there were concerns about the physical working environment in the new structures. In addition, however, they were also concerned about the impact on their professional role, or more precisely, about whether decentralisation would help or hinder their ability to effectively carry out their job as they currently perceived it. This concern was focused on their relationships, both with other professionals working in the Authority, but particularly with the service users. There was also an issue over the extent to which their specialised professional identity might be undermined by the genericism within decentralisation. Linked to this was an anxiety about the extent to which decentralisation would result in a diminution of their professional status and their ability to influence, shape, or control welfare provision either in the way needs were determined or satisfied.

Workers also wanted to assess the likely impact of decentralisation on the NALGO Branch. The ease with which workers could meet and organise effectively in their own collective structures was very much part of their working lives, almost part of their conditions of service. Indeed there was some feeling that decentralisation should be opposed simply on the grounds of its impact on trade unionism and that any restrictions on their ability to organise in an appropriate manner should become part of the agenda of items to be negotiated in both neighbourhood and authority-wide forums. In particular workers were concerned about the impact of decentralisation on the union structures, on the consequent difficulties of organising and communicating across the Branch, and the enforced changes on their identity as trade unionists. Thus, the extent to which their trade unionism had been related to their identification with an occupational role, rather than through their employment as a local authority worker, had significant implications under decentralisation, requiring a re-orientation both to their colleagues and to their self-perception as trade unionists. Overall, such considerations over working conditions inevitably raised questions and dilemmas about the nature of public service trade unionism and the extent to which their interests as workers should, if necessary, be sacrificed in favour of a better service for users.

The impact on the service user

The impact of decentralisation on the service user was another important consideration for the activists. They focused on both the immediate impact on service delivery - were users getting more and/or better services, more quickly, and in a more effective manner - and the possible implications for the relationship between workers and consumers. In this last respect the key issues were: changes to their immediate relations, described as proximity to the consumer, which included the potential for user violence, as well as the more long-term implications over who was to control service provision and the manner of its delivery. This was highlighted by the establishment of the Neighbourhood Forums. Having established that overall there were improvements to be had from closer, more personal contact between service provider and user, which could help to dismantle unproductive barriers between them, there remained a desire to retain sufficient personal defensible space. Workers wanted to maintain a distinction between, what Goffman (1959) described as, front and back region, between the place where performance is given and the place where 'performance is knowingly contradicted as a matter of course' (p 114), and where backstage languague can be used. In the new open-plan offices workers were very conscious about what they experienced as over-exposure to the public. In addition, workers were very aware of the difficulties of having insufficient resources, despite increases in expenditure during the early years of decentralisation, when service users had been promised a more effective service, and which many would interpret as meaning that more resources would be available more quickly. In such circumstances it was feared, and experienced, that front line staff would have to take the brunt of any dissatisfaction or anger of frustrated users. Again workers were aware of the need to find the right balance between closer proximity, ease of access, and adequate cover for any of the services, against spreading services so thinly that users ended up receiving a poorer service.

Finally, there were issues that arose from the introduction of neighbourhood based Forums, and the implications these might have for professional control over service provision and managerial accountability. The Forums offered the greatest opportunity to challenge and transform existing welfare social relations. They created a public arena in which professional definitions of social need, priorities, patterns of service delivery, and modes of behaviour in respect of both public service users overall, and specific user groups, could be explicitly identified, questioned and altered. Ultimately they were arenas in which the personal, as well as the collective, competence of workers could be brought to account. Irrespective of whether or not the Forums had direct powers of hiring and firing, they had the potential to exert considerable influence if sufficiently organised and purposeful in their behaviour. Workers had not considered the Forums' potential, but had managed their arrival by both questioning the legitimacy of the participants, and defining their purpose in ways that did not directly impinge upon themselves. Thus, Forums were seen either as a public relations exercise for elected members and managers, or as a talking shop for unrepresentative but vociferous community organisations who wanted to feel part of the process of local government. Neither of these definitions were felt to be of immediate concern to the front-line staff, and thus there was no need to see the Forums as a point of accountability, or necessitating their participation.

Nevertheless, the presence of the Forums, as an alternative power base in local social welfare planning and service delivery, raised questions about the role of public service trade unions. Not least of these was whether as a trade union they should participate in the structures, thereby acknowledging their legitimacy, and also creating the possibility for new, albeit informal, avenues for negotiation over industrial relations issues, as well as being drawn increasingly into service delivery issues. Thus to seek such participation would have significant implications for the bargaining machinery and the nature of trade union concerns. Yet to avoid doing so could, should the Forums gain in strength and influence, leave the trade union weakened, and less able to influence policy formulation. This would leave them confined to a reactive role, but having to contend not only with their formal employers but also with organised local user and citizen groups. Many of the respondents expressed confidence in getting support from users and the public at large when they were engaged in industrial action. In future, with a well organised Forum lobby united with the elected members this assumed support may no longer be forthcoming. However, this does presuppose that the competing interests within the Forums can find a sufficiently strong and sustainable unity of interest amongst themselves, and one which coincides with the interests of the councillors.

The experience of the authority

Finally a factor which was central to the respondents' judgement of decentralisation was their experience of the Authority, divided between their experience of the elected members and the professional officer management. Although their perception of councillors and managers in relation to the planning and implementation of decentralisation, was important, this was not the only concern. In judging the politics and practice of the Authority, workers took account of a number of factors including: commitment to other key policy areas; relations with central government, which was perceived as the primary obstruction to successful social welfare policy at a local level; and finally, in relation to the workforce and the trade union, which theoretically they were committed to recognising and striving to work with in a co-operative manner. Such considerations were not time restricted to the post-decentralisation period, but included both what the Authority had stated was to be its overall strategic approach, and the extent to which an overall consistency of practice could be identified during its time in office.

In respect of their own representative body, NALGO, respondents took account of: the extent to which the Authority facilitated the effective functioning of the union; the degree to which it consulted and negotiated over industrial relations issues; and the extent to which it was seen to publicly acknowledge the positive role and importance of the union both in its representative function and as a legitimate voice on matters of public service practice. In relation to the Authority's attitude to themselves as workers, there was, for example, an acute awareness of the contradiction between the language of alliances and the avowed care of the workforce, with the perceived inadequate levels of awareness, lack of interest, and actual practice over safety and personal security at work. Examples were frequently given which were felt to be illustrative of a management that was not committed to its workforce, despite the rhetoric. These included: the then emergent policy on sickness, which was experienced as punitive; managements' denial of the stress involved in front-line service delivery; and the lack of adequate training workers had received when the decentralisation policy had been first introduced. Similarly, they did not perceive the councillors adopting their own emphasis on greater accountability but rather felt that it was they, as the workers with the most direct contact with the service user, who had to cope with both much greater levels of exposure to user frustration, and being held to account for all the shortcomings which they believed were largely beyond their control.

In the area of the Authority's overall strategy, the respondents had a clear sense of the linkages between a range of initiatives including equal opportunities and anti-discriminatory practice, the homelessness policy, low pay strategy, the rate-capping campaign and decentralisation. Disappointment over any one of these may not have produced an overall negativity, although both the equal opportunities policy and the rate-capping campaign were seen as bench marks by which the overall strategy might be judged. However, a sense of disillusionment over a number of these strategically important issues did lead to a questioning of the Authority's commitment both to the overall approach and to its genuineness in respect of any one initiative. Since decentralisation lay at the heart of the strategy, and had generated a considerable volume of discussion around policy values and goals, it was not surprising that any questioning of commitment or genuineness focused very sharply on this particular policy. It was after all the Authority's self-declared flagship, the personification of what they represented and stood for. Therefore, any doubt in either the implementation of the policy itself, or in other important policy areas or political action, would lead to a questioning of motives not only of decentralisation but the Authority itself. Not surprisingly such an analysis posed questions for the respondents about what could be achieved in the current political climate: what were the possibilities and limitations of progressive change in the context of the 'new right', and indeed what should be their strategy as trade unionists to the Authority in this context. Respondents faced the dilemma of how much leeway should be given to an authority, elected on a 'no cuts' ticket, but which then declared that it had no alternative but to bow to government pressure. Further, once the Authority had chosen to continue in office, as a 'dented shield', respondents asked if this raised any fundamental questions in relation to its professed principles: did it merely reflect the absence of principles in political practice, or simply a realistic assessment of the lack of power to carry out their principles. Whatever the conclusion, it raised questions about the usefulness of treating the Authority's principled statements with any degree of seriousness. Clearly, not all, or even a majority, of respondents took the view that the elected members should have either resigned, or taken action that might have resulted in their removal from office. Nevertheless the period in which decentralisation was introduced coincided with, and was partly an outcome of, renewed debate about political practice in and by the state. It is not surprising, therefore, that the behaviour of Islington's councillors should come under critical scrutiny, and that this heightened level of interest in politics should have an affect on the smooth implementation of a policy such as decentralisation, which was in part centrally concerned with issues of values and political practice.

The case study revealed a high level of commitment to public collective provision, and subsequently a concern for the way in which such services are provided. Workers in the front line of service delivery are well placed to recognise, as did many respondents, both their shortcomings and the ways in which services could be improved. However, how, and to what extent, such understandings are articulated by public service trade unionists will vary, because they are equally concerned about themselves, as workers. The conditions under which they have to labour, their relations with their employer, and what they could be expected to tolerate in changing their professional practice, have all to be considered. Such workers have to deal with and manage the day to day impact of any new policy initiative and are, therefore, understandably cautious or critical, rather than idealistic, about the possibilities of specific policies. Policies also have to be evaluated against their impact on other policies and practices. Furthermore, workers have both a history and a current experience of management and their employers which they also utilise in their evaluation of any proposed strategy. Similarly, they have a current experience of the service users, and of themselves as providers, and this too impacts forcefully on their perception of the limits and possibilities for changing the social relationships involved. They may see themselves as the guardians of the public good, of desirable and appropriate behaviour, but they also have few opportunities in their work to experience the user in any other relationship other than that of client, supplicant, or dependent. This does little to facilitate the competing image of the user as a citizen with rights, who has a central role in the shaping of social welfare. Even if they feel the need to establish more equal relations with service users there are few opportunities for doing so, breaking free from their own contradictory relationship to the user as citizen and the user as client poses many difficulties.

Finally, it should be remembered that it is difficult to speak of an overall single union response. The case study, for example, revealed differences of attitude and approach between: activists and ordinary members, different departments and occupational groupings within them; those who had been decentralised and those who had not; and between workers on different points on the proletarianised-ambiguously located continuum. The union's character, itself constantly evolving, was strongly shaped at any one point in time by the influence of those segments within the union that had managed to secure a powerful place within its structures. Such segments, as in for example radical social work, brought their own particular work cultures, patterns, identities and history, as well as their local political traditions and allegiances. However, the influence and strength of specific sections varied over time, and other groups took over as the makers of union character.

NALGO Islington - A typical response to decentralisation?

The 'neutral but cautious' response by the Islington Branch of NALGO to the decentralisation scheme - "ultra-traditionalist" and "a crude reactive role" according to Sharron (1984) - was not in itself uncommon in relation to trade union colleagues in other areas across the country. This was recognised at a national level by NALGO (1984) when, speaking in the context of social work, and giving a broad welcome to the devolution of services to a more local level it noted the overall caution of branches in their response, but also supported this by conditioning its own approval thus,

> Providing adequate resources, staffing, training, etc. is forthcoming and provided that it is accompanied by a shift in the balance of influence over the provision and development of services back to social work practitioners and away from purely managerial staff. (p 51)

It also noted, with reference to the possible development of local welfare advisory committees which included 'community representatives', and which could just as easily refer to those local structures such as the Forums in Islington, that they should not become, "bodies to which individual social workers are held accountable" (p 51). The same document also expressed the union's concern over, "voluntary organisations' increased role in policy making ... at the relative lack of public accountability by voluntary organisations, and that the services which voluntary organisations provide are not likely to be as well monitored as those provided by local authorities" (p 50). Similarly, Ivan Beavis (1985), the then NALGO London Regional Secretary commented that,

> Like most worthy causes, NALGO is in favour of decentralisation in principle so long as it can be demonstrated that it will lead to an improvement in the standard of local authority services and that such a process is not achieved at the expense of the workforce. ... Trade unions exist primarily to protect and advance the interests of their own membership. This applies to local government just as much as it does to the manufacturing sector or anywhere else. ... Labour councillors have forgotten this simple fact ... wanted us to forget ... all the principles and procedures of consultation and bargaining which the unions see as essential in order to protect their members' interests ... we approached decentralisation in the same way as any reorganisation. (p 12)

Responses by other branches were not too dissimilar from that of Islington. Thus, in Walsall, the first authority to decentralise, the unions initially refused to cooperate when the council was unable to guarantee any loss of jobs, but were subsequently found to be too weak to sustain their position, and quickly gave way to the authority, after a number of workers were suspended for refusing to comply. The Tower Hamlets NALGO Branch, in response to their Borough's decentralisation proposal, raised 19 points of concern (Tower Hamlets Decentralisation Committee 4/9/86), which were not dissimilar from the concerns expressed within Islington, concluding with a request for "a written interpretation of the concept of decentralisation since no clear view or perspective has been expressed".

In Hackney, NALGO's response was if anything a much tougher one to that in Islington. Here the Branch refused to cooperate over decentralisation in a convincing vote of 836 to 139 in favour of non-cooperation on the grounds that, "the conditions of work of NALGO members will be radically altered". The baseline position as agreed by the Branch Executive was that, "staff see decentralisation as an issue relating to pay, conditions of work and job content, duties and responsibilities" (NALGO Emergency Committee Minutes May 1983). Hackney NALGO put forward a set of 12 demands which it said would have to be met prior to the first stage of decentralisation being introduced. The demands, which were virtually ignored by the Council, included a range of issues designed to improve conditions of service but which were not necessarily directly related to decentralisation. For example, they wanted workplace nurseries to be attached to all workplace sites; all temporary posts, including those employed under the then Manpower Services Commission, to be made permanent; and all vacant posts and those readily identifiable to be filled. Beavis (1985), speaking of the Hackney situation, noted that in his view, "the Labour Council adopted ... the same familiar postures and reasoning of all employers. There was no radical new industrial relations initiative introduced. ... Over 20 different disputes raged during the period 1982 to 1984. To this day the union has refused to conclude an agreement to allow decentralisation to proceed in Hackney just because we do not believe that any such agreement will be honoured" (p 13).

As we saw earlier, NALGO and the NUPE Officers Branch in Hackney were also to come into dispute with the local Tenants Federation, and affiliated Tenants Associations, who had been vigorously promoting their own decentralisation initiative. When the tenants occupied a local housing office complaining of delaying tactics the unions took industrial action, to put pressure on the Authority to end it as swiftly as possible, and subsequently closed all 27 area housing offices to the public, withdrawing all council services from the council estates in the area of the occupation. Tenants accused the unions of 'corruption' and 'gangster style tactics' whilst according to Community Action (1984), UCATT and TGWU stewards continued to support the tenants. The tenants claimed that their occupation had revealed explicit racist and sexist material on display and evidence that repair work was being given to a select group of private contractors at inflated prices. The occupation was ended by the retaking of the property by local government workers having, according to the tenants, been 'tipped-off' about the small number in occupation at a particular moment. Earlier, NALGO had been accused of deliberately deceiving the tenants into signing an agreement on the promise of a meeting with the unions which they subsequently refused to hold. Tyrrell (1984), Chairperson to the Federation, argued that the councillors had failed to tackle either the professional management or the white-collar unions, "Elected councillors must confront management if they are to be able to run local government for the benefit of the people. As socialists we must get rid of the syndrome that unions are always right." Representatives from Islington's management have stated that there was never any industrial action in the Borough over decentralisation. Strictly speaking this is true, in the sense that the unions were not in dispute over either the objectives or principles of decentralisation. However, there were a number of disputes that were directly linked with the implementation of the policy. These included: the boycotting of the first Neighbourhood Officer posts; stoppages over staff safety in the neighbourhood offices; social worker action over the conditions under which they entered the local offices; a strike over the reorganisation of the Home Help Organisers into the neighbourhood offices; a prolonged dispute over the career grade proposals for Chief Executive administrative staff, and over the Borough's initial proposal not to have a designated receptionist in the neighbourhood offices. In addition, there were disputes over Borough-wide issues that have involved neighbourhood office workers e.g. the Nursery Nurses and Priority Based Budgeting disputes. Finally, there were other disputes that were seen as being central to the implementation of the principles espoused within decentralisation although having wider ramifications, which might have occurred irrespective of decentralisation, but nevertheless take on a greater significance because of decentralisation (e.g. the racism dispute). Such disputes were not atypical either in their frequency or intensity, and led Sharron (1984) to describe the aftermath of the Nursery Nurses dispute as leaving, "a legacy of bitterness ... in the socialist Borough of Islington where there is a regime which is probably as friendly to local government trade unions as any in the country" (p 10).

It was not unusual then to find industrial unrest associated with those authorities who attempted, or aspired to, radical socialist policy reforms. A number of writers have commented on this apparent paradox, and on the range of disputes that took place in those authorities where the new urban left was influential. Wolmar (1984) referred to the "remarkable wave of strikes in over half the 16 Labour authorities scheduled to be rate-capped" (p 13) and commented that, "these councils are facing political oblivion and their workforce mass redundancy" (p 13). Gyford (1985) stated that it was noticeable that "a number of left-wing councils have found themselves involved in industrial disputes" (p 101) and referred to Sheffield, St. Helens, Camden, Lewisham, and Southwark, as well as Hackney and Islington. Weinstein (1986) adds Haringey and Lambeth to the list and Walsall, Norwich, Manchester, Liverpool, and Tower Hamlets could also be included. Thomas (1985), adding Birmingham, refers to decentralisation as being, "seriously delayed and, at worst, killed by frustrating and often bitter negotiations with NALGO". Lansley et al. (1989) commented that "ironically, the new Left councillors often had a worse industrial relations record than other authorities ... It was the new policy initiatives of the left councillors which provoked the greatest number of disputes" (p 111) and suggest that "public sector trade unions have traditionally been over-defensive about radical change ... proved unwilling to adapt to change or even co-operate in measures to improve service delivery" (p 203). Hoggett (1987) stated that, "local government unions have tended to resist all attempts at decentralisation over the last few years". Pilkington (1985) spoke of Labour-controlled authorities being, "racked by some of the most bitter industrial disputes in local government this decade". Sharron (1985) referred to the "generalised industrial unrest in left-wing Labour authorities, particularly those where attempts are being made to radically reorganise services" (p 17) whilst Ingham (1985) made a more general point suggesting that the propensity for local government workers to take industrial action is directly related to the strength of the Labour Party in the authority.

In addition to the regularity of disputes, there were also a number of recurring themes, many of which have appeared in Islington. A common concern was that the councils attempted to by-pass traditional mechanisms of industrial relations, speaking over the heads of the representatives and appealing directly to the workforce, or indeed a fear that councils were committed to seriously weakening the unions as an end in itself. The introduction of new technology was also a source of tension as was the regrading of posts, differences over the number of new appointments that would be necessary in the proposed structure, the level of cover for localised staff, opening hours, the speed of implementation, the degree of cross-departmental work proposed or generic work within a departmental structure. As the Islington Joint Trades Union Council expressed it,

The Trade Unions will not accept any attempt to undermine or reduce the effectiveness of job-descriptions by the introduction of generic worker posts in the Neighbourhood Offices. Skill and training in different fields is not inter- changeable between employees.

Further, the role and powers of the neighbourhood committees or Forums, the design and security of neighbourhood offices, the lines of managerial accountability, guarantees over redundancy and protection of existing service conditions, managerial inexperience and impatience to push the proposed changes through quickly, the filling of vacant posts, and concern that it was simply a disguised process of 'do-it-yourself cuts' were all sources of anxiety and conflict. In theory none of these issues should have proved insurmountable, and indeed might have been predicted given the extent of some of the proposed changes, but in reality they are symbolic of a much deeper conflict that has existed between the white-collar workers and the new urban left.

By contrast, blue-collar unions in local government have not always reacted in the same way as their white-collar colleagues in NALGO. Indeed one of the first initiatives on decentralisation in Hackney came jointly from the Hackney Tenants Federation and the building workers employed in the Authority's Direct Labour Organisation. In Walsall, where the DLO was said to be "rotten from tip to toe" (Sharron 1984) it nevertheless, according to Powell the then leader of Walsall Council, produced its own "package of revolutionary reforms" (quoted in Sharron 1984) after it had been warned of the possible loss of jobs. John Newman (1985), Convenor of the Islington DLO wrote in favour of decentralisation and despite voicing some regret that as a trade unionist they had "sacrificed a degree of solidarity by agreeing to local repairs ... an element of competition is creeping in which is unhealthy from a union point of view", nevertheless felt that the right decision had been taken because,

We can now offer a better service to tenants which we as unionists believe is essential if we are to rally people round in defence of the DLO and local government in general. (p 10)

Manual workers in Islington did, however, successfully negotiate, although only after a four day stoppage, an improved flat-rate pay scheme, outside the national basic rate, plus a local bonus system. Livingstone (1982) also spoke positively of the blue-collar response to the implementation of the GLC's manifesto promises, "we carry the bulk of them with us on most issues. The blue-collar unions are much better generally" (p 22) and compared them with the white-collar staff association which was he said, "a total roadblock to everything we try to do". The TGWU as part of its own 'Link-Up' campaign with the voluntary sector sponsored a publication by Labour Community Action (undated), a pressure group within the Labour Party. This argued for the adoption of a community development strategy by the Party, which would include a duty on local authorities to consult with the community sector, a requirement to draw up a "local strategy for community development" (p 11), and legislation requiring all grant supported voluntary groups to adopt an equal opportunities policy.

Whilst there may be some exaggeration involved in some of the above comments, and some possible political point scoring given traditional rivalries between white and blue-collar workers, there are nonetheless good reasons why manual workers may see improved services and localised delivery as something to be supported. It is after all quite likely that those manual workers will themselves be the recipients of public services and will live locally; hence they, their families, and friends stand to make a direct gain. This is less likely with those professionalised white-collar workers, who may not reside within their local authority employer's boundaries, and who are less likely to be dependent on such a wide range of public services, that are essential to their material well-being, and whose absence leaves them without alternative means. Many of the administrative and clerical white-collar workers would though undoubtedly be in a similar position to their blue-collar colleagues, and in the case-study their responses to the policy were more favourable, and they were less supportive of the Branch's position. Manual workers may also improve their working conditions as a consequence of decentralisation, especially when it encourages multi-skilled team work in a fixed neighbourhood in place of an individualised impersonal mono-skilled approach.

However, it is worth noting that whilst this white-collar conservatism and defensiveness might reflect the overall picture it is not universally true and white-collar public service trade unionists have also supported such initiatives. Thus, a joint publication (albeit in the context of a Conservative authority) by the Roehampton District Tenants Associations and the Wandsworth NALGO Housing Shop Stewards acknowledged that there was, "no shortage of criticism of the qualitative deficiencies in local authority housing provision", and went on to propose the setting up of multi-disciplinary teams, estate based surgeries, evening opening, guaranteed availability of housing officers, a more personal and friendly manner by staff, a district office shop guides for new tenants, tackling rent arrears quickly and personally rather than by letter, and a locally based advisory service. Such examples are, however, rare.

Conclusion

This chapter has attempted to draw together the areas of concern that effect the response of white-collar public service trade unionists to policy initiatives in service delivery. Although decentralisation has been the focus of the study, it has been suggested that the variables identified, the objectives of the policy iself and its underlying principles, its impact on working conditions, the consequences for the service user, and the workers' experience of the Authority in respect of other policies and its ability to manage effectively, are all likely to be significant in any similar policy innovation. Workers do not respond to policies in isolation but locate them within a broad context that is both complex and dynamic. It has also been argued that industrial disputes in those authorities characterised by new urban left councillors have been commonplace, and perhaps more so than in other authorities. Further thought is given to this observation in the next chapter. Here, it has been noted that the intensity and relatively large number of disputes involving NALGO in the Borough of Islington have not been atypical but are indeed illustrative of that particular period. Underneath much of the conflict lies a deep sense of disappointment and frustration with the limited achievements of those urban left councils with whom many of the public service trade union activists felt a lot in common. Whilst for some of these activists it was the personal failings, weaknesses, or tactical errors that stunted or halted socialist progress in the local state, any shortcomings need also to be considered in the wider context of political developments. The negative evaluation of the Authority and its policies fed into and reinforced the union's priority of pursuing its own sectional interests.

12 Understanding the conflict

This chapter is concerned with examining the various explanations that have been offered to account for the high levels of industrial conflict involving public service unions in radical Labour authorities. Three broad approaches are identified. The first tends to isolate the two main protagonists, unions and employers, and seeks explanations in their separate attitudes and behaviours, ultimately making one side more responsible than the other. The second approach, an extension of the first, recognises the relational element involved in the conflict and, whilst also identifying particular problems specific to either party, attempts to identify how each can move toward the other, thereby reducing the possibility of future conflict. In this second approach there is less concern for identifying a guilty party. The third approach attempts to locate the principal parties in the wider socio-political context, and seeks explanations in the difficulties the parties had in operating within this.

In this last approach two theories can be identified in the literature. The first explains the conflict by reference to the tension between trade unionism and socialist transformative politics. The second seeks an explanation in the breakdown of the traditional styles of industrial relations in local government brought about by the fiscal crisis. Whilst both offer some interesting insights neither are fully satisfactory and a third explanation is offered here. This argues that those attempts that confine themselves to the area of industrial relations are too limited, and that it is more useful to see the public service industrial conflicts during the 1980s in the context of the efforts of the urban left to mobilise a new political force. The industrial relations conflicts are but one aspect of the failure of that project to materialise due to the multiple variables and their specific characteristics that needed to be harnessed together, but which were also in some important respects beyond the control of those pursuing the strategy. The area of industrial relations became an important focal point not only because there were some important, immediate, and practical, work-related issues to be resolved for state employed workers and their managers, and indeed these issues at times completely dominated the agenda, but also because it was the most important institutionalised setting in which the ideas for the proposed political formation were advanced and their feasibility tested. All the other potential public arenas involving the different participants that might be concerned with such a project were still very much in the making. Thus we should see the industrial relations conflicts both as an expression of the difficulties of negotiating work-related change in a particularly hostile climate for local authorities and, as a reflection of the tensions involved in the exploration of a political project, at the centre of which lay an argument for transforming the social relations of state provided services.

Finally, we consider three possible scenarios for the future of public service white-collar trade unionism. I conclude by suggesting that the future is likely to be one of a continuing mixture of reactive, 'conditions of service' trade unionism, with spasmodic attempts at more pro-active inroads into areas of public sector provision and the social relations contained therein. At best such activity will be uneven in its growth and development but it is likely nevertheless to have a continuing impact on public service trade unionism. Ultimately, given favourable conditions, it may lead to a radical transformation of relationships in the public services, based on a democratic mandate for social intervention by state employed workers and rooted in relationships of citizenship rights with service users and their organisations. However, for this to materialise, public service trade unions need to address the limitations of the particular form of politics that has developed amongst significant sections of the membership.

There are some difficulties in adopting this approach for although the three broad approaches identified do reflect real positions and mark out significant differences in addressing the problem, they are also to some extent artificially created. Most writers appear to be quite happy moving between the different explanations, utilising discrete aspects, and have not felt the need to distinguish clearly between them. Consequently, it is not always possible to identify specific writers as belonging exclusively to one or the other approach. Nevertheless, this process of filtering through the mixed explanations does, I believe, provide us with a clearer understanding of the competing tendencies within the literature. It is, however, important to acknowledge that each of the broad explanations have important contributions to make to our understanding although it is my contention that to date these have only been partial explanations.

Isolate the parties involved in the conflict

(i) The failures of management

The political and professional management within those radical local authorities have been accused of being either too weak and naive, or too uncompromising in their approach to their white-collar unions. They have been too weak in failing to tackle the unacceptable practices in local government, and naive in assuming too readily that unions would be sympathetic to the idea of improving public services in an effort to counter the New Right's anti-collective welfare politics. Simultaneously they are said to have been too uncompromising towards the unions, failing to sufficiently acknowledge the need for greater worker participation in management. In either case they are accused of being ineffective, incompetent or just plain inexperienced. Thus according to Lansley et al. (1989),

> Left councils conspicuously failed to address the problem of, let alone resolve, the tension between the interests of producers and the interests of consumers; or to develop clear priorities between policies to improve service provision for the local community and measures to better terms and conditions of staff. This was because the rhetoric of the left constantly confused the two. The struggle that councils engaged in was 'to defend jobs and services' which were seen as inseparable. The

uncomfortable reality that services could be protected while jobs were lost, or vice versa, was not confronted. (p 107)

They suggest that the new councillors were uncomfortable with their role as employers especially when it came to making difficult decisions between different forms of spending. They quote Sullivan, leader of Lewisham Council 1985-87, as saying that councillors failed to manage effectively because they were confused between the requirements of management and ideas about workers' control and industrial democracy. For Lansley et al. there were also, "more fundamental management failures" within the professional managerial group, pointing to the absence of structures that could cope with expansion and change, and speaking of managers as being "often ill-equipped and unskilled at implementing change" (p 115), clinging to traditional methods and being unable to effectively translate policy ideas into working practices, provide proper training, or offer effective means of communication to ensure that workers were fully cognisant to the policy ideas and their implications.

Hoggett (1987) was similarly critical of the way local government operated saying that it was, "virtually impossible to get a coordinated response from all council departments to a common problem. Councils are organised on the basis of (usually warring) professional empires ..." He identified a second approach to the tendency of leaving it to the expert, which is the attempt by the elected members to deal directly with the trade unions, by-passing senior management and thereby, "effectively given the unions a veto over council policy and management in the belief that this is the correct thing to do" (p 32). Wolmar (1984, 1985) spoke of the councillors' lack of preparation to manage large numbers of staff, indeed failing to perceive management as a key task, and finding it difficult to resolve their dual role as representatives of the labour movement and employer of thousands of people. This, he says, was reflected in their ineffective negotiations which were amateurish and given low priority, "the average Labour Party activist ... probably knows as much about industrial relations as about the mechanical structure of a dustcart. Worse, the last thing they ever dreamed of in their wildest nightmare is to be an employer" (Wolmar 1984, p 13). In addition, he argues that elected members failed to provide training for managers and shop stewards, had no proper mechanism for discussing policy objectives with the workforce, and were short of direct contact with the trade unions of which they had an idealistic understanding. For Pilkington (1985) the new Left councillors, with their community activist background, "had little or no experience of traditional trade union functions and practices". Hoggett (1987) expressed a similar view commenting, "Workerist assumptions that unions play a progressive role may be good for inner party Brownie points but do not always square with the reality" (p 35). Like Wolmar, he argues that radical change requires, "a political commitment, sagacity, dogged determination and imagination" (p 33) and identifies those councillors who took a tough stand, as being positive role models in the task of overcoming NALGO's 'dynamic conservatism'.

Sharron (1985) meanwhile pointed to disputes in St Helens and Sheffield as arising as a result of the councillors' failure to maintain the traditional pattern of industrial relations, which had led over the years to a situation where the unions had a veto over policy developments and had acquired some very favourable agreements. Here the problem on the management side was said to be "dynamic, impatient and perhaps managerially inexperienced Labour groups needing to stamp out what they saw as sloppy management, and to impress on the workforce their right to carry through radical reorganisations." (p 20).

Yet Heery (1988) speaks of the councillors in Islington and the GLC, when faced with "trade unions unwilling to grant open-ended support for their policies ... have tended to lurch towards a much harder position ... decided to impose change ... there was a conviction that an electoral mandate gave the council the right to override the sectional interests of trade unions. The result was ... to generate a crisis in industrial relations" (pp 210-211). Certainly the Islington case-study, although focused on the experience of trade unionists, highlights a marked shift in strategy towards greater Taylorist styles of managerial control by both senior officers and elected members. This was experienced by workers in relation to both specific policies and employment practices, such as that on homelessness or sick leave, as well as a general re-assertion of the "right to manage". Whilst this was partly as a consequence of their experience of industrial relations, it was largely as a result of Labour's 1987 electoral defeat, and the decision by Labour local councillors to remain in office, either as a dented shield to protect vulnerable individuals and communities, or due to a reluctance to give up power, and the need to secure their political futures by appealing over the workforce to the electorate. Thus, left Labour authorities increasingly adopted the "new public sector managerialism" (Newman and Clarke 1994) instigated by the Conservative government.

(ii) White-Collar local authority trade unions: conservative and self-interested or simply protecting their legitimate interests in a hostile climate?

For those writers focusing on what responsibility should the white-collar unions bear for the industrial unrest there are broadly two schools of thought. The first argues that unions such as NALGO are inherently conservative, intent on defending their own narrow interests at any cost, and clinging to outmoded practices. This traditionalism is seen as gaining support from the hard left within the union who themselves tend to be conservative in their trade unionism and who have, during the years of growing industrial militancy, developed a rank and file politics that is unreservedly hostile to any top-down political or managerial initiatives. Linked to such a perspective is usually a call for trade union reform (Sawyer 1984, Wolmar 1984). The second approach sees the unions as defending their legitimate interests and, having weighed up the risks and benefits of the policy initiatives, decided on a cautious approach. Here it is argued that the unions resisted policies that might undermine their strength, and that they needed to weigh up the advantages of pre-figurative policies against the need for self-protection. Further, as they were never accorded a legitimate place in the politics of the urban left they could therefore never be confident as to the real intentions of the politicians seeking to implement the policies associated with it.

Hodge (1988) noted that the greatest resistance to Islington's decentralisation programme came from the trade unions because, "even the most radical local government officers are afraid of change." Wolmar (1984) argues that in general the role of British trade unions has "always been narrowly defined and defensive. Unions are not necessarily socialist". Of NALGO, he reflects that its conservatism is indicated by it having "repeatedly voted by large majorities not to affiliate to the Labour Party" (p 14) and whose practices can amount to an "unacceptable neo-Luddism" (p 15). The Labour Coordinating Committee (1984) commenting that the unions had "declined the invitation to step outside their normal traditional role", preferring instead "to assume the more passive role of responding to others' proposals in order to maintain the usual employee/employer relationship", reflected that "sadly public sector unions seem to be lagging some way behind some of their private sector counterparts when it comes to asserting control over the labour process their members are engaged in" (pp 24-25) and called for them to "transcend that rather narrow attitude" or fear the consequences of themselves not being supported in the face of cuts and privatisation (p 25). Sharron

(1985) concludes that when faced with the challenge of change, "NALGO's instincts were defensive and crude. It was unable either to take account of the benefits and opportunities offered ... or to make allowances for the councils' fraught relations with central government: its narrow field of vision was fixed on relatively minor issues of conditions of service linked to reorganisation" (p 20). Heery (1988) too suggests that in Islington the unions, "refused to countenance" a change in the nature of industrial relations by rejecting the council's desire to "replace the conventional, adversarial system ... with a more co-operative relation ..." (p 204), and their overall response is described as "sceptical and wary" and as devoting "their attentions to minimising any adverse consequences for the workforce ... delayed the implementation of the policy ... slowed the process of change ... increased the cost of the policy ... knocked some of the radical edges off the council's proposals" (pp 206-207).

Such traditional conservatism in NALGO, which has often in the past been put down to the influential presence of senior officers in the membership, has more recently been linked to the politics of left-wing political groupings, particularly the Socialist Workers Party. These groups have often been held responsible for much of the industrial conflict (Puddephat 1984, Blunkett, quoted in Sharron, 1985, also Campbell 1985). Thus Shields and Webber (1986) in their summing up of the conflict in Hackney conclude that, "in common with other inner-city NALGO branches, the active membership was dominated by a few highly motivated members of hard-line revolutionary organisations whose acknowledged strategy is the undermining of all left Labour initiatives. They were able to take advantage of the natural apprehensions of the rank and file members when faced with such radical and wide sweeping proposals ..." (p 138). Sharron (1985), like Wolmar (1984), notes the irony of the similarity between far left trade-unionism and NALGO's traditional 'non-political' approach. The trade unionism of such left groups is described as "confrontation at all costs with employers, whether they are big multi-nationals or progressive socialist authorities ... continually to press home the union's advantage in sympathetic councils, despite any financial or political difficulties those councils may be facing" (pp 20-21). Wolmar believes that the SWPs interest is in, "boosting their membership at the expense of a disillusioned and beaten Labour left" (p 14). However, Lansley et al. (1989) express some caution, and whilst noting that the role of the SWP in promoting industrial action has been well publicised, "not least by the SWP itself", warn against exaggerating their influence as far more powerful have been "those trade unionists who were also active Labour Party members and who saw accelerating industrial action as a way of mobilising workers and preventing cuts" (p 114). A similar point was made by Hodge (1988) and other councillors in Islington, who have complained about the way NALGO members have used the local Labour Party to pursue their interests particularly in industrial disputes.

The Islington research did find that a number of the Neighbourhood Shop Stewards belonged to the Socialist Workers Party and indeed that in some sections, such as the Housing Advisory Service, they were by far the largest grouping. In addition a number of respondents, as noted earlier, indicated that the SWP were responsible for getting on to the Branch agenda items that were not seen as being immediately relevant to the broad membership, and proposing solutions to problems that were not shared by the majority. However, my conclusions are, like Lansley et al. that it is indeed easy to exaggerate their influence. Firstly, the SWP figured no more significantly than other left of centre organisations, especially the Labour Party and Communist Party, in the respondents' comments on influential political groupings in the Branch. Secondly, whilst they may have been influential in some occupational groups their presence was noticeably absent in many other groups, and the numbers of SWP activists involved overall was relatively small compared to activists from other political groups, a point confirmed by the Chairperson of the Neighbourhood Service Sub-Committee. Thirdly, what was striking about the comments was, in fact, how aware respondents were of attempts by the SWP to 'take advantage' of a situation, indeed how predictable they were, and therefore, how easy it was to spot their manoeuvrings. Furthermore, such predictability enabled other activists to more easily recognise what they perceived as the sensible aspects of SWP politics. It is somewhat too easy, not to say paternalistic, to suggest that workers are unable to make up their own minds about political strategies and only support them because they have been misled by one particular political group

Other writers have argued that there is a specific form of militancy within NALGO, which is not directly related to a political party but to the inappropriate copying of what is perceived of as industrial workplace rank-and-file politics. The most developed position is that advanced by Joyce et al. (1988) in a study of radical trade unionism amongst social workers. Here they, incorrectly I would suggest, try to distinguish between the specific form of social work trade unionism and those of other workers in the public sector, developing an argument around a particular brand of rank-and-filism in social work trade unionism to explain their specificity. What set social workers apart was, it is claimed, their self-activity aimed at making NALGO "better suited ... to the purpose of providing for their collective representation" (p 8), and which was objectified in a union character that was, "activist, militant and sectionalist" (p 8). Social workers, they suggest, were faced with the question of whether they would develop new forms of struggle or go with old ones. In the end they chose the latter and the authors comment, "we believe that initially they made the mistake of seeing their own fractional experience as in some way representing the whole union, and once or twice even the whole working class" (p 4).

Joyce et al. argue that the early militancy of social work developed as much in opposition to the union leadership which was, for them wrongly, perceived as conservative or reactionary, seeking "a docile, impotent form of trade unionism". The most significant tactic adopted was said to be that of 'rank-and-filism', "a potent political doctrine in social workers' trade unionism" (p 239). Here rank-and-filism is defined as the self organisation of workplace members who organise on a delegate basis, the latter being subject to direct election and recall by the workers they represent, and it was this tendency which they suggest led to autonomous action by grass roots social workers within NALGO. Its ideal form was seen as a kind of "competitive militancy. Vanguardism is meant to spark off more grass roots initiatives as other workers realise the validity of direct, spontaneous action" (p 256). Furthermore, there was always some uncertainty around the relationship between these social work activists and their local government colleagues as they preferred to concentrate on issues specific to social work. Such perceptions are said to have changed by the end of the 1970s but the particular brand that was social work trade unionism had a major impact on the union which, the authors conclude, was permanently changed especially in respect of a different attitude to industrial action. For their part, the social work "vanguardism of earlier days has given way to a more refined tactical repertoire in the mid-1980s" (p 162).

There can be no denying either uneven and variable developments in a trade union or the influence of social workers in NALGO. They have been prominent in campaigns against public sector cuts and the centre of two of the union's biggest disputes, the field and residential social worker strikes, as well as being active in local branch organisations. In Islington, social services was seen as one of the strongest departments in trade union terms. However, I believe it is incorrect to speak of a distinct social work trade unionism. Indeed, there is not one but a number of brands of trade unionism within social work, and attitudes to trade unionism amongst social workers will vary according to such factors as geographical location (shire based against metropolitan), age, education and qualification, position within the hierarchy, and service orientation. Rather, what is being described is a significant, but fractional, tendency within social work, but one which was also evident, although with varying degrees of strength and vociferousness, within other local government occupational groups, such as planning and public health. Such tendencies were organised both within the occupational groups (e.g. Case Con in social work, PHAS in public health) and across the union overall (NALGO Action Group). Moreover, the influence of such groups within their local branches and the union generally varies over time so that in Islington the most powerful group in the Branch in the late 1970s was the libraries section which was dominated by the Communist Party. Within the neighbourhood offices, there were very few social worker representatives in workplace steward roles and it was the housing department that was a growing and powerful influence. Thus, the growth of militant trade unionism amongst social workers is better understood in the context of a more general trend within the public services and affecting a wide range of occupational groups including some of the more emergent groups such as those in equal opportunities, economic development, urban regeneration, arts and culture, along with community development.

What is significant is not the identification of some occupational specificity, especially since the occupation is itself internally segregated, but the identification of differentiating factors that cut across occupational groups. These are understood as being related partly to a worker's position in relation to the delivery of state welfare provision, partly to shared positions in terms of work and market relations, and partly to common influences outside of the productive process. Thus Lash and Urry (1987) suggest some common developments within trade union politics overall since the late 1960s, in the form of what they describe as "radical individualism" in union struggles, as well in the new social movements. This is "rooted in shop floor struggles which often opposed official union channels. These were viewed as decentralised struggles against the union as well as the capitalist hierarchy, and labelled as 'anarchic'. This radical individualism is, for Lash and Urry, based on public rights connected to the state and "involves mistrust of and deep hostility to 'authority' whether that is of the employer, the state, the union or the class." What is clear is that the character of NALGO's growing militancy has to some extent been shaped by a strongly activist, grass roots and at times anti-managerialist culture amongst many of its shop stewards and activists. The roots of this culture may be different for different occupational groups and fractions within them, but they have been increasingly brought together by changes within the public sector affecting all occupational groups. Furthermore this militant rank-and-filist character itself went through a process of reformulation during the 1980s, particularly in those areas concerned with equal opportunities and anti-discriminatory practice. This has to date produced what might be described as a radical individualism that is no longer 'anarchic' but is disciplined, not by any one party, but by the mandarins of a new moralism.

The resultant politics are often symbolic and authoritarian. For example, rather than being anti-managerial as in the 1970s, it demands that management be accountable, for not only ensuring that rules and procedures governing access to jobs, services and resources are non-discriminatory, but should involve positive targeting towards particular social categories, notably black and ethnic minorities, women, those with disabilities, and gays and lesbians, in order to put right past injustices against them, but now at the expense of current applicants. The union then sees its role as monitoring such practices and punishing those who transgress, including its own members. This aspect of the new rank-and-filism has an element of policing the broad trade union membership, as well as other non-union colleagues, and insists that management fulfils its responsibilities by taking action that may not be in the immediate interests of the current union membership. Indeed, NALGO was prepared to make judgements about which union member was "correct", or what level of punishment should be handed out, but often without the necessary expertise and structures to ensure that this could be done fairly. It has also led both to the introduction of bureaucratic solutions to the problem of inequality and disadvantage to ensure that particular interests are represented, and to arguments about who is the most disadvantaged and therefore whose interests deserve the highest priority, which has often resulted in further differentiation and division within the union. Thus NALGO Islington has a number of 'self-organised' groups including a Women's Group, a Black Workers' Group, a Gay and Lesbian Group, and an Irish Workers Group, the latter being more of a Borough-wide body than one restricted to NALGO members. Such groups however, do not necessarily reflect the self activity of their potential membership or arise in response to a demand from such groups. Rather, these were groups which the branch leadership deemed as necessary and for whom it reserved seats on the Executive Committee, despite the fact that neither the Black Workers' nor the Women's Group were in any sense functioning. Their value was more in the symbolic message they projected about the 'correctness' of the union's politics.

Some of Islington NALGO's industrial disputes in the mid-1980s reflected the common confusions and sectional conflicts that have arisen within the new rank-and-filism. For example, the attitude of many of the respondents to the low level of union activity amongst the chief executive administrative workers is revealing of the often symbolic and unintegrated nature of the new politics. The administrative section of the chief executive's department within the neighbourhood offices comprised mainly low-paid, low status, female workers, a significant proportion of whom were black women. The interview material revealed a marked failure by NALGO to understand the nature of this group, with their reluctance to actively engage in trade union politics, which was usually explained away as 'apathy'. Few of those interviewed made any connection between, for example, the reluctance to engage in strike action with the relative low pay of these workers, and, therefore, whether they were literally able to afford to lose a day's pay to strike for something that was not always of immediate benefit to them. Similarly nobody appeared to consider that the disruption of public services might be more immediately damaging to these workers and their families: that they might be simultaneously both workers and service users. This is not to argue that trade unions should not engage in industrial action because of the impact on particular groups of workers but to suggest that some acknowledgement of the real material differences between workers is necessary when planning the kind of action to be taken, and to ensure that some workers are not scapegoated for their reluctance to participate in certain forms of action by those who are not called upon to make the same degree of sacrifice. The irony is to be found in having a militant rank-and-filism now cloaked in anti-racism and anti-sexism, that appears at times to take insufficient account of the interests of its lowest paid female and black members, in order to satisfy the symbolic gesture politics of its more favoured members.

The status tensions between workers appeared to be most sharply visible when they involved relations between the administrative workers and their professionalised colleagues. NALGO successfully argued against the Council's proposal not to have receptionists in the neighbourhood offices on the grounds that being a receptionist was a skilled job which would not be done properly by other workers too busily engaged in other tasks. Yet this impeccable traditional union defence of posts, and retaining discrete job descriptions, can also reinforce traditional status, power and class relations. In the running of decentralised neighbourhood offices it is the receptionists who are in the front-line of consumer frustration and anger, and indeed it is they who were on the receiving end of most abuse that occurred there. Other professionalised workers either resented having to undertake such duties or steadfastly refused to do so, 'not part of the job description', but offered no solution to those workers expected to cope with situations for which they are inadequately prepared or rewarded. Neither tackling the problem together, as colleagues, nor arguing for greater authority for receptionists, especially in relation to other professional workers, were seen as solutions.

There is then within NALGO a paradox in its militancy toward urban left authorities in that the traditional conservatism of the white-collar professionals is often to be found in an unholy and unspoken alliance with the rank-and-filist militancy of the left wing activists, themselves influenced by particular features of new left politics. The resultant politics, in the face of proposals for radical change, are narrowly defined and self-interested. They are intent on defending the existing division of labour within the public sector, and ensuring that any improvements to service delivery are brought about primarily by an extension of services, and therefore jobs, and not by an improvement to the quality of existing services or any transformation in the social relations between service producers and users. In response a number of leading politicians in Islington argued that such a position was both unrealistic and indefensible, and concluded that they should push ahead with policy initiatives, if necessary at the expense of the white-collar unions, and again ironically pursuing strategies closely similar to the market-oriented "new managerialism" sweeping other parts of local government.

(iii) The unions respond in the only realistic way possible

An alternative scenario recognises the resistance of the white-collar trade unionists to the political strategy and specific policy manifestations of the urban left, but argues that this was a realistic and understandable response in the context of a hostile central government, and the much reduced ability of local government to deliver the resources necessary for the successful implementation of progressive policies. Thus, in the current financial and political climate what is at issue here is the extent to which local authorities were using decentralisation, not only to retain control of strategic decisions, but to shift responsibility for inadequate services to devolved units, thereby making it more possible to survive. In such circumstances it is the workers who are exposed to, and are expected to deflect customer frustration, which may include physical assault. They are left to manage and allocate devolved but reduced budgets, but now with an additional neighbourhood based public body able to exert greater and immediate pressure from below, and dispute the increasingly difficult decisions that have to be taken as resources are withdrawn from vulnerable groups. Such devolved decision-making would in the circumstances add up to no more than do-it-yourself cuts, whilst allowing councillors to avoid responsibility as they refer to, and defer to, locally-based decisions that reflect local need. Further, given that many public service workers do have a genuine commitment to responding to and meeting the needs of the vulnerable, they are likely to feel under increasing pressure to make up any shortfall by working harder themselves, a form of self-regulated unpaid overtime. Thus, the argument is that a balanced weighing-up of the potential risks and benefits involved suggested that active pursuit of the policy was not worthwhile, and that the subsequent failure of local authorities to defeat the Government over rate-capping vindicated the union's position.

In addition, there is the view that there was little evidence from past relationships with councillors to make trade unionists feel that they had any option but to treat them first and foremost as employers and to look upon any pronouncements of an alliance with extreme caution. According to Simpkin (1983), speaking about social workers, "whatever their intentions, the councillors remain social workers' employers and few seek to win any sort of trust from their employees; instead like so many trade union convenors turned personnel managers, their sympathy cannot be relied on because they are often much more rigid and dangerous enemies than those who have always been part of management" (pp 165-166). For Burn, then Branch Secretary of NALGO Islington, speaking after the nursery nurses dispute,

> ... there will inevitably be a lot of distrust. We are not interested in maintaining divisions, but members will be very reluctant to join the Council in the fight against rate-capping when they have been seen to hammer relatively low paid workers for so long. The prospects for total unity have been seriously damaged. (quoted in Sharron 1984, p 11)

Some writers, such as Weinstein (1986), argue that the trade union activists showed themselves to have a more sophisticated understanding of organising for political change in contrast to "many of the new generation of socialists who ... belong more to that section of the left who seek shortcuts to socialism" (p 58).

Rather, for such writers, the period is understood to be one of 'retreat' for the 'working class', which the collective strength of the unions can at best 'slow down'. Such an analysis argues that the likely short-term nature of 'pre-figurative' experiments should in itself be a good reason for caution, and reluctance to respond to requests to abandon tried and trusted defensive methods of organisation and action. Simpkin (1983) not wanting to reject either the need for new approaches to trade unionism or the usefulness of demonstrating one's political ideas, nevertheless remains cautious. He comments that,

> Islands of socialism rarely survive long without considerable compromise ... I am not a great believer in the possibility of 'prefigurative' institutions as solid achievements, particularly within the state. But I do not underestimate their importance as part of the ideological war ... socialists cannot afford to abandon their organisation, nor some of their traditional weapons ... the unions must be changed; and we need to develop a wider range of tactics ... We may want to widen the scope of union business and make it more accessible, but we cannot afford to forget the need for self-defence (p 184).

More generally it can be argued that it is part of the nature and essence of trade unions to examine carefully any proposal for change that impacts upon existing conditions of service or the labour process. It is certainly not a wise policy for unions to take at face value what is offered solely because it emanates from a self-proclaimed socialist employer. Thus, given the far reaching implications of decentralisation, in terms of where workers were to be located and what duties they were expected to perform, one should not be surprised that they demand considerable time to inspect the details of any proposal. Caution was further demanded by the fact that the language of decentralisation was similar to both earlier localised solutions to the problems of urban management and to those proposals, such as patch based services, simultaneously being advocated by right-wing local authorities. Trade unions could rightly claim time to compare the proposals of those radical authorities with other more conservative versions as well as reflecting upon past experiences. In Islington, the concept of participation had been a central theme for some time and had been institutionalised in the form of a 'Participation

Officer' only to be later dropped. Unions could legitimately want to know what was to be different about the new package.

This argument has been further advanced by those who believe that NALGO had no choice but to protect itself once local authorities appeared to have decided that the union was a major obstacle to change and had to be defeated. What began as a trade union's prerogative to examine any proposed change from the point of view of their members becomes a defense of the union. Thus, Darke and Gouly (1985) suggest that, "it is easy for councillors to identify the white-collar staff, organised by NALGO, as a major obstacle in implementing new policies. Confrontation with NALGO is seen as a prerequisite to change ..." This sense of being under attack, a view voiced by a number of activists in Islington and not, as we have seen, denied by some key councillors should, however, be understood as something that emerged over time and was only obviously apparent after the defeat of Labour in the 1987 election. Thus, it is unlikely that the councillor, quoted by Wintour (1989) as saying, "Councils have got to realise that, in London, the Socialist Workers Party still run NALGO. They are the enemy. It's them against us. There is no middle way", would have been particularly representative in the 1980-85 period. Yet councillors have not always demonstrated sympathy towards the unions, as the leaders in Walsall acknowledged, even if in retrospect regretting their failure "to consult staff ... we were just carried away with enthusiasm; we thought everyone would feel the same." (Dave Church former Chair of Housing Walsall, quoted in Seabrook 1984, pp 123-125). Again Sharron (1984) notes in relation to Islington, "There was clearly a desire ... to take the unions on" and he quotes the Branch Secretary as saying, "One of the councillors actually said that if we can beat the unions on the Nursery Nurses, we can beat them on decentralisation" (p 11).

Furthermore, it can be argued that not only did councillors have a poor track-record of progressive management, and express increasingly hostile views about trade unions, but also that white-collar trade unions were never, in fact, a central part of the new urban left strategy. Consequently it was difficult for unions to have any sense of a shared ownership of the project, and understandable that they were defensive. Although the rainbow coalition proposed by the urban left included the public service unions their role was secondary to those of the elected members, the service users and community based organisations (Campbell and Jacques, 1986). However it could be argued with some justification that there was no blueprint as to the significance of any of the potential parties, and that there was nothing preventing the unions playing an influential part had they so chosen. Nevertheless, the urban left's strategy was in part a response to a growing sense of fragmentation amongst the traditional working class, and a view of the trade unions as no longer able to exert the kind of power they once had. In the context of white-collar unions there has also for some time been the feeling that they were not 'a proper union' (Darke and Gouly 1984) which further reduced the significance they were given. Furthermore, the strategy included a left critique of public sector services and how they are delivered, and the unions, whilst they represented the interests of their members as workers, were also in their role as welfare professionals, the ones being criticised. It was never going to be easy to keep the two separate, to support people as trade unionists but to be critical of their professional practice.

A final part of this particular scenario is to argue that, in fact, the white-collar public service unions are not conservative and reactive forces at all but have been, and continue to be, involved in developing progressive practices, either in respect of their own internal organisation (Brenton 1978), or in alliances with others. Thomas (1985), for example, argues it is possible to exaggerate the union's conservatism and points to

Birmingham where he says, "NALGO has agreed, in return for higher gradings, to break down departmental boundaries in part of the neighbourhood offices". He quotes a local union official as saying that, "NALGO wanted local area committees to have more power over neighbourhood offices" (p 366). Daniel and Wheeler (1989) although acknowledging that, "The involvement of community groups in the formulation of a popular plan based on social need is not very widespread in social services", point to the example of the 'Leeds Social Workers' Action Group' which began meeting in 1978. It arose as a defensive body out of the social workers strike but developed further, outlining alternative policies in the areas of service provision for those with a mental or physical disability. The result was said to be,

> New and more positive relationships with councillors ... a springboard for opening up debate on the service among the wider community ... a possible focus for developing the demands of users, community groups and the rest of the labour movement (pp 136-137).

They also refer to two attempts by social workers within Wandsworth, the 'Balham Network' and 'Working For Children in Wandsworth', to get involved with community groups to identify both local need and those related to specific user groups (see also Simpkin 1983). Similarly, Murray (1989), reports on the 'Haringey Schools Campaign' to improve the quality of school meals as well as defend jobs. This initiative was organised by Haringey Womens' Employment Project but grew to involve, "all the differing and often suspicious or conflicting interests together in an effort to forge an alliance of support - parents, workers, trade unions, school meals service management, councillors, teachers, community organisations" (p 108).

Again in Wandsworth, NALGO along with officials from NUPE, and the blue-collar GMBATU, worked with 'Services to Community Action and Tenants' and 'Public Service Action' magazine to jointly publish a report, entitled 'Public Jobs For Private Profit' (Benlow et al. 1983) on the joint industrial campaign against the privatisation of public services in the borough. The report acknowledges the importance of joint user-worker action and is critical of its own campaign for failing to act quickly enough in this respect but argues that,

> Public sector trade unionists can only begin to win mass support and protest if we are seen to be arguing for new ways of organising and improving public services ... for better services, for much greater tenant, user and worker control over decision-making and for a much less hierarchical organisation at work (p 24).

However, the report also points out that the joint trade union solidarity was in the end broken by NALGO's withdrawal as a consequence of the drying up of the local strike fund and a failure by NALGO's National Emergency Committee to provide enhanced strike pay along with a lack of confidence in the conflict. Ascher (1987) in reviewing the trade unions' overall response to the threat of privatisation suggests that, "the unions remain convinced of the importance of building grass roots support" (p 124) and acknowledges their attempts to work with organisations and community groups, referring to efforts in Basingstoke and Coventry which drew together councillors, community organisations and the unions (p 122). Nevertheless, she concludes that such action was seriously weakened by disagreements within the unions over the most appropriate strategy, an absence of central leadership with the political direction being left to the branches, and inter-union conflict which was on at least some occasions related to differently perceived class positions of white and blue-collar workers, summed up in the conflict between 'careers' and 'jobs'.

Cohen and Fosh (1988), in a study on the attitudes of five white and blue-collar unions, found that,

The NALGO organisation in our research took the prize ... in showing the most consistent commitment to all aspects of workplace trade union democracy (pp 22-23),

Although they did qualify their praise by noting that, "they occasionally left the members behind". As an example of this unevenness they considered the strong policy of opposition to rate-capping adopted by the branch under study and referred to "an impressive series of mass turnouts". This they describe as an opportunity "to use effective local trade union action to advance a wider political objective." However, it ultimately failed because of an increasing gap between "a highly ideologically-motivated leadership" and a "more pragmatic membership" (p 25) which was increasingly demoralised by their failure to make any impact upon the government.

NALGO has increasingly become involved in what traditionally have been regarded as 'professional' issues. In a report from a weekend policy meeting in November 1979 (National Services Conditions Committee on Local Government November 1979) it was noted that,

It could be argued that there is a difference between purely professional consultation and trade union consultation but in practice such a distinction is highly contentious and where possible it is suggested that professional as well as trade union consultation should take place with the membership.

It suggested this could best be done through advisory panels at branch rather than national level. A 1984 NALGO report entitled, 'The Personal Social Services' reviewed both the current state of funding and policy developments, and made recommendations for the future. These included a growing emphasis on the rights of individual clients, support for local welfare advisory committees, the devolution of services to "self-sufficient teams with a community focus" (p 52), and developing the ethnic awareness of the social services. In addition, NALGO has also commented on the developments in professional training, the application of the mental health legislation, and given evidence to the Barclay Committee on community social work, where it agreed that "there is an increasing demand in some areas of public life for greater participation and accountability" (National Service Conditions Committee on Local Government May 1982).

The union is also recognised as taking a leading proactive role in the field of equal opportunities, with the first conference policy on positive action being made in 1981. Later in the decade the National Executive Council's report to the 1988 Annual Conference on Positive Action within the union (NALGO 1988) stated that, "trade unions have become complacent about their commitment to equality" (p 5) and accepted "the importance of setting a clear lead at national level" (p 15). The Working Party responsible for the report stated its belief that,

All its policies, activities and structures should reflect its commitment to equality for women, black and minority ethnic people, lesbians and gay men, those with disabilities and all others facing discrimination and disadvantage ... a programme of positive action is required (p 28).

The report endorsed the 1984 policy of promoting and facilitating "the development of self-organised groups at all levels within the union" (p 12) and argued that such groups could help develop policies on equal rights, ensure that the full membership is represented in the union, provide a specific focal point for new members, be a resource for the training of stewards, and represent individual members. In fact, the report did not deal with the proposal to establish reserved places on the NEC for all minority groups, which it deferred, but was nevertheless an ambitious attempt by a union to deal with low levels of participation by disadvantaged groups. However, as we have seen earlier, although the union at national level and those active in the branches may support and understand the policies around positive action there may well be both a considerable gap between them and the broad membership and a degree of symbolism about such policies. Nevertheless, in the consultation process leading to the formation of Unison, NALGO members appeared to be both actively involved and continuing to develop equal opportunities policies (NALGO 1991).

Carpenter (1994) in his extensive review of public service unions in relation to community care is able to identify a number of attempts by NALGO to intervene in the policy debates, not least during the last 15 years. Although many of these interventions, such as a critique of local authority community care plans, or an attack on the pay and conditions of services found in many voluntary agencies (NALGO 1993) can be seen as merely a continuation of their normal role of defending member interests, there are some examples when they have gone beyond this. However, Carpenter's conclusion that, "New trade union and socialist approaches have responded to the new public management by increasingly seeking a new compact with users" (p 90) or that "industrial relations and social policy users have become inextricably enmeshed as unions ... have sought common cause with users and pressure groups in the campaign for well-funded, publicly run, quality public services, which are responsive to the needs and wishes of users" (p 108) is perhaps a little over optimistic when applied to NALGO. Nevertheless there are some examples, such as the research sponsored by NALGO (Mackie, 1992) into users' experiences of community care, to highlight what might be part of an emergent new politics.

It is thus possible to point to an increasing range of examples of public service white-collar unions going beyond their traditional concerns about conditions of service. This has happened to some extent in a number of ways, such as, the development of their own alternative professional policy measures, attending to questions involving their own internal democratic structures, and forming short-term alliances with elected members, service users and community organisations. It is also likely that these trends will continue, although no doubt unevenly and inconsistently. Nevertheless, it still remains the case that unions such as NALGO are first and foremost concerned with service conditions and that for a considerable number of members that is the limit of their trade unionism. However many examples were listed of attempts to move beyond this traditional approach they would still be small, fragile, underdeveloped, and relative to the range of potential issues with which it could engage.

This first approach, by focusing on the two key protagonists, unions and employers, attempts to apportion responsibility for the conflict by identifying their relative weaknesses or failings. The employers, and specifically the elected members, are seen as being either too weak in the face of unreasonable trade union resistance, or too uncompromising and insensitive to union grievances and concerns. For their part, the unions are seen as conservative, adopting an inappropriate form of rank-and-filism, and intent only on pursuing their sectional interests. Alternatively they are depicted as responding in the only reasonable way possible given the inexperience of the newly elected councillors and the hostile political climate. Furthermore, the white-collar unions are seen as being as progressive in their policies and actions as any other sectional grouping. The difficulty with this approach, however, is that not only does it not give much attention to the broader context in which the two parties found themselves, or consider the policy that was at issue, but also provides little guidance on how to decide on which of the competing perspectives is the most accurate or who must accept the responsibility. It is no doubt possible to find examples of each and all of these characteristics but it is unlikely that each authority shared the same characteristics or that these appeared in a pure or undiluted form.

Searching for mutual gain

The second approach to explaining the conflict is to a large extent an extension of the first. However, whilst acknowledging 'faults' or unhelpful tendencies on both sides it does not seek to apportion blame to either one, but suggests that both have failed to recognise the need to move towards the other. Underlying this view is the belief that both sides stand to gain by cooperating and that difficulties came about because neither sufficiently identified these mutual benefits or, to paraphrase Pilkington (1985), found a common language. The focus of such relational arguments is, on the one hand, the need to give greater recognition to the potential value and expertise of front-line workers in policy development, and the need for both management and unions to move towards greater workplace democracy. On the other hand, advocates stress the importance of giving greater weight to the consumers' definition of need and solutions to social problems. Shifts in both directions will it is suggested require changes on the part of both unions and management and it is the failure to do so which was a major cause of the hostile impasse between them.

Industrial democracy and the value of the workers: the responsibility of management

When discussing the role that can be played by management in facilitating a more co-operative approach to negotiation, three points are raised: (i) the need to give greater recognition to the knowledge of workers; (ii) the need to re-examine industrial relations in local government; and (iii) the need to introduce workplace democracy into the overall strategy of democratising public services. A number of writers have highlighted the absence of, and need for, a greater recognition of the value of local authority workers in the policy initiatives (Kendall 1984, Morrell and Bundred 1984, Epstein 1990). Stoker (1888), for example, argues that, "What is required is a new relationship ... One which avoids collapsing into the formula of 'the management's right to manage', and which recognises the positive contribution to service delivery and development that grass-roots local authority workers can make" (p 262). Similarly, Thomas (1987), suggests that much of the conflict arose because councillors seemed to think that "once they are in control of the 'machine' they have the right to run the council as they like" and goes on to argue for an injection of workplace democracy in local authorities and hence a more constructive relationship between the councillors and the unions. Amongst his ten point approach to a new public economy, Murray (1986) calls for a new type of manager who has, "the capacity of running a creative enterprise, and the imagination to develop alternative social relations within the workplace". Callaghan (1990) recognises that, "the behaviour of front-line employees deeply affects the way services are experienced by users" (p 5) and that their commitment is essential, "for the adaptability of public services in the 1990's". Public service managers, therefore, "need to realise the value of the resource they have in their employees and the potential for improving the services by learning from their experiences and ideas" (p 5). They must do this, he argues, by involving those workers in the decisions about service delivery and by not attempting to by-pass or undermine union bargaining processes. Other writers too have been keen to identify practical steps that management might take to bring about better industrial relations (Graves and Pilkington 1989, Daniel and Wheeler 1989), and improved staff morale (Robertshaw 1986).

Such arguments and suggestions should not be under-valued, yet the whole issue of introducing greater workplace democracy or re-evaluating the processes of industrial relations in local authorities was noticeably absent from the new urban left programme, although not from the rhetoric, and especially from the decentralisation policy in those authorities that have recognised the need for the democratisation of services. Such an absence was undoubtedly a major weakness when attempting to convince trade unions of one's commitment to the transformation of social relations. Its introduction, and a consistent approach to its implementation, would be a significant step towards demonstrating not only an appreciation of the knowledge and potential contribution of front line workers but also of a willingness to share, and therefore, first of all give up, some power.

Reforming the unions

The central issue raised in relation to the white-collar unions, and it is one that has been applied more generally to all trade unions, is the need to 'modernise' and to recognise the extent to which a "negative style of trade-unionism" (Sharron 1985) has led to considerable resentment amongst their potential allies. In the context of public service unions, modernisation is to take the form of a greater interest in the nature of the welfare 'product', and how the social relations of welfare can be related to socialism, a greater emphasis on the needs of the consumer as defined by the consumer, by extending union democracy, and a greater commitment to developing models of welfare agencies that combine workers' and users' control with democratic accountability (Carpenter 1994). Again such arguments have included checklists to assist union's to assess proposals or guide their future direction (Simpkin 1983).

Sawyer (1984) considers it, "essential for trade unions to rethink their purpose and methods" and amongst other things calls for them to, step beyond "short-term problems", and offer a "vision of society". He goes on to assert the need for greater internal democracy and member participation in the unions themselves, a view echoed by the Labour Co-ordinating Committee (1984). In a general article on the need for a new role for trade unions, but applicable to the public sector, Lane (1987) comments that they "have not normally and as a matter of habit concerned themselves with the logic of the enterprise ... isolated instances apart, it is not common for workers or their representatives to express concern about what is produced, where and how, until crisis has loomed" (p 21). On the basis that it is important for unions to form the best possible relationship with progressive councils, whilst avoiding incorporation, Thomas (1987) similarly argues that "NALGO and other white-collar unions need to take, and be seen to take far more interest in ensuring that socialist principles inform the content of their work" (p 87). Meanwhile, Davies (1988) describing it as "vital", calls for, "A politicised interpretation by trade unionists of professional autonomy as workers' control, based on confident assertions of who can establish the greatest legitimacy and credibility with consumers" (p 212). He argues that in a situation where services are either being destroyed or reoriented, "Restricted trade union perspectives ... are ... in need of urgent extension ... a concern about the quality of 'the product' is needed ... as an essential political intervention, some of the traditional professional preoccupation with the standard of service being offered may be required" (pp 213-214). Callaghan (1990), having already commented on the need for management to reform its ways suggests that, "Trade unions ... need to take a bold and innovative stance ... convincing their members that changes in the way services are provided are sometimes necessary and desirable" (p 5). They will, he continues, "need to develop new strategies which aim, in the long term, to ensure that users' interests do not conflict with those of employees" and "explore and encourage new forms of management theory and practice which are specifically designed to endorse the values and enhance the quality of public services" (pp 6-7). Stewart (1990) believes there are "deep issues for the trade unions ... that ... require a degree of flexibility amongst staff that we have not been used to" (p 11).

Although not going as far as other writers, Epstein (1990), calls for a shift in the balance of power between providers and consumers more in the direction of the latter, agreeing with Smith (1986) that, "The balance of forces between producers and consumers is in need of correction ... We suffer from producerism: the custom of planning economic, industrial and social strategy in exclusive accordance with the wishes and convenience of producers" (quoted in Epstein p 75). Nellis (1989), addressing social workers specifically, argues for a "major revaluation of trade unionism" (p 117) declaring that workers, "need to retain (or build) their links with the powerholders on the left, however fragmented, draw support, contribute ideas and provide evidence of the deleterious effects of Thatcher's social and economic policies" (p 116) and goes so far as to suggest that the strike weapon should not be used in support of services because they have already demonstrated that "they are rarely of direct benefit to clients" and that to be seen as acting purely on the basis of worker self-interest would be, "an act of political suicide". Croft and Beresford (1989) seeking to address this problem of working more closely with the consumer call for "a great debate that engages all the key stakeholders who have so far been left out of the discussion" (p 18). Such moves to modernise and extend their areas of concern are seen by Graves and Pilkington (1989) as very much within the union's own interest for they argue that the trouble with reactive trade unionism is that the union thereby, "effectively consigns itself to a position of perpetual resistance ... and denies itself the opportunity to shape the proposals on the basis of its members' long term interests", a point we have seen accepted in retrospect by leading officers in Islington NALGO.

Thus, despite the influence of the new urban left within both the council chamber and the white-collar public service trade unions, it is argued neither side sufficiently considered the implications of the new political alliance as it applied to themselves and their relationships with each other. This failure to move toward the other in order to find common ground and a new language was a major cause of the continuing and escalating industrial unrest in radical local authorities. However, the difficulty with such an approach is that it remains more of a combination of description and a prescription of what should happen in the future rather than an explanation as to why this failure occurred.

Change in a hostile climate

A third approach is one which attempts to locate the industrial conflict in the wider context in which the two principal parties find themselves. Three alternatives are identified here: one that sees it as a conflict between two different approaches to change

- trade unionism and socialist politics; one that suggests that what we witnessed was a breakdown of normal industrial relations as a result of the inability of the local authorities to maintain a sufficient level of trust with the unions, principally by meeting their demands for expansion, whilst pushing ahead with policy developments; and a third which suggests that we must look beyond the industrial relations field and consider the failure to develop an alliance between trade unions and radical councillors as a failed political strategy related to the conditions in which it was attempted, the failure to sufficiently think through or address central aspects of the programme, and the difficulty of harnessing together a number of variables some of which were beyond the control of the participants.

(i) Socialism and trade unionism

The first attempt to locate the disputes in a wider context is one which identifies a structural problem for those attempting to introduce political changes through the medium of industrial relations. This arises as a consequence of the limitations of trade unionism in any transformative politics, the tension between holding on to what you have and moving into the unknown where you may be or emerge in some sense weaker.

Thus, Stoker (1988), whilst recognising NALGO's anxiety over the changes implied by decentralisation undertaken in the context of a hostile climate and financial constraint, suggests that a more fundamental problem was the, "long-standing uncertainty about the relationship between socialism as a political objective and the role of trade unionism" (p 213). He points to the contradiction between the unions' aim of securing the best deal from existing circumstances, modifying but not transforming, and those "strategies for transforming society and developing a new social and economic order" (p 213). Similarly, Simpkin (1983) speaks of the unions as being "irredeemably tied to the economy which engendered them. Unions were not formed to overthrow capitalism ... but to defend workers from the onslaughts of employers so that they could gain as many as possible of the fruits of capitalism for themselves" (p 157). Calvert (1987), describes trade unions as being, "powerfully shaped by the broader social and political environment within which they function: they do not seek to supplant the employer but rather establish appropriate limitations on the exercise of managerial authority." He goes on to argue that unions, especially those in the public sector, where government and employers have been influential in shaping the bargaining process, are primarily organisations which provide bargaining and arbitration services. Unions have been further restricted in their vision, Calvert suggests, by the way in which they came to conceptualize the practice of internal democracy which was one that deterred participation by the members.

The structural limitations of trade unionism have long been a subject of debate amongst a range of marxist writers and the tensions, identified by Stoker and others, are not confined to the relationship between trade unions and politicians advocating socialist politics, but are also to be found within the trade unions themselves. Thus there were in NALGO Islington countervailing forces holding, with varying degrees, a commitment to personal and organisational change, and to the principle of both the decentralisation and the democratisation of services. Indeed, many of the activists had joined the authority precisely because of those transformative politics. Consequently, the outcome of any particular situation cannot be simply 'read off' from the structural position of trade unions. Nevertheless, for trade unions to move away from the security of making the best out of the current situation to the unchartered waters of transformative politics they need to have some degree of confidence in the level of support and likely success of such a venture, both within the wider community and in the union itself. This is difficult in a union such as NALGO with competing interest groups and social categories. Such unity of purpose appears to be noticeable only by its absence according to the work of Marshall et al. (1988), who found that despite the fact that the majority of their respondents acknowledged the absence of a unified moral order in society, did not approve of social injustice, could "conceive both of a more just society and the means by which it might be achieved", and endorsed those efforts towards redistribution, nevertheless judged these as being, "unlikely to be forthcoming given existing social, economic, and political arrangements." They conclude that, "past experience has bred a cynicism towards the very socio-political agencies who would necessarily be involved in accomplishing the envisaged social changes" (p 161). This disaffection with political structures embraces trade unions, and effectively places a check on collective action. Thus although there is a structural tension between trade unionism and transformative politics it is not one that in and of itself prevents an alliance as envisaged by the urban left. Rather this research suggests that it is a demonstration in practice, that the new politics are both genuinely held and consistently applied, which plays a significant part in the evaluation of and commitment to any political strategy.

(ii) Local government retrenchment and public sector industrial relations

The most comprehensive attempt to date to place the conflict in the context of existing industrial relations, and the expectations that these had generated for both councillors and trade unions, but which could not be accommodated in a period of resource constraint, is that of Heery (1988) and Laffin (1989). It is Laffin who provides the most detailed analysis. His premise is that local authorities are best conceptualised as 'negotiated orders' (Strauss et al. 1963), the institutional structures being depicted as "constructs formed out of the diverse goals or purposes that actors bring to their involvement in the organisation" and hence both sides to industrial relations are engaged in a process of "mutual adjustment" (p 19) and wish to avoid an all out power struggle. However, their ability to reach and maintain mutual agreements is constrained by the wider context. Laffin argues that the key problem for the councillors, as managers, is "how to pursue or even maintain their objectives without destroying the organisational means whereby those objectives can be obtained" (p 22) which he defines as the problem of "balancing policy against trust", between "managing now and preserving the possibility of managing in the future" (p 35). Drawing from more general industrial relations theory, management in local government is seen as having to reconcile two aims, that of implementing new policies in response either to their own values or to a changing environment, and maintaining trusting relationships with the trade unions. In the past this was made easier by a normative consensus between the two sides, the existence of a fairly stable local political climate, and the effective operation of institutionalised consultative machinery. Underpinning all of this were the finances to sustain growth in services and improved working conditions, so that any proposed change could be brought about by adding to the existing provision and providing rewards to the workforce. However, the fiscal crisis seriously undermined these relationships of trust and introduced considerable uncertainty over future developments in local government, making it very difficult for management to negotiate either retrenchment or growth.

Laffin suggests that traditional patterns of management were thus disrupted both by the growing competition over the allocation of increasingly scarce resources and the election of a new breed of ideologically committed and educated councillors. Furthermore, increased instability was introduced by the invigoration of local politics by a range of active interest groups, and a central government imposed financial squeeze resulting from the fiscal crisis. Additionally, the growing activity of front line workers made the job of management and control even more difficult and the legitimacy of the institutional arrangements for the negotiation of change were subsequently under increasing pressure. Consequently, it was, he argues, increasingly difficult, in the absence of financial growth to buy acceptance for policy changes, or to manage the tension between policy and trust, as new policies tended to be implemented either as a straight switch of resources or a cut in services. In such circumstances, management are said to be driven towards a strategy of either conciliation or confrontation in their dealings with unions, as opposed to those of co-optation or collaboration, both of which having either been questioned by the unions themselves or require too high a price from management in the current period of constraint. The problem for the union leadership on the other hand is, according to Laffin, one of "finding a balance between too much confrontation and too much collaboration" (p 67), between trusting the council too much and too little, as local government unionism became increasingly militant and defensive in the face of increased fiscal pressures. In one of his two local authority case studies Laffin considers the relationship between NALGO and a radical Labour group. He assesses the latter as "experiencing growing problems in accommodating new policy initiatives within increased financial constraints. Financial constraints not only limited such initiative but also reduced the ability of management to gain the co-operation of staff through regrading and career incentives" (p 97). However, there was nevertheless a feeling amongst the Labour councillors, that NALGO ought to cooperate both in the wider interests of the labour movement, and as a 'thank you' for the earlier generous agreements that had been made with them. NALGO saw things differently, believing that they had a genuine grievance, and doubtful of the councillors' ability to resist government and maintain existing service provision. Consequently, they felt the need to put pressure on the council to keep them from cutting services, which further reduced the levels of trust between them. As the external pressure on the local authority intensified, after the defeat over rate-capping, the local authority saw the situation in terms of their own survival and thus the problems of negotiating change have again increased.

The issue becomes, for Laffin, how and to what extent can local authorities negotiate about retrenchment, as employers have fewer resources to offer in the bargaining process and, "almost inevitably retrenching employers come to place duress on the unions implying or even threatening unilateral action unless the unions accept the management case" (pp 125-126). However, such steps towards confrontation contain high risks for they destroy trust, but some trust must be retained "as a basic level of organisational workability is still required" (p 127). Finally, Laffin points to the way in which the scope of bargaining in local authorities is limited by the "highly institutionalised decision-making structures" thereby reducing the scope of industrial relations decision-making to one of the process of policy change, and excluding discussion on the substance or outcome of policy proposals. Attempts by the council to open up the process of planning change may create better opportunities for taking the unions with them, but may also make the unions more effective should they resist the changes and if the council is unable to co-opt them with additional rewards.

Laffin's analysis adds to our understanding of the escalating conflict between white-collar public service unions and radical Labour authorities. However, there are some difficulties with it. Firstly, Laffin places too much emphasis on the impact of the fiscal crisis. As has already been shown, the policy developments in the early 1980s were actually taking place in the context of financial growth and expansion, with rewards being offered for accepting policy changes, despite central government attempts to control and eliminate this. It was not until the latter part of the decade that local authority spending was severely restricted. This does not take away from the fact that since the mid-1970s the reduction in public spending has been a major priority for both Labour and Conservative governments and that there have been uneven reductions in terms of both service areas and geography. It is, therefore, reasonable to suggest that the climate of public service trade unionism was no longer one where there was an expectation of growth, or confidence that councils would prove capable of, or willing to, maintain standards let alone meet new needs. Further, councils were not unknown for threatening reductions if unions were unco-operative. This may have produced a climate in which hard bargaining was more the rule than the exception.

Secondly, Laffin places too great an emphasis on the making of concessions as the price for innovative policy changes to the exclusion of everything else. The Islington research demonstrates that the 'bottom line' for the unions was not to see a deterioration in service conditions. In addition, for many of the activists there were a number of past grievances they wanted to have addressed. However, a commitment to tackling these was as much about a demonstration of consistency of the espoused principles in the decentralisation policy as it was about making a 'material deal' in exchange for policy development. Activists were also concerned about the substance of the policy itself, and its relationship to other policies which were seen as making up a coherent approach. It is suggested rather that whilst public service white-collar workers certainly do have a concern for wages and conditions, although not always or solely their own (in Islington there was considerable support for the improvement of the lower paid and no demands were made for additional financial resources for the professionalised staff), they also have a concern for ensuring other changes which are not so dependent on a growth budget. Thus, in Islington, there were strong feelings about the successful implementation of equal opportunities policies.

In addition, whilst one might agree with Laffin that the institutionalised industrial relations machinery does tend to focus on the process, rather than the substance or outcome of change, the Islington research again demonstrates that both substance and outcome were very much at the forefront of the activists' concerns and deliberations. Thus one of the initial concerns, which was maintained throughout, was on the effectiveness of having so many neighbourhood offices and a concern that the monies spent on building new offices could have been more effectively spent by being reallocated to other service areas. The significance of concerns such as these, however, is that they highlight a fundamental weakness with Laffin's approach in that he restricts his analysis to traditional industrial relations bargaining and by doing so he ignores two things. Firstly, that a significant sector of those engaged in human service work are genuinely concerned about the human product of their labours, i.e. ensuring that needs are satisfied or that some beneficial change has taken place. Secondly, it ignores the wider political context and the relationship of the two parties to this. It is to this that I will now turn as I consider it to be a more fruitful way for explaining the conflict between the white-collar unions and the urban left councils.

The collapse of a political strategy

Laffin has identified the range of pressures that face negotiators in a constrained financial climate, making industrial relations no easy task. Yet writers such as Stoker, by highlighting the tension between trade unionism and socialist transformative politics, remind us that what we have been studying cannot simply be contained within, or fully explained by, an industrial relations model. Certainly radical versions of decentralisation require a drastic reorganisation of service delivery and working arrangements for those involved, and, therefore, are clearly a matter of some considerable importance for industrial relations bargaining. However, they were also the centre piece of a political strategy designed to reinvigorate socialist political life through the building of a new alliance capable of acting as an agency for socialist change. The strategy not only required public service workers to accept changed, though not necessarily poorer, working conditions, it also proposed that they enter into new more egalitarian and democratic relationships. This applies both externally, with the users and recipients of public services, with neighbourhood and interest based community and voluntary organisations, and internally with their professional managers, elected members, and finally within their own trade union. To do so workers would have to engage in critical self-reflection and dialogue with the other parties involved, over the quality of service delivery and their own personal and collective practice. For their part, the unions needed to have some confidence firstly, in the possibility and worthwhileness of the proposed strategy and secondly, and of equal importance, some confidence in the promoters' ability to see the strategy through in adverse circumstances, and to apply the espoused principles of the strategy to a range of policies and practices.

These political concerns are of a different order to those normally contained within industrial relations, and even though they were primarily played out through the medium of industrial relations, and were constantly inter-woven with the more usual trade union matters, nevertheless the politics of decentralisation, and the political context in which this was being attempted, were never far away from the activists' considerations. The industrial conflicts and the resultant, often unstable and unfinished settlements, that surrounded decentralisation represent, not only the increasing difficulties of reaching long-term industrial agreements, but also the failure of a political strategy whose success depended upon public service trade unions and elected councillors finding a 'new language' and common practice both in the short-term, in their mutual opposition to central government, and in the long-term, in their desire for some more widespread and fundamental social transformation. It was a strategy which failed firstly, and primarily, not because of disagreements over the principles contained within it but because of the difficulties of implementing it in the particular circumstances of the time, and with little external support. Secondly so many of the key variables that had to be mobilised were beyond the control of the key actors. Thirdly, some of the key elements over which they did have some influence were insufficiently addressed. Finally, the key actors failed to properly apply the principles of the strategy to their own practice.

Despite, or perhaps because of, the political difficulties in the early 1980s, this was a time when there was felt to be real possibilities for successfully constructing new political relationships and movements which would be based more on localised grass-roots democratic organisation in place of the centrally determined top-down statist approach of both the Labour Party and the other fringe left political parties. Such optimism was fuelled by the emergence of a new breed of councillors who had both ideological commitment and the ability to articulate a coherent strategy. In addition, they came with a wealth of experience from a wide range of settings both within local government and in community politics, although significantly there is little evidence that many came with a strong industrial trade union background. Within the white-collar public service unions there was a growing body of members with experience of industrial militancy and collective assertiveness, and many possessed additional experience of campaigning in community and voluntary organisations as well as the new social movements. Activists within the union were generally committed to preserving and developing public services and a significant number had been drawn to work not only in the metropolitan areas but also to those councils which espoused progressive policies. In addition, such workers were receptive to the idea of working with and alongside community organisations, although the practical application of this idea was often limited. However, there were also significant problems which were to prove insurmountable for those wishing to participate in the project.

Firstly, amongst each of the principal parties, councillors, trade unions and consumers, there were conflicting interests and agendas, and those promoting the strategy within any one constituency never represented more than a fraction of its total membership Councillors had different agendas, for example, in relation to how they saw trade unions and the extent to which they were prepared to devolve power and control, as well as services. Consumers were divided over whether their primary objective, especially in the face of increasing poverty and social decline amidst already busy and stressful lives, was to have services delivered quickly and efficiently, or to be involved in the democratic running of services, with the likelihood of having to make decisions over cutting provision. Trade unionists were divided, for example, over the degree of commitment towards socialist politics, and many of the membership would be openly hostile to the concept of a trade union pursuing any political strategy, as opposed to protecting and promoting the employment interests of its members, as well as the degree to which they valued community involvement, or felt the need for greater public accountability of their work.

In addition, there were a number of outstanding conflicts and tensions between the parties that needed, but did not receive, considerable attention for a new alliance to form. Most crucially, the role of trade unions in the proposed transformative project was never coherently articulated either specifically in relation to public service trade unions or more generally in relation to the traditional labour movement. The new urban left strategy effectively marginalised or even rejected traditional trade unionism as being itself part of the problem. If the strengths, as well as the shortcomings, of trade unionism, had been seriously addressed at the outset, the conflicts of interest between public service workers and their employers would have come to the forefront at an earlier stage in the process, rather than as happened after a number of damaging industrial disputes which left both parties feeling frustrated and bitter towards each other. Further, it might also have led to the inclusion of workplace democracy in the overall strategy. It is indeed remarkable that in a strategy concerned with the democratisation of public services, workers' control and its meaning in the context of public services should have been virtually excluded from consideration, not even raised as part of the long term agenda.

Similarly, whilst the devolution of budgets, responsibilities and management to the neighbourhood level along with the development of generic work were all seen as central to the project, collective work within teams was not seriously explored. It would appear that the new urban left councillors were not as willing to pursue actions that would have reduced or modified their own power as they were prepared to tackle the relationships between workers and consumers. Yet it has been argued by those libertarian radicals in the public sector that collective work is a necessary prerequisite for altering the worker/consumer relationships. As Stanton (1990) points out social relations among workers have a deep effect on the relationships between an agency and the people who use it (p 124). He refers to the research into social services which has consistently highlighted, "fragmented uncooperative work groups and departments ... staff tend to work mainly as individuals; often feeling unsupported and distrustful ... suspicious of what they label as 'the hierarchy' or 'management' " (p 125). He argues that "closed, controlling, hierarchical staff relations undermine attempts to work openly, equally and in ways that respect the rights of people who use the agency" (p 125). In effect, the new urban left councillors and the professional managers failed to enable or encourage the service producers, who were not themselves demanding the opportunity, to devise collaborative working relations as a step towards entering into a critical dialogue with service users. Had this happened, it is likely that both councillors and progressive workers would have been better equipped to both respond to the considerable levels of criticism, and to change their working practices but also would have found themselves in very different relations of power to each other and to service users. Had such steps been taken, it is also less likely that the controlling and repressive nature of a significant portion of public services would have been so neglected. This may have avoided the tendency to either idealise the user, or depoliticise them in the language of the 'consumer'. By imposing the language of the market on the social relations of the welfare state, both the real meaning of some of those relations and the variations between different transactions were ignored. To obscure the relationships in this way resulted in councillors having an unrealistic set of images about the user, their circumstances, and the degree to which they always welcomed in their lives interventions, of any kind, by the state. From the workers' point of view, this could only be understood as a combination of naivety, a lack of concern for the difficult circumstances in which they as workers had to operate, and ignorance of the real dangers to which they were sometimes exposed. More significantly, in the long term, it exposed a major weakness in the strategy, namely the assumption that the existing 'moral order' and underpinning assumptions of social welfare intervention were seen as legitimate by the citizens, both service users and non-users, to whom they were ostensibly accountable. The desire to alter the relationships between service producers and users has not been matched by a commitment to develop a democratic mandate for state intervention in the specific service areas. To have raised such questions as, at what point and in what circumstances should the state intervene, or what kind of responses should the state be able to make, and how should its actions be monitored and controlled, would have required all three parties to move towards an intervention strategy for the future, and to face the inadequacies of the past. Such an exercise would certainly involve, as Hall and Held (1989) argue, "breaking with any assumption that the state can successfully define citizens' wants and needs for them, and become the 'caretaker of existence' " (p 23). For this, neither the elected members nor the unions appeared prepared.

In respect of the specific relationship between the trade unions and the authorities, the Islington research suggests that councillors failed to see the importance of consistency of actions and philosophy between a number of linked policies. Further, they failed to see the importance of acknowledging when they had not been consistent, or felt unable to be so. Perfection was not expected, but in the context of their espoused principles, openness and honesty might have been. Thus, the 'true' commitment of the councillors to democratisation and improvements in the quality of service provision was, in part, measured by their practice in relation to equal opportunities policies, both in staffing matters and service delivery; in their responses to the needs of low-paid workers, in respect of both wages and training; their behaviour as employers, both in the context of industrial disputes and their willingness to tackle outstanding trade union grievances; and specifically, in how far they were prepared to apply their politics in the dispute with central government over rate-capping. From the perspective of many of the NALGO activists, the councillors had been found wanting in these areas, generating enough doubt about their commitment and capacity to push through the policies in the face of strong opposition so as to make them wary of committing themselves to forming any alliance.

For their part, many of these same activists were ultra-defensive in their response to the policy development, prepared only to accept the changes of decentralisation if conditions of service were protected and new resources were found. There was very little evidence to suggest that many activists were willing to consider a reorganisation of existing resources in order to implement the decentralisation policy and, equally, that there was either a serious questioning of the professional assumption that they as workers knew what was best for the users, or a desire to make links with user organisations in situations other than those where it was of immediate interest to the trade unions to do so, and which never seemed to imply any commitment to their long-term development. Murray (1988) taking a sympathetic view, and speaking more about a wider industrial programme, but which has equal relevance to the public sector, notes that few unions have "had the resources to develop alternative strategies and build coalitions of communities and users around them" but goes on to argue that, "this is now a priority if unions are to reclaim their position as spokespeople of an alternative economy rather than defenders of a sectional interest" (p 13). Moreover, the union activists operated in a strong culture of rank-and-filism, which was distrustful of hierarchy both within the authority and the union itself, and which also made for an extremely cautious and short-term approach. In turn, the management were themselves inexperienced as employers, which combined with growing frustration led to escalating confrontational tactics when under pressure. In addition, they too had different agendas in respect of the role of the unions and whether or not it was necessary to somehow defeat them in order to get the decentralisation policy in place.

In themselves these issues would constitute considerable obstacles to the im-plementation of radical policies. However, the policy was also being developed in a period when local authorities were having to defend themselves against continuous attempts by central government to firstly reduce and curtail, and then restructure, their activities. Radical local authorities not only had to spend considerable energy defending the material basis of their services but were also having to defend the very principles of local authority service provision. They attempted to introduce wide ranging policy developments in a climate that was often dominated, at least at the ideological level, by reductions in public expenditure and when public sector morale was extremely low. As the decade progressed, the situation for radicals in local government deteriorated and the perceived prospects for radical change receded, not only as a result of the two post-1979 general election defeats for the Labour Party, but also with the defeat of the GLC's, 'Fare's Fair Campaign', the failure of those local authorities resisting attempts to restructure local government finance to agree on a unified strategy and the subsequent acquiescence to government pressure, the abolition of the GLC and the Metropolitan County Councils, and beyond the town hall, the 1985 defeat of the National Union of Mineworkers following their year long strike. Widening inequalities also placed additional burdens on local authorities to ensure that services were delivered effectively and efficiently with minimum delay. Understandably, service user priorities were inevitably and increasingly focused on ensuring that basic services were delivered and reliable, thereby removing some of the pressure on themselves, as insecurities around employment, wage levels and income maintenance increased for many.

Circumstances such as these, especially when combined with the problems within and between the central parties to the strategy as outlined, were not particularly conducive to experimentation in social relations. However, it is still possible to envisage a situation in which the radical decentralisation proposals could have formed a central plank both in the opposition to central government, and in the longer term goal of socialist transformation. Such a scenario may have been feasible had there been a national voice that addressed the concerns, but also transcended the specificity, of service users, public service unions, workers, and local councillors. Not surprisingly, given its history, the Labour Party at national level, was unable on its own to promote a strategy that was centred on the dynamism, variety and autonomy of the local, as opposed to the central state, and which recognised the importance of independent extra-parliamentary organisations and movements. Yet, given this and the circumstances in which it was attempting to implement policy developments, it is both significant, and a serious failing by the new urban left that they conspicuously failed to cultivate a national leadership.

Murray (1988) recognises the need for some centralised coordination and direction alongside decentralised units with considerable autonomy. Firstly, he urges, in the context of a policy for full employment, for

> Detailed local plans, decentralised public services ... and secondly, that Labour should, develop a network of social industrial institutions, decentralised, innovative, and entrepreneurial. For each sector and area there should be established one or more enterprise boards ... channels for long-term funds, for new technology, for strategic support across a sector, for common services, and for initiatives and advice on the social priorities (p 13).

No doubt had a serious effort been made by the urban left to create such a parallel national focus, considerable resistance and obstruction would have been placed in its way. Yet without some centralised coordination and leadership, which holds the respect of the local participants, the vitality and energy of local political development is always vulnerable to parochial and sectional interests. The urban left may have revived the level of interest in local politics and given it a new sense of importance but in so doing it seems to have forgotten the lessons of those earlier attempts at bottom-up social change, and particularly the need to engage those national bodies, including the trade unions, that are influential in setting priorities and agendas both for specific policy developments and broader political strategies.

Future scenarios

Three scenarios for the future direction of white-collar public service trade unionism can be identified. The first is one in which the unions retreat into the narrow confines of traditional industrial relations concerns. The second, the polar opposite to the first, is one in which they simultaneously, actively seek a radical transformation of their social relationships with other key actors in the public sector and undertake a process of self-transformation, based on the development of a democratic mandate for state intervention in social welfare. The third, and I suggest most likely, option is one in which they continue in an uneven and contradictory way to engage in professional issues, but to do so in an opportunistic way, guided primarily by a desire to protect their particular sectional interests.

The first scenario, of retreating back into a narrow trade unionism, remains possible given further threats to the material well-being, job security, social status, and fragmentation of the public sector workforce. However, I would suggest this is an unlikely route, and certainly not one that is easily or freely adopted. NALGO, as we have seen, had become increasingly involved in professional or service-related issues; indeed it has been so involved that in some areas, such as equal opportunities, it would consider itself as having a leading role. Again, the trade unionism of the NALGO activists, and no doubt many of the ordinary members too, already extends beyond concerns relating to service conditions. Indeed many are involved, as citizens, in political activities, such as the politics of race, gender, sexuality, as well as collective consumption, which inevitably raise questions for them as public service workers about how such services are delivered and to what degree of quality. Furthermore, many bring with them a commitment to sustaining and extending public provision for the meeting of social need, and do not see their employment solely as a means to a livelihood. It is likely that the need to defend such collective non-market provision will continue for some time, and with this likewise the need to provide good quality services and to be seen to be open to and promoting positive changes. Public service trade unions will continue to need allies and supporters, and to ensure that these are forthcoming they must themselves demonstrate their willingness to develop relationships both with user representatives but also elected members, who not only have their own basis of legitimacy in the form of an electoral mandate but who as employers wield considerable power. Finally, the merger into UNISON of the white and blue-collar public service unions of NALGO, COSHE and NUPE is also likely to ensure that a retreat into narrow trade unionism is unlikely as it increases the possibility of a closer integration, within the same organisation, between the public service trade unionist as producer and as user, as well as making it more likely that the issues that divide white and blue-collar workers, the ambiguously located and the more obviously working class, will be more directly addressed. Yet in order to avoid a future of narrow sectionalist trade unionism an internal process of critical re-examination of the rank-and-filist politics inappropriately borrowed from capitalist production will be necessary. The articulation of a new public service trade unionism remains an urgent task facing UNISON. Thus, whilst the first scenario is unlikely to be the one pursued, it nonetheless remains more likely than its polar opposite. Here it is the trade unions who actively seek the transformation of social relations with service users and local authorities, whilst also consciously revolutionising themselves and engaging in a process designed to produce a more democratic mandate for their interventions in social life as state employees. Yet such a development, whilst long overdue, is unlikely to materialise substantially, at least not without the development of a national political movement. The historic and continuing power of public service professionalised workers, many of whom continue to see their interests as best served by advancing their privileges in alliance with the more powerful, and at the expense of the less well-organised, to significantly influence both the nature of specific policy developments and the values that underpin these, will otherwise conspire against it. However, there are elements, albeit small ones, of progressive developments in some aspects of public service unionism. Furthermore, the development of sectional, but significant, political movements, despite their limitations, such as the self-organisation of black political groups, are also likely to continue to exert pressure within UNISON, to reassess internal structures, practices and culture, and to engage more directly with black and ethnic minority service users about the quality and provision of public services. Similarly, it is possible that through increased involvement in Europe, public service unions in the UK will be influenced by both their European counterparts and by political developments in other countries or Europe as a whole.

In the foreseeable future it is, however, the third scenario which seems to be the most likely route to be followed by public service trade unions. Here we can expect to see UNISON continue to be drawn into, and to even take an increasingly active role in, areas that are traditionally thought of as professional, and therefore beyond its normal remit. It is likely that those forces, already referred to above, both within and outside the union will drag both the more conservatively inclined broad membership, and the activists into discussions and negotiations around service quality issues. However, this will not be a one way process of increasing commitment to a radicalised service ethic. Rather it will be faltering, uneven and no doubt contradictory, conditioned as much by self-interest as by the desire to transform existing welfare relationships. Until and unless there is a powerful external social force that is pressurising and pushing public service unions into wider political directions, it seems unlikely that anything but short-term opportunism will dictate how and to what extent they engage with service users and local authority employers.

Furthermore, public service unions are subject to internal divisions and conflicting interests amongst the membership, manifested both at national and branch level, and who are themselves to varying degrees, organised in sub-groups within the union. As Offe (1985) notes, unions, "can only successfully defend the interests of the 'well organised' groups who 'set the agenda' of discussion by simultaneously accepting impairment of the interests of other groups and segments" (p 157). The development of UNISON may have the effect of highlighting differences between groups and segments within the workforce, but this may lead to less rather than more greater representation of their common interests, making it more difficult for it to mobilise, what Offe describes as, "a common willingness to act that flows from a notion of shared collective identities and mutual obligations of solidarity" (p 187). The new union will also have to balance such competing internal sectional demands against those of organised service users, community organisations and social movements, as well as political parties, for better quality services, yet without necessarily gaining an automatic increase in resources, and greater involvement in the determination of social welfare policies and organisational structures and practices. It is likely, especially given the ebb and flow of such social forces at least in their local manifestation, that UNISON will attempt to play a calculating game that protects as much of what it has, and is careful about what it trades in, in return for any changes to working practices.

Conclusion

This chapter has reviewed the different explanations offered for the relatively high levels of industrial conflict in those local authorities led by the urban left of the Labour Party, and has focused in particular on the conflicts surrounding the implementation of a radical decentralisation policy. The varying explanations, which have often been prescriptive in nature, have been categorised into three broad headings: those who tend to blame either one or other of the key participants; those who have argued that both parties need to avoid talking past each other and re-evaluate how best their mutual interests might be served; and those which seek explanations by pointing to the socio-political context in which the decentralisation initiative was launched. Within the third category two distinct theories were considered. The first focused on the limitations of trade unionism in socialist transformative politics. The second identified widespread problems with public sector industrial relations in the context of a fiscal crisis. However, it was argued that, despite the insights offered by these approaches, it is more useful to consider a third that took industrial relations conflicts as but one, albeit important, feature of an attempt to construct a new political formation.

The arena of industrial relations became an important focal point both because there were significant matters of industrial relations to be resolved, and because it was the institutionalised setting within which the ideas for the proposed new political formation could be tested out. It has been argued that insufficient attention was given to some of the principal components within the strategy, and that some crucial factors were excluded. In particular, this included: its localised focus and the need to establish a national leadership; the need to review the assumptions within the welfare relationships and to seek a new democratic mandate for such interventions; the need to manage the tension between introducing greater democratisation from above and how such opportunities might be used by those who participate; the need to directly address, re-evaluate and, where possible, identify alternative ways of meeting the competing interests of the key participants and to address the conflicts within any one interest group; the need to tackle existing conflicts between the principal parties, and to consider the concept of workers' control, collective work, and the role of trade unions within the strategy.

Finally, in considering possible future scenarios in the development of UNISON, it was suggested that the union is likely to continue, but in an uneven essentially self-interested and opportunistic way, to become involved in areas that go beyond those traditional trade union concerns that focus exclusively around the narrow economic and employment needs of the membership. UNISON will have much to do to overcome sectional interests within it and mobilise common interests based on shared identities, along with re-examining relationships with service users.

Appendix 1
Methodology: Sample details and selection criteria

The interviewees:

A total of 43 trade union NALGO activists were interviewed (Table 1), 39 of whom were based in the neighbourhood offices. Of the 31 Neighbourhood Office Shop Stewards (NOSS) then in post, 28 were interviewed, two were on sick leave and the third was not available for interview. In 11 of the neighbourhood offices where there was only one NOSS, ten were interviewed. In the ten neighbourhood offices where there were two NOSS, 18, were interviewed. This left three neighbourhood offices with no NOSS, although interviews with Departmental Representatives took place in one of these. Of the remaining 15 activists interviewed, eight were former NOSS; two were current Departmental Representatives (DR); two were former DR's; one was a current representative from the Women's Self-Organised Group who was also a member of the Branch Executive in that capacity; one was a current representative from the Black Workers' Self-Organised Group and a member of the Branch Executive in that capacity; and one was the full-time Branch Secretary. In addition to the above positions, a number of those interviewed wore more than one union hat so that two were members of the Islington Irish Workers' Self-Organised group, one was a member of the Black Workers Self-Organised Group, five were currently members of the Branch Executive and four were former members of the Executive.

NALGO activists interviewed (Table 1)

Neighbourhood Shop Stewards	28
Ex-Neighbourhood Office Shop Stewards	8
Departmental Representatives	2
Ex-Departmental Representatives	2
Self-Organised Group Representatives	2
Branch Officers	1
Total Interviewed	43

Distribution by neighbourhood office:

Interviews were carried out in 20 of the 24 neighbourhood offices. In only six of these was there one interview. Two interviews took place in each of ten offices, three occurred in each of three offices and in one office, four interviews were carried out. Of the ten offices with only one NOSS to be interviewed, five other activists in four of these offices were interviewed. These were two former NOSS, both of whom worked in the same Neighbourhood Office, two former Departmental Representatives, and one Self-Organised Group representative, who was also a current member of the Branch Executive. In one Neighbourhood Office that was without any NOSS, two Departmental Representatives were interviewed. In contrast, within three of the nine neighbourhood offices with two current NOSS there were also four former NOSS, all of whom were interviewed. Four people were interviewed who were located outside the neighbourhood offices: the Branch Secretary, who worked from the Branch Office; two former NOSS, who were currently working in the central Housing Office; and one Self-Organised Group representative who was employed in one of the neighbourhood libraries.

Distribution according to gender:

Of the 43 interviewed, an appropriate gender balance was obtained with 22 women and 21 men. Of the men interviewed, (Table 2) 11 were currently NOSS, one of whom was a current Executive member and one was a member of a self-organised group; five were former NOSS, of whom two were members of the Executive and one was a former member; two were currently DR, one of whom was a former Executive member; one was a former DR, having also been a member of the Executive; one was a self-organised group member and currently a member of the Executive; and finally, the Branch Secretary was male. Of the women interviewed, (Table 3) 17 were current NOSS, two of whom were also members of self-organised groups; three were former NOSS, one of whom had been a Departmental Representative and a former Branch Executive member; one was a former DR; and one was a representative of the Women's Self-Organised group and a member of the Executive in that capacity.

Of the 31 NOSS then in post, 18 were women, 17 of whom were interviewed, whilst of the 13 men who were NOSS, 11 were interviewed.

Male activists interviewed (Table 2):

Neighbourhood Office Shop Stewards	11
Ex-Neighbourhood Office Shop Stewards	5
Departmental Representatives	2
Ex-Departmental Representatives	1
Self-Organised Group Representatives	1
Branch Officers	1
Total	21

Female activists interviewed (Table 3):

Neighbourhood Office Shop Stewards	17
Ex-Neighbourhood Office Shop Stewards	3
Ex-Departmental Representatives	1
Self-Organised Group Representatives	1
Total	22

In the light of the still predominant view of the woman worker as less likely to be a member of a trade union, and less active within it if she does join, than her male colleague, the high profile of women activists in the neighbourhood offices is striking. Overall, of the 43 activists interviewed, 22 were female. Out of the current 31 NOSS, 18 were women and 13 men. Furthermore, women outnumbered men in NOSS positions in all three major departments. Finally, women outnumbered men in the leading occupational functions amongst the activists. Thus, for example, of the 11 Principal and basic Advisory Workers eight were women, and of the five Welfare Rights workers three were women.

Distribution according to department:

Forty-two of the 43 interviewed were departmentally based, the exception being the Branch Secretary. What is immediately striking about the departmental spread of the interviewees is the high number of neighbourhood office activists based in the Housing Department, and, similarly, given its low reputation for trade union consciousness and activity, from the Chief Executives Department, in comparison with the Social Services Department, who had a reputation for strong trade unionism within the Branch. However, a closer inspection of the job functions of those activists reveals, for example, that within the Chief Executives, trade union activism was not evenly spread across functions and grades, with most of the stewards being employed in the more professionalised posts. The departmental distributon of the 42 neighbourhood based activists is given below:

Housing	23	(12 women, 11 men)
Chief Executives	11	(5 women, 6 men)
Social Services	6	(4 women, 2 men)
Environmental Health	1	(1 male)
Libraries	1	(1 female)

Of the 28 current NOSS the pattern remains the same, as can be seen from the table below.

Housing	15	(9 women, 6 men)
Chief Executives	8	(5 women, 3 men)
Social Services	4	(3 women, 1 male)
Environmental Health	1	(1 male)

Similarly, of the eight former NOSS interviewed, Housing dominates with six, whilst the Chief Executives and Social Services both produced one each. Although not all former NOSS were interviewed there was no reason to feel that the overall pattern amongst current NOSS had in any way changed drastically. The interview material would suggest that the explanation for the relatively small number of Social Service workers in NOSS posts is both a reflection of their declining strength and their reluctance to commit themselves to the neighbourhood workplace as the basis for trade union organisation as their earlier unionism had been strongly related to their occupational role.

Distribution according to occupational role:

Current activists interviewed were not drawn equally from across the full range of job functions within each of the Departments. Indeed, what is noticeable is the preponderance of only a very limited number of job functions amongst the activists, especially in both Housing and the Chief Executives, as can be seen below:

Housing:

Job function	Activists interviewed
Housing Advisory	10
Principal Advisory	1
Housing Benefits	3
Estate Manager	3
Senior Estate Manager	1
Lettings Officer	2
Improvements Officer	2
Housing Co-ops Officer	1

Although these numbers do reflect to some extent the numerical distribution of job functions within each office, e.g. one would only expect to find one Lettings Officer, Improvements Officer or Co-ops Officer per Neighbourhood Office, they also reflect some active trade union organising amongst Advisory workers, who are numerically similar to Estate Managers and Benefits Officers.

Chief executives:

Job function	Activists interviewed
Welfare Rights Worker	5
Community Worker	2
Neighbourhood Officer	1
Administrative Officer	3

Clearly it is those in the professionalised roles who take a leading trade union role in the Chief Executives with the number of welfare rights workers acting as a NOSS far exceeding their proportional distribution as there is but one such worker per neighbourhood office compared with some nine or ten administrative workers.

Within Social Services, of the six activists interviewed, four were fieldwork Social Workers, one was an Occupational Therapist and the other was a Home Care Organiser.

Distribution by time employed by Islington Borough Council:

The activists interviewed were in the main experienced workers who had been employed for some time by the Borough. They could not be said to be newcomers, although the majority had been employed by the Authority since the introduction of the decentralisation initiative. Nevertheless, nine had been Islington employees for ten years or more, and ten had worked there between five and ten years. Not surprisingly, given the trade union roles they occupied, only two had been employed by Islington for less than a year.

Length of Service in IBC

Less than 1 year	2
1-3 years	11
3-5 years	11
5-10 years	10
More than 10 years	9

Clearly, the great majority (30), had been employees of the Borough for the whole of the period in which decentralisation had been operational. In addition, a significant number had worked in the Borough prior to joining the Authority, whilst others had worked in neighbouring authorities and, therefore, their amount of knowledge of the Borough's history was quite substantial.

Distribution by time holding union office:

These were also activists, however, who were relatively inexperienced as trade unionists holding a formal union office position within the Branch, although the majority had at least 2.5 years experience in their current post:

Activists Length of Time in Union Office:

Less than 1 year	2
1-3 years	31
3-5 years	8
5-10 years	1
More than 10 years	1

In addition, 12 referred to union positions prior to joining the Authority and 13 mentioned their involvement in political organisations.

Reasons for working in Islington:

The great majority of activists mentioned either Islington's reputation (16 responses) or its policies (22 responses) as being an important reason in their decision to work for the Borough. Of those who mentioned specific policies as having attracted them, decentralisation and equal opportunities came out as joint first both receiving ten mentions. Eight stated that they positively chose to work in Islington and 12 said they would describe the Borough as 'progressive'.

Activists' perceptions of Islington NALGO:

Of the 43 interviewed, 33 described Islington NALGO as 'militant'. However, 17 also mentioned a gap in the outlook and politics between the Branch Officers, activists, and the ordinary membership. Political parties were seen as playing a significant role in relation to their contributions to union discussions, although not in respect of the formulation of Branch policies. Seventeen mentioned the Socialist Workers Party as being very vocal in union debates, whilst nine others referred to other political groups including the Communist Party, Socialist Organiser and the Labour Party as all influential and organised within the Branch. However, it was the differential levels of trade union consciousness and activism between departments which was perhaps seen as being more important. Within the neighbourhood structure, Social Services (30 responses) and Housing (26 responses) were consistently identified as being the stronger departments whilst the Chief Executives was equally consistently (25 responses) identified as the weakest. Amongst the centralised departments, the Libraries, with nine responses, was the only other department to be mentioned as being particularly powerful, although by no means as strong as it had been at the end of the 1970s when it had controlled a number of the Branch Officer posts. Respondents recognised that current strengths and weaknesses were not permanent but changed over time. Thus, Social Services was seen as being less powerful than it had been, whereas Housing was seen as having grown, and continuing to grow, in strength. In addition, it was acknowledged that within each department there would be some sections that were more conscious and more active in their trade unionism than others. This was often related to the nature of the occupational role being undertaken, so that it was felt by many that having a job that related to other people's rights almost inevitably drew you into active trade unionism in defence and promotion of your own rights.

The questionnaire

The questionnaire was divided into five sections. Section 'A' was designed to elicit background information on the respondents in relation to their workplace, length of service, nature of their position and occupation, as well as relevant biographical details. In order to gain some insight into the motivating forces behind their trade unionism and to produce a personal profile of the NALGO activist, Section 'B' focused on their backgrounds, seeking information on parental status and socio-economic class, and enquiring about attitudes to politics and levels of political and social activity. Section 'C' sought additional information on the respondent's views on government and trade unions as well as finding more detail on job situation. Section 'D' looks more closely at the respondent's engagement with trade unionism, their attitudes to public service trade union activity, and draws out attitudes and perceptions of management. Finally section 'E', looks specifically at the policy of decentralisation, exploring the respondents' views on the theoretical possibilities contained within it, their actual experience of it in practice, and the process of union-management negotiations. Occasionally, similar questions were asked in different sections with a view to testing out levels of consistency in the answers. There were 72 substantive questions in the questionnaire but many of these either had secondary questions within them or required the respondent to respond to a range of options, making a total of 265 separate items to be addressed. The questionnaire took approximately one and a half hours to complete, and undoubtedly some of the respondents found this a heavy demand on their time. This compares with the 106-item questionnaire, on Union Democracy, given to Sheffield NALGO members and the 214 items given to NALGO stewards in Sheffield by Nicholson et al. (1981), and the 199-item questionnaire of academic staff at Polytechnics carried out by Social and Community Planning Research (1989). In drawing up the questionnaire on decentralisation I used ten of the questions from the Sheffield survey as well as developing and modifying some others to make them relevant to my purposes.

That part of the questionnaire going to the neighbourhood offices was distributed through the stewards in each of the offices. Reliance upon a second party voluntarily undertaking the distribution obviously raises problems of reliability and efficiency and although an alternative would have been to have the stewards draw up a list of union members to whom I could then personally mail the questionnaire, there was some reluctance from some of the stewards to do this and a preference on their part to be responsible for distribution. An attempt to make the questionnaire more meaningful and personal was done by attaching a letter explaining its purpose and providing a contact point for anyone should they wish to discuss it. A further, reminder letter was sent, again via the steward, during the completion period. Respondents were asked to return the completed questionnaire to the steward, from whom I collected them. A 'postal' questionnaire is not the most satisfactory method for conducting such data collection and a better return can be achieved by getting the respondent to complete the questionnaire with the researcher present. However, both time and resource constraints as well as the difficulties of organising such a task potentially involving 250 people in six locations prohibited any other approach. Contact with the Branch Exectutive members was made through the Branch mailing distribution.

A 25% sample of the neighbourhood offices was chosen for the questionnaire. The sample was not determined on a random basis as the objective was to ascertain the views of NALGO members taking account of both differential membership levels and degrees of trade union activism in each office, and a range of criteria connected with the workplace which might impact upon the views and perspectives of the trade unionists. The following criteria were, therefore, used in the selection of neighbourhood offices:

1 The opening date for the neighbourhood office
2 The size of the neighbourhood office
3 The level of consumer demand
4 The level of expressed consumer satisfaction
5 The geographical location within the Borough
6 The political representation within the ward served by the office
7 The level of industrial relations activity within the office

The intention was not so much to make comparisons between the different offices against each of the separate data but rather to ensure that an overall representative sample was achieved. Ultimately, it was assumed that whilst there would be some response variations related to workplace this would not be a significant factor. Other variables, such as occupational role, departmental location, hierachical position in the organisation, material reward, and most importantly the very fact of having been decentralised, as opposed to continuing to work from the centralised departments, would be at least as significant in determining attitudes to the decentralisation policy.

The following neighbourhood offices were selected for the questionnaire:

1   Julie Curtin
2   Cally Road
3   Gillespie
4   Durham Road
5   Tufnell Park
6   Clerkenwell

Two hundred questionnaires were distributed in the neighbourhood offices. This represented the total number of NALGO members within the six offices, as provided by the stewards. There were a total of 248 posts in the six offices, although not all of these were occupied at the time of the research. In all 24 offices there were 995 posts. Fifty-one questionnaires were completed and returned, a 25.5% return of the NALGO members in the six offices. However, as a result of feedback from the first stage distribution about the time taken to complete the questionnaire, the number of sections to be completed was reduced in the second stage where the focus was more specifically on reactions to the decentralisation initiative. Only ten of the 51 responses completed this shortened version which required them to complete only sections 'A' and 'E', and which had been printed separately. Thus 41, or 20.5%, completed the full five sectioned questionnaire. In addition to the returns from the neighbourhood offices, 25 full questionnaires were distributed to the Branch Executive and nine of the eligible members completed the full questionnaire. Thus there was a total of 62 completed questionnaires, a 27.5% return rate overall. Six of those who completed the questionnaire were also amongst those interviewed.

Opening times for the neighbourhood offices:

The neighbourhood offices were opened over a three year period, between March 1985 and March 1987, although the programme began initially with only four offices, all opening in March 1985, followed by 11 coming on stream mid to late 1985, with a further eight starting during 1986, and the final office opening in March of the next year. It was, therefore, important to ensure that the questionnaire covered offices that had come into operation at different points in the process on the assumption that lessons may have been learnt by the end of the cycle from the inevitable teething problems of the early openers. Equally, the early starters would be more bedded down, being by now 'old hands' at decentralisation, with more time to reflect upon it as an effective way of delivering services and altering social relations with consumers and managers. Both Cally Road and Julie Curtin were early starters (March 1985), Tufnell Park and Gillespie were both late arrivals (March and May 1986), whilst Clerkenwell and Durham Road were in the middle range, becoming operational in July and November 1985 respectively. Information on opening times was supplied by the Borough's Decentralisation Unit.

Size of neighbourhood office:

Inevitably, the size of each office varied according to the size of the defined neighbourhood, and the number of posts in each office varied, at the time of the research from between 33 and 53, with a total of 248 and represented 25% of the total number of posts across all 24 offices. Again the information related to office size was supplied by the Decentralisation Unit. Not all posts were occupied at the time of the research and no automatic relationship is assumed between NALGO membership and total number of posts available. The 80% NALGO membership level in the six chosen offices may by slightly higher than that for all the neighbourhood offices as the level of steward reported union membership and activity in the sample was assessed as above average. Nevertheless it was thought important to cover a range of office sizes partly just to get an overall spread of office type but also since workplace size has long been identified as an important variable in trade union consciousness. It was acknowledged, however, that even the largest office would still be considered a small workplace in general terms, and that the actual employer, Islington Borough Council, could only be classified as a large employer. Furthermore, despite the decentralised structures, it was likely that it would be the Borough's overall policies that would have an impact on trade unionism amongst its employees rather than the local management within a single decentralised unit. Nevertheless, the behaviour of local management was considered important and indeed was commented upon by those interviewed, and was consequently taken into account when selecting offices. Gillespie and Julie Curtin were both small offices (34 posts in each), Tufnell Park and Durham Road, each with 39 posts, were of average size, whilst Cally Road, with 49 posts and Clerkenwell with 53 were both large offices.

Consumer demand:

Consumer demand on local authority services via the neighbourhood offices varied according to such indices as: socio-economic position, the level of public sector housing available in each office's neighbourhood, and the age distribution within the population. It was assumed that levels of consumer demand would have an important determining effect on workers perceptions of the effectiveness of decentralisation in reaching users and its ability to respond to demand. The MORI survey (1988) carried out for the Borough Council between July and December 1987, on 'Service Provision and Living Standards in Islington', was used to identify the range of demand levels across the Borough's 24 offices. Across the Borough as a whole the MORI study showed that 53% of Islington's residents had used their neighbourhood office on at least one occasion, although the usage rates varied between offices from 69% to 35% of the local neighbourhood populations. In fact, Durham Road, Cally Road, Clerkenwell and Julie Curtin were all busy offices, with high levels of usage whilst Tufnell Park was ranked 14th in its usage and Gillespie had a low usage, being ranked 22nd (MORI p 134). The level of Council housing also varied between neighbourhoods, and as housing was the service in most demand in the neighbourhood offices it was again felt important to have a range which reflected this distribution. Thus council tenure was high in Clerkenwell, Cally Road and Durham Road, around average in Julie Curtin and Tufnell Park and low in Gillespie. Similarly, unemployment levels can be assumed to affect the usage of Council services and of the six chosen offices Clerkenwell and Tufnell Park had high levels of unemployment, with Cally Road and Gillespie showing average levels, whilst Julie Curtin and Durham Road were experiencing low levels.

Consumer satisfaction:

The MORI survey found that overall 44% of Islington residents were satisfied with the way the Council was being run. However, satisfaction levels varied across the Borough.

Gillespie rated the highest satisfaction level with 60%, whilst Durham Road ranked 6th, with 48%, and Tufnell Park 8th, with 47%. At the bottom, Julie Curtin was ranked 23rd, with 35%, whilst Clerkenwell and Cally Road were also both in the lower half, 15th and 16th respectively. Similarly, in relation to expressed dissatisfaction levels, Julie Curtin, Cally Road and Clerkenwell all ranked high, being 2nd, 3rd, and 4th respectively. Durham Road was ranked 10th, whilst Tufnell Park and Gillespie both received low rankings of 21st and 24th respectively. The six chosen neighbourhood offices are similarly distributed across the consumer satisfaction levels in relation to Housing services.

The level of consumer satisfaction with both the treatment received when visiting a neighbourhood office and with the result of their visit again varied according to the local office used, although MORI noted that the vast majority, four in five, were satisfied with the treatment received and three in five with the result of their contact (MORI p 135). However, dissatisfaction levels varied, in relation to result, between 20 and 46% across the neighbourhood offices, and between five and 22% in relation to treatment. Again it was assumed that variable levels of consumer dissatisfaction would be related to both levels of worker satisfaction, especially in relation to the treatment offered to service users, and resources available to meet demand. It was further assumed that this would influence the workers' evaluation of the policy and may highlight differences in their attitude towards users and, therefore, the degree to which they felt a need to work more closely with them. Gillespie and Tufnell Park were given low rates of dissatisfaction in relation to both treatment and result, (ranked 20th and 24th and 17th and 19th respectively) in contrast with Durham Road and Clerkenwell who both came out badly on both counts (Durham Road was ranked 3rd and 2nd highest respectively and Clerkenwell was ranked highest in relation to treatment and 8th in relation to outcome). Cally Road was rated badly (ranked 3rd) on dissatisfaction with the treatment received but was average (ranked 14th) in relation to the outcomes. Finally, Julie Curtin was rated average on dissatisfaction over outcome (ranked 12th) and had high levels of dissatisfaction over the treatment received (ranked 7th). Not surprisingly, low levels of council tenure, and therefore lower levels of demand are positively correlated with higher levels of satisfaction in relation to both overall Council services and the treatment and outcomes of contact with neighbourhood offices.

Geographical location:

In order to obtain a reasonable sample of the 24 offices, in a Borough with marked contrasts between its northern and southern sections, it was important to have a wide geographical spread. Durham Road, Gillespie and Tufnell Park are located in the northern part of the Borough, whilst Clerkenwell is in the southern end, with Cally Road and Julie Curtin in the middle at the western and eastern ends of the Borough.

Political representation:

Although the Labour Party held a considerable majority on the Council, it was nevertheless important to include an area where representation of the other political parties was reasonably strong, especially since this may highlight differential attitudes by workers towards the elected members for their neighbourhood. Clerkenwell was chosen from those six wards, all in the southern part of the Borough, which in 1986 all had SDP representation, but which was the only ward to also have an SDP candidate elected in 1982. There is currently no Conservative Party representation.

Trade union activity:

It was thought to be important to identify neighbourhood offices according to levels of trade union activity. However, such data is not measurable in the same way as the other criteria and the views of the Branch officials and shop stewards were relied upon to identify current union membership levels, longer term trends of engagement in trade union action, and the current occupancy rate of steward positions. On this, admittedly impressional basis, Durham Road, Cally Road and Julie Curtin were identified has having a high level of trade union activity whilst the remaining three, Tufnell Park, Gillespie and Clerkenwell were assessed as average. Given that the objective was to uncover the views of active NALGO members, the priority was to target those offices with an average or above level of trade union engagement.

A profile of the respondents:

Occupational role:

The respondents to the questionnaire cover a wide range of occupations found in the neighbourhood offices. A list of the occupations and the number of full-time equivalent respondents involved is given below.

Housing Advisory Officers	9
Estate and Senior Estate Managers	6
Housing and Senior Housing Benefits Officers	6.5
Trainee Housing Benefits Officers	1
Lettings Officers	2
Improvements Officers	2
Social Workers and Senior Social Workers	8
Community Workers	1
Welfare Rights Workers	3.5
Administrative Workers	6
Assistant Neighbourhood Officers	1
Neighbourhood Officers	5
Principal Environmental Health Officers	1

The additional occupations of those Branch Executive members who responded and were not neighbourhood based were:

Administrative Workers	2
Architects	1
Policy Development Officers	1
Trainee Legal Assistants	1
Storekeepers	1
Research Workers	1
Senior Technical Accountants	1
Senior Employment Officers	1

One respondent failed to identify their occupation.

In relation to the respondents' departmental distribution, within the neighbourhood offices, the majority were employed within Housing (28 responses), followed by the Chief Executives (15), Social Services (9), and Environmental Health (1). The Branch Executive members came from the Chief Executives (3), and one each from Housing, Legal, Finance, Architects, and Building Works.

Place of residence:

The great majority of the respondents (47) lived outside of the Borough, with 25 residing in another Inner-London borough, 17 within an outer borough and three outside of London.

Employment in the Borough:

The majority (40) of respondents had worked for the Borough for between one and five years as can be seen from the table below. In fact this was, overall, a stable group of workers for a comparison with their length of service in local government reveals that 41 of the 61 had only worked for the Borough of Islington during their local government career. Employment by Islington Borough Council:

Less than one year	8
1-3 years	23
4-5 years	17
6-10 years	10
11-15 years	2
16-20 years	0
More than 20 years	1

Employment within local government:

The average length of employment in local government, between four and ten years for the majority (38), is slightly longer than that for employment by the Borough with 20 of the respondents indicating that they had worked for other local authorities.
Employed within local government for:

Less than one year	3
1-3 years	13
4-5 years	17
6-10 years	21
11-15 years	7
16-20 years	0
More than 20 years	1

Distribution according to age:

This was a relatively young group of repondents. The majority (41 or 66%) were clustered in the ten-year age band of 25-35 years, 24 (38%) of these being between 25 and 30 years. These compare with the 39% in Nicholson et al. 1982 study who were in the 26-40 age band and the 19% in their 26-30 group. In Islington there were few respondents at either the very young age band (18-24) or the older age category (46 and upwards), as can be seen below:

18-24 years	5
25-30 years	24
31-35 years	17
36-40 years	8
41-45 years	6
46-50 years	1
51-55 years	0
55+ years	1

Distribution according to gender:

The respondents produced an equitable gender balance with a slightly larger number of female respondents (33) and at 53.2% compares with the Borough's percentage of women officers of 51.4%.

Ethnic origin of respondents:

When asked to describe their own ethnic origin, a large majority (43) listed themselves as 'white British', whilst seven classified themselves as black (i.e. Afro-Caribbean [2], African [2], Asian [3]), eight as Irish, two as white European non-British, and two as 'other'. The 12.9% response from black people does not compare well with the Borough's overall figure of 21.2% black and ethnic minority officers, although a sizeable proportion of these are employed within Social Services Day and Residential Division where they account for 38.6% of the staff.

Distribution according to educational qualifications:

This was a highly well-qualified group of respondents with 37 possessing a degree and eight of these having a post-graduate qualification. These 45 (72%) compare with 40% in the Nicholson et al. study. Five others had some other form of further education. Conversely, only three of the respondents possessed no qualifications, four had less than five GCSE's or its equivalent, and three had five or more GCSE's, but had proceeded no further.

Distribution by parental background:

Exactly half the respondents described at least one of their parents (18 of the father and eight of the mothers) as having either a professional/managerial job or being self employed. Five fathers and 11 mothers were described as having supervisory or similar and routine non-manual jobs. Thirteen fathers and one mother were described as having a skilled manual job whilst nine fathers and 12 mothers were said to have been in semi or unskilled manual jobs. Eleven of the mothers were described as never having held or generally not in paid employment. This distribution is again different from that of Nicholson et al. (1982) who found that "around half have parents in blue-collar occupations and over half of those from white-collar backgrounds fall in the 'professional' or 'managerial' categories" (p 78). In Islington, a large number (35 representing 67% described their parents as working class (30) or lower middle class (5), with nine describing them as either middle or upper middle. The politics of the respondents' parents were also slightly more to the left of the political spectrum. Twenty-three described their fathers and 21 their mothers as being politically 'centre left', 'left' or 'far left'. Nineteen of the fathers and 18 of the mothers were described as being either 'centre right' or 'right'. No one was said to be 'far right'.

The respondents' politics

The respondents themselves had clearly moved even further to the left of the political spectrum compared to their parents. In addition a significant number were politically active and for many this activity was not confined to any one particular arena. Thus, 12 described themselves as 'far left', 25 as 'left' and ten as 'centre left'. Nobody described themselves as being anywhere right of centre. Forty-three respondents stated that their interest in politics was either fairly strong (24) or very strong (19) with only six saying it was fairly weak. Indeed, 22 (43%) stated that they would like to be more involved in politics and the majority (19) indicated that a lack of time was one reason for not being able to pursue this.

Exactly 50% of the respondents stated that they were members of a political party and 80% of these said that they attended party politcal meetings either occasionally (11) or regularly (9), with only two never attending. Eighteen respondents had participated in campaigning for their party in the local elections, 17 having done so for national elections. Eleven stated that they "actively participate in local party activities" and six held an office in the party. Their political interests were not limited to party politics, however, and a number indicated an interest in political issues that to some extent reflect those of the new urban left. Thus, 37 stated that feminism or women's movement politics were either very important or important to their own politics. Thirty-nine declared the same in relation to race and black struggles; whilst 26 said that was the case for issues of sexuality and gay and lesbian politics; and 24 felt that environmental or green issues were important or very important for them politically.

In addition, nine respondents were members of a national pressure group, such as Shelter or Child Poverty Action Group; 15 were members of a national campaigning body, such as Anti-Abortion or Anti-Apartheid; five were members of a local community action group and four were members of a local voluntary service providing group. Respondents were given a range of options to best describe their membership of such bodies, ranging from the non active member, member, occasional participant to active member, and in all cases the majority of those who were involved described themselves simply as 'members'. Finally, respondents were asked to indicate how many of their friends outside work shared their views. Forty-one stated that either most (21) or a significant number (20) of their non-workplace friends shared their political views.

Twenty-one stated that either most (15) or a significant number (6) of such friends were also active trade unionists, although 13 stated that this was so with only very few of their friends. However, the majority of such non-workplace friends were not employed by the Authority. Twenty-eight said that very few worked for the Authority and five said that none did. Only one said that most of their non-workplace friends worked for the Borough whilst 14 said that a significant number did so.

Thus, a significant number of these respondents saw themselves as on the left of the political spectrum, with a politics that goes beyond mere party politics encompassing those of the contemporary social movements, are actively involved through a variety of organisations in pursuing their political interests, and who move in a social environment in which many of their friends share their ideals and their trade union activism.

Employment status:

Fifty-nine of the 62 respondents worked in full-time posts, which is not surprising given the poor history of the professionalised occupations in providing part-time or job-share posts. Eighteen of the respondents identified themselves as having some formal managerial responsibilities attached to their posts, although three others supervised other workers without having, or acknowledging, any managerial responsibility. Nine respondents were responsible for supervising between one and five workers, whilst eight had such a responsibility for between six and ten workers.

Work situation:

Fifty-one respondents, 42 of whom worked in neighbourhood offices, completed section 'C', which asked questions on work situation. One of the striking features of their responses (question C2) is that despite the emphasis on generic team work within decentralisation, only seven respondents said they were part of "a highly integrated team" although all of these came from the decentralised teams. The majority described their work situation primarily in terms of "a loosely integrated team" (22, all but two coming from the NO) or working "alongside but largely independent of others" (14, eight from the decentralised offices), whilst five stated that they worked mainly on their own.

When asked (question C3) to say whether the people they were in daily contact with did the same or very similar work the respondents were divided between the 26, who said that either none or very few did, and the 18 who said that most or almost all of them did. However, once the non-neighbourhood office workers are removed from the figures, most of whom worked in close proximity to colleagues doing the same or very similar work, the picture for the decentralised workers is one where virtually twice as many of them were working alongside people, very few of whom were engaged in similar activity. No doubt this is a direct consequence of highly decentralised structures with necessarily only one or a few occupational roles in each office.

Finally, when questioned (C4) about the nature of their contact with the service user, of the 51 respondents, only ten had very little or no face to face contact with the consumer, and eight of these were not working in neighbourhood offices. Thirty-nine were engaged in providing a caring service, and for 21 of these this was their primary task. Thirty-two provided material benefits to the consumer, and 39 had jobs that required them to ensure that statutory requirements were enforced. This typically mixed social welfare profile, of work that has elements of caring, material benefits and direct social control, contrasted sharply with the non-neighbourhood office based Branch Executive members who had very little or no direct consumer contact, and were engaged either entirely with policy development or ensuring that statutory requirements were enforced.

Trade union membership:

There was a close correspondence for the respondents between membership of NALGO and employment within local government. In only nine of the 62 responses was there a discrepancy between the length of service in local government and the length of membership in NALGO. In three cases only one of the two questions was answered. However, in the remaining 50 cases the answers were identical (questions A5 and A19). The table below gives the length of time the respondents had been trade union members.

Less than one year	4
1-3 years	16
4-5 years	17
6-10 years	15
11-15 years	6
16-20 years	0
More than 20 years	1
Did not respond	3

Clearly, not everyone joined NALGO as soon as they did local government, and some will leave the union during their employment and may rejoin later. However, the close overlap between the figures suggests that for the vast majority of respondents joining NALGO went with joining local government. Thirty-seven of the respondents stated that they had also been a member of another trade union, whilst 23 had only been members of NALGO. Although one of the stated aims of the questionnaire was to identify the views of the ordinary NALGO members, only 13 respondents (ten of whom were women), of the 52 who completed the full questionnaire, described themselves as being "ordinary members who had never held a union office". Of the remaining 34 who answered, 19 said they were either currently a shop steward or Branch Officer, and 15 said they were either a former steward or Branch Officer. In addition, six also identified themselves as belonging to the Black Workers Self-Organised Group, six to the NALGO Women Members Group, four to the NALGO Gay and Lesbian Group and nine to a NALGO Special Interest Group, which for the majority was most likely to mean the Irish Workers group. Of course not all NALGO members would be eligible to join an existing self-organised group and 14 specifically mentioned this. Finally, six also stated that they had been members of NALGO Action Group, which was now no longer functioning.

Virtually all the respondents (44), regardless of whether or not they had held a union post, described themselves as union activists of one sort or another. Twenty-five stated that their activism was an extension of their political, religious or ideological beliefs, whilst the remaining 19 declared that although they did not get involved most of the time there were issues which they were concerned about and involved with. Thirty-four of the respondents were either current or former holders of a union position, and only 13 had never held office in the union. The great majority indicated that their union activism (ranging from occasional involvement through frequent to very often) included, voting in union elections (45), attending union rallies (45), attending Branch meetings (38), attending departmental or site union meetings (48), and raising an issue or grievance with a union representative (23).

Union membership was seen by 36 respondents as linking them with the wider labour movement, and valued it as such. A significant 45 out of 51, valued their membership for the protection it offered to their work related interests. However, a majority of respondents did not feel that the union should restrict itself to conditions of service issues. Thus 32 disagreed that the union should confine itself to defending its members' jobs and pay levels, and 28 disagreed that it should limit itself to improving pay and conditions of service. Conversely, 43 indicated that the union should engage with issues around the quality of service provision and 37 said it should produce policy guidelines on how services should be provided. Despite their activism within the union, and therefore a greater likelihood of influencing and shaping Branch policies and direction, these respondents did not express high levels of satisfaction with the Branch's ability to effectively pursue its members' interests. Thus, only four said they were 'very satisfied' with the Branch action in general, although 21 said they were 'satisfied'. However, 14 said they were either 'not satisfied' or 'very dissatisfied'. In relation to the decentralisation policy the number of those expressing some level of dissatisfaction rose to 22, and only eight expressed any form of satisfaction. Over equal opportunities policies, there was more of an even divide with 23 expressing some satisfaction and 19 being dissatisfied.

In comparison with those activists, as measured by their current or former occupation of formal union roles, ordinary members did not register strong connections between trade unionism and belief systems. Nevertheless their pragmatic engagement with union politcs (37.25% of the ordinary members giving this as their response in comparison with 26.3% of the activists) produced a level of engagement that is beyond merely being a passive member content to receive the benefits of trade unionism without having any interest in trade union activities. The Nicholson et al. (1982) study noted likewise that "apathy cannot be said to be the norm" (p 86) although they describe 34.7% as being 'passive dues-payers' and only 4.5% as 'ideological activists'. This sharply contrasts with the Islington sample where 37% classified themselves as 'selective activists' and 49% as 'ideological activists' to use the Nicholson et al. phrase. Furthermore, when asked more about their attitudes to trade unionism (question D5), eight of the 13 ordinary members agreed, five of them strongly, that they valued being a union member because it identified them with the labour movement (a 61.5% response in comparison with a 73% response of the activists); 12 agreed, seven strongly, that they valued the union because it protected their interests at work (a 92.3% response which is slightly higher than the 86.8% activist response and is to be expected emphasising the relative differences between a pragmatic and ideological emphasis given by the two groups). In contrast, 11 of the ordinary members disagreed, seven of them strongly, that being a union member increased one's personal status and power, a 84.6% response which interestingly compares with the 57.8% response of the activists, revealing perhaps real differences between those who do and those who do not occupy union posts. They did, however, see their union membership as providing them with an opportunity to discuss their views with their colleagues. Ten agreed with this statement, a 76.9% response compared with a virtually identical 76.3% response from the activists. They also gave a significantly higher rating than that of the activists (61.5% against 47.4%) to the statement that they valued being a union member because it is part of their contact with other people. When asked (question C1) on whether or not they viewed the policies of the present government as a direct threat to local government services and workers, these ordinary members again responded in similar fashion to their colleagues with experience of union positions (92.3% against 86.8%), although a smaller percentage (53.8% against 65.8%) of ordinary members agreed that public services needed to be democratised. However, there were signs that when it came to defining the scope of legitimate trade union activity, the ordinary members were more inclined towards the view that the union should confine itself to improving the pay and conditions of service to all members: 45% agreed with this, in comparison with 31.6% of the formally defined activists and conversely, only 38.5% disagreed compared with 60.5% of the activists.

Appendix 2
Tables

Table 6.1: *External Factors Shaping Attitudes to Trade Unionism*
   Results in Numbers

External Factors:	Influential	Not Influential
Current Government Policies	47 (29 very)	2
Other Trade Unionists	40 (18 very)	8
Economic Climate	39 (17 very)	9
High Unemployment	38 (20 very)	10
Education	36 (15 very)	12
Political Party	29 (20 very)	27
Gender	25 (7 very)	23
Media	23 (7 very)	24
Ethnic Origin	20 (7 very)	26
Membership of Pressure Group	17 (8 very)	29

Table 6.2: *The Influence of Market and Work Situation*
   Results in Numbers

	Influential	Not Influential
Working Conditions	36	12
Work Colleagues	36	13
Pay Levels	35	12
Management Policies and Attitude	34	13
Role in the Authority	26	19

Table 8.1: The Potential Benefit of Decentralisation to the Service User
Results in Numbers

	Strongly Agree	Agree on Balance	Not Sure	Disagree on Balance	Strongly Disagree
Consumers having better access to workers	33 N = 56	20	1	2	0
Consumers having better understanding why certain decisions taken	17 N = 56	16	13	9	1
Consumers having better understanding of problems facing workers	12 N = 56	15	15	10	4
Consumers getting a voice in service delivery	13 N = 56	21	8	13	1
Consumers having more power in service delivery	13 N = 57	20	8	15	1
Consumers feeling that services belong to them	11 N = 56	20	10	14	1

Table 8.2: The Potential of Decentralisation to Challenge Working Relationships
Results in Numbers

	Strongly Agree	Agree on Balance	Not Sure	Disagree on Balance	Strongly Disagree
Breaking down departmental barriers	19 N = 56	23	5	9	0
Enabling workers to share knowledge/skills	16 N = 55	26	7	6	0
Helping workers better understand colleagues	18 N = 56	30	6	2	0

	Strongly Agree	Agree on Balance	Not Sure	Disagree on Balance	Strongly Disagree
Helping to break down professionalism	9 N = 56	18	21	7	1
Challenging a top-down approach to service delivery	12 N = 55	16	12	12	3
Breaking down white/blue-collar workers	9 N = 56	16	6	21	4
Helping to bring about a better relationship between workers and users	10 N = 55	22	11	11	1
Producing a more participatory and democratic welfare service	11 N = 56	17	11	14	3
Providing a better working environment	11 N = 56	13	11	13	8

Table 8.3: The Potential Impact on Strategic Policies and Resources Results in Numbers

	Strongly Agree	Agree on Balance	Not Sure	Disagree on Balance	Strongly Disagree
Making authority wide resources easier to get hold of	13 N = 55	21	9	7	5
Undermining effectiveness of appropriate centralised planning and monitoring	4 N = 54	6	16	21	7
Undermining Equal Opportunities policies	3 N = 55	10	14	20	8

Table 8.4: The Potential to Politically Mobilise in Defence of Collective Welfare
Results in Numbers

	Strongly Agree	Agree on Balance	Not Sure	Disagree on Balance	Strongly Disagree
Enabling workers to defend and revitalise the public sector	8 N = 54	13	11	16	6
Helping to recapture lost confidence in the public sector	9 N = 55	18	7	17	4
Helping to unite the opposition to attacks on local government because if offers something positive	10 N = 55	16	9	15	5
As a strategy it is unclear and lacks political credibility	10 N = 56	13	13	16	4
There is nothing new in the idea of decentralisation	10 N = 56	25	9	10	2
It has the potential for bringing about substantial social change	9 N = 56	6	10	18	13
It is a potentially misplaced strategy in the absence of a vibrant mass socialist movement	8 N = 59	13	13	16	9

Table 8.5: The Extent to Which Decentralisation Has in Practice Led to a General
Improvement in Service Provision
Results in Numbers

	Improvement	Same	Don't Know	Decrease
An improvement in the relationship between service provider and user	21 N = 55	16	6	12
An improvement in the efficiency of service offered	22 N = 54	10	7	16
Improvement in the quality of service offered	20 N = 53	10	11	12

	Improvement	Same	Don't Know	Decrease
Improvement in the level of service offered to the consumer	22 N = 55	10	11	12

Table 8.6: *Workers Under Pressure*
    Results in Numbers

	Strongly Agree	Agree on Balance	Not Sure	Disagree on Balance	Strongly Disagree
The Authority is making workers more accountable to users but is itself no more accountable to either workers or users	19 N = 49	18	9	3	0
Workers have been left in the firing line of user dissatisfaction	33 N = 49	16	0	0	0
It has idealised the user and placed workers under increased personal risk	15 · N = 48	23	5	4	1
Workers have had to get too close to the user	4 N = 47	7	11	19	6

Table 8.7: *Managing Inadequate Resourcing*
    Results in Numbers

	Strongly Agree	Agree on Balance	Not Sure	Disagree on Balance	Strongly Disagree
It has been impractical in a period of resource constraint	16 N = 48	15	9	7	1
It has shifted attention away from the Authority's inability to provide real services	16 N = 48	12	6	12	2

	Strongly Agree	Agree on Balance	Not Sure	Disagree on Balance	Strongly Disagree
It is essentially about the management of scarcity in a recession	8 N = 48	15	11	9	5
It has been used to cover up an inadequate service	13 N = 48	13	10	10	2

Table 8.8: Impact on Job Satisfaction
Results in Numbers

	Strongly Agree	Agree on Balance	Not Sure	Disagree on Balance	Strongly Disagree
It has led to a greater sense of job satisfaction	3 N = 47	7	6	16	15
It has given workers new responsibilities but insufficient rewards	14 N = 49	25	5	5	0
It has meant more work for fewer people	20 N = 48	12	10	4	2
It has led to a reduction in time to undertake complex tasks	11 N = 48	18	10	7	2
It has reduced the possibility of long-term development work	13 N = 48	7	17	9	2
It has enriched our daily work	2 N = 51	11	6	16	16
It has offered little power to workers	15 N = 49	23	4	7	0

Table 8.9: *Decentralisation and Deskilling*
    Results in Numbers

	Strongly Agree	Agree on Balance	Not Sure	Disagree on Balance	Strongly Disagree
It has led to a loss of skill in our work	8 N = 49	7	10	20	4
It has undermined our professional position	6 N = 47	5	11	19	6
It has led to a loss of autonomy for workers	3 N = 49	17	14	12	3

Table 8.10: *Increased Managerial Control*
    Results in Numbers

	Strongly Agree	Agree on Balance	Not Sure	Disagree on Balance	Strongly Disagree
It increased managerial control	9 N = 47	17	9	11	1
It is more about managerialism than democratisation	11 N = 47	15	11	6	4
It has offered new hope for working with elected members	2 N = 47	4	12	21	9

Table 8.11: *Overall Reflections on the Initiative in the Present Context*
    Results in Numbers

	Strongly Agree	Agree on Balance	Not Sure	Disagree on Balance	Strongly Disagree
It has been too ambitious given a government intent on destroying the power of local authorities	9 N = 48	17	7	9	6

	Strongly Agree	Agree on Balance	Not Sure	Disagree on Balance	Strongly Disagree
It has been vague and half-baked	8 N = 48	12	16	10	2
It has undermined good practice in other important areas such as equal opportunities	12 N = 49	7	14	13	3
It has not gone far enough in decentralising services	9 N = 48	14	7	12	6

Table 8.12: General Views on Management Results in Numbers

	Strongly Agree	Agree on Balance	Not Sure	Disagree on Balance	Strongly Disagree
Management should always be trusted	0 N = 48	4	2	20	22
It is a real disadvantage to understand management's point of view	1 N = 44	5	7	18	13
When workers participate in managerial decision-making it confuses roles and management are likely to get their own way	3 N = 46	5	16	12	10

Table 8.13: Engaging With Management Results in Numbers

	Strongly Agree	Agree on Balance	Not Sure	Disagree on Balance	Strongly Disagree
Management do not like to have their authority challenged	24 N = 45	15	3	3	0

	Strongly Agree	Agree on Balance	Not Sure	Disagree on Balance	Strongly Disagree
Management are open to criticism, welcoming of new ideas	0 N = 45	3	10	19	13
There is insufficient access to management	10 N = 46	15	10	10	1

Table 8.14: Perceived Management Commitment to the Workforce Results in Numbers

	Strongly Agree	Agree on Balance	Not Sure	Disagree on Balance	Strongly Disagree
Management always want to minimise the influence of trade unions	18 N = 47	16	6	5	2
Management are not committed to an equal relationship with trade unions	22 N = 45	12	10	0	1
When resources are scarce management will always attempt to reduce the workforce and undermine existing arrangements	30 N = 47	10	4	3	0
Management do not properly recognise their responsibilities to the workforce	20 N = 45	12	6	6	1
Management are insufficiently sensitive to the needs of workers with childcare responsibilities	11 N = 44	14	7	9	3

Table 8.15:   Perceived Managerial Commitment to Good Practice
Results in Numbers

	Strongly Agree	Agree on Balance	Not Sure	Disagree on Balance	Strongly Disagree
Management's first commitment is to the provision of high quality services	6 N = 46	7	6	16	11
Management are committed to equal opportunities	1 N = 45	5	10	20	9
Management are committed to improving the position of the low paid	1 N = 45	1	6	13	24

Table 9.1:   Councillors' Involvement in Policy Implementation
Results in Numbers

	Strongly Agree	Agree on Balance	Not Sure	Disagree on Balance	Strongly Disagree
Councillors have a right to be involved in policy implementation	9 N = 44	23	6	5	1
Councillors are essentially amateurs and should leave questions of practice to the professionals	6 N = 45	10	7	20	2
Councillors have a legitimate right to influence working practices	5 N = 45	8	8	13	11

Table 9.2: Union Views on Council Behaviour During Implementation Process
  Results in Numbers

	Strongly Agree	Agree on Balance	Not Sure	Disagree on Balance	Strongly Disagree
Elected members were inexperienced as employers and ignored normal industrial relations	8 N = 41	11	15	6	1
It was incompetent in how it introduced such a far-reaching change	8 N = 42	17	7	8	2
It displayed undue haste	10 N = 42	15	5	10	2
Elected members had some idealised view of the community and believed the unions to be resistant to change	12 N = 41	22	6	0	1
It was unwilling to listen to union advice	6 N = 42	20	9	5	2
It showed little respect for the negotiators	6 N = 42	18	11	6	1
It ignored the union's willingness to co-operate	4 N = 41	12	19	6	0
It got frustrated at what they saw as slow progress	6 N = 41	20	6	7	2
It acted in a high-handed and authoritarian way as soon as it encountered any resistance	6 N = 41	13	12	9	1
It deliberately sent out false information about the union's position	5 N = 41	6	20	10	0

*Table 9.3: Perceptions of Councillor Attitudes to the Union
Results in Numbers*

	Strongly Agree	Agree on Balance	Not Sure	Disagree on Balance	Strongly Disagree
Councillors are committed to ensuring that the union is properly consulted	0 N = 44	6	10	11	18
Councillors are sensitive and responsive to the views and advice of the union	0 N = 44	4	13	11	16
Councillors are ultimately only interested in their own personal power and their careers	9 N = 45	14	10	11	1
Demonstrated more concern for staff feelings about change	26 N = 50	12	10	2	0
Offered opportunities to any disgruntled group of staff to air their views	22 N = 50	13	12	3	0

*Table 9.4: The Influence of Better Working Conditions on a Union-Councillor Alliance
Results in Numbers*

	Strong Influence	Slight Influence	Not Sure	Not Influenced
Improvements in career structure of lower paid	37 N = 50	11	2	0
Improvements in training opportunities	34 N = 50	13	2	1
Improved working conditions	34 N = 50	13	2	1

Table 9.5: Influence of the Process of Negotiated Change on an Alliance Results in Numbers

	Strong Influence	Slight Influence	Not Sure	Not Influenced
Joint union-management timetable for implementing change	24 N = 50	19	2	5
Regular, well-publicised meetings with union members at all levels of structure	24 N = 50	19	4	3
In-depth response to union concerns about proposals	27 N = 53	19	4	3
Positive responses to accumulated union grievances	25 N = 50	14	5	5
Greater acknowledgement given to stress caused by such major changes	28 N = 50	14	3	5
Provide the unions with additional resources to better participate	21	15	7	6
Greater thought to the needs and aptitudes of individuals in fitting people into new jobs	27 N = 50	15	5	3
Greater respect for shop stewards	21 N = 48	7	12	8
Long period of consultation prior to policy formulation	24 N = 50	9	12	5
Given more attention to difference between consultation about ideas and policies	19 N = 49	13	10	7

*Table 9.6: Influence of Authority's Relations with Individual Staff Members
Results in Numbers*

	Strong Influence	Slight Influence	Not Sure	Not Influenced
Maintained active commitment to other major policy areas contained within manifesto	23 N = 48	13	8	4

*Table 9.7: Influence of Decentralised Structure on an Alliance
Results in Numbers*

	Strong Influence	Slight Influence	Not Sure	Not Influenced
More accountable management	23 N = 50	20	3	3
Energetic and well-organised programme of filling vacancies	29 N = 49	14	3	3
Programme of regrading and upgrading posts	23 N = 49	19	5	2
Growth in staffing	22 N = 48	19	5	2
Broader, flatter management structure	13 N = 48	16	12	7
Lump sum payment as compensation for changes in working conditions	16 N = 47	11	10	10

Table 9.8: Influence of Managerial Processes and General Policy Orientation
  Results in Numbers

	Strong Influence	Slight Influence	Not Sure	Not Influenced
Actively sought your views	23 N = 48	13	5	7

Table 9.9: Influence of Authority's Role in Wider political Context
  Results in Numbers

	Strong Influence	Slight Influence	Not Sure	Not Influenced
Been more vigorous in pursuing a campaign against central government	27 N = 49	7	9	6
Acknowledged the limitations of decentralisation as a political strategy	16 N = 50	17	16	1

Table 9.10 Influence of Opportunities Provided for the Union to Engage with External
  Bodies
  Results in Numbers

	Strong Influence	Slight Influence	Not Sure	Not Influenced
Broader, flatter management	13 N = 48	16	12	7
Provided unions with opportunities to meet with community organisations	19 N = 49	10	11	8
Provided opportunities for unions to meet with consumers	19 N = 49	9	12	9
Greater respect for shop stewards	21 N = 48	7	12	8

	Strong Influence	Slight Influence	Not Sure	Not Influenced
Lump sum payment as compensation for changes in working conditions	16 N = 47	11	10	10

Table 10:1 The Role of Public Sector Unions
Results in Numbers

	Strongly Agree	Agree on Balance	Not Sure	Disagree on Balance	Strongly Disagree
Want the Branch to confine itself to defending my job and present pay level	2 N = 47	6	7	15	17
Branch to confine itself to improving pay and conditions of service to all members	11 N = 48	7	2	15	13
People should leave their political beliefs at home when they go to work	6 N = 48	7	3	7	25
Public Service unions should stick to bread and butter issues of industrial tribunal	1 N = 48	2	8	13	24
It is not the job of trade unions to produce policy guidelines on how services should be provided	3 N = 48	2	6	14	23
Union should not involve itself in quality of service provision unless it affects the number of jobs available to its members	1 N = 47	1	2	13	30

Table 10.2: *Industrial Action in the Public Sector*
   Results in Numbers

	Strongly Agree	Agree on Balance	Not Sure	Disagree on Balance	Strongly Disagree
Public Service unions should not undertake strike action if it adversely affects service users	3 N = 48	3	4	17	21
Unions should be free to undertake whatever industrial action is necessary in pursuit of their interests	26 N = 48	10	3	6	3
Unions should attempt to minimise the impact on consumers when undertaking industrial action	11 N = 47	17	8	7	4
Unions should attempt to work with service users when undertaking industrial action	25 N = 49	17	2	2	3

NEIGHBOURHOOD AREAS IN ISLINGTON

Beaumont
Rise

St John's

Archway

Hanley

Irene
Watson

Durham
Road

St George's

Tuffnell
Park

Sobell

Gillespie

Quadrant

Clock
Tower

Drayton Park

Highbury

Julie Curtin

Rosedale

Canonbury
West

Cally

Upper Street

Canonbury
East

St Peter's

Calshot

Clerkenwell

Finsbury

 Neighbourhood offices participating in questionnaire

Bibliography

N. Abercrombie and J. Urry (1983). *Capital, Labour and the Middle Classes*. G
Allen & Unwin

N. Abercrombie and A. Warde (1988). *Contemporary British Society*.
Polity Press.

R. Adams (1977). 'Bain's Theory of White-collar Union Growth: A conceptual
critique'. *British Journal of Industrial Relations*, vol. 15, pp 317-21.

P. Alcock and P. Lee (1981). 'The Socialist Republic of South Yorkshire'. *Critical
Social Policy*, vol. 1, no. 2, Autumn.

M. Alexander, D. Cooper and R. Dean (1982). *Women in Local Government: The
Neglected Resource*. Local Government Organisation Resource Unit Report no. 1.

J. Allen (1988). 'Fragmented Firms, Disorganised Labour'. In: J. Allen and D.
Massey (eds), *The Economy in Question*. Open University Press.

J. Allen (1988). 'Towards a Post-Industrial Economy?'. In: J. Allen and D. Massey
(eds), *The Economy in Question*. Open University Press.

J. Allen and D. Massey (eds) (1988). *The Economy in Question*.
Open University Press.

V. Allen (1967). 'The Paradox of Militancy'. In: R. Blackburn and
A. Cockburn (eds), *The Incompatibles*. Penguin.

P. Anderson (1967). 'The Limits and Possibilities of Trade Union Action'.
In: R. Blackburn and A. Cockburn (eds), *The Incompatibles*. Penguin.

P. Anderson (1968). 'Components of the National Culture'. *New Left Review* no. 50,
July-August.

C. Andrews (1978). 'BASW and Trade Unionism'. *Social Work Today* vol. 9, no.
35, 9th March.

J. Angel (1971). *The Radical Therapist*. Ballantine Books.

R. Argue, C. Gannage and D.W. Livingstone (eds) (1987). *Working People and
Hard Times*. Garamond Press, Toronto.

P. Armstrong (1986). 'Work Supervision and Trade Unionism'. In:
P. Armstrong et al. (eds), *White-collar Workers, Trade Unions and Class*. Croom
Helm.

P. Armstrong, B. Carter, C. Smith and T. Nichols (1986). *White-collar Workers,*

Trade Unions and Class. London, Croom Helm.

P. Arnold and I. Cole (1988). 'The Decentralisation of Local Services: Rhetoric and Reality'. In: P. Hoggett and R. Hambleton (eds), *Decentralisation and Democracy.* School of Advanced Urban Studies.

K. Ascher (1987). *The Politics of Privatisation.* Macmillan.

R. Bailey and M. Brake (eds) (1975). *Radical Social Work.* Edward Arnold.

R. Bailey and M. Brake (1975). 'Case Con Manifesto'. In: R. Bailey and M. Brake (eds), *Radical Social Work.* Edward Arnold.

R. Bailey and M. Brake (1980). 'Contributions to a Radical Practice in Social Work'. In: M. Brake and R. Bailey (eds), *Radical Social Work and Practice.* Arnold.

G.S. Bain (1966). 'The Growth of White-collar Unionism in Great Britain'. *British Journal of Industrial Relations*, vol. 4. no. 3, pp 304-305.

G.S. Bain (1970). *The Growth of White-collar Unionism.* Oxford, The Clarendon Press.

G.S. Bain and R. Price (1972). 'Who is a White-collar Employee?' *British Journal of Industrial Relations*, vol. X, no. 3, November.

G.S. Bain and R. Price (1972). 'Union Growth and Employment Trends in the U.K. 1964-70'. *British Journal of Industrial Relations*, vol. 10, November, pp 336-381.

G.S. Bain, D. Coates and V. Ellis (1973). *Social Stratification and Trade Unionism.* London, Heinemann.

G.S. Bain and R. Price (1980). *Profiles of Union Growth: A Comparative Statistical Portrait of Eight Countries.* Oxford, Basil Blackwell.

G.S. Bain and R. Price (1983). 'Union Growth in Britain: Retrospect and Prospect'. *British Journal of Industrial Relations*, vol. 21, no. 1, March, pp 46-68.

G.S. Bain and P. Elias (1985). 'Trade Union Membership in Great Britain: An Individual-level Analysis'. *British Journal of Industrial Relations*, vol. 23, pp 71-92.

G. Bamber (1986). *Militant Managers?* Gower.

A. Barnett (1973). 'Class Struggle and the Heath Government'. *New Left Review.* M. Barrett (1984). 'Unity is Strength? Feminism and the Labour Movement'. In: J.Siltanen and M. Stainworth (eds), *Women and the Public Sphere.* Hutchinson.

K. Bassett (1984). 'Labour, Socialism and Local Democracy'. In: M. Boddy and C. Fudge (eds), *Local Socialism.* Macmillan.

R. Baxandall, E. Ewen and L. Gordon (1974). *The Working Class has Two Sexes.* Monthly Review Press.

R. Beacham (1984). 'Economic Activity: Britain's Workforce'. *Population Trends*, no. 37, pp 6-14.

P.B. Beaumont (1992). *Public Sector Industrial Relations.* Routledge.

I. Beavis (1985). 'Sacrificing the Unions - Who Shot NALGO?' *Going Local?* no. 2, April.

V. Beechey (1982). 'The Sexual Division of Labour and the Labour Process: A Critical Assessment of Braverman'. In: S. Wood (ed), *The Degradation of Work? Skill, Deskilling and the Labour Process.* Hutchinson, London.

V. Beechey (1982). 'Women's Employment in Contemporary Britain'. In: V. Beechey and E. Whitelegg (eds), *Women in Britain Today.* Open University Press.

J. Benington (1976). *Local Government Becomes Big Business.* Community Development Projects Information and Intelligence Unit.

D. Benlow, P. Ramage, M. French, D. Simmonds and D. Whitfield (1983). *Public Jobs for Private Profit.* Wandsworth Trade Union Publications.

P. Beresford and S. Croft (1982). *Democratising Social Services, Battersea*

Community Action. Paper given at the 1982 Labour Co-ordinating Committee 'Beyond Welfare' Conference.

P. Beresford and S. Croft (undated). *Towards a Social Strategy*. Battersea Community Action.

P. Beresford and S. Croft (1986). 'All We Are Saying'. *Going Local?* no. 6, November, pp 20-21.

K. Beuret and G. Stoker (1986). 'The Labour Party and Neighbourhood Decentralisation: Flirtation or Commitment'. *Critical Social Policy* Issue 17, Autumn.

H. Beynon (1973). *Working for Ford*. Open University Press.

H. Beynon and R. Blackburn (1984). 'Unions: The Men's Affair'. In: J. Sittanen and M. Stainworth (eds), *Women and the Public Sphere*. Hutchinson.

Birmingham Women and Social Work Group (1985). 'Women and Social Work in Birmingham'. In: A. Davis and E. Brook (eds), *Women, the Family and Social Work*. Tavistock.

J. Black, R. Bowl, D. Burns, C. Critcher, G. Grant and D. Stockford (1983). *Social Work in Context*. Tavistock.

P. Blackburn (1984). 'Towards the Unitary State: Tory Attacks on Local Government'. *Critical Social Policy*, Issue 10, Summer.

R. Blackburn (1971). 'The Heath Government: A New Course for British Capitalism'. *New Left Review* no. 70.

R. Blackburn and A. Cockburn (eds) (1967). *The Incompatibles: Trade Union Militancy and the Consensus*, Penguin Special/New Left Review.

R.M. Blackburn and K. Prandy (1965). 'White-collar Unionisation: A Conceptual Framework'. *British Journal of Sociology* vol. XVI, June, pp 111-122.

D. Blunkett (1981). 'Struggle for Democracy'. *New Socialist*,September/ October.

D. Blunkett (1981). 'Towards a Socialist Social Policy'. *Local Government Policy Making*, vol. 8, pp 95-103.

D. Blunkett (1984). 'How the Other Half Lives'. *Marxism Today*, July.

D. Blunkett, M. Hodge, J. Beecham and D. Hatton (1984). 'State of Siege'. *New Socialist*, May/June.

D. Blunkett and B. Crick (1988). 'The Labour Party's Aims and Values'. *The Guardian*, 1st February.

P. Blyton and G. Ursell (1982). 'Vertical Recruitment in White-Collar Trade Unions: Some Causes and Consequences'. *British Journal of Industrial Relations*, vol. 20, no. 1, March.

J. Boateng (1985). 'Politicisation was not an Issue before Tyra'. *Community Care* 17th October, p.2.

M. Boddy and C. Fudge (eds) (1984). *Local Socialism*. Macmillan.

M. Boddy and C. Fudge (1984). 'Labour Councils and New Left Alternatives'. In: M. Boddy and C. Fudge (eds), *Local Socialism*. Macmillan.

S. Bolger, P. Corrigan, J. Docking and N. Frost (1981). *Towards Socialist - Welfare Work*. Macmillan.

J. Bourne (1987). 'The Shape of Things to Come?' *New Socialist*, March.

S. Box (1971). *Deviance, Reality and Society*. Holt, Rinehart and Winston.

M. Brake and R. Bailey (eds) (1980). *Radical Social Work and Practice*. Edward Arnold.

H. Braverman (1974). *Labour Power and Monopoly Capital*. Monthly Review Press.

H. Braverman (1982). 'Capitalism and the Division of Labour'. In: A. Giddens and D. Held (eds), *Classes Power and Conflict*. Macmillan.

M. Brenton (1978). 'Worker Participation and Social Service Agency'. *British Journal of Social Work* vol. 8, no. 3.

L. Bridges (1982). 'Keeping the Lid on: British Urban Social Policy 1975-81'. *Race and Class* vol. XXIII, Autumn/Winter.

M. Brogden and M. Wright (1979). 'What about the Workers'. *Social Work Today* vol. 10, no. 37, 22nd May.

M. Brogden and M. Wright (1979). 'Reflection on the Social Work Strikes'. *New Society*, 4th October.

E. Brook and A. Davis (1985). *Women, the Family and Social Work*. Tavistock.

P. Braham, A. Rattansi, R. Skellington (1992). *Racism and Anti-Racism*. Sage/OUP. London.

C. Brown (1984). *Black and White in Britain*. Policy Studies Institute.

C. Brown (1992). 'Same Difference: The Persistence of Racial Disadvantage in the British Employment Market' In: P Braham et al., *Racism and Anti-Racism*. London Sage/OUP

R. Brown (1976). 'Women as Employees: Some Comments on Research in Industrial Sociology'. In: D.L. Barker and S. Allen (eds), *Dependence and Exploitation in Work and Marriage*. London, Longman.

R. Brown (1984). 'Women as Employees: Social Consciousness and Collective Action'. In: J. Siltanen and M. Stainworth (eds), *Women and the Public Sphere*. Hutchinson.

A. Bryman (1989). *Research Methods and Organisation Studies*. Unwin Hyman.

A. Brym, S. Goss, A. McDougall, H. Ousley, L. Smith, D. Sullivan, S. Twigg and M. Ward (1988). *Labour Councils in the Cold: A Blueprint for Survival*. Labour Co-ordinating Committee, January.

N. Buck (1985). 'Service Industries and Local Labour Markets: Towards an Anatomy of Service Employment', Regional Science Association Annual Conference, September. Quoted by J. Allen, 'Towards a Post-industrial Economy?' In: J. Allen and D. Massey (eds) (1988). *The Economy in Question*. Sage/Open University Press.

Building Trades Operatives Shop Stewards Committee and the Federation of Hackney Tenants Association (1980). 'Hackney Building Workers and Tenants Report (unpublished).

M. Buraway (1979). 'Thirty Years in Making Out'. In: R.E. Pahl (ed), *On Work*. Blackwell.

D. Burns (1987). 'Voluntary Sector Participation'. *Going Local?*.

D. Burns (1989). 'Decentralisation? When?'. *Going Local?*, no. 12, March, pp 8-10.

D. Burns and E. Roberts (1986). 'Decentralisation', Islington NALGO, February/March (unpublished).

A. Butcher (1986). 'The Community Practice Approach to Local Public Service Provision'. *Community Development Journal*, vol. 21, no. 2.

D. Byrne (1982). 'Class and the Local State'. *International Journal of Urban and Regional Research*, vol. 6, no. 1, March.

H. Cain and N. Yuvat Davis (1990). 'The Equal Opportunities Community and the Anti-Racist Struggle'. *Critical Social Policy* Issue 29, Autumn.

B. Callaghan, A. Coote, G. Hulme and J. Stewart (1991). *Meeting Needs in the 1990s*. Institute of Public Policy Research, Social Policy Paper no. 2. Institute of Public Policy Research/Trades Union Congress.

A. Callinicos (1983). 'The New Middle Class and Socialist Politics'. *International*

Socialism 2:20, Summer.

J. Calvert (1987). 'Uncharted Waters: The Labour Movement's Dilemma in Developing a New Role beyond the Bargaining System'. In: Argue et al. (eds), *Working People and Hard Times*. Garamond Press, Toronto.

B. Campbell (1984). 'Politics, Pyramids and People'. *Marxism Today*, December.

B. Campbell (1987). 'Charge of the Light Brigade'. *Marxism Today*, February.

B. Campbell and M. Jacques (1986). 'Goodbye to the GLC'. *Marxism Today*, April.

C. Cannan (1972). 'Social Workers: Training and Professionalism'. In: T. Pateman (ed), *Counter Course*. Penguin Education Special.

N. Canver and E. Yaylali (1987). 'Decentralisation: Has it Helped? *Going Local?*, March, p.7. Decentralisation Research and Information Centre, School of Advanced Urban Studies, University of Bristol.

Capital and Class Editorial Collective (1982). *A Socialist GLC in Capitalist Britain?* Capital and Class.

G. Carchedi (1975). 'On the Economic Identification of the New Middle Class'. *Economy and Society*,Re vol. 4, no. 1, March.

G. Carchedi (1977). *On the Economic Identification of Social Classes*. Routledge & Kegan Paul. London.

M. Carpenter (1988). *Working for Health: The History of COHSE*. Lawrence & Wishart.

M. Carpenter, R. Elkan, P. Leonard and A. Munro (1987). *Professionalism and Unionism in Nursing and Social Work*. ESRC Research Project (unpublished). University of Warwick, March.

M. Carpenter, R. Elkan, P. Leonard and A. Munro (1990). *Professionalism and Unionism in Nursing and Social Work*. Revised End-of-Award Report to Economic and Social Research Council, University of Warwick, Department of Applied Social Studies, December.

B. Carter (1979). 'Class, Militancy and Trade Union Character'. *Sociological Review*, vol. 27, pp 297-316.

B. Carter (1985). *Capitalism, Class Conflict and the New Middle Class*. Routledge & Kegan Paul.

B. Carter (1986). 'Trade Unionism and the new Middle Class: The Case of ASTMS'. In: P. Armstrong et al. (eds), *White-collar Workers, Trade Unions and Class*. Croom Helm.

P. Carter, T. Jeffs and M. Smith (eds) (1989). *Social Work and Social Welfare*. Open University Press.

CASE-CON: A Revolutionary Comic for Social Workers.
  Vol. 1, Spring 1970
  Vol. 2, Autumn 1970
  Vol. 3, March 1971, p.12
  Vol. 4, June 1971, pp.11-12
  Vol. 10, January 1973, p.18
  Vol. 13, Autumn 1973, pp.26-27
  Vol. 17, Autumn 1974 - training issue
  Vol. 20, September 1975, p.16 - community work issue

M. Castells (1977). *The Urban Question*. Edward Arnold. London.

A. Cawson (1982). *Corporatism and Welfare*. Heinemann Educational.

A. Cawson and P. Saunders (1983). 'Corporatism, Competitive Politics and Class Struggle'. In: R. King (ed), *Capital and Politics*. Routledge and Kegan Paul.

J. Childs (1985). 'Managerial Strategies, New Technology and the Labour Process'. In: D. Knights, H. Willmott and D. Collinson (eds), *Job Redesign: Critical Perspectives on the Labour Process*. Gower, Aldershot.

D. Clapham (1985/86). Management of the Local State: The Example of Corporate Planning'. *Critical Social Policy* Issue 14, Winter.

G. Clapton (1977). 'Radicalism - What does it all add up to?' *Social Work Today*, vol. 8, no. 28, 19th April.

T. Clark and D. Jaffe (1973). 'Towards a Radical Therapy', Gordon & Breach, New York. Quoted in Simpkin, *Trapped within Welfare*, Macmillan (2nd edition).

J. Clarke and M. Langan (1993). 'Restructuring Welfare: The British Welfare Regime in the 1980s'. In: A. Cochrane and J. Clarke (1993). *Comparing Welfare States*. Sage/Open University Press.

J. Clarke, A. Cochrane, E. McLaughlin (1994). *Managing Social Policy*. Sage.

M. Clarke and J. Stewart (1985). *The Service Programme*. Local Government Training Board. Local Government and Public Services: Working Paper 2. October.

S. Clarke (1977). 'Marxism, Sociology and Poultantzas' Theory of the State'. *Capital and Class*, no. 2, Summer.

T. Clarke and L. Clements (1977). *Trade Unionism under Capitalism*. Fontana.

P. Clayton, M. Brogden, M. Wright and O. Keidan (1979). 'Looking Back on the Strikes'. *Social Work Today*, vol. l0, no. 37, 22nd May.

H. Clegg (1985). *A History of British Trade Unionism Since 1889. Vol II 1911-1933*. Clarendon Press. Oxford.

A. Cochrane (1985). 'The Attack on Local Government: What It Is and What It Isn't'. *Critical Social Policy* Issue 12, Spring.

A. Cochrane (1986). 'Community Politics and Democracy'. In: D. Held and C. Pollitt (eds), *New Forms of Democracy*. Open University Press.

A. Cochrane (1989). 'Restructuring the State: the Case of Local Government'. In: A. Cochrane and J. Anderson (eds), *Restructuring Britain: Politics in Transition*. Open University Press/Sage.

A. Cochrane and D. Massey (1989). 'Developing a Socialist Urban Policy'. In: P. Alcock, A. Gamble, I. Gough, P. Lee and A. Walker (eds), *The Social Economy and the Democratic State*. Lawrence and Wishart.

A. Cochrane and J. Anderson (eds) (1989). *Restructuring Britain: Politics in Transition*. Open University Press/Sage.

A. Cochrane and J. Clarke (1993). *Comparing Welfare States*. Sage/Open University Press.

A. Cochrane and D. Welsby (1989). *Decentralisation and Corporation in English Local Government*. Paper presented at the Urban Change and Conflict Conference, Bristol.

A. Cockburn and R. Blackburn (1969). *Student Power*. Penguin Special.

C. Cockburn (1977). *The Local State*, 1st edn. Pluto. (3rd edn. 1980).

C. Cockburn (1971). *Brothers - Male Dominance and Technological Change*. Pluto.

S. Cohen (1971). *Images of Deviance*. Pelican Original. Penguin.

S. Cohen and P. Fosh (1988). *You Are the Union: Trade Union Workplace Democracy*. Workers Education Association.

D. Cohn-Bendit (1969). *Obsolete Communism: The Left-wing Alternative*. Penguin Special.

Collective Design/Products (eds) (1985). *Very Nice Work If You Can Get It: The Socially Useful Production Debate*.

J. Collingridge (1986). 'The Appeal of Decentralisation'. *Local Government Studies* May/June, 9-17.

Commission for Racial Equality (1982). *Ethnic Origins of Nurses Applying for and in Training*. Commission for Racial Equality.

Commission for Racial Equality (1983). *Ethnic Minority Hospital Staff*. Commission for Racial Equality.

Communist Party (1982). *London District Congress*, no. 27 and 28, Document 6: Local Councils and Decentralisation, November.

Community Action Magazine no. 18, 'On the Buses', 1975.

Community Action Magazine no. 23, 'Better Bus Services and Running Your Own', 1975.

Community Action Magazine no. 33, 'Fares Fair', 1977.

Community Action Magazine no. 35, 'Leeds Council Defeated over Fares Increase', 1978.

Community Action Magazine no. 37, 'Any More Fares?', May/June 1978.

Community Action Magazine no. 66, 'Going Local in Walsall, Islington and Hackney', August/September 1984, pp. 14-25.

Community Action Magazine no. 68, 1984. 'Will Labour Doff its Cap?', December 1984.

Community Action Magazine no. 68, 'Standing Alone: the Struggles of Tenants in Hackney', December 1984.

Community Development Project (1974). *'Inter-Project Report'*.

Community Development Project (1975). *'Forward Plan'*.

Community Development Project (1975). *The Costs of Industrial Change*, January.

Community Development Project (1977). *Gilding the Ghetto*. CDP Inter-Project Editorial Team.

Conference of Socialist Economists Editorial (1982). *'Socialist GLC in Capitalist Britain'*. C.S.E. 18, Winter, pp.117-135.

R.W. Connell (1989). 'A Critique of the Althusserian Approach to Class'. *Theory and Society* 8(3). In: Giddens and Held (eds), *Classes Power and Conflict*, Macmillan.

D. Conyers (1986). 'Decentralisation and Development: A Framework for Analysis'. *Community Development Journal* vol. 21, no. 2.

P. Cooke (ed) (1989). *Localities: The Changing Face of Urban Britain*. Unwin Hyman.

P. Cooke (1989). 'Locality, Economic Restructuring and World Development'. In: P. Cooke (ed), *Localities: The Changing Face of Urban Britain*. Unwin Hyman.

P. Cooke (1989). 'The Local Question - Revival or Survival'. In: P. Cooke (ed), *Localities: The Changing Face of Urban Britain*. Unwin Hyman.

M. Cooley (1980). 'Architect or Bee?', *Hand and Brain*.

M. Cooley (1985). 'After the Lucas Plan'. In: *Collective Design/Projects 'Very Nice Work If You Can Get It'*. Spokesman.

D.M. Cooper (1980). 'The Seebohm Transition'. In: B. Glastonbury, D.M. Cooper and P. Hawkins (eds), *Social Work in Conflict*. Croom Helm.

D.M. Cooper (1980). 'Salaries and Hierarchy'. In: B. Glastonbury, D.M. Cooper and P. Hawkins (eds), *Social Work in Conflict*. Croom Helm.

D.M. Cooper and B. Glastonbury (1980). 'The Dilemma of the Professional Employee'. In: B. Glastonbury, D.M. Cooper and P. Hawkins (eds), *Social Work in Conflict*. Croom Helm.

D. Corkey and G. Craig (1978). 'CDP: Community Work or Class Politics? In: P. Curno (ed), *Political Issues and Community Work*. Routledge & Kegan Paul.

P. Corrigan (1982). 'The Marx Factor'. *Social Work Today*, vol. 13, no. 20, 26th January.

P. Corrigan and P. Leonard (1978). *Social Work Practice under Capitalism:A Marxist Approach*. Macmillan.

C. Cousins (1987). *Controlling Social Welfare*. Wheatsheaf Books.

Coventry, Liverpool, Newcastle, North Tyneside Trades Councils (1982). *'State Intervention in Industry: A Workers Enquiry'*. Spokesman, 2nd edn.

J. Cowley (1977). 'State Employees, Professionals and Radicalisation'. In: J. Cowley, A. Kaye, M. Mayo and M. Thomson (eds), *Community or Class Struggle*. Stage One.

J. Cowley, A. Kaye, M. Mayo and M. Thomson (eds) (1977). *Community or Class Struggle*. Stage One.

A. Coyle and J. Skinner (1988). *Women and Work*. Macmillan.

S. Croft and P. Beresford (1989). 'Decentralisation and the Personal Social Services'. In: M. Langan and P. Lee (eds), *Radical Social Work Today*. Unwin Hyman.

S. Croft and P. Beresford (1989). 'Time for Social Work to Gain New Confidence'. *Social Work Today*, 13th April.

S. Croft and P. Beresford (1989). 'User Involvement, Citizenship and Social Policy'. *Critical Social Policy* Issue 26, Autumn.

R. Crompton (1976). 'A Critique of the Industrial Relations Approach'. *Sociology* vol. 10, September.

R. Crompton (1976). 'Approaches to the Study of White-collar Unionism'. *Sociology* vol. 10, pp 407-26.

R. Crompton (1979). 'Trade Unionism and the Insurance Clerk', *Sociology* vol. 13, p. 406. Quoted in B. Carter (1985). *Capitalism, Class Conflict and the New Middle Class*. Routledge & Kegan Paul.

R. Crompton (1993). *Class and Stratification*. Polity Press.

R. Crompton and J. Gubbay (1977). 'The Political Economy of Class', extract from *Economy and Class Structure*. Macmillan. Reproduced in Hyman and Price (1983). *The New Working Class? White-collar Workers and their Organisations*. Macmillan.

R. Crompton and G. Jones (1984). *White-collar Proletariat*. Macmillan.

F. Croner (1962). 'Soziologie der Angestellten Kiepenheuer und Witsch', Cologne. Quoted in G.S. Bain and R. Price (1972). *British Journal of Industrial Relations* vol. X, no. 3, November.

C.S.E. State Apparatus and Expenditure Group (1979). *Struggle Over the State*. CSE Books, London.

J. Dale (1987). 'Decentralisation: Grounding the Debate'. *Community Development Journal* vol. 22, no. 2, April.

P. Daniel and I. Wheeler (1989). *Social Work and Local Politics*. BASW/ Macmillan.

J. Darke and K. Gouly (1985). 'United We Stand'. *New Socialist*, February.

I. Davey (1977). 'Radical Social Work: What does it Mean in Practice?', *Social Work Today* vol. 8, no. 23, 15th March.

B. Davies (1988). 'Professionalism or Trade Unionism? The Search for a Collective Identity'. In: T. Jeffs and M. Smith (eds), *Welfare and Youth Work Practice*. Macmillan.

J.G. Davies (1972). *The Evangelistic Bureaucrat*. Tavistock.

J.G. Davies (1988). 'From Municipal Socialism to Municipal Capitalism?' *Local Government Studies*, March/April.

A. Davis (1987). 'Hazardous Lives - Social Work in the 1980s: a View from the Left'. In: M. Loney et al. (eds), *The State of the Market*. Sage.

A. Davis and E. Brook (1985). 'Women and Social Work'. In: A. Davis and E. Brook (eds), *Women, the Family and Social Work*. Tavistock.

M. Davis, B. Misrah, R. Shield, K. McDonnell, P. Hoggett and R. Tyrrell (1984). *Go Local to Survive*. Labour Co-ordinating Committee, August.

N. Deakin (1984). 'Two Cheers for Decentralisation'. In: A. Wright, J. Stewart and N. Deakin, *Socialism and Decentralisation*. Fabian Tract 496, London.

N. Deakin (1985). 'The Fashionable Choice'. *Community Care*, 18th April, 12-14.

The Decentralisation Research and Information Centre (1986). *Decentralisation: An Information Pack*, June. Polytechnic of Central London/GLC.

J. Dearlove (1979). *The Reorganisation of Local Government: Old Orthodoxies and a Political Perspective*. Cambridge University Press.

Department of Employment (1991). 'Ethnic Origins and the Labour Market'. *Employment Gazette*, February, pp.59-72. HMSO. London.

J. Diamond (1989). 'Tower Hamlets: Views from Within'. *Going Local?* 13, pp 7-9.

J. Dobbin and M. Martin (1989). 'Metro Rochdale: Putting the Rhetoric into Practice: A Radical Approach to Decentralisation'. *Going Local?* no. 14. November, pp 8-11.

L. Dominelli (1992). 'An Uncaring Profession? An Examination of Racism in Social Work'. In: P. Braham et al. *Racism and Anti-Racism*. Sage/OUP. London.

L. Dominelli and E. McLeod (1989). *Feminist Social Work*. Macmillan.

L. Doyal, Hunt and Mellor (1981). *Migrant Workers in the NHS: Part I*. A report for the Social Science Research Council.

S.S. Duncan and M. Goodwin (1982). 'The Local State and Restructuring Social Relations'. *International Journal of Urban and Regional Research* vol. 6, no. 1, March.

P. Dunleavy (1980). *Urban Political Analysis*. Macmillan.

P. Dunleavy (1984). 'The Limits of Local Government'. In: M. Boddy and C. Fudge (eds), *Local Socialism*. Macmillan.

P. Dunleavy and B. O'Leary (1987). *Theories of the State*. Macmillan.

D. Edgar (1988). 'When the Hardline is Right'. *Marxism Today*, February.

R.C. Edwards (1979). *Contested Terrain: The Transformation of the Workplace in the Twentieth Century*. Heinemman. New York.

B. and J. Ehrenreich (1974). *Work and Consciousness*. Monthly Review Press.

B. and J. Ehrenreich (1977). 'The Professional-Management Class'. *Radical America* vol. 11, no. 2 (March-April), pp 12-17. Reproduced in Hyman and Price (eds) (1983), *The New Working Class? White-collar Workers and their Organisations*. Macmillan.

H. Elcock (1986). 'Decentralisation as a Tool for Social Services Management'. *Local Government Studies*, July/August, pp 35-49.

H. Elcock (1988). 'Alternatives to Representative Government in Britain: Going Local'. *Public Policy and Administration* vol. 3, no. 2, June, pp 38-50.

J. Epstein (1990). *Public Services: Working for the Consumer*. European Foundation for the Improvement of Living and Working Conditions.

Equal Opportunities Commission (1993). *Men and Women in Britain 1993*.

P. Fairbrother (1980). Review Article of 'In and Against the State'. *Capital and Class*, Summer.

P. Fairbrother (1984). *All Those in Favour*. Pluto.

P. Fairbrother (1988). 'Flexibility at Work: The Challenge for Unions'. *Workers Educational Association Studies for Trade Unionists* vol. 14, no. 55. December.

P. Fairbrother and J. Waddington (1990). 'The Politics of Trade Unionism: Evidence, Policy and Theory'. *Capital and Class*, 41, pp.15-56.

Federation of Hackney Tenants Association (1982). *Decentralisation - As Viewed by the Federation of Hackney Tenants Association*.

Federation of Hackney Tenants Association (1983). *Report on Tenant Representation to Hackney Borough Council*, April.

A. Ferner (1985). 'Political Constraints and Management Strategies: the Case of Working Practices in British Rail'. *British Journal of Industrial Relations* vol. 23, pp 47-69.

N. Fielding and P. Seyd (1984). 'Cities in Revolt'. *New Socialist*, September.

A. Fleming (1989). 'Employment in the Public and Private Sectors. *Economic Trends*. no. 34. December.

T. Flynn (1981). 'Local Politics and Local Government'. *Capital and Class* 13, Spring.

M. Folin (1981). 'The Production of the General Conditions of Social Production and the Role of the State'. In: M. Harloe and E. Lebas, *City, Class and Capital*. Edward Arnold.

P. Foot (1968). *The Politics of Harold Wilson*. Penguin Special.

M. Foucault (1971). *Madness and Civilisation*. Tavistock, Social Science Paperbacks.

K. Fox, M.J. Hetzel, T. Riddell, N. Rose and J. Sazama (eds) (1981). *Crisis in the Public Sector*. Monthly Review Press/Union for Radical Political Economics.

B. Frankel (1979). 'On the State of the State: Marxist Theories of the State after Leninism'. In: A. Giddens and D. Held (eds), *Classes, Power and Conflict*. Macmillan.

B. Friedan (1966). *The Feminine Mystique*. Penguin.

A. Friedman (1976). 'Responsible Autonomy Versus Direct Control Over the Labour Process'. *Capital and Class* vol. 1, no. 1.

A. Friedman (1986). 'Developing the Managerial Strategies Approach to the Control Process'. *Capital and Class* Gilroy, no. 30, Winter.

M. Friedman and R. Friedman (1980). *Free to Choose*. London: Secker and Warburg.

N. Frost and M. Stein (1989). 'What's Happening in Social Services Departments?' In: Langan and Lee (eds), *Radical Social Work Today*. Unwin Hyman.

B. Fryer, T. Manson and A. Fairclough (1978). 'Employment and Trade Unionism in the Public Services: Background Notes to the Struggle against the Cuts'. *Capital and Class* 4.

R.H. Fryer (1989). 'Public Service Trade Unionism in the Twentieth Century'. In: R. Mailly, S.J. Dimmock and A.S. Sethi (eds), *Industrial Relations in the Public Services*. Routledge.

C. Fudge (1984). 'Decentralisation: Socialism Goes Local?' In: M. Boddy and C. Fudge (eds), *Local Socialism*. Macmillan.

D. Gallagher (1987). 'Affirmative Action'. In: *Working People and Hard Times*. Garamond Press, Toronto.

A. Gamble (1986). *Britain in Decline* (2nd edn.). Macmillan.

M. Garrett (1973). 'Islington Strikes Again'. *Case Con* 13, Autumn.

M. Garrett (1980). 'The Problem with Authority'. In: M. Brake and R. Bailey (eds), *Radical Social Work and Practice*. Edward Arnold.

A. Giddens (1980). 'Class Structuration and Class Consciousness'. In: A. Giddens and D. Held (eds), *Classes, Power and Conflict*. Macmillan.

A. Giddens and D. Held (eds) (1982). *Classes, Power and Conflict*. Macmillan.

A. Giddens and D. Held (1982). 'Contemporary Theories of Class and Class Conflict (Introduction)'. In: A. Giddens and D. Held (eds), *Classes, Power and Conflict*. Macmillan.

P. Gilroy (1987). *There Ain't No Black in the Union Jack*. Hutchinson.

R. Girod (1961). *Etudes Sociologiques sur les Couches Salariees: Ouvriers et Employes*. Marcel Riviere. Quoted in G.S. Bain and R. Price, 1972) *British Journal of Industrial Relations* vol. X, no. 3, November.

B. Glastonbury, D.M. Cooper and P. Hawkins (1980). *Social Work in Conflict (The Practitioner and the Bureaucrat)*. Croom Helm.

A. Glyn and J. Harrison (1980). *The British Economic Disaster*. Pluto Press.

282 *Public Service Trade Unionism and Radical Politics*

J. Godbout (1981). 'Producers and Users: the Dynamics of Change'. In: M. Harlow and E. Lebas (eds), *City, Class and Capital*. Edward Arnold.

Going Local (1984). 'Hackney - Strange Fruit'. *Going Local?* no. 1, December.

Goldberg. 'Dilemmas in Social Work'. *Journal of Psychomatic Research* vol. 18, p.268.

E.M. Goldberg and R.W. Warburton (1979). *Ends and Means in Social Work*. National Institute of Social Work/G. Allen & Unwin.

P. Goldblatt (1983). 'Changes in Social Class between 1971 and 1981: Could these Affect Mortality Differences among Men of Working Ages?' *Population Trends* no. 51, pp 9-17.

J. Goldthorpe (1982). 'On the Service Class, its Formation and Future'. In: A. Giddens and G. Mackenzie (eds), *Social Class and the Division of Labour*. Cambridge University Press.

J. Goldthorpe and C. Payne (1986). 'Trends in Intergenerational Class Mobility in England and Wales 1972-83'. *Sociology* vol. 20, no. 1, pp.1-24.

J. Goldthorpe, C. Llewellyn and C. Payne (1987). *Social Mobility and Class Structure in Modern Britain* (2nd edn.). Clarendon Press, Oxford.

J.H. Goldthorpe, D. Lockwood, F. Bechhofer, J. Platt (1969). *The Affluent Worker in the Class Structure*. Cambridge University Press.

J. Goldup (1977). 'How Radicals are Kept in Check'. *Community Care* no. 23, 14 September.

M. Goodwin (1989). 'The Politics of Locality'. In: A. Cochrane and J. Anderson (eds), *Politics in Transition*. Oxford University Press/Sage.

M. Goodwin, S. Duncan and S. Halford (1989). *Urban Politics in the 'PostFordist' Economy*. Paper presented to Seventh Urban Change and Conflict Conference, University of Bristol.

P. Gordon and A. Newmham (1986). *Different Worlds*. Runnymede Trust.

S. Goss (1988). *Local Labour and Local Government*. Edinburgh University Press.

S. Goss, J. Hillier and J. Rule (1988). *Labour Councils in the Cold: A Blueprint for Survival*. Labour Co-ordinating Committee, January.

I. Gough (1979). *The Political Economy of the Welfare State*. Macmillan.

I. Gough (1983). 'Thatcherism and the Welfare State'. In: S. Hall and M. Jacques (eds), *The Politics of Thatcherism*. Lawrence & Wishart.

I. Gough and L. Doyal (1989). 'Socialism, Democracy and Human Needs'. In: P. Alcock, A. Gamble, I. Gough, P. Lee and A. Walker (eds), *The Social Economy and the Democratic State*. Lawrence and Wishart.

F. Gould and B. Roweth (1980). 'Public Spending and Local Policy: The UK 1950-1977'. *Journal of Social Policy* 9, no. 3, pp 337-357.

J. Le Grand (1990). 'The Welfare State'. In: J. Hills (ed), *The State of Welfare: The Welfare State in Britain Since 1974*. London Oxford University Press.

D. Graves and E. Pilkington (undated). *Decentralisation: the Implications for Trade Unions*. Polytechnic of Central London, Decentralisation Research and Information Centre.

J. Gray. 'The Empire Builders Strike Back - the Response of NALGO to Proposals for Radical Decentralisation of Local Government'. Unpublished essay, School of Advanced Urban Studies.

G. Green (1987). 'The New Municipal Socialism'. In: M. Loney, R. Bocock, J. Clarke, A. Cochrane, P. Graham and M. Wilson (eds), *The State or The Market*. Open University Press.

G. Greer (1971). *The Female Eunuch*. Paladin.

S. Gregory and J. Smith (1986). 'Decentralisation Now'. *Community Development*

Journal vol. 21, no. 2.

J. Gyford (1983). 'The New Urban Left: A Local Road to Socialism'. *New Society*, 21st April.

J. Gyford (1985). *The Politics of Local Socialism*. George Allen & Unwin.

J. Gyford (1987). 'Pluralist or Collectivist?'. *Going Local?* no. 8, July, p. 23.

J. Gyford (1987). 'Decentralisation and Democracy'. In: P. Willmott (ed), *Local Government, Decentralisation and Community*. Policy Studies Institute.

J. Gyford (1991). *Citizens, Consumers and Councils*. Macmillan.

J. Gyford, S. Leach and C. Game (1989). *The Changing Politics of Local Government*. Unwyn Hyman.

G. Hackett and S. Weir (1984). 'State of Siege'. *New Socialist*, May/June.

R. Hadley, P. Dale and P. Sills (1984). *Decentralising Social Services*. Bedford Square Press/NCVO.

R. Hadley and M. McGrath (1984). *When Social Services are Local*. National Institute of Social Work Library no. 48. George Allen & Unwin.

C. Hakim (1979). *Occupational Segregation*. Department of Employment Research Paper 9.

C. Hakim (1981). 'Job Segregation: Trends in the 1970s'. *Employment Gazette*, December.

S. Hall (1980). 'Reformism and the Legislation of Consent'. In: National Deviancy Conference (ed), *Permissiveness and Control*. Macmillan.

S. Hall (1984). 'The State in Question'. In: G. McLennan, D. Held and S. Hall (eds), *The Idea of the Modern State*. OUP.

S. Hall (1984). 'The Crisis of Labourism'. In: J. Curran (ed), *The Future of the Left*. Polity Press/New Socialist.

S. Hall (1984). 'Face the Future'. *New Socialist*, September.

S. Hall (1984). 'The State - Socialism's Old Caretaker'. *Marxism Today*, November.

S. Hall (1988). 'Brave New World'. *Marxism Today*, October.

S. Hall, C. Critcher, T. Jefferson, J. Clarke and B. Roberts (1978). *Policing the Crisis*. Macmillan.

S. Hall and D. Held (1989). 'Left and Rights'. *Marxism Today*, June.

A.H. Halsey (1987). 'Social Trends Since World War II'. *Social Trends* vol. 17, pp 11-19.

R. Hambleton (1987). 'Developments, Objectives and Criteria'. In: P. Willmott (ed), *Local Government, Decentralisation and the Community*. Policy Studies Institute, Discussion Paper no. 18.

R. Hambleton (1989). 'Back in the USA. America: Are we Heading the Same Way?' *Going Local?* 12, March, pp 17-19.

R. Hambleton (1989). *The Decentralisation of Public Services to Local Level*. Position Statement: London Borough of Islington. School of Advanced Urban Studies, September.

R. Hambleton and P. Hoggett (1984). 'Decentralisation: Themes and Issues'. In: R. Hambleton and P. Hoggett (eds), *The Politics of Decentralisation: Theory and Practice of a Radical Local Government Initiative*. SAUS Working Paper 46, School of Advanced Urban Studies.

R. Hambleton and P. Hoggett (1984). The Politics of Decentralisation: *Theory and Practice of a Radical Local Government Initiative*. SAUS Working Paper 46, School of Advanced Urban Studies.

R. Hambleton and P. Hoggett (1988). 'Beyond Bureaucratic Paternalism'. In: P. Hoggett and R. Hambleton (eds), *Decentralisation and Democracy*. School of Advanced Urban

Studies.

R. Hambleton and P. Hoggett (1988). 'The Democratisation of Public Services'. In: P. Hoggett and R. Hambleton (eds), *Decentralisation and Democracy*. School of Advanced Urban Studies.

J. Hanmer and D. Statham (1988). *Women and Social Work - Towards a Woman-Centred Practice*. BASW/Macmillan.

K.J. Harrop et al. (1978). *The Implementation and Development of Area Management*. Institute of Local Government Studies, University of Birmingham.

M. Hart-Landsberg, J. Lembake and S. Marotto (1981). 'Public Sector Workers and the Crisis of Capitalism'. In: Fox et al. (eds), *Crisis in the Public Sector*. Monthly Review Press/Union for Radical Political Economics.

H. Hartman (1976). 'Capitalism, Patriarchy and Job Segregation by Sex'. In: M. Blaxall and B. Reagan (eds), *Woman and the Workplace*, University of Chicago Press.

D. Harvey (1973). *Social Justice and the City*. Edward Arnold.

S. Hatch and S. Humble (1980). *Towards Neighbourhood Democracy*. Association of Researchers in Voluntary Action and Community Involvement, Pamphlet no. 2.

B. Hearn (1985). 'Local Alliance'. *Community Care* 18, 32-34.

J. Hearn (1982). 'Radical Social Work - Contradictions, Limitations and Political Possibilities'. *Critical Social Policy* vol. 2, no. 1, Summer.

J. Hearn (1987). *The Gender of Oppression: Men, Masculinity and the Critique of Marxism*. Wheatsheaf Books.

A. Heath and S.K. McDonald (1987). 'Social Change and the Future of the Left'. *Political Quarterly* vol. 58, no. 4, pp 364-377.

E. Heery (1984). 'Decentralisation in Islington'. In: R. Hambleton and P. Hoggett (eds), *The Politics of Decentralisation*. SAUS Working Paper 46, School of Advanced Urban Studies.

E. Heery (1988). 'A Common Labour Movement? Left Labour Councils and the Trade Unions'. In: P. Hoggett and R. Hambleton (eds), *Decentralisation and Democracy*. School of Advanced Urban Studies.

D. Held (1984). 'Critical Perspectives on the Modern State'. In: G. McLennan et al. (eds), *The Idea of the Modern State*. OUP.

D. Held (1984). 'Power and Legitimacy in Contemporary Britain'. In: G. McLennan, D. Held and S. Hall (eds), *State and Society in Contemporary Britain*. Polity Press.

D. Held (1987). *Models of Democracy*. Polity Press.

D. Held and J. Keane (1984). 'Socialism and the Limits of State Action'. In: J. Curran (ed), *The Future of the Left*. Polity Press/New Socialist.

D. Heptinstall (1985). 'There Must be Trust' *Community Care*, 18th April, p. 25.

J. Heritage (1980). *Feminisation and Unionisation: A Case Study From Banking*. University of Warwick, Mimeo.

J. Heron (1988). 'Validity in Co-operative Inquiry'. In: P. Reason (ed), *Human Inquiry in Action*. Sage.

R. Hill (1978). 'Social Workers and Industrial Action'. *Social Work Today* vol. 9, no. 35, 9th May.

R. Hill (1978). 'A Trade Union Role for BASW - Yes or No? The Case For ...', *Social Work Today* vol. 10, no. 3, 12th September.

J. Hills (ed), 1990. *The State of Welfare: The Welfare State in Britain Since 1974*. London, Oxford University Press.

B. Hindess (1973). '*The Use of Official Statistics in Sociology*. British Sociological

Association/Macmillan Press.

M. Hodge (1988). 'Central/Local Conflicts: The View from Islington' (based on a paper presented in 1985). In: P. Hoggett and R. Hambleton (eds), *Decentralisation and Democracy*. School of Advanced Urban Studies

M. Hodge (1989). Talk given at School of Advanced Urban Studies.

M. Hodge (1991). Interview with Paul Hoggett.

M. Hodgson (1984). Overstating the State'. *Marxism Today*, June.

P. Hoggett (1984). 'Decentralisation, Labourism and the Professionalised Welfare State Apparatus'. In: R. Hambleton and P. Hoggett (eds), *The Politics of Decentralisation: Theory and Practice of a Radical Local Government Initiative*. SAUS Working Paper 46, School of Advanced Urban Studies.

P. Hoggett (1985). 'A Long Wave to Freedom?' *Chartist* No. 106, October/ November, pp.25-28.

P. Hoggett (1987). 'Waste Disposal - Making Municipal Socialism Work'. *New Socialist*, March.

P. Hoggett (1988). *Reflecting on Local Socialism*. Unpublished paper.

P. Hoggett (1988). 'A Farewell to Mass Production? Decentralisation as an Emergent Private and Public Sector Paradigm'. In: P. Hoggett and R. Hambleton (eds), *Decentralisation and Democracy*. School of Advanced Urban Studies.

P. Hoggett (1988). 'Political Parties, Community Action and the Reform of Municipal Government in Europe'. In: P. Hoggett and R. Hambleton (eds), *Decentralisation and Democracy*. School of Advanced Urban Studies.

P. Hoggett (1990). 'Modernisation, Political Strategy and the Welfare State: An Organisational Perspective'. *Studies in Decentralisation and Quasi-Markets 2*. School of Advanced Urban Studies.

P. Hoggett and R. Hambleton (1984). 'Decentralisation Strategies for Achieving Change'. In: R. Hambleton and P. Hoggett (eds), *The Politics of Decentralisation: Theory and Practice of a Radical Local Government Initiative*. SAUS Working Paper 46, School of Advanced Urban Studies.

P. Hoggett, S. Lawrence and C. Fudge (1984). 'The Politics of Decentralisation in Hackney'. In: R. Hambleton and P. Hoggett (eds), *The Politics of Decentralisation: Theory and Practice of a Radical Local Government Initiative*. SAUS Working Paper 46, School of Advanced Urban Studies.

P. Hoggett and R. Hambleton (1988). *Decentralisation and Democracy*. Occasional Paper 28, School of Advanced Urban Studies (2nd edn.).

P. Hoggett, R. Hambleton and F. Tolan (1988). *The Decentralisation of Public Services to Local Level* (a proposal for evaluation research and dissemination to ESRC). Unpublished, April.

P. Hoggett and I. McGill (1988). *Labourism: Means and Ends*. Critical Social Policy no. 23, Autumn.

J. Holloway and S. Picciotto (eds) (1978). *State and Capital: A German Debate*. Edward Arnold, London.

J.M. Holmwood and A. Steward (1983). 'The Role of Contradictions in Modern Theories of Social Stratification'. *Sociology* vol. 17, no. 2.

D. Howe (1986a). *Social Workers and Their Practice in Welfare Bureaucracies*. Gower.

D. Howe (1986b). 'The Segration of Women and their Work in the Personal Social Services'. *Critical Social Policy*, Issue 15, Spring.

A. Hudson (1989). 'Changing Perspectives: Feminism Gender and Social Work'. In: M. Langan and P. Lee (eds), *Radical Social Work Today*. Unwin Hyman.

P. Hunt (1984). 'Workers Side by Side: Women and the Trade Union Movement'. In:

J. Siltanen and H. Stanworth (eds), *Women and the Public Sphere*. Hutchinson.

M. Hutchinson-Reis (1989). 'And For Those of Us who are Black? Black Politics in Social Work'. In: M. Langan and P. Lee (eds), *Radical Social Work Today*. Unwin Hyman.

U. Huws (1985). 'Challenging Commoditisation: Producing Usefulness Outside the Factory'. In: Collective Design Products (ed), *Very Nice Work If You Can Get It*. Spokesman.

R. Hyman (1980). 'White-Collar Workers and Theories of Class'. In: R. Hyman and R. Price (eds), *The New Working Class? White-collar Workers and their Organisation*. Macmillan.

R. Hyman and R.H. Fryer (1977). 'Trade Unions: Sociology and Political Economy'. In: T. Clarke and L. Clements (eds), *Trade Unions Under Capitalism*. Fontana.

R. Hyman and T. Elger (1981). 'Job Controls, the Employers Offensive and Alternative Strategies'. *Capital and Class* 15, Autumn, pp.115-148.

R. Hyman and R. Price (1983). *The New Working Class? White-collar Workers and their Organisation*. Macmillan

M. Ingham (1985). 'Industrial Relations in British Local Government'. *Industrial Relations Journal* vol. 16, no. 1, Spring, pp 6-16.

Islington Borough Council (undated). *Guidelines for the Establishment of Neighbourhood Forums*.

Islington Borough Council (undated). *Neighbourhood Forums: Public Guidelines*.

Islington Borough Council (undated). *Recommended Constitution for Neighbourhood Forums*.

Islington Borough Council (1986). *Going Local: Decentralisation in Practice*. Conference Report.

Islington Borough Council (1986). *Decentralisation, Black Needs, Black Concerns*. Conference Papers.

Islington Borough Council (1986). Equal Opportunities Joint Committee. *Officers Headcount*, November.

Islington Borough Council (1987). *Going Local: Decentralisation in Practice*.

Islington Borough Council (1988). *Gillespie Neighbourhood Forum Constitution*.

Islington Borough Council (1989). Kevin Thompson - personal correspondence.

Islington Borough Council (1991). 'The Composition of Neighbourhood Forums Findings of a Survey Conducted in June 1990'. Islington, June.

R. Jack (1988). 'Getting it Right'. *Insight*, 30th August.

M.P. Jackson (1987). *Strikes: Industrial Conflict in Britain, USA and Australia*. Wheatsheaf Books.

M.P. Jackson (1988). *Trade Unions* (2nd edn.). Longman.

S. Jefferys (1979). 'Striking into the 80s - Modern British Trade Unionism, its Limits and Potential'. *International Socialism* 2:5, Summer, pp 1-52.

D.J. Johnson and C. O'Donnell (1981). 'The Accumulation Crisis and Service Professionals'. In: Fox et al. (eds), *Crisis in the Public Sector*. Monthly Review Press/Union for Radical Political Economics.

T. Johnson (1972). *Professions and Power*. Papermac.

T. Johnson (1977). 'The Professions in the Class Structure'. In: Scase (ed), *Industrial Society, Class Cleavage and Control*. George Allen & Unwin.

T. Johnson (1982). 'The State and the Professions: Peculiarities of the British'. In: A. Giddens and G. Mackenzie (eds), *Social Class and the Division of Labour*. Cambridge University Press.

P. Johnston (1981). 'Public Sector Unionism'. In: Fox et al. (eds), *Crisis in the Public*

Sector. Monthly Review Press/Union for Radical Political Economics.

R.J. Johnston (1990). 'Local State, Local Government and Local Administration'. In: J. Simmie and R. King (eds), *The State in Action*. Pinter.

C. Jones (1983). *State Social Work and the Working Class*. Macmillan.

C. Jones (1989). 'The End of the Road? Issues in Social Work Education'. In: P. Carter et al. (eds), Social Work and Social Welfare. Open University Press.

P. Joyce, P. Corrigan and M. Hayes (1988). *Striking Out: Trade Unionism in Social Work*. Macmillan.

A. Kakabase (1982). *Culture of the Social Services*. Gower.

M.P. Kelly (1980). *White-collar Proletariat: The Industrial Behaviour of British Civil Servants*. London: Routledge & Kegan Paul.

A. Kendall (1984). 'Decentralisation: Promise or Delusion'. *Going Local?* December.

I. Kessler (1989). 'Bargaining Strategies in Local Government'. In: R. Mailly, S.J. Dimmock and A.S. Sethi (eds), *Industrial Relations in the Public Services*. Routledge.

U. Khan (1989). 'Islington: Is the Red Flag Flying There?' *Going Local?* no. 13, June, pp. 12-14. Decentralisation Research and Information Centre, School of Advanced Urban Studies, Bristol University.

D.S. King (1989). 'The New Right, the New Left and Local Government'. In: J. Stewart and G. Stoker (eds), *The Future of Local Government*. Macmillan.

Labour Community Action (1991). *Labour and the Voluntary Sector*. Transport and General Workers Union, Link-up Campaign.

Labour Co-ordinating Committee (1984). *Go Local to Survive*. Labour Coordinating Committee.

M. Laffin (1989). *Managing Under Pressure*. Macmillan.

R.D. Laing (1965). *The Divided Self*. Pelican.

R.D. Laing (1969). *Self and Others*. Pelican.

T. Lane (1987). 'Unions: Fit for Active Service?' *Marxism Today*, February.

M. Langan and P. Lee (1989). *Radical Social Work Today*. Unwin Hyman.

M. Langan and P. Lee (1989). 'Whatever Happened to Radical Social Work'. In: M. Langan and P. Lee (1989). *Radical Social Work Today*. Unwin Hyman.

S. Lansley, S. Goss and C. Wolmar (1989). *Councils in Conflict: The Rise and Fall of the Municipal Left*. Macmillan.

S. Lash and J. Urry (1987). 'The End of Organisation'. *New Statesman*, 6th March.

R. Lees and M. Mayo (1984). *Community Action for Change*. Routledge & Kegan Paul.

V. I. Lenin (1973). What is to be Done. Foreign Languages Press, Peking.

J. Lewis (1979). 'British Capitalism, the Welfare State and the First Radicalisation of State Employees'. In: J. Cowley, A. Kaye, M. Mayo and M. Thompson (eds), *Community or Class Struggle?* Stage One.

Lewisham Council's Women's Committee (undated). *No Room at the Top?* Lewisham Borough Council.

M. Lipsky (1980). *Street-level Bureaucracy*. Russell Sage, New York.

C.R. Littler and G. Salaman (1982). 'Braverman and Beyond: Recent Theories of the Labour Process'. *Sociology* 16, no. 2, May, pp 251-69.

C.R. Littler and G. Salaman (1984). *Class at Work*. Batsford Academic and Educational Limited.

K. Livingstone (1982). 'People's London Defiant'. *New Socialist*, January/ February.

K. Livingstone (1984). 'Renaissance Labour Style'. *Marxism Today*, December.

K. Livingstone (1987). 'Power to the People - The Radical Manifesto'. *New Statesman* 4th September.

D. Lockwood (1958). *The Blackcoated Worker*. London Unwin University Books.

J. Lojkine (1981). 'Urban Policy and Local Power: Some Aspects of Recent Research in Lille'. In: M. Harloe and E. Lebas (eds), *City, Class and Capital*. Edward Arnold.

London-Edinburgh Weekend Return Group (1980). *In and Against the State*. Pluto (2nd edition).

S Lukes (1975). *Power: A Radical View*. London, Macmillan.

R. Lumley (1973). *White-collar Unionism in Britain*. Methuen & Co.

R. Lumley (1978). 'Could BASW be an Effective Trade Union?' *Social Work Today*, vol. 9, no. 35, 9th May.

J. McDonnell (1984). 'Decentralisation and New Social Relations'. *Going Local?*, December.

L. McDowell (1989). 'Gender Divisions'. In: C. Hamnett, L. McDonnell and P. Sarre (eds), *The Changing Social Structure*. Open University Press.

G. McLennan (1984). 'Capitalist State or Democratic Polity? Recent Developments in Marxist and Pluralist Theory'. In: G. McLennan et al. (eds), *The Idea of the Modern State*. OUP.

L. Mackie (1992). *Community Care: Users' Experiences*. NALGO.

R. Mailly, S.J. Dimmock and A.S. Sethi (1989). *Industrial Relations in the Public Services*. Routledge.

R. Mailly, S.J. Dimmock and A.S. Sethi (1989). 'The Politics of Industrial Relations in the Public Services'. In: R. Mailly, S.J. Dimmock and A.S. Sethi (eds), *Industrial Relations in the Public Services*. Routledge.

H.J. Maroney (1987). 'Feminism at Work'. In: J. Mitchell and A. Oakley (eds), *What is Feminism*. Basil Blackwell.

G. Marshall and D. Rose (1988). 'Proletarianisation in the British Class Structure?' *British Journal of Sociology* vol. XXXIX, no. 4, pp 498-518.

G. Marshall, D. Rose, H. Newby and C. Volger (1988). *Social Class in Modern Britain*. Unwin Hyman.

S. Marshall (1987). 'Confrontation and Consultation: The Organisational Objectives and Strategies of Two Public Sector Unions'. In: Argue et al. (eds), *Working People and Hard Times*. Garmond Press, Toronto.

P. Y. Martin (1984). 'Trade Unions, Conflict and the Nature of Work in Residential Service Organisations'. *Organisational Studies* 5/2, pp 169-185.

K. Marx (1948). *Communist Manifesto*. New York International Publishers.

K. Marx (1963). *The Eighteenth Brumaire of Louis Bonaparte*. New York International Publishers.

K. Marx (1968). 'The Civil War in France'. In: K. Marx and F. Engels, *Selected Works*. Lawrence and Wishart.

K. Marx (1968). 'Wages, Price and Profit'. In: K. Marx and F. Engels, *Selected Works*. Lawrence and Wishart.

K. Marx and F. Engels (1968). *Selected Works*. Lawrence and Wishart.

K. Marx (1971). *A Contribution to the Critique of Political Economy*. London, Lawrence and Wishart.

D. Massey, L. Segal and H. Wainwright (1984). 'And Now for the Good News'. In: J. Curran (ed), *The Future of the Left*. Polity Press/New Socialist.

J.B. Mays (1967). *Crime and the Social Structure*. Faber.

R. Means (1984). 'Decentralisation and the Personal Social Services'. In: R. Hambleton and P. Hoggett (eds), *The Politics of Decentralisation: Theory and Practice of a Radical Local Government Initiative*. SAUS Working Paper 46, School of Advanced Urban Studies.

R. Means and R. Smith (1988). 'Implementing a Pluralistic Approach to Evaluation in

Health Education'. *Policy and Politics* vol. 16, no. 1, pp 17-28.

R. Meegan (1988). 'A Crisis of Mass Production'. In: J. Allen and D. Massey (eds), *Economy in Question*. Open University Press.

P. Meiksins (1987). 'White-collar Workers and the Process of Class Formation'. In: Argue et al. (eds), *Working People and Hard Times*. Garmond Press.

D.E. Mercer and D.T. Weir (1972). 'Instrumental Collectivism and Occupational Sectionalism'. In: R. Hyman and R. Price (eds), *The New Working Class? White-collar Workers and their Organisations*. Macmillan (1983).

C. Miliband (1969). *The State in Capitalist Society*. Weidenfeld & Nicolson.

C.J. Miller (1981). 'Area Management: Newcastle's Priority Areas Programme'. In: C. Smith and D. Jones (eds), *Deprivation, Participation and Community Action*. Routledge & Kegan Paul.

F. Milson and A. Fairbairn (1970). *Youth Work in the 1970s*. Routledge & Kegan Paul.

M. Mitchell and D. Russell (1989). 'Race and Racism'. In: P. Brown and R. Sparks (eds), *Beyond Thatcherism*. Open University Press.

D. Montgomery (1976). 'Workers Control of Machine Production in the 19th Century'. *Labour History*, Fall, pp 485-509.

MORI (Market and Opinion Research International) (1988). *Service Provision and Living Standards in Islington*.

F. Morrell and S. Bundred (1984). 'No Short Cut'. *New Socialist*, September.

M. Mullard (1987). 'Decentralisation and Local Control - A Centralist Critique'. *Community Development Journal* vol. 22, no. 2, April.

F. Murray (1983). 'The Decentralisation of Production - the Decline of the Mass-Collective Worker'. *Capital and Class* 19.

N. Murray (1985). 'View from the Ground'. *Community Care*, 18th April, pp 26-30.

R. Murray (1986). 'Public Sector Possibilities'. *Marxism Today*, July.

R. Murray (1988). 'Life after Henry (Ford)'. *Marxism Today*, October.

U. Murray (1989). 'Public Sector Jobs and Services for Community Needs'. *Community Development Journal* vol. 24, no. 2.

T. Nairn (1965). 'Labour Imperialism'. *New Left Review*, no. 32, July/ August.

NALGO *Emergency Committee Minutes 1972-86*. NALGO.

NALGO (1979). *Industrial Action - An Alternative View*. NALGO.

NALGO (1984). *The Personal Social Services*. NALGO.

NALGO (1985). *Residential Workers Dispute*. NALGO.

NALGO (1988). *The National Executive Council's Report on Positive Action*. Annual Conference, NALGO.

NALGO (1991). 'Towards a New Union'. *NALGO Update: Consultation Exercise - What You Think*. March.

NALGO (1993). *Community Care: Handbook for Local Government Branches*.

NALGO, Islington Branch (1984). *Report on Children's Day Centre Industrial Action 1984*.
1st Report 16th April
2nd Report 17th July
Letter

NALGO, Islington Branch (1985). *Strike Action by Islington Branch Members 5.8.1985 - 11.9.1985*. Islington NALGO.

NALGO, Islington Branch (1986). *Decentralisation*, 13th March. NALGO, Islington Branch.

NALGO, Islington Branch (1987). *Report for Greater London Whitley Council Joint Secretaries/Disputes Committee*. Housing Advisory Workers Regrading Dispute and

Lock-Out. NALGO, Islington Branch.

P. Nanton (1989). 'The New Orthodoxy: Racial Categories and Equal Opportunity Policy'. *New Community* 15(4), July.

M. Nellis (1989). 'Social Work'. In: P. Brown and R. Sparks (eds), *Beyond Thatcherism*. Open University Press.

J. Newman, J. Clarke (1994). 'Going About Our Business? The Managerialisation of Public Services'. In: J. Clarke, A. Cochrane, E. McLaughlin *Managing Social Policy*. Sage.

K. Newton and T.J. Karran (1985). *The Politics of Local Expenditure*. Macmillan.

N. Nicholson et al. (1980). 'Background of White-collar Shop Stewards'. *British Journal of Industrial Relations* vol. XVIII, July, pp 231-239.

T. Nichols (1986). 'Introduction'. In: P. Armstrong et al. (eds), *White-collar Workers, Trade Unions and Class*. Croom Helm.

N. Nicholson, G. Ursell and P. Blyton (1981). *The Dynamics of White-collar Unionism*. London Academic Press.

O.E.C.D. (1982). *Employment in the Public Sector*. O.E.C.D. Paris.

J. O'Connor (1973). *The Fiscal Crisis of the State*. St. Martins Press, New York.

C. Offe (1975). 'The Theory of the Capitalist State and the Problem of Policy Formation'. In: L. Lindberg, R.R. Alford, C. Crouch and C. Offe (eds), *Stress and Contradiction in Modern Capitalism*. Lexington Books.

C. Offe (1982). 'Some Contradictions of the Modern Welfare State'. *C.S.P.* vol. 2, no. 2, Autumn.

C. Offe (1984). *Contradictions of the Welfare State*. Hutchinson.

C. Offe (1985). *Disorganised Capitalism*. Polity Press.

C. Offe and V. Ronge (1982). 'Theses on the Theory of the State'. In: A. Giddens and D. Held (eds), *Classes, Power and Conflict*. Macmillan.

M. Oppenheimer (1973). 'The Proletarianisation of the Professional'. In: P. Halmos (ed), *Professionalism and Social Change*. University of Keele.

H. Ouseley (1985). 'Treating them all the Same - Decentralising Institutional Racism'. *Going Local?*, April.

H. Ouseley, D. Silverstone and U. Prashar (1981). *The System*. Runnymede Trust and South London Equal Rights Consultancy.

L. Panitch (1980). 'The State and the Future of Socialism'. *Capital and Class* no. 11, Summer.

L. du Parcq (1987). 'Neighbourhood Services: The Islington Experience'. In: P. Willmott (ed), *Local Government Decentralisation and Community*. Policy Studies Institute, Discussion Paper no. 18.

P. Parma (1989). 'Other Kinds of Dreams'. *Feminist Review* no. 31, Spring.

N.C.A. Parry and J. Parry (1976). *The Rise of the Medical Profession: A Study of Collective Social Mobility* Croom Helm.

N.C.A. Parry and J. Parry (1977). 'Professionalism and Unionism: Aspects of Class Conflict in the NHS'. *Sociological Review* 25, pp 823-41.

N.C.A. Parry and J. Parry (1979). 'Social Work, Professionalism and the State'. In: N. Parry, M. Rustin and C. Satyamurti (eds), *Social Work, Welfare and the State*. Edward Arnold.

T. Pateman (ed) (1972). *Counter Course*. Penguin Education Specials.

G. Pearson (1973). 'Social Work as the Privatised Solution of Public Ills'. *British Journal of Social Work* vol. 3, no. 2, Summer, pp 209-25.

G. Peters (1985). 'Different Routes - Same Goal'. *Community Care*, 18th April.

E. Pilkington (1985). 'Looking for New Friends'. *New Statesman*, 5th April.

R. Pinker (1985). 'Against the Flow'. *Community Care*, 18th April, pp 20-22.

A. Pithouse (1990). 'Guardians of Autonomy: Work Orientations in a Social Work Office'. In: P. Carter, T. Jeffs and M. Smith (eds), *Social Work and Social Welfare Yearbook 2*. Open University Press.

Policy Studies Institute (1986). *Ethnic Minorities in Public Housing in Islington* Policy Studies Institute.

A. Pollert (1981). *Girls, Wives and Factory Lives*. Macmillan.

C. Posner (1968). *Reflections on the Revolution in France: 1968* Pelican

N. Poulantzas (1973). Political Power and Social Classes'. *New Left Review*.

N. Poulantzas (1973). 'On Social Classes'. *New Left Review* 78. In: Giddens and Held (eds) (1982), Classes, Power and Conflict. Macmillan.

N. Poulantzas (1975). 'The New Petty Bourgeoisie'. From: *Classes in Contemporary Capitalism*. New Left Books. Reproduced in R. Hyman and R. Price (1983). *The New Working Class? White-collar Workers and their Organisation*. Macmillan.

N. Poulantzas and R. Miliband (1972). 'The Problem of the Capitalist State'. In: R. Blackburn (ed), *Ideology in Social Science*. Fontana.

K. Prandy, A. Stewart and R.M. Blackburn (1983). *White-Collar Unionism*. Macmillan.

E. Preteceille (1981). 'Collective Consumption, the State and the Crisis of Capitalist Society'. In: M. Harloe and E. Lebas (eds), *City, Class and Capital*. Edward Arnold.

R. Price (1983). 'White-collar Unions: Growth, Character and Attitudes in the 1970s'. In: R. Hyman and R. Price (eds), *The New Working Class? White-collar Workers and their Organisation*. Macmillan.

R. Price and G.S. Bain (1976). 'Union Growth Revisited: 1948-74 in Perspective'. *British Journal of Industrial Relations* vol. XIV, no. 3, November.

R. Price and G.S. Bain (1983). 'Union Growth in Britain - Retrospect and Prospect'. *British Journal of Industrial Relations* vol. 21, no. 1, March.

J.M. Prottas (1978). 'The Power of the Street-Level Bureaucrat in Public Service Bureaucracies.' *Urban Affairs Quarterly* vol. 13, no. 3, March.

M. Pryce (1977). 'Do Social Workers Need their Own Trade Union?' *Social Work Today* vol. 9, no. 1, 30th August.

M. Pryce (1979). 'How BUSW is Facing Up to the Realities of Trade Unionism'. *Social Work Today* vol. 10, no. 25, 20th February.

A. Puddephatt (1984). 'Out of the Defeatist Ghetto Labour Councils and the S.W.P.', *Chartist* 98, January/February.

A. Puddephatt (1985). 'Shaping our Socialism'. *Chartist* 104, May/June.

A. Puddephatt (1988). 'Local State and Local Community: The Hackney Experience'. In: P. Hoggett and R. Hambleton (eds), *Decentralisation and Democracy*. School of Advanced Urban Studies.

K. Purcell (1984). 'Militancy and Acquiescence among Women Workers'. In: J. Siltanen and M. Stanworth (eds), *Women and the Public Sphere*. Hutchinson.

Radical Therapist Collective (1974). *The Radical Therapist*. Pelican.

C. Rallings (1983). 'White-Collar Workers, Unionisation and Political Behaviour'. *Industrial Relations Journal* vol. 14, no. 2, pp 60-73.

G. Rankin (1970). 'Professional Social Work and the Campaign against Poverty'. *Social Work Today* vol. 1, no. 10, p 21.

P. Reason (ed) (1988), *Human Inquiry in Action*. Sage.

P. Reason (1988). 'The Co-operative Inquiry Group'. In: P. Reason (ed), *Human Inquiry in Action*. Sage.

P. Reason and P. Hawkins (1988). 'Storytelling as Inquiry'. In: P. Reason (ed), *Human Inquiry in Action*. Sage

C. Reich (1970). *The Greening of America*. Penguin.

K. Renner (1978). 'The Service Class' (English Translation [1958]). In:
  T. B. Bottomore and P. Goode (eds), *Austro-Marxism*. Oxford, Clarendon Press.

A. Rivers (1988). 'Training for Change in Newham's Housing Service'. In: P. Hoggett
  and R. Hambleton (eds), *Decentralisation and Democracy*. School of Advanced Urban
  Studies.

K. Roberts, F. Cook, S. Clark and E. Semeonoff (1973). *The Fragmentary Class
  Structure*. Heinemann.

S. Robertshaw (1986). 'Negotiating Change'. *Housing*, December, p.10.

G. Robinson (1981). 'A Class Analysis of State Workers'. In: Fox et al. (eds), Crisis
  in the Public Sector. Monthly Review Press/Union for Radical Political Economics.

Roehampton District Tenants Association and Wandsworth NALGO Housing Shop
  Stewards Committee (undated). *A Better Housing Service*.

J. Roemer (1982). *A General Theory of Exploitation and Class*. Cambridge Mass.:
  Harvard University Press.

D. Rose and G. Marshall (1986). 'Constructing the (W)right Classes',
  Sociology vol. 20, no. 3. Reprinted in E.O. Wright *The Debate on Classes*, Verso.

G. Routh (1980). *Occupation and Pay in Great Britain 1906-79*. Macmillan.

S. Rowbotham (1984). 'Sharing the Caring'. *New Statesman*, 13th January.

S. Rowbotham (1989). 'Left Out of the Argument by Ideological Gift-Wrap'. *The
  Guardian*.

J. Rubery (1978). 'Structured Labour Markets, Worker Organisation, and Low Pay'. In:
  A. Giddens and D. Held (eds), *Power, Classes and Society*. Macmillan.

M. Rustin (1984). 'Opening to the Future'. *New Socialist*, October, pp 11-16.

P. Sarre (1989). 'Recomposition of the Class Structure'. In: C. Hamnett, C. McDowell
  and P. Sarre (eds), *The Changing Social Structure*. Open University Press.

C. Satyamurti (1981). *Occupational Survival*. Blackwell, Oxford.

P. Saunders (1980). 'Local Government and the State'. *New Society*, 13th March, pp
  550-551.

P. Saunders (1984). 'Rethinking Local Politics'. In: M. Boddy and C. Fudge (eds),
  Local Socialism. Macmillan.

T. Sawyer (1984). 'Politics Will Make the Unions Strong'. *New Socialist*, September.

T. Schuller and D. Robertson (1983). 'How Representatives Allocate their Time: Shop
  Steward Activity and Membership Contact'. *British Journal of Industrial Relations*
  vol. 25. no. 1, March.

J. Seabrook (1984). *The Idea of Neighbourhood*. Pluto.

Lord Seebohm (1968). *Report on Allied Personal Services*. HMSO.

N. Shah (1989). 'It's Up to You Sisters: Black Women and Social Work'. In:
  M. Langan and P. Lee (eds), *Radical Social Work Today*. Allen & Unwin.

H. Sharron (1980). 'NALGO: State of the Union'. *Social Work Today* vol. 11, no. 38.

H. Sharron (1984). 'Islington's Legacy of Bitterness'. *Social Work Today*, 30th July.

H. Sharron (1984). 'Pulling the Town Hall to Pieces'. *The Guardian*, 5th December.

H. Sharron (1985). 'Overcoming Trade Union Resistance to Local Change'. *Public
  Money*, March.

R. Shield (1982). 'Decentralisation and Socialism: Power to the People?' *Chartist* no.
  91, June/August, pp 10-14.

R. Shield (1983). 'The Socialist Case for "Going Local"'. *Chartist* no. 93,
  November/January, p 21.

R. Shield and J. Webber (1986). 'Hackney Lurches Local'. *Community Development
  Journal* vol. 21, no. 2.

J. Siltanen and M. Stanworth (eds) (1984). *Women and the Public Sphere*. Hutchinson.

M. Simpkin (1983). *Trapped within Welfare* (2nd edn). Macmillan.

M. Simpkin (1989). 'Radical Social Work: Lessons for the 1990s'. In: P. Carter, T. Jeffs and M. Smith (eds), *Social Work and Social Welfare* Yearbook. Open University Press.

A. Sivanandan (1983). *A Different Hunger*. Pluto.

J. Skinner and C. Robinson (1988). 'Who Cares? Women at Work in Social Services'. In: A. Coyle and J. Skinner (eds), *Women and Work*. Macmillan.

Skeffington (1969). *People and Planning*. HMSO.

N. Small (1987). 'Putting Violence Towards Social Workers into Context'. *Critical Social Policy* Issue 19, Summer.

B.C. Smith (1985). *Decentralisation: The Territorial Dimension of the State*. George Allen & Unwin.

B.C. Smith (1988). *Bureaucracy and Political Power*. Wheatsheaf.

C. Smith (1987). *Technical Workers: Class, Labour and Trade Unionism*. Macmillan Education Ltd.

D. Smith (undated). *From Seebohm to Barclay: The Changing Political Nature of the Organisation of Social Work*. Department of Social Administration, University of Manchester.

L. Smith (1980). 'The Promotion of Neighbourhood Projects in Islington'. In: S. Hatch and S. Humble (eds), *Towards Neighbourhood Democracy*. Association of Researchers in Voluntary Action and Community Involvement, Pamphlet no. 2.

L. Smith (1981). 'Public Participation in Islington - a Case Study'. In: L. Smith and D. Jones (eds), *Deprivation, Participation and Community Action*. Macmillan.

L. Smith and D. Jones (eds) (1981). *Deprivation, Participation and Community Action*. Macmillan.

M. Smith (1986). 'The Consumer Case for Socialism'. *Fabian Tract* 513, Fabian Society, July.

Social Trends 25 (1995). Central Statistical Office HMSO.

Social Work Today, 'Guidance to Members on NALGO Overtime Ban', vol. 8, no. 26, 5th April 1977.

Social Work Today, Letters page, vol. 8, no. 28, 19th April 1977.

Social Work Today, Comment, vol. 10, no. 3, 12th September 1978.

Social Work Today, Comment, vol. 10, no. 5, 26th September 1978.

Social Work Today, 'No Affiliation with TUC', vol. 10, no. 27, 6th March 1979.

Social Work Today, 'BUSW Comes under Fire at NALGO AGM', vol. 10, no. 31, 3rd April 1979.

Social Work Today, 'BUSW is a Mistake says Branch Resolution', vol. 10, no. 34, 1st May 1979.

Social Work Today, Letters page, vol. 10, no. 36, 15th May 1979.

A. Stanton (1990). 'Empowerment of Staff: a Prerequisite for the Empowerment of Users?' In: P. Carter, T. Jeffs and M. Smith (eds), *Social Work and Social Welfare Yearbook*. Open University Press.

D. Stark (1980). 'Class Struggle and the Transformation of the Labour Process: A Relational Approach'. In: Giddens and Held (eds), *Classes, Power and Society*, Macmillan.

D. Statham (1978). *Radicals in Social Work*. Routledge & Kegan Paul.

M. Stein, N. Frost and P. Haynes (1982). 'Personal Social Services under the Conservatives'. *Critical Social Policy* vol. 3, Spring, pp 52-54.

G. Stevenson (1976). 'Social Relations of Production and Consumption in the Human

Service Occupations'. *Monthly Review*, p 28.

A. Stewart, K. Prandy and R.M. Blackburn (1980). *Social Stratification and Occupations*. Macmillan.

J. Stewart (1984). 'Bureaucracy and Decentralisation in the Delivery of Local Services'. In: R. Hambleton and P. Hoggett (eds), *The Politics of Decentralisation: Theory and Practice of a Radical Local Government Initiative*. SAUS Working Paper 46, School of Advanced Urban Studies.

J. Stewart and G. Stoker (eds) (1989). *The Future of Local Government Beyond the Centre Series*. Macmillan.

G. Stoker (1987). 'Decentralisation and Local Government'. *Social Policy and Administration* vol. 21, no. 2, Summer, pp 157-169.

G. Stoker (1988). *The Politics of Local Government*. Macmillan.

G. Stoker (1989). 'Creating a Local Government for a Post-Fordist Society: The Thatcherite Project?' In: J. Stewart and G. Stoker (eds), *The Future of Local Government Beyond the Centre Series*. Macmillan.

P. Stubbs (1985). 'The Employment of Black Social Workers: from Ethnic Sensitivity to Anti-Racism?' *Critical Social Policy* Issue 12, Spring.

J. Suddaby (1979). 'The Public Sector Stake in Camden'. *New Left Review*, Winter.

P. Sutton, C. Bower, J. Hammerton and M. Willis (1980). 'The Social Work Front in Counter Attack'. *Social Work Today* vol. 12, no. 9, 28th October.

Lord Swann (1985). *Education for All: The Report of the Committee of Enquiry into the Education of Children from Ethnic Minority Groups*. Cnd 9453, London HMSO, March.

T.S. Szasz (1972). *The Myth of Mental Illness*. Paladin.

L. Tasker and A. Wunnam (1977). 'The Ethos of Radical Social Workers and Community Workers'. *Social Work Today* vol. 8, no. 23, 15th March.

D. Taylor (1989). 'Citizenship and Social Power'. *Critical Social Policy* Issue 26, Autumn.

M. Taylor (with the Newcastle and Sheffield Tenants' Federations) (1986). 'For Whose Benefits? Decentralising Housing Services in Two Cities'. *Community Development Journal* vol. 21, no. 2, April, pp 126-133.

R. Taylor (1978). *The Fifth Estate - Britain's Unions in the Seventies*. Routledge & Kegan Paul.

M. Terry (1982). 'Organising a Fragmented Workforce: Shop Stewards in Local Government'. *British Journal of Industrial Relations* vol. 20, no. 1, March.

D. Thomas (1984). 'The Job Bias against Blacks'. *New Society*, 1st November.

D. Thomas (1985). 'Tortoise in the Works'. *New Society*, 7th June.

H. Thomas (1987). 'A Response to J. Weinstein "Angry Arguments across the Picket Lines: Left Labour Councils and White-collar Trade Unionism", CSP June 17th 1986" in "Feedback"'. *Critical Social Policy* Issue 20, Autumn.

E.P. Thompson (1970). *Warwick University Ltd*. Penguin Education Special.

R. Thorpe and J. Petruckenia (1985). *Community Work or Social Change*. (Interview with Fran Hayes - Australian Social Welfare Union National Organiser 1977-80). Routledge & Kegan Paul.

M. Tomlinson (1986). 'A State of Decentralisation'. *Going Local?* no. 5, July, pp 16-17.

J. Urry (1973). 'A Highly Significant Intermediate Class' from 'Towards a Structural Theory of the Middle Class'. *Acta Sociologica* vol. 16, no. 3, pp 180-3. Reproduced in R. Hyman and R. Price (eds) (1983), *The New Working Class? White-collar Workers and their Organisation*. Macmillan.

S. Usher (1987). 'Unions and Social Issues'. In: Argue et al. (eds), *Working People and Hard Times*. Garamond Press, Toronto.

D. Volker (1966). 'NALGO's Affiliation to the TUC'. *British Journal of Industrial Relations* no. 4.

K. Walsh (1982). 'Local Government Militancy in Britain and the United States'. *Local Government Studies* 8, p 6.

K. Walsh, B. Hinings, R. Greenwood and S. Ranson (1981). 'Power and Advantage in Organisation'. *Organisational Studies* 2/2, pp 131-152.

G. Walton (1978). 'NALGO Gives Support for All-Out Strikes'. *Social Work Today* vol. 9, no. 48, 15th August.

G. Walton (1978). 'Employers Study Pay as Strike Threat Spreads'. *Social Work Today* vol. 10, no. 4, 19th September.

G. Walton (1978). 'All Standing Firm in 8th Week of Strike'. *Social Work Today* vol. 10, no. 6, 3rd October.

G. Walton (1979). 'Strike in 22nd Week Continues to Spread'. *Social Work Today* vol. 10, no. 19, 9th January.

G. Walton (1979). 'NALGO Leaders to Urge Strike Settlement'. *Social Work Today* vol. 10, no. 20, 16th January.

G. Walton (1979). 'Strikers Urge Rejection of NJC Pay Proposal'. *Social Work Today* vol. 10, no. 21, 23rd January.

G. Walton (1979). 'Both Sides Agree on Formula to End Strikes'. *Social Work Today* vol. 10, no. 24, 13th February.

G. Walton (1979). 'The Strikes: Special Meeting at NJC Sought'. *Social Work Today* vol. 10, no. 25, 20th February.

G. Walton (1979). 'NALGO Withdraws its NJC Meeting Request'. *Social Work Today* vol. 10, no. 26, 27th February.

G. Walton (1979). 'Cheshire Social Workers go back to Work'. *Social Work Today* vol. 10, no. 27, 6th March.

G. Walton (1979). 'No Holds Inquest as Strikes Drag On'. *Social Work Today* vol. 10, no. 28, 13th March.

G. Walton (1979). 'No Attempts to Break Strike Deadlock'. *Social Work Today* vol. 10, no. 29, 20th March.

G. Walton (1979). 'Four Areas Return as Strike Talks Continue'. *Social Work Today* vol. 10, no. 30, 27th March.

G. Walton (1979). 'No Hope in Sight in Tower Hamlets Settlement'. *Social Work Today* vol. 10, no. 37, 22nd May.

R. Walton (1975). *Women and Social Work*. Routledge & Kegan Paul.

M. Ward (1985). 'Making the Organisation Work for Members'. *Local Government Survey*, July.

A. Webb and G. Wistow (1983). 'The Personal Social Services: Incrementalism, Expediency or Systemic Social Planning?' In: M. Loney, D. Boswell and J. Clarke (eds), *Social Policy and Social Welfare*. Open University Press.

J. Weinstein (1986). 'Angry Arguments Across the Picket Lines: Left Labour Councils and White-Collar Trade Unionism'. *Critical Social Policy* 17, Autumn.

S. Weir (1984). 'Raiders of the Local State'. *New Socialist* January/February, pp 23-27.

S. Westwood (1984). *All Day Every Day*. Pluto Press.

N. White (undated). *Whitleyism or Rank and File Action*. NALGO Action Group.

P. Wilding (1982). *Professional Power and Social Welfare*. Routledge & Kegan Paul.

R. Williams (ed) (1968). *May Day Manifesto*. Penguin Special.

P. Willmott (1987). 'Introduction'. In: *Local Government Decentralisation and*

Community. PSI Discussion Paper no. 18. Policy Studies Institute.

P. Wintour (1983). 'Breaking the Chains'. *New Statesman*, 14th January.

P. Wintour (1989). 'Service Lifts Locally'. *The Guardian*, 17th February.

C. Wolmar (1984). 'Divided We Stand'. *New Socialist*, December.

C. Wolmar (1985). Paper given at the 'Moving the Monolith' Seminar at School of Advanced Urban Studies, University of Bristol, 17th September.

C. Wolmar (1985). 'Strike Against Harassment'. *New Statesman*, 27th September.

C. Wolmar (1987). 'The Fresh Face of the Capital's Politics'. *New Statesman*, 18th September.

P. Wood (1985). 'A Critical Tension'. *Community Care*, 18th April, pp 36-37.

S. Wood (1982). *The Degradation of Work? Skill, Deskilling and the Labour Process*. Hutchinson.

S. Wood and J. Kelly (1988). 'Taylorism, Responsible Autonomy and Management Strategy'. In: R.E. Pahl (ed), *On Work*. Blackwell.

A. Wright (1984). 'Decentralisation and the Socialist Tradition'. In: A. Wright, J. Stewart and N. Deakin (eds), *Socialism and Decentralisation*. Fabian Tract 496, London.

E.O. Wright (1976). 'Class Boundaries in Advanced Capitalist Societies'. New Left Review no. 8.

E.O. Wright (1978). 'Class Boundaries and Contradictory Class Locations'. *From Class, Crisis and the State*, New Left Books. In: A. Giddens and D. Held (eds) (1983), *Power, Classes and Society*. Macmillan.

E.O. Wright (1985). *Classes*. Verso.

E.O. Wright (1989). 'Rethinking Once Again, the Concept of Class Structure'. In: E.O. Wright (ed), *The Debate on Classes*. Verso.

E.O. Wright (1989). 'A General Framework for the Analysis of Class Structure'. *Politics and Society* vol. 13 no. 4 (1984), reprinted in E.O. Wright et al. (eds), *The Debate on Classes*. Verso.

E.O. Wright et al. (1989). *The Debate on Classes*. Verso.

M. Yates (1981). 'Public Sector Unions and the Labour Movement'. In: Fox et al. (eds), *Crisis in the Public Sector*. Monthly Review Press/Union for Radical Political Economics.

Index